# Great Sanskrit Plays

*in Modern Translation*

# Great Sanskrit Plays

in New English Transcreations by

## P. Lal

*Shakuntala*
*The Toy Cart*
*The Signet Ring of Rakshasa*
*The Dream of Vasavadatta*
*The Later Story of Rama*
*Ratnavali*

A New Directions Book

Manufactured in the United States of America
New Directions books are printed on acid-free paper
First published clothbound and as New Directions Paperbook 142 in 1964
Published simultaneously in Canada by Penguin Books Canada Limited

New Directions Books are published for James Laughlin
by New Directions Publishing Corporation
80 Eighth Avenue, New York 10011

FIFTH PRINTING

To Fanny and Harry

# CONTENTS

# ACKNOWLEDGMENTS

The translation of these plays began in 1955 and would never have been accomplished without the encouragement of James Laughlin. He went through them with meticulous care, checking the improvements in style suggested by Sherry Mangan, Hayden Carruth, and Robert Fitzgerald, in order to establish the "neutral" tone of transcreation which I felt was called for if the plays were to mean anything significant to the three kinds of readers I kept in mind when on the job: American, English and Indian.

Many friends, among them gurus, have helped at various stages and in various ways. It gives me pleasure to acknowledge varying degrees of debt to Reverend R. Antoine, S.J., Professor in St. Xavier's College, Calcutta, who carries his Sanskrit scholarship with as much charm as lightness; William Hull, Professor of English at Hofstra University; Dr. V. Raghavan, whose erudition in Sanskrit one can only hope vainly to emulate; Mr. Hiran Kumar Sanyal, for his enlightening discussions with me; Dr. Kalidas Nag, for helping me with some of the biographical and historical details recorded in the introductions; David McCutchion, Professor of Comparative Literature at Jadavpur University, and *il miglior fabbro;* J. van Buitenen, Professor of Sanskrit at the University of Chicago and Professor Sadhan Kumar Ghosh, for stimulating discussions on the theory and nature of drama. I am grateful to Robert Stein for valuable suggestions on the myth, symbol, and image clusters in *Shakuntala,* which I have embodied in the introduction to the play.

The transcreations of *Shakuntala* and *The Dream of Vasavadatta* have appeared in the *Orient Review,* Calcutta; the introduction to *Shakuntala* is expanded from the original which was published in the *Statesman,* Calcutta, in 1957. The general introduction on Sanskrit drama, which has appeared in *Quest,* is based on a lecture delivered at Columbia University in November 1962; and the individual introductions to the five other plays are based on lecture notes made during my tenure as Special Professor at Hofstra University in 1962–1963.

Finally, for all that wives deserve thanks for, I thank my wife; and, in particular, for her help with the notes at the end of this book.

# INTRODUCTION

The subcontinent of India has absorbed three major invasions in its history, each bringing with it a powerful army, a mature religious culture, and a refined language. The first of these, the Aryan, took place some time between 3000 and 2000 B.C., and brought Sanskrit (literally, "the language of the cultured," "the perfected tongue") and the scriptures known as the Vedas; the Muslim, c.1000 A.D., brought Persian and the Koran; and the British, about three hundred years ago, introduced English and Protestant Christianity.

One of the Indo-European family of languages, Sanskrit originated in central Asia, and during the early period of its growth in India changed from a relatively simple structure in the Vedic songs (2000 B.C.) to the considerable technical and philosophical sophistication we see in the Upanishads and the Gita (1000 B.C.). During the time of the Buddha, around 500 B.C., Sanskrit in its pure form became an elite language, used in courts by nobles and in temples by Brahmins, and used also by the pandits who kept alive the oral tradition (we have no evidence of written records till the time of Asoka's reign, 273–232 B.C.); but a variant of Sanskrit—in the eyes of purists a corruption—took shape around this time and, in its Prakrit form by Hindus and Pali form by Buddhists, began to be used extensively as a lingua franca in India. After the Muslim invasions in the tenth and succeeding centuries, the use of Sanskrit as a creative language almost died out, though it continued to be a prestigious unifying agent in Hindu ritual and philosophical discussion.

Today the use of Sanskrit is restricted almost exclusively to religious ritual and academic study, and it serves the Indian vernaculars and their literatures in much the same way as Greek and Latin serve the European vernaculars. It is said that Panini, the grammarian of Sanskrit, at once established and killed Sanskrit by excessively stressing its fearfully complex system of linguistic rules and principles; now a dead "living" language, spoken by a negligible and dwindling minority and cherished by scholars, it is doubtful that Sanskrit can ever regain its former glory.

Some idea of Sanskrit's extraordinary richness and diversity can be had by glancing at a few of the important works it has produced: the two epics, the *Ramayana* (the story of Rama) and the *Mahabharata* (the story of the war between the Pandavas and the Kauravas); the pre-Aesop fables in the *Hitopadesa* and the *Panchatantra*; the tales and novellas in *The Great Ocean of Rivery Stories* and *The Ten Princes;* the songs of religious praise in the four Vedas (*Rig*-Veda, *Yajur*-Veda, *Sama*-Veda, and *Atharva*-Veda); the subtle metaphysical speculations in the Upanishads, especially the *Isha, Katha, Chandogya* and *Brihadaranyaka;* the six philosophical systems, among them Nyaya and Yoga; the treatise on sex by Vatsyayan, *Kama-Sutra*, and the erotically symbolical poem, *Gita-Govinda* by Jaya-deva; together with a very large, and untranslated, number of minor poems, riddles, chants, treatises and commentaries (called *tikas*), social tracts (Manu's *Laws* and Kautilya's *Arthashastra*), and folk tales in Prakrit and Pali.

## ORIGINS OF SANSKRIT DRAMA

The origins of Sanskrit drama are lost in the obscurity of myth and legend, and very little is known about the nature of the *acted* drama. Bharata, the first great theoretician of Sanskrit drama, is supposed to have lived sometime during the first century B.C., and his *Natyashastra*, or *The Art of the Play*, is the clearest discussion and exposition of dramatic nature and practice that we possess. He declares that the theories he lays down for the composition and performance of plays were obtained from the practical experience he gained when he directed the nymphs of heaven, the Apsaras, in plays produced for the edification of the gods. The *Mahabhasya*, an earlier treatise (circa 150 B.C.), says that a play dealing with the marriage of Lakshmi, the consort of Vishnu, was performed before the gods. In legend, Krishna and the *gopis* perform the drama of the *rasa-lila*, the cowherdesses dancing to the strains of his divine flute. The *Dasharupaka*, a much later discussion of dramatic theory than the *Nat-yashastra*, says that drama is described as a *natya* (the Sanskrit root word *nritta* means dance) because the *nata*, the actor, imitates and mimics various kinds of heroes; but the play is also called *rupa* (Sanskrit for visual form and beauty) because objects are offered for the visual delectation of the audience.

There seems little doubt, however, that the earliest representations of Sanskrit drama were in the nature of religious performances. If we go back to the drama implied in the dialogue-hymns of the *Rig*-Veda, especially the frog hymn (VII:103), in which men disguised as frogs dance and sing in order to invoke the rain god, or the gamblers' hymn (X:34), in which dancers represent the leaping and falling of dice, the first influences seem to lie in ceremonial practices. In fact, the *Mahavrata* (the Great Vow) ritual which is mentioned in the religious tract *Sankhyayana Aranyaka* (c. 1000 B.C.), one of highly dramatic abuse between a Brahmin pupil and a hetaera, contains elements which later appear to have entered into the Sanskrit play. During the *Mahavrata* ceremony girls dance round the sacred fire to invoke fertility for the land. The Vedic marriage ceremony and the horse sacrifice mentioned repeatedly in the epics are extremely dramatic performances.

The point to note is that Sanskrit drama developed independently of foreign influences (from the Greeks, who were in northwestern India in Alexander's time, it apparently borrowed only a word—*yavanika,* from *yavana,* meaning "foreigner"—to signify a stage divider), and is deeply rooted in the myths, legends, and rituals of India.

TYPES OF SANSKRIT DRAMA

Sanskrit plays are divided into two groups—*Rupaka* (major drama) and *Upa-rupaka* (minor drama). There are ten kinds of *Rupaka*; the seven considered most important and in general use are:

1. The *Nataka*. This is the most common type and may contain anywhere from five to ten acts. If it contains ten, it deserves the honor of being called a *Maha-nataka* (super-play). All the plays included in this volume, except *The Toy Cart* and *Ratnavali,* are *Natakas*.

2. The *Prakarana*. This type resembles the *Nataka* in structure, but the plot is invented, not adapted from myth and legend. *The Toy Cart* and Bhavabhuti's *Malati and Madhava* are good examples; among

the lesser known, and dramatically inferior, are the seventeenth-century dramatist Uddandinnatha's *Mallika-maruta* and the ten-act *Kaumudimitrananda* by Ramachandra, a disciple of Hemchandra (born 1173).

3. The one-act *Prahasana* or Farce. Examples: Jagadishvara's *Hasyarnava* (c. fifteenth century) and King Mahendravarman's *Matta-Vilasa* (c. seventh century). *Shringara-bhushana* by Vamana Bhatta Bana (born 1500) is a monologue Bhana; and Bhasa's thirteen well-known ones, discovered by Pandit Ganapati Shastri in 1913, are all one-acters but not *Prahasanas*.

4. The one-act *Vyayoga*. This deals with heroic themes or the *vira rasa*. Examples: *Partha-parakrama* by Prahladana Deva (born 1163) and *Saugandhi-kaharana* by Vishvanatha (born 1310).

5. The four-act *Ihamriga*. Partly based on legend, partly invented, this type deals with the pursuit by the hero of an unattainably divine lady. Example: Vatsaraja's *Rukminiharanam*.

6. The four-act *Dima*. This deals with gloomy and calamitous events, and the hero is a demon, demigod, or deity. Example: Vatsaraja's *Tripuradaha*.

Another kind, strictly speaking, stands midway between the *Rupaka* and *Upa-rupaka*. Harsha's *Ratnavali* is also an example of a play built on another, and is therefore minor drama. There is no need here to go into the intricate types of *Upa-rupaka*, of which eighteen are described by different commentators on the drama.

PLOT STRUCTURE

Commentators are generally agreed that the action of a drama involves five stages of development. First, there is the desire to attain something (known as *arambha*), which leads to the organized effort (*prayatna,* the second stage) to achieve the goal. The third stage admits the possibility of success (*prapti-sambhava*) in relation to the input of effort and the obstacles to be surmounted, followed by the certainty of success (*niyatapti*) and the actual attainment (*phalagama,* the fifth stage).

Parallel with these five stages of progressive dramatic action are the five elements that constitute a plot: the germ (*vija*), the drop (*bindu*), the episode, the incident and the dénouement. In addition, there are the five critical meeting points (*samdhi*) of plot: the opening (*mukha* or protasis), progression (*pratimukha* or epitasis), development (*garbha*, meaning "deepening," or catastasis), pause (*vimarsha* or peripeteia), and conclusion (*nirvahana* or catastrophe).

## CHARACTERISTICS OF SANSKRIT DRAMA

1. Since the law of *karma* mechanically dispenses a kind of cosmic justice for every thought, word, and deed, no occurrence in human life can be considered as really tragic—hence the entire absence of tragedy as an art form. Bharata, in fact, forbids the representation of death on the stage.

2. Sanskrit (literally, "cultivated" or "perfected") is spoken by all Brahmin and noble characters in the play, while Prakrit (the vernacular) is reserved for menials and, generally, women.

3. Lyrical stanzas in strict Sanskrit meters alternate with frequent use of prose. Since it is difficult to manipulate Sanskrit metrics to suit the needs of Prakrit, no woman normally expresses herself in verse.

4. The jester normally has a prominent role and closely resembles Shakespeare's wise clown.

5. Unities of time and space are observed up to a point (see the Preface to *The Toy Cart*). More important, however, is the tendency to portray not real characters but ideal types, without losing the qualities that go into the making of characters as separate, unique personalities.

6. A benediction (*nandi*) opens each play and, generally, closes it. This is spoken by the Stage Manager and invokes blessings on the audience. Some benedictions have been omitted in these transcreations, because they are not always organically related to the plays.

7. The main sentiment or flavor (*rasa*) tends to be either heroic or erotic (see the exposition under RASA AND CATHARSIS).

8. The number of acts varies from one to ten, and the play falls in any one of the ten major or eighteen minor categories of drama.

9. Scenes are indicated by the entrance of one person and the exit of another. There is, strictly speaking, no front curtain, though the use of one in modern presentation will not affect the dramatic movement (see THEATER PRODUCTION OF SANSKRIT DRAMA).

## RASA AND CATHARSIS

The theory of *rasa* is central to an appreciation of Sanskrit drama. Bharata propounds it in a way that does not make for easy understanding, but the general ideas can be quickly summarized. Poetry (*kavya*), dance (*nritta*), and mime (*nritya*) produce emotion (*bhava*) of the "romantic" type; they treat aspects of the *lila* (play) of life, and may involve people who enjoy them in personal, even gushy, feelings. Only drama (*natya*), because it is the fifth Veda, produces *rasa* (the essence of impersonal emotion). Nothing, certainly not pity and terror, needs purging; what is required is the creation of a dispassionate delight in the minds of the audience who have been able to look at life steadily and see it whole as a result of the dramatist's skill in presenting before them the eight major sentiments arranged in a harmonious spectrum.

The following eight are involved in this artistic complex, and Bharata implies that every Sanskrit play should indicate its familiarity with these basic human feelings by embodying them in various situations as the plot develops:

1. desire, affection, erotic longing (*rati* or *sringara*).
2. laughter, comic or farcical joy (*hasa* or *hasya*); but not laughter involving cynicism or scorn.
3. anger (*krodha* or *raudra*) arising from the feeling of ill-treatment.
4. sadness (*shoka* or *karuna*) as a result of separation from a loved one.
5. pride (*utsaha* or *vira*) in one's own powers, leading to the display of energetic enterprise, bravery, charity, or forgiveness.
6. fear (*bhaya* or *bhayanaka*) of reproach or attack.
7. aversion or loathing (*jugupsa* or *bibhatsa*).
8. wonder (*vismaya* or *adbhuta*) in the connotation of an encounter with anything that stimulates childlike surprise.

These eight *bhavas* are "stable" sentiments. There are thirty-three "un-stable" or transitory sentiments which, says Bharata, are usable within a play but have significance only in relation to the eight stable ones. Transcending both, of course, is the ninth *bhava*, the *rasa bhava*, which is not included in the list of stable *bhavas*, because the stable *bhavas* have significance in relation to it; it is *santa* (peace, serenity, the feeling of one-ness arising from a sense of wholeness), and therefore indescribable and supernatural. Here we are caught up in the pattern of Hindu metaphysics, and the conception of ideal art being a fleeting experience of the divine. In *The Sanskrit Drama*, A. B. Keith explains beautifully that *rasa* is "one, it is a single, ineffable, transcendental joy, but it can be subdivided, not accord-ing to its own nature, but according to the [eight] emotions which evoke it."

The thirty-three "unstable" sentiments are: discouragement, weakness, apprehension, weariness, contentment, stupor, joy, depression, cruelty, anxiety, fright, envy, arrogance, indignation, recollection, death, intoxica-tion, dreaming, sleeping, awakening, shame, demonic possession, distrac-tion, assurance, indolence, agitation, deliberation, dissimulation, sickness, insanity, despair, impatience, and inconstancy. These play "chancy" roles in the play, emerging as the situation demands, and remaining in the background when not required.

The balancing of the eight sentiments in harmony is the ideal of Sanskrit drama, because this produces *rasa*. The purging, simultaneously, of pity and terror is the Aristotelian ideal, and such shock therapy requires the imitation of an *action*. Bharata defines drama as "the imitation or repre-sentation of conditions and situations." In this connection one might point to the insular, indolent, and refined nature of Indian society at the time that Bharata wrote; free from military threat, it could devote itself to the pursuit of the ideal, the spiritual, and the blissful. Greek society, threatened with the ever-present Persian tiger outside its gates, produced an art form which properly purged pity, the impulse to approach sentimentally, and terror, the impulse to retreat sentimentally, because these are emotions highly undesirable in a martial society—and all Athens was a standing army. In addition, the idea of the "stamp of one defect, oft breaking down the pales and forts of reason," as a result of which the hero, "in the general censure, takes corruption," pertains specifically to the Judaeo-Greco-Chris-tian world-view, and posits the absolute moral choices which create the tragic—the "damned"—or the happy—the "saved"—condition. In the Hindu world-view, the chief sin being ignorance, *rasa* became a form of enlightenment through participation in esthetic ritual.

THEATER PRODUCTION OF SANSKRIT DRAMA

The recent discovery of the dance theater at Ramgarh in the southwest of Bengal spurred interest in further research in Indian theater architecture and design, a field completely neglected and one in which dependable source material is extremely scarce.

The *Natyashastra* offers many pointers. Bharata speaks of three types of theaters, the rectangular (*vikrashta*), the square (*chaturasra*), and the triangular (*triasra*). Each of these is further divided into the large, the medium-sized, and the small; presumably the large was for major plays, the medium for one-acters, and the small for monologues. The ideal, says Bharata, is one that measures thirty-two yards in length and sixteen in width. When divided into two equal areas, this becomes a 16-yard square for the audience, with the remaining square redivided into two halves of 16 x 8 yards each. A further halving of the front 16 x 8 rectangle results in two rectangles, each measuring 4 x 16 yards. The 4-yard square at the center of the back half of these two portions is the *rangashirsha* (the retiring room). The front half, measuring 4 x 16, becomes the stage proper; the portion measuring 8 x 16 at the back of the retiring room becomes the green room with two entrances. It is separated from the stage by a curtain, but there is no curtain between the stage and the audience. The commentator Abhinavagupta says there are eighteen different kinds of stages; the one described is presumably the most satisfactory.

The stage is, of course, on a slight elevation; Bharata speaks of *dvibhumi*, or two levels, the raised level for the stage and the other for the audience; in the *Sangita-Ratnakara,* a treatise on the arts, there is a detailed description of one such theater: "It should be covered over by an awning, supported by pillars richly decorated and hung with garlands. The master of the house should take his seat in the center, on a throne: the occupants of the private apartments should be seated on his left and persons of rank on his right. Behind each group are the chief officers of the state or household, and poets, astrologers, physicians, and men of learning are to be seated in the center. Female attendants, selected for their beauty and figure, are to be present with fans and chowries, while persons carrying sticks are to be stationed to keep order, such armed guards to be placed in different directions. When all are seated, the musicians enter and play, after which the chief dancer advances from behind the curtain, and after saluting the audience, scattering at the same time flowers among them, she displays her skill."

What is described here is a dancer's performance, but attention needs to be given to her "advancing from behind the curtain." This is the curtain that divides the stage proper from the green room and the retiring room, the place from which emanate the noises and shouts so often to be found in the plays in this volume. H. H. Wilson, in his work on the Hindu theater, states, "It seems possible that curtains were suspended transversely, so as to divide the stage into different portions, open equally to the audience, but screening one set of actors from the other. . ."

Of the five hundred plays that we possess knowledge of, it is calculated that about four hundred were actually staged in various courts and in various parts of the country. Theater-going was an occupation of the *nagaraka,* the town sophisticate; the villagers had their own folk drama to delight in.

SUGGESTED BOOKS FOR FURTHER READING

*The Sanskrit Drama. Its Origin, Development, Theory and Practice,* A. Berriedale Keith (*Oxford University Press*). The standard work on the subject, a model of scholarship, clarity and thoroughness. Some of Dr. Keith's remarks have been challenged by Dr. V. Raghavan in various magazine articles, but the bulk of his study continues to be extraordinarily impressive; especially recommended are the chapters, "The Characteristics and Achievement of the Sanskrit Drama" and "The Sentiments."

*The Theatre of the Hindus,* H. H. Wilson, V. Raghavan, K. R. Pisharoti, and Amulya Charan Vidyabhusan (*Susil Gupta, Calcutta*). A reprint of Wilson's *Select Specimens of the Theatre of the Hindus* (1871), with additional material on the South Indian theater and theater architecture by Indian scholars. Especially useful for its excellent summaries of the major extant Sanskrit plays, it has an excellent chapter on "Objects of Dramatic Representation."

*Drama in Sanskrit Literature,* R. V. Jagirdar (*Popular Book Depot, Bombay*). A recent study of the poetic qualities of Sanskrit dramatists, to counterbalance the critics who present them as "purveyors of the epic or

traditional stories with some embellishments," this book is excellent on
Bhavabhuti, and has interesting accounts of the social and historical
background.

*A History of Sanskrit Literature,* Arthur A. Macdonell (*Munshiram
    Manoharlal, Delhi*). A reprint of the extremely useful general study
    which first appeared in 1900, containing a capsule though not very
    illuminating survey of Sanskrit drama.

*Theater in India,* Balwant Gargi (Theater Arts, New York). This general
    study appeared in 1962 and contains an interesting appreciation of
    *The Toy Cart* from the viewpoint of socialist realism.

*Theater in the East,* Faubion Bowers (Nelson, New York). Subtitled "A
    Survey of Asian Dance and Drama," this is an excellent general intro-
    duction to the traditions which Indian drama embodies.

*The Vidusaka,* G. Bhat (New Order Book Company, Ahmedabad). Mr.
    Bhat studies the role of the Jester in Sanskrit drama.

*Contributions to the History of Hindu Drama,* Manomohan Ghosh (K. L.
    Mukhopadhyay, Calcutta). An analysis of the "origin and diffusion" of
    Sanskrit drama.

*Sanskrit Drama: Its Origin and Decline,* Indu Sheykhar (E. J. Brill,
    Leiden). This book was published in 1960 but was presented as a thesis
    at Utrecht University in 1954.

*Drama in Ancient India,* S. Bhatt (Amrit Book Company, New Delhi).

*The Indian Theatre,* Chandra Bhan Gupta (Motilal Banarsidass, Benaras).
    A thesis offered under the title "Presentation of Sanskrit Plays" in 1949;
    useful for details on actual theater production.

*The Classical Drama of India,* Henry W. Wells (Asia Publishing House,
    New York).

*The Indian Theater,* E. P. Horrwitz (First published, Glasgow 1912; re-
    issued, Benjamin Blom, New York, 1967).

*Indian Drama,* Sten Konow (General Printers and Publishers, Calcutta).
    A standard study, translated from the German *Das Indische Drama*
    by S. N. Ghosal.

# SHAKUNTALA

by

## KALIDASA

# Preface

There are many reasons why Kalidasa's classic has remained unavailable in an actable English translation for so long, but one strikes me as especially significant. Rhapsody in criticism begins very often where precision and intelligent judgment leave off, and *Shakuntala* has been unfortunate in receiving periodic doses of honeyed comment. Some of this has come from usually reliable sources, which has not, however, helped to mitigate the harm done by excessive adulation: Goethe explained in verse that *Shakuntala* "charms, enraptures, feasts and feeds" the soul, and Rabindranath Tagore, in a devoted essay, tried to bring out "the inner meaning" of the play by describing it as an allegory in which the fibers of physical passion are toughened by pain and separation into a deep, domestic, semispiritual love.

The play is, of course, concerned chiefly with exploring the range of *sringara rasa,* but Tagore's zealously argued point is illuminating in another way: it reminds us—and this needs constant reminding—that Kalidasa, in writing *Shakuntala,* was also summing up, unconsciously, an entire *dharma*, a code of humane values. Here begins the translator's first headache. Translation is often easy, *traduttori traditori* notwithstanding, and literal translation absurdly so; but perplexing problems arise when a perfectly orderly set of conventions and values of one way of life has to be made perfectly orderly and comprehensible to readers accustomed to values often slightly, and sometimes totally, different.

Take the scene where Mother Gautami, and Sarngarava and Saradvata, the hermits of Kashyapa's ashrama, bring the veiled Shakuntala before King Dushyanta. She is pregnant, and the hermits hope that Dushyanta, whose Kshatriyan propriety is well known, will accept her as his wife. They do not know that an irascible hermit has placed a curse on the king, making him forgetful of the immediate past; they have only Shakuntala's word to go by, and Shakuntala, evasive at first, admits that Dushyanta married her by Gandharva rites in the ashrama.

"You look happy, hermits," says the guard. "I hope your news is pleasant." Dushyanta, who is at a distance on the left of the stage and who has an eye for good looks, turns to the female guard at his side, and whispers, "Who is that veiled lady? She stands out like a glistening bud among brown leaves." Although not exactly a risqué remark, it gives the guard a chance to flatter the royal taste: "I couldn't say, sire," she remarks. "But she is very lovely." By this time Shakuntala has approached near enough for the king to note that her head is covered, and he realizes quickly that he has overshot the limits of Kalidasan decorum. "Hold your tongue," he orders. "She may be married." Which is not only good stage sense, but excellent Hindu sense as well.

I shall have cause to refer again to this self-correcting moral mechanism in *Shakuntala*: it faces the translator on nearly every page, and is the most important quality he must somehow succeed in conveying to his reader. It might be helpful here to digress a little. The difference between journalistic invention and imaginative representation is clear enough: the latter is merely intelligent, the former sensible. But the difference between imaginative writing and creative writing is, because subtle, more important: the first is esthetically organic, the second esthetically and *morally* unified. It is a question of the difference between the titillating, entertaining writer and the elevating writer—and there *is* such a difference.

To an audience thoroughly familiar with Sanskrit, *Shakuntala* is all of a piece, possessing a clean, bracing ethics; but to English readers the scenes and incidents which best embody the ethics can appear incongruous and even farcical if a translator goes about his job ignorantly or condescendingly. Even on the purely technical level, his job is not easy. In the first place, the play is full of irritating *dei ex machina*; stage divisions are not into acts and scenes but parts and interludes, fluid, interwoven— seven altogether; asides, whispers, soliloquies, and chantable slokas abound; good middle-class Sanskrit, "pure" sloka Sanskrit (for the Brahmin and Kshatriya Establishment), and pidgin servants' Sanskrit (called Prakrit) all rub shoulders. Then there are naive bits of melodrama (as when Shakuntala starts crying because she has to leave the ashrama), adolescent chivalry (when Dushyanta rushes out from behind the tree in order to swat the bee that has been annoying Shakuntala), and trivial bits of school-girlishness (when the two maids, Priyamvada and Anasuya, tease Shakuntala about falling in love). There is also an impossible jester called Mathavya who, in punning and wise ludicrosity, is very Shakespearean but who, to the Indian mind, is lovable chiefly because he is an insatiable bundle of gastronomical desires.

Faced by such a variety of material, the translator must edit, reconcile, and transmute; his job in many ways becomes largely a matter of *trans-creation*. The sage who lifts his right hand and says:

> This is a sacred place, sir, and the stag is a sacred beast. Hunting sacred beasts is sinful.
> This stag is not a scrap of paper, for boys to set fire to.
> The very thought is sinful: a tender animal matched against your lightning-like arrows.
> Put the arrow back in your quiver, sir.
> It is meant to guard the distressed, not harm the innocent.

has to be made credible; and so has the king who replies meekly, "I am sorry." Once that is done, the picture of a pattern of culture in which the sage can occasionally give orders to a king and get away with it is complete.

Take other examples. The fact that the birth of a son, Bharata, to Dushyanta has already been predicted, and the birthmarks that help to reconcile the king to Shakuntala are in that sense required only for the sake of working out a happy ending for the play, is not incongruous within the play's ethical structure, however much it may appear so to a foreigner. The Indian knows in advance the legend which Kalidasa makes use of for the purposes of his "plot."

Again, when an Indian critic interprets the play within the requirements of Hindu metaphysical theory, suggesting that it has a circular development of theme beginning with *santa* (the peaceful hermitage in Act I), developing into *sringara* (love seen as rajas, the quality of passion seeking fulfillment, in Acts II–III), moving further into *karuna* (repudiation, seen as tamas, the quality of dark, tragic passion in Acts IV–VI), and finally *santa* once more (in the reunion scene, the quality of sattva in Act VII), this appears perfectly plausible too, though to a mind grooved in a different cultural pattern it must surely appear farfetched and abstruse.

One could go on in this fashion—expanding on Tagore's erotic-to-domestic-love interpretation, or suggesting the antithesis posited in the play between the verities of ashrama life and the hypocrisies of the court, a theme dear to the creative artists of all forest civilizations—but in each case the key point to an understanding of the interpretation would necessarily have to refer to the harmony that Kalidasa achieves, whatever the significance we attach to the play. *Shakuntala* is a delicately balanced play, with no technical or emotional loose ends, spinning within its own moral framework like a gravity-defying gyroscope.

It is a matter of the self-correcting moral mechanism again when Sarngarava in Act V argues with Dushyanta to have Shakuntala lawfully accepted as his queen. This scene is an extremely delicate one. When Mother Gautami says, "You are aware of the exceptional circumstances of the case. She kept her love to herself; you didn't tell us either. It's difficult for a third person to interfere with a private arrangement," the king protests, "I don't understand." Sarngarava, who despite his ashrama training is a bit of a hothead, steps forward: "We don't either. You know the custom, sire. We cannot keep her in the ashrama. We know she is pure, but what will people say? A wife must stay with her husband." Sense overtakes Dushyanta: "Are you implying that I'm married to her?" Sarngarava cushions the shock by saying, "You may have made a mistake, but duty comes first to a king." Dushyanta snorts, "You're presumptuous." Sarngarava instantly loses his head: "I do not like the tone of your voice, sire. You speak like one drunk with power." But almost instantly he cools down and employs sarcasm: "You are no adulterer; it's Father Kashyapa who's to blame for giving his daughter in honor to the robber who stole her." Surprisingly enough, the king takes all this calmly. He must follow the tradition, and play his small part in the harmonious system of courteous and moral checks which go into the making of *Shakuntala*.

Or consider the famous, remarkably tender last scene where the king, now in his senses, recognizes Shakuntala as she moves slowly toward him. In Laurence Binyon's version, published in London in 1920, which is a condensed paraphrase in iambic pentameter, the finest lyrical phrases are cut and the remainder turns into a sloppily sentimental encounter:

BHARATA. Mother, who is this man? He embraced me and called me his son.

SHAKUNTALA. O my heart! Is it my lord indeed?

KING. O my beloved!

SHAKUNTALA. Victory! Victory! (*her voice breaks*)

KING. Tears choke the words that you would greet me with. I have found you. I have found you. All is won.

BHARATA. Who is he, mother?

SHAKUNTALA. Ask of Fate, my child.

KING. O ease your soul, Love, of its bitterness. My mind was darkened,
when I knew you not.

SHAKUNTALA. Rise, husband, noble husband. . .

Binyon missed the point. A husband falling at the feet of his wife com-
municates an experience of extraordinary poignance to an Indian. Shakuntala's "Ask of Fate, my child" means much more than just that in Sanskrit:
it involves the idea of karma and of the stars influencing human life. To
suggest this I translated it as: "My son, a star is dancing;" but I would
refer the reader to the entire passage as I think it should be translated

The second problem is the question of style. Even if Binyon's English is
unobjectionable, his style fails to convey the Indian "spirit." There have
been other translators too, and among them many Indians, with the result
that succulent silliness has often resulted from an overly meticulous attention to the Sanskrit. Take the well-known love scene. I am afraid it is in
many ways similar, so far as amorous technique goes, to what Indian movie
moguls find excellent for box-office success: coyness, rapid and irrepressible
eye movements and an unfulfilled clinch. The translator has to make all
this appear natural, for to a Sanskrit-knowing and tradition-conscious
audience it is not corny at all; and I do not see how this is possible if
Shakuntala, seeing her friends leave, exclaims (in the P. K. Roy version):
"How! Gone indeed!" The king is at her side, however, and murmurs,
"Away with anxiety. This person, the server, stands indeed by your side.
Shall I work the lotus-leaf-fan whose breeze is moist with particles of
water that allay lassitude; or, O thou, with-thighs-like-the-outer-edge-of-
the-palm-of-the-hand, having placed your lotus-red feet in my lap, shall
I press them as is agreeable to you?"

Shakuntala, perturbed by the ungrammatical sweet nothings of this
hyphenated ardor, replies, "I shall not cause this self of mine to offend
against those that deserve respect," and wants to get up and leave. "O fair
one," continues the chivalrous Dushyanta, "the day is not yet extinguished,
and this your condition. Having left the bed of flowers in which lotus-
leaves serve to cover up the breasts how can you go out in the sun with
your limbs delicate through suffering?" He stops her. Shakuntala appeals

to his family honor. "O descendant of Puru," she implores, "respect decorum. Though smitten by love, I cannot command myself." But the king is adamant. "O timid one, off with respect for your superiors. Having known of you, his worship, the lord of anchorites, who is aware of the shastras, will not take offense at it. Besides, several daughters of royal sages are as married by the Gandharva rites and welcomed by their fathers."

In spite of the fact that he calls Father Kashyapa "his worship," Shakuntala will not relent. "Do release me. I will yet again honor my friends." And the king says, "Well, I will release." "When?" asks Shakuntala. The king puts all he has in the speech that follows: "Meanwhile, O fair one, as is done of the fresh flower by the bee, the flavor of your tender and untouched lower lip is being gently tasted by me longing for a sip." This is nonsense, for he is only about to begin to kiss her when a voice offstage announces that it is time for good girls to go to bed. Shakuntala leaves.

The same scene can be better translated without violating its "Indianness." An excellent literal version, such as the one from which I have quoted, sounds like a ghastly parody, and reading it becomes a comical experience. Binyon attempted to get away from such unimaginative jejuneness. But I cannot imagine a king, however Edwardian, uttering true love in metronomic verse pattern:

> When, like the bee on the just-opened bud,
> I have tasted that untasted sweet, your lips,
> And for one heavenly moment have assuaged
> The thirst that parches me, Shakuntala!

Such thirst passeth understanding, and it is small wonder that Shakuntala responds so tardily to passion expressed in mealy prose and gelatin verse!

Neither method will do the trick. Both believe that the Sanskrit "flavor" needs to be preserved, and that English can be "exotified" enough to do this. This halfway house is a dream castle. The thing to do is to attempt to preserve not the Sanskrit language but the Hindu tradition which it enshrines; in fact, I would suggest that the best way to translate *Shakuntala* is to have the translation as far removed from the coils of Sanskrit as possible. Sanskrit is an extremely disciplined yet intricate and metaphorical weapon in Kalidasa's hands, resembling an *alpona* pattern. Within the strict outlines, the ascetic grammar, the exacting sloka form, there is amazing virtuosity in idea, image, and metaphor. What is required of the translator is that he be able to comprehend the tightness of the pattern and communicate it rather than the dazzling displays of linguistic and imaginative skill. These are incommunicable; the history of translation is littered with the débris of incommunicables.

Quoting Sanskrit critics, Professor Ingalls explains how poetry is supposed to possess three kinds of *dhvani* (or "overtone"). Every word, in fact, has three kinds of radiating meaning. "Ganges" by itself means just a holy river in India, but the moment the word is used in context (such as "a village on the Ganges"), the second meaning—a village on the *bank* of the Ganges—comes into operation; the word means more than itself. But there is a third meaning too: the word "Ganges" associated with a village on its bank suggests coolness and holiness. "Our difference from the Sanskrit poets really comes down simply to this: we rely on the magic of the spoken tongue to bring about these sudden expansions of the mind, whereas the Sanskrit poet has chosen to use linguistic and rhetorical devices that are more controllable and more consciously rational." The translator, in other words, has one major task to perform: he must divine, discover, or guess the *effect* Kalidasa was trying to create, and then attempt to re-create it with the resources of the English language.

At the same time, he could profitably keep in mind the system so beloved of the New Critics: associations of ideas and clusters of images. In the first act, symbols of fertile feminine beauty recur: deer, flowers, the spring creeper, the mango tree, and a bee. "The vine has budded prematurely," explains Robert Stein, "symbolising Shakuntala's entry into womanhood. The creeper has chosen a mate—the mango tree which will symbolize the stable and true aspect of Dushyanta's character." The third act repeats the lotus symbol, "a self-sustaining flower which grows from filth," thereby suggesting the "all-consuming, destructive, romantic love, which will lead directly to the curse of non-recognition."

In the fourth act, the central symbol is the ritual fire, representing romantic love and also the god Agni, "the dispeller of night," dispeller of ignorance and confusion, foreshadowing the final recognition of Shakuntala. Shakuntala's impending motherhood is suggested by the pregnant doe, and by the trees bringing forth fine garments and jewelry for her to wear. The song heard by the king in the fifth act—about a mango tree, a bee, and a lotus—refers the audience back to the initial meeting of the two lovers. Later, there are references to a sterile spring, because the king has ordered that there be no celebration on account of his grief. And so on, till the final act, with its clear, white light of recognition, the gold peak, and the images of motherhood introduced as we meet Kashyapa and Aditi, the parents of the gods. The play is completed in the *santa rasa,* "there is absence of passion, perfect illumination, blissful consciousness, and complete concentration of attention (as laid down in the *Sahitya-darpana, The Mirror of Art* )." "And may I be released from further lives."

KALIDASA

*Birthplace:* Central India, most probably Ujjain, the capital of the kingdom of Chandragupta II (also known as Vikramaditya). Legend, however, identifies Kalidasa with Matrigupta, king of Kashmir, in north-west India.

*Date of birth:* Unknown, varying with different scholars between the second century B.C. and the fourth century A.D. According to K. M. Pannikar: in the reign of king Agnimitra (second century B.C.); traditionally: 56 B.C. (Kalidasa is supposed to be one of the "nine gems" adorning the court of Vikramaditya). According to Professors Lassen and Weber: second century A.D.; Max Muller and Dr. Bhandarkar put him in the sixth century. Keith, Bloch, Pandit Ramavatara Sharma and Kokileswar Sastri prefer the fourth century.

# SHAKUNTALA

# Characters

A Charioteer, *to Dushyanta*

King Dushyanta, *ruler of India*

A Sage, *of Kanva's ashrama*

Shakuntala, *foster-daughter of Kanva*

Anasuya } *friends of*
Priyamvada } *Shakuntala*

Jester, *Mathavya, Dushyanta's friend*

A Guard, *of the King's camp*

General, *of King Dushyanta*

Two Hermits } *of Kanva's*
Novices } *ashrama*

Mother Gautami, *matron of the ashrama*

Hermit Women } *of Kanva's*
Hermit Boys } *ashrama*

Kashyapa, *a holy sage*

Sarngarava, *hermit of the ashrama*

Chamberlain, *of Dushyanta*

Female Guard, *of the palace*

Saradvata, *hermit of the ashrama*

Priest, *of Dushyanta*

Officer of City Police }
Januka, a constable } *of the capital*
Suchaka, a constable }

Prisoner

Sanumati, *a nymph*

Two Maidservants, *of the royal garden*

Chaturika, *a maid of the palace*

Matali, *Indra's charioteer*

Hermit Girls

Maricha, *a holy sage*

Voices, Voices of the Court Poets, Voice of the Trees, etc.

# ACT I

*Enter* KING DUSHYANTA'S *chariot. The* KING *is armed with a bow and arrow.*

CHARIOTEER. You are like Siva on a deer hunt:
   Bow and arrow in search of the antelope.

KING. This clever beast leads us a wild-goose chase.
   Look, charioteer,
   There, open-mouthed and foaming: grass falls from his mouth half
      chewed,
   He fears the arrow and pulls in his neck,
   He leaps like a breath of air, gracefully,
   Turning his neck toward the chariot.
   But now I'm afraid I'm losing him, though I saw him clearly a minute
      back.

CHARIOTEER. He gave us the slip on that bumpy ground. I had to rein
in tight then. But he won't get far.

KING. Faster!

CHARIOTEER. This is the fastest I can, your Majesty. *He loosens the
reins.*

   Look at them go! Taut, intolerant, and emulous,
   Ears straight and steady, careless of the kicked-up dust.

KING. They excel even the gods.
   This speed is a miracle, it plays tricks with my eyes—
   Small objects put on size, the crooked becomes straight.
   I seem to be nowhere and everywhere.
   There he is! Slow down, charioteer.

*The* KING *aims an arrow. Shouting voices are heard offstage.*

VOICES. The sacred stag! The sacred stag! Who would kill the sacred
stag?

CHARIOTEER, *looking and listening.* I see holy men everywhere, Your Majesty. Exactly where you were going to shoot.

KING, *quickly.* Stop the horses.

*The chariot stops. A* SAGE *enters, followed by a number of disciples.*

SAGE, *lifting his right hand.* This is a sacred place, sir,
   and this stag is a sacred beast. Hunting sacred beasts is sinful.
   This stag is not a scrap of paper, for boys to set fire to.
   The very thought is sinful: a tender animal matched against your
      lightning-like arrows.
   Put the arrow back in your quiver, sir.
   It is meant to guard the distressed, not harm the innocent.

KING. I am sorry.

SAGE. Nobly done, sir. You prove yourself a Puru.
   My blessings on you: may your son be like you.

KING. I am honored.

SAGE. We were out to gather sticks for the sacrificial fire. The ashrama of our guru Kanva is over on the other side, sir, on the left bank of the Malini. If it isn't interfering with your plans, may we ask you to join us for a while? We'd be happy to perform the sacred rites in your presence.

KING. Is Sage Kanva there?

SAGE. Not at the moment. He's away on a pilgrimage to ward off the evil eye from his daughter. But Shakuntala is receiving his guests, and she will be pleased if you accept her hospitality.

KING. Then I'll come. She will speak of me to her father when he returns.

SAGE. We will see you there.

*The* SAGE *and his disciples leave.*

KING. The horses, charioteer! We shall go to the ashrama.

CHARIOTEER. Yes, Your Majesty. *He clucks to the horses.*

KING. No one briefed me, but I think I can make out where I am.
   This is the edge of the Forest of Penance. It's simple really.

Here are grains near the tree roots, dropped from the beaks of wild
  parrots.
Fruit lies rotting, with no one to pick it.
The deer gaze nonchalantly at our strange chariot.
And the paths to the pond are wet: the sages have been bathing.

CHARIOTEER. That is true.

KING. We mustn't spoil their peace, you know. Stop the chariot here.
I'll walk the rest of the distance.

CHARIOTEER. Your Majesty.

KING, *getting down.* Nor should we expect fanfare. Here, hold these.
*He hands his bow, quiver, and golden ornaments to the* CHARIOTEER. See
that the horses are washed and fed by the time I get back.

CHARIOTEER. Certainly, Your Majesty. *He drives off.*

KING, *glancing around.* Is this the entrance? Anyway, here I go!
  But this is a strange omen—my arm is trembling.
  Why should my arm tremble. . .here in the disciplined tranquillity of
    an ashrama?
  But I dare not ask: fate has doors everywhere.

VOICES, *offstage.* Don't be silly! . . .Come on. There! . . .Of course I'm
right.

KING, *listening.* Near that clump of trees, I think.

*He goes forward and looks.*

Ashrama girls with pitchers watering the plants.
Prettier than I would have expected.
What an extraordinarily beautiful girl!
Palace vines don't hold a candle to forest creepers.
I may as well look on.

SHAKUNTALA *enters with two friends.*

SHAKUNTALA. I told you I was right. This is the spot.

ANASUYA. Your father loves these creepers more than he loves you.
That's why he asks you to water them.

SHAKUNTALA. How clever you are! I love them too. And I love my father. So there!

KING, *aside*. If this is Kanva's daughter, Kashyapa's a bad judge to put her in an ashrama.
    Teaching her penance? He might as well cut soma sticks with lotus leaves.

SHAKUNTALA, *stopping*. This is much too tight. Please, Anasuya, help me with this impossible dress! Priyamvada is always playing silly tricks like this.

ANASUYA, *helping her*. There.

PRIYAMVADA, *giggling*. Priyamvada is not playing silly tricks. Your figure's getting better, that's what it is, Shakuntala.

KING, *aside*. It really doesn't fit her; but that doesn't mean it's not right for her.
    The lotus is lovely though filth-covered,
    The moon prettier for her dark spot.
    Anything extra helps the substance, provided the substance exists!

SHAKUNTALA. And now this *kesava* tree. Poor thing! *She sprinkles the tree with water.*

PRIYAMVADA. How pretty you look, Shakuntala. Stay there—no, next to the *kesava*—that's it. You'd think the tree was blessed with a flowering creeper when Shakuntala is near it.

SHAKUNTALA. You're good at flattery, aren't you, Priyamvada?

KING, *aside*. Sweet, yes—but it's the truth.
    Her lips glisten like new leaves,
    Her arms are shoots,
    And her youth sprouts a glory of glittering flowers.

ANASUYA. You are forgetting the light-of-the-forest, twining like a bride round that tree. It's the loveliest creeper for miles around.

SHAKUNTALA. I'd forget myself first. *She looks at the creeper.*
    This tree and creeper are well married:
    The light-of-the-forest is young and in flower,

The tree grows strong in a network of branches.

ANASUYA. Well, well. Have you any idea, my dear Priyamvada, why Shakuntala waters the light-of-the-forest?

PRIYAMVADA. No.

ANASUYA. She thinks, Priyamvada—she thinks, "If I were a creeper, if I could only find a strong handsome tree. . ."

SHAKUNTALA, *overhearing*. Very clever. But keep your daydreaming to yourself. *She continues sprinkling.*

KING. This girl could not possibly be low-caste. What a silly idea! She is fit for a Kshatriya, a real warrior—or why am I pulled toward her like this? When in doubt, one's own impulses are the safest guide. But I must find out about her.

SHAKUNTALA, *speaking in agitation*. Drat this bee! Shoo! Scat! Why don't you fly back to the creeper? *She fans her hands in commotion.*

KING. Lucky rascal,
        You taste the sweetness of her lips, while I stand thirsting.
        We chase meaning, you have the fruit:
        Her flashing eyes, a whisper in her ears.

SHAKUNTALA. Shoo! *She moves away but the bee follows.* Oh, no! Not here too! Please go away. For heaven's sake, do something, Anasuya!

ANASUYA, *laughing*. Call Dushyanta. He is responsible for guarding the ashramas!

KING, *aside*. All right, here's where I come in. *He steps forward but then stops suddenly.* Now there's no reason at all to be afraid but—*He muses.* I mustn't give the game away. Let's see. Well—

SHAKUNTALA. Here too! *She steps aside, walking fast.* Shoo, you idiot! Scat!

KING, *emerging from behind the tree*. Who dares to disturb the peace of the ashrama girls? Be it known that I am a descendant of Puru, a friend to the distressed and foe of the discourteous.

*At the* KING's *sudden appearance, the girls are confused.*

ANASUYA. Oh, sir, it's nothing, sir, nothing serious. Only a bee, sir—worrying our friend here. *She points to* SHAKUNTALA.

KING, *facing* SHAKUNTALA. I'm glad it's nothing serious. Are the holy rites also safe?

SHAKUNTALA, *confused, is unable to speak.*

ANASUYA. Indeed, sir, all is well. The more so since you've arrived, sir. Shakuntala, do bring this gentleman some fruit. I'll wash his feet.

KING. You are too gracious. Please don't. Your words are hospitality enough.

PRIYAMVADA. But you must sit down, sir. It's so hot. There's a cool and shady spot under the *saptaparna* tree—over there. *She points.*

KING. You must be tired too. I notice you've been watering the plants.

ANASUYA. Let's all sit down, Shakuntala.

*They all do so.*

SHAKUNTALA, *aside.* Why is there such a feeling in my heart? He is our guest. And I certainly mustn't lose my head in an ashrama.

KING. I'm glad to find myself in such charming company.

PRIYAMVADA, *aside.* He speaks nobly. Who can he be? Such manners and dignity!

ANASUYA, *aside to* PRIYAMVADA. I wish I knew. I'll ask him. *Aloud.* I hope you will not mind, sir, but it's the confidence you have given us that prompts me. Where do you come from? Which country laments your absence? And if I'm not being too impertinent, what brings you here, sir, tired and alone?

SHAKUNTALA, *aside.* I must keep calm. She takes the words out of my mouth.

KING, *aside.* This is getting ticklish. I must hide myself and reveal myself too. Well. . .*Aloud.* I am a special officer of the king, madam, empowered by him to ascertain if the holy rites at his kingdom's ashramas are proceeding undisturbed.

ANASUYA. It's good to hear that.

SHAKUNTALA's *two friends notice her shyness.*

ANASUYA, *aside*. If your father comes back today, Shakuntala. . .

SHAKUNTALA, *aside*. Well?

ANASUYA, *aside*. He will honor his guest with all he has.

SHAKUNTALA, *aside*. Very clever. But magpies jabber better.

KING. And now may I ask a question?

ANASUYA. Sir?

KING. I was told that the holy hermit Kashyapa was wedded to lifelong celibacy. Then how is it that he has a daughter?

ANASUYA. That's easily answered, sir. You've heard of a royal sage named Kausika?

KING. Yes.

ANASUYA. Shakuntala is *his* daughter. Kashyapa only adopted her after she was abandoned.

KING. Abandoned?

ANASUYA. It's a long story, sir. Kausika was a most remarkable sage. In fact, he was so devout that the gods grew jealous of his austerities and sent the nymph Menaka to tempt him.

KING. I'm told the gods are nervous people.

ANASUYA. It was spring then, sir, and Menaka was a very lovely nymph, and—*She stops short, embarrassed.*

KING. I see. I should have guessed.

ANASUYA. Yes, sir.

KING. It's understandable—she could only be the child of a nymph. Lightning isn't born in the earth's bowels.

SHAKUNTALA *remains shyly silent. The other girls smile knowingly at her.*

PRIYAMVADA, *to the* KING. I'm sorry, sir. You were saying?

*Covertly,* SHAKUNTALA *shakes a warning finger at* PRIYAMVADA.

KING. Yes, of course, of course—may I ask another question?

PRIYAMVADA. We are ashrama girls, sir, we're used to answering questions.

KING. Will your friend stay in the ashrama only until betrothal, or has she taken a lifetime vow?

PRIYAMVADA. She follows her father's instructions, sir. But I believe he wants to see her happily married.

KING, *aside*. It's possible then. I feed on hope.
    This is not fire, but a gem:
    I must shape her and make her mine.

SHAKUNTALA, *angrily*. I must be getting along, Anasuya.

ANASUYA. Whatever for?

SHAKUNTALA. I don't like the way Priyamvada is talking. I think I'd better tell Mother Gautami.

ANASUYA. But you know it's not proper to desert a guest, Shakuntala.

*Nevertheless,* SHAKUNTALA *moves away. The* KING *rises, but then checks himself.*

KING, *aside*. A lover's a pitiable creature.
    I almost caught her, but courtesy interfered.
    I've let her go without so much as rising.

PRIYAMVADA, *catching* SHAKUNTALA. You mustn't, Shakuntala.

SHAKUNTALA. Why not?

PRIYAMVADA. You owe me two plants. Remember the ones I watered for you? Pay your debt, then you can go.

KING. Please don't press her. She is tired.
    Her shoulders droop and her palms are red.
    She breathes heavily and small drops dot the *sirisha* flowers in her hair;

Her knot is loose, almost falling.
Let me free her of her debt.

*He gives* SHAKUNTALA *a ring. The two friends see the royal seal and stare at each other.*

A gift from the king.

PRIYAMVADA. If that can't free you, nothing will! *She laughs lightly.* I free you, Shakuntala, or the king frees you, or this kind gentleman.

SHAKUNTALA, *aside.* If only I could give her what she deserves! *aloud* You make an excellent arbiter, Priyamvada.

KING, *aside, watching* SHAKUNTALA. Is it possible that she feels for me in the same way I do for her? Has God granted my prayer so soon?
   She doesn't talk to me, but listens carefully to all I say.
   She doesn't return my glances, but she wants to look at me when she
      thinks I'm not watching her.

VOICES, *offstage.* Be ready to receive King Dushyanta, O hermits:
   He comes on a hunt.
   Round up the sacred animals.
   His horses are kicking up brown dust which settles like a film of
      locusts on the ashrama trees
   Where our clothes are hanging.
   What's worse, an elephant is scattering the deer;
   The king's chariot unnerves him, and he is lunging at the trees;
   Now he is blinded by torn creepers, he is charging into the holy huts.

*The* KING *and the girls listen in fear.*

KING, *aside.* I must slip away and see what I can do. My officers apparently have no respect for the peace here.

ANASUYA. Will you excuse me, sir? The elephant may cause damage.

KING, *speaking anxiously.* Of course. I'm sorry for this.

*They rise.*

ANASUYA. We're sorry we couldn't receive you properly. We feel ashamed to ask you to visit the ashrama again.

KING. I've never been better received in my life.

SHAKUNTALA. Wait, Anasuya. My foot's pricked—just a thorn—but wait. And my dress—wait, I'll be with you in a minute. *She looks at the* KING *and goes out slowly.*

KING. I don't think I'll go back to the camp after all. I'll find the officers and have them camp somewhere nearby. This girl is too much in my thoughts: I walk away, but my mind is a silk pennant that streams in the wind and must go back to her.

*He walks out slowly.*

C U R T A I N


# ACT II

*The* JESTER *enters, sighing and making a long face.*

JESTER. This king will be my death! What a hunter—he does nothing but hunt! "There goes a stag!" "Hey! that boar!" "Hey! that tiger!" And he drags us along on one hunt after another—under the hot sun—where even the trees give no shade—the streams are full of leaves and mud—not a healthy living drop in sight—and you eat at the oddest hours—the meat stinks—and I'm all one big backache from the infernal riding—damn it, I can't even get a decent night's sleep! And he's at it again bright and early. First those blasted birds he's snared, squealing away, the bastards. Oh, my back's sore—damn my luck! And yesterday he sees this girl Shakuntala, and now he's made camp here and won't budge for all the world. I'll have nightmares from now on, I suppose. But I'll just have to grin and bear it. *He grins.* Let's see if he's up yet. *He shades his eyes and looks offstage.* He's up all right. Here he comes with a covey of beauties around him—bows in their hands and garlands of flowers. I'll have to pretend I have the rheumatism or something. *He leans on his stick as the* KING *enters.*

KING, *aside*. I know she can't be an easy prize,
Â Â Â Â But it's a comfort to see she likes me too.
Â Â Â Â Liking each other is pleasure enough:
Â Â Â Â Fulfillment's another matter.

*He smiles gently.*

Â Â Â Â This is the way a lover fools himself:
Â Â Â Â He paints her as he wants her, not as she is.
Â Â Â Â The way she looked out of the corner of her eyes—
Â Â Â Â The light step she took, turning her body—
Â Â Â Â Her quick anger when about to depart—
Â Â Â Â The lover thinks they were all meant for him.

JESTER, *leaning clumsily on his stick*. Forgive me, Your Majesty, if I cannot bow. I greet you with words.

KING. Mighty fast work, this stiffness of yours.

JESTER. Yes, Your Majesty. But you shouldn't ask how. My eyes drop tears, but you send the clouds.

KING. I don't understand.

JESTER. Tell me, sire: does the reed bend by itself, or does the current push it?

KING. The current, of course.

JESTER. You have pushed me, sire. *He weeps profusely.*

KING. Come, come.

JESTER. I can't. I can't stand it any more. You live here in the forest like a peasant, Your Majesty. Hunting has killed me. I'm nervous as a rattle. Let me have rest, sire—*He sighs.* Lots of rest.

KING, *aside*. Hunting bores him. But it bores me too—at least since I met Shakuntala. It's so. . .so ruthless killing the deer she raised with her own hands. *He smiles.* They have borrowed innocence from her.

JESTER, *looking intently at the* KING. Your mind is elsewhere, sire. I have asked in vain.

KING, *smiling*. No, you didn't. We shall camp here, and you will have a well-deserved rest.

JESTER. Thank you, thank you, thank you. *He is about to move away.*

KING. I haven't finished.

JESTER. I'm sorry, I'm sorry, I'm sorry.

KING. When you've rested, I think I could do with your help for a bit. No hard work, of course.

JESTER. If it's eating something sweet, sire, I'm your man.

KING. We'll see. Guard!

*A* GUARD *enters.*

KING. Bring my commanding officer here.

*The* GUARD *goes out and returns with the* GENERAL, *saying, "This way, sir."*

GENERAL. Good morning, sire.
    Hunting's a dubious sport, but you've done well.
    I never saw Your Majesty look better.
    I'm told it's pulling the bowstring that does the trick—
    Absolutely great for developing the biceps.

*He approaches nearer the* KING.

    The beaters have already started into the forest.
    Shall we follow, sire?

KING. I'm afraid I can't. My friend here doesn't approve of hunting.

GENERAL. He's a fool. Why, look at you, sire! Fit as a fiddle, and hunting has done it for you. The hunt's a splendid thing. You get to know how animals behave in tight corners. Your own skill comes out: knocking down a running beast isn't eating cake. Anyone who doesn't approve of hunting is crazy.

JESTER, *heatedly*. Oh, go away! Go make love to a she-bear, we're not budging.

KING. I'm sorry, but I've made up my mind. We're camping here.
Let the beasts enjoy themselves today, shall we?
The buffalo can churn the ponds with their horns if they wish,
The deer can stand quiet in the shade,
The boars can dig roots in the shallow lakes.
I'd like to give this bow of mine a holiday too.

GENERAL. Of course, sire.

KING. Call back the beaters. And tell the soldiers to go easy here; this is an ashrama and I'd like to see it respected. Besides, the hermits are quite unpredictable: quiet on the surface, but very tense inside. Worrying them is asking for trouble.

GENERAL. Yes, Your Majesty.

JESTER. Remember the she-bear!

*The* GENERAL *goes out. The* KING *addresses his officers.*

KING. Take off those hunting outfits and get into something more comfortable. And you, guard, see that you keep good watch here.

*The officers depart.*

JESTER. Good riddance! They collect like flies around sugar. Let's sit down, sire, in the shade. It's nice and cool over there.

KING. Lead on, sir.

*The* JESTER *leads the way to a shady spot, where they sit down.*

KING, *continuing.* You're a queer fellow—you miss everything that's worth seeing.

JESTER. I do not. I see you very clearly.

KING. Anyone can be pleased with what he's used to. I meant you haven't seen Shakuntala.

JESTER, *aside.* I won't give him the chance. *Aloud.* Are you in love with a hermit's daughter?

KING. No—I'm not that harebrained. Anyway she's really a nymph's daughter, only brought up by Kashyapa. Talk about white flowers falling on dry branches!

JESTER, *laughing*. You have the pick of the girls in the palace, sire. You lose your head over trifles.

KING. You haven't seen her.

JESTER. She must be ravishing indeed if she can attract you!

KING. Words are poor things.
   God made her as beautiful as a painting.
   She is flawless, created out of whatever is lovely, precious, and simple.

JESTER. The other girls had better brush up their charms!

KING. I should think so.
   She's a virgin flower, a serene leaf,
   An uncut diamond, untasted honey.
   Whoever gets her is a lucky fellow.

JESTER. Get her yourself then, before some oil-smeared hermit takes her.

KING. Her father isn't here. I'd have to ask his permission.

JESTER. Tell me, did she look your way?

KING. She glanced at me.

JESTER. How?

KING. You know how. She's not used to flirting; she looked at me but when I caught her eye she turned away. I thought she smiled, but that may have been my imagination. . . . She didn't encourage me, if that's what you mean.

JESTER. It takes time, sire.

KING. Of course I did think she showed some emotion when she was leaving. She took a few steps and hesitated, complaining that her foot had been pricked. And she pretended to free her dress from a jutting branch when it wasn't caught at all.

JESTER. If you don't watch out you'll be turning this ashrama into a harem.

KING. The trouble is they all know me now. I wonder how I might manage to slip in unnoticed. . . .

JESTER. Easiest thing in the world! Next time come as the king, to collect your taxes—order the hermits to bring one sixth of their grain, as others do.

KING. That's foolish. Their payment is more precious than gold. The taxes we collect come and go, but their tax is their prayer and penance—things that are imperishable.

VOICE, *offstage*. At last!

KING. Deep and rich—that sounds like a hermit's voice.

GUARD, *entering and bowing*. Two young hermits, Your Majesty, who wish to see you.

KING. Bring them here.

*The* GUARD *goes out and re-enters with the two* HERMITS.

GUARD. This way, please.

*Both* HERMITS *look intently at the* KING.

FIRST HERMIT. He's very handsome. And virtuous too. In the first place, he camps near an ashrama; second, he promises to look after us. No wonder the poets write songs in his praise!

SECOND HERMIT. Is this King Dushyanta, Gautama?

FIRST HERMIT. It couldn't be anyone else.

SECOND HERMIT. I guessed as much. I have heard a great deal about him.

THE HERMITS, *approaching nearer the* KING. Our blessings, sire.

KING, *rising*. I am grateful for them.

*They offer fruit, which the* KING *accepts*.

KING, *continuing*. What can I do for you?

FIRST HERMIT. We thought we might ask you to protect us from the demons that have been harassing us since our guru Kanva went away. Stay with us for a few days.

KING. You flatter me.

JESTER, *aside*. Naturally.

KING, *smiling*. Guard, have my chariot and bow brought here.

GUARD. Yes, Your Majesty. *He goes out*.

THE HERMITS, *joyfully*. We knew you'd agree. It runs in the blood of the Purus.

KING, *bowing*. I won't keep you. I'll follow you as soon as the chariot arrives.

*The* HERMITS *leave*.

KING. Would you like to come and see Shakuntala?

JESTER. Not if the demons are still there.

KING. Oh come, come, little chicken—I'll be with you.

JESTER. That might make me change my mind.

*The* GUARD *re-enters*.

GUARD. The chariot's ready, sire, but there's a messenger from the queen just arrived.

KING. *speaking quickly*. From my mother?

GUARD. Yes, sire.

KING. Bring him here immediately.

GUARD. Yes, sire. *He goes out and returns with the* MESSENGER.

MESSENGER. Greetings from the queen mother, Your Majesty. She wishes to remind you that the Fast of the Son's Homage is four days from now, and she must have you by her side then.

KING. On one side, the hermits; on the other, my dear mother. I can't very well refuse either.

JESTER. Then stand in the middle, as Trishanku did.

KING. I wish I could, but I can't. And I can't be in two places at the same time.

I'm like a stream that's cut in two by an obstinate rock.

I can't make up my mind.

*He thinks deeply.*

I'll make the best of a bad job. Look here, my mother treats you like a son, doesn't she? Well, tell her I'm very busy here, and do whatever's necessary about the fast.

JESTER. I could. But won't you think I'm just leaving to escape from the demons?

KING. How could I? *He smiles.*

JESTER. Well, I shall go as your brother.

KING. In fact, you may take all my officers with you too. I don't like them here upsetting the peace.

JESTER. I'll go like a prince!

KING, *aside.* But the fellow's a gossip—he'll probably give my secret away to the palace ladies. *He takes the* JESTER *by the hand and speaks aloud.* You realize, of course, that I'm staying here simply to help the sages, not because of that silly girl I mentioned. I'm a king, after all, while she just plays with deer all day and understands nothing of love-making. You knew I was only joking all along, didn't you?

JESTER. But of course.

*They both leave.*

C U R T A I N

INTERLUDE

*The action takes place on the fore-stage in front of the curtain. A novice from the ashrama enters, carrying kusha grass.*

NOVICE. The king's a wizard—not one demon has troubled us since he set foot here. The twang of his bowstring strikes terror everywhere, like a lion's growl. *He acts as if someone is approaching.* It's Priyamvada. *He steps toward her.* For whom do you carry medicine and lotus blossoms, Priyamvada? What?—is Shakuntala sick? A heat stroke? Nurse her well, Priyamvada, she is the soul of our guru. I'll perform her duties in the meantime and offer holy water to Mother Gautami.

*They leave.*

# ACT III

*The* KING *enters, looking very lovesick.*

KING, *sighing.* I know something of self-discipline.
　I also know she has a father.
　Nevertheless my heart longs for her.
　O brilliant god of arrows and flowers,
　O Moon, how many of the lovesick you deceive!
　Your arrows are not flowers, nor is moonlight cold.
　It burns, and the arrows are sharp as rock.
　O fish-god, have mercy:
　I am wounded by two black eyes.

*He paces back and forth in distress.*

The rites are over, the hermits no longer need me.
One look from her could cure me.

*He sighs.*

I must find her.

*He looks at the sun.*

It's getting on toward noon.
She will be on the banks of the Malini, in the garden of creepers.

*He examines the trees.*

She passed this spot not long ago, and took flowers:
The cut stalks are still oozing,
And the young buds spill milky juice.
What a lovely spot!
Sick limbs can bathe in the lotus-scented breeze
That comes carrying cool spray from the Malini.

*He looks around.*

I'll find her in this cane bower: here are her footprints, shallow in front and deep at the back: she must be very tired. Let me look. *He peers among the reeds, and then smiles.* At last! *Shakuntala is seen lying on a stone slab, attended by her friends.* My darling resting on a bed of stone, flowers over her head, friends to care for her. . . . I'll hear their secrets now!

ANASUYA, *fanning* SHAKUNTALA *with a lotus leaf.* Is the breeze enough for you, Shakuntala?

SHAKUNTALA. Are you fanning me?

ANASUYA *looks helplessly at* PRIYAMVADA.

KING, *aside.* She's terribly tired. Or is she lovesick like me?

*He gazes at* SHAKUNTALA *longingly.*

I've never seen her prettier than at this moment.
Her breasts rise and fall slowly, the lotus in her hair has slipped—
Sunstroke and love play havoc with girls,
But sunstroke doesn't make them so pretty!

PRIMYAMVADA, *aside.* She's been like this since she met that officer.

ANASUYA, *aside.* I thought so too. I'll ask her. *Aloud.* Are you in pain, Shakuntala?

SHAKUNTALA, *raising her head.* Well? What—?

ANASUYA. I know very little about love, but I've read poems and—and romantic stories. . . . You must be in love, Shakuntala, isn't that it? I can't give you medicine until I know what the trouble is.

KING, *aside*. My diagnosis exactly.

SHAKUNTALA, *aside*. What can I possibly tell her?

PRIYAMVADA. Tell us, Shakuntala. We mean well. You've been losing weight every day. You haven't been yourself at all.

KING, *aside*. How right she is:
> Her cheeks are pale, her breasts tired;
> Her waist thinner and shoulders drooping.
> Lovesick, she is lovely—like the *madhavi* creeper
> Blown by the wind, but fresh.

SHAKUNTALA. You are so kind to me. But I don't want to put you to any trouble.

ANASUYA. That's just it. Tell us what is upsetting you. It's easier to bear sorrow if you share it.

KING, *aside*. She can't get out of it now. . . . I was so eager to know at first, why am I apprehensive now?

SHAKUNTALA. It happened when I saw the officer. . . . *She pauses, embarrassed.*

ANASUYA *and* PRIYAMVADA. Go on, Shakuntala. Go on.

SHAKUNTALA. I wasn't the same afterward. . . . Every time he crosses my mind, this happens.

KING, *joyfully*. That's all I wanted!
> The god of love gave me sorrow, but he can heal it too,
> Like black clouds that burst in rain.

SHAKUNTALA. If you could arrange a meeting. . .But if not, there's no use carrying on with the cure.

KING, *aside*. I must do something about this.

PRIYAMVADA, *aside*. A pretty hopeless case, Anasuya. We mustn't delay. That officer—he looked high-caste to me. Couldn't we do something?

ANASUYA, *aside*. I guess we could.

PRIYAMVADA. You're lucky to have fallen in love with him, Shakuntala, he's just the man for you. It's as inevitable as a river flowing into the sea or the *shakara* tree having an *armukta* creeper.

ANASUYA. How do we go about it? We must cure her soon—and in secret.

PRIYAMVADA. The "soon" is as good as done, but secrecy is another matter.

ANASUYA. Why?

PRIYAMVADA. You can't hide such feelings. And I thought the officer looked a bit weak and lovesick too.

KING, *aside*. So right, so right. My arm bracelet doesn't seem to stay in place any more.

PRIYAMVADA, *thoughtfully*. Why not a love letter? I'll put it in the flowers and see that it reaches him.

ANASUYA. Fine. Yes, that will do nicely. *To* SHAKUNTALA Well?

SHAKUNTALA. I'll do anything you say.

PRIYAMVADA. Think out a poem—and see that it has you in it.

SHAKUNTALA. I'll try. I hope he won't take it amiss.

KING, *aside*. Amiss? I would rush to you if I could. SHAKUNTALA *sits up*. Thank God, I've not been able to sleep these days, or I might have missed all this. There is love in her eyes as she thinks out the poem.

SHAKUNTALA. I think I have it, but I've nothing to write with.

PRIYAMVADA. Scratch the words with your nails on a lotus leaf. It's soft as a parrot's breast.

SHAKUNTALA *does so, speaking as she writes.*

SHAKUNTALA. How does this sound?
 I can't tell your desire,
  Try as I may,
 But my heart burns with fire
  Night and day.

KING, *emerging from his hiding place.*

> The lily endures the sun,
>> But the moon—no;
> Your heart's the distressed one,
>> Mine is aglow.

ANASUYA *and* PRIYAMVADA. You come in the nick of time, sir.

SHAKUNTALA *tries to get up.*

KING. Don't rise. This is no time to be formal.

ANASUYA. Sit down here, sir, on this stone.

*The* KING *sits down.* SHAKUNTALA *is silent.*

PRIYAMVADA. You know how you feel about each other now. But I'd like to put in a word, if you don't mind.

KING. Please do. I like the way you speak your mind—it prevents misunderstandings.

PRIYAMVADA. I recognize you now, sire. You are the king himself, not one of his officers. And I know that the king protects whoever is in trouble.

KING. That is my highest duty.

PRIYAMVADA. She is in trouble, sire, and the god of love is responsible. Please take good care of her.

KING. Of course. But thank you for the advice.

SHAKUNTALA, *looking at* PRIYAMVADA. I don't see why you must press him so, Priyamvada. He must be wanting to get back to the palace ladies.

KING. I love you, Shakuntala. If you think I am trifling with you, you wound me doubly.

ANASUYA. Kings have many wives, Shakuntala. You must make allowance for that. See that she doesn't come to grief, sire.

KING. I cannot break tradition, but I assure you I now hold two loyalties above all—Shakuntala and my kingdom.

PRIYAMVADA, *looking around.* Let us go, Anasuya. We'll take that lost fawn to its mother.

ANASUYA *and* PRIYAMVADA *get up to leave.*

SHAKUNTALA. Don't leave me alone.

PRIMYAMVADA. Alone, she says!

*The two girls depart.*

KING. You have nothing to worry about as long as I'm here. Shall I fan you with the lotus leaf? Would you rather I pressed your tired feet?

SHAKUNTALA. I am giving you unnecessary trouble. *She tries to leave.*

KING. It's blazing hot, Shakuntala, and you're in no condition to walk alone. You won't be able to stand the sun after your bed of lotus leaves. *He catches her by the arm.*

SHAKUNTALA. Please, sire. I am a woman. It's not my fault I'm in love. What will the others think?

KING. Don't be afraid. Your father knows the shastras. There have been cases when girls have married according to the Gandharva rites. They weren't ostracized.

SHAKUNTALA. Please let me go, sire. I must join my friends.

KING. I will—in a minute.

SHAKUNTALA. Please.

KING. After I have kissed you, as a bee kisses a flower.

*He lifts her face, but she turns away.*

VOICE, *offstage.* Night approaches. To bed, hermits.

SHAKUNTALA, *alarmed.* It must be Mother Gautami, come to look for me. Hide yourself, sire, quickly—in the bush there.

*The* KING *does so.* GAUTAMI *enters, with a pot in her hand.* PRIYAMVADA *and* ANASUYA *follow.*

GAUTAMI. How are you, child?

SHAKUNTALA. Much better, mother, thank you.

GAUTAMI. Take this water, child, it will help you. *She sprinkles holy water from the pot on* SHAKUNTALA's *head.* It's late now; you should be in bed. *She starts to leave.*

SHAKUNTALA, *aside.* When I had my chance, I was coy. Now I have only regret. *Aloud.* I will return, ivy bower: you were my best doctor.

SHAKUNTALA *departs with the others. The* KING *emerges from his hiding place with a sigh.*

KING. Obstacles all the way!
　I almost kissed her, even as she said no.
　Now it's over.
　These are the flowers she lay on,
　This the letter her nails wrote out,
　This the lotus her fingers dropped—
　Small mercies: I shall stay here and relish them.

VOICE, *offstage.* Help us, O king!
　The demons are attacking us.
　The purple clouds are gathering around the sacred fire.

KING. Not a minute to lose!

*He departs hastily.*

C　U　R　T　A　I　N

INTERLUDE

ANASUYA *and* PRIYAMVADA *enter the fore-stage and begin plucking flowers.*

ANASUYA. A Gandharva marriage is good enough. I'm glad she has found such a fine man. . . . But I have misgivings, Priyamvada.

PRIYAMVADA. Why?

ANASUYA. The hermits have sent him away today; now he is back with his palace ladies. I wonder if he will remember her long.

PRIYAMVADA. Of course he will. You can tell good breeding. What I'm worried about is how Father Kashyapa will take it.

ANASUYA. He won't mind.

PRIYAMVADA. What makes you think so?

ANASUYA. After all, he did want to find a suitable husband for her. If fate gives him a helping hand, so much the better.

PRIYAMVADA, *looking in her basket.* Enough flowers for today!

ANASUYA. Just a few more! we'll offer them on Shakuntala's behalf.

PRIYAMVADA. Good.

*They continue picking flowers.*

VOICE, *offstage.* Is anybody in?

ANASUYA, *listening.* It sounds like a guest.

PRIYAMVADA. Shakuntala is there to receive him. . .*Aside.* . . . though her mind's somewhere else!

ANASUYA. I think these are more than enough. Let's go.

*They turn to depart.*

VOICE, *offstage.* This is an insult! Why is there no one to receive me? A curse on whoever is stealing your thoughts! He will be reminded, but he won't remember—like a madman who cannot recall what he has just said.

PRIYAMVADA. Oh, no! This is terrible. The worst has happened—Shakuntala has unknowingly insulted a holy guest. *She looks in the direction of the voice.* It's that bad-tempered hermit Durvasas—there he goes hopping away!

ANASUYA. Hurry. Throw yourself on your knees before him! Bring him back, while I get the holy water and fruit ready.

PRIYAMVADA. I hope I can catch him. *She runs out.*

ANASUYA, *stumbling on a root.* Oh dear, I've dropped the basket! I'm in such a dither. *She stoops to pick up the flowers.*

PRIYAMVADA, *re-entering.* He won't give in. But I've cooled him down a bit.

ANASUYA, *smiling.* What does he say?

PRIYAMVADA. I begged him: "O holy one, please forgive us." "No!" he said. "Please, O holy one, this is the first time it's happened, she's like your own daughter, only very silly. Please forgive her."

ANASUYA. Yes, yes, but what happened?

PRIYAMVADA. Why, he disappeared into thin air, and I heard a voice saying out of the sky: "I can't take back my words, but the curse will be broken when he recognizes a sign."

ANASUYA. At least that's something. And she has the royal ring, you remember? He gave it to her before he left. Shakuntala has the remedy in her own hands!

PRIYAMVADA. Let's go, Anasuya; we'll be late for prayers.

*Again they prepare to leave.* PRIYAMVADA *pauses a moment, observing something offstage.*

PRIYAMVADA. Look at her, Anasuya—lost in thought as usual, like a painted picture, her face cupped in her left hand. She doesn't know herself these days. How could you expect her to greet Durvasas properly?

ANASUYA. Let's keep this to ourselves. We mustn't get her mixed up in a scandal—she's so sensitive.

PRIYAMVADA. Of course not, silly. One doesn't sprinkle roses with dishwater.

*They both leave.*


## ACT IV

*A* NOVICE *enters, just arisen from sleep. He speaks to himself.*

NOVICE. Kashyapa asks me to find out the time—at this hour of the night too! *He looks at the sky.* Why, it's dawn already. There's the moon on the hill, and the bright sun behind the forest. When the moon is vanishing, the lily lives in memory, and recalling her is pain. A lover gone away is greater pain. Look, the sun touches the dew on the jujubes. The peacock wakes on the roof of the hut, and the stag, weary from the mud-bath, stretches himself in the sun. The moon drops suddenly. There is a time for decline. And the brightest, I am told, fall lowest.

ANASUYA, *offstage.* The hermits may not know it, but he's played her false.

NOVICE. I'll tell Kashyapa it's time for prayers. *He leaves.*

ANASUYA, *entering.* I feel so helpless. Why should a girl fall in love with a deceiver? It's all that Durvasas' fault! And why doesn't the man write? It's ages since he left. He certainly fooled her—took her in completely. *She stands and thinks.* We could send him the ring though. Only there's no one to take it. And I don't dare tell Father Kashyapa that she's married —and pregnant! It's her fault, after all. Oh me, what a mess I've landed her in!

PRIYAMVADA, *entering and speaking joyfully.* Hurry, Anasuya—Shakuntala's leaving.

ANASUYA, *bewildered.* Where? How?

PRIYAMVADA. I saw her not a minute ago; I went round to find out how she was.

ANASUYA. Well?

PRIYAMVADA. Father Kashyapa was there with her, blessing her as she stood before him—all blushes. Can you believe it? "You're lucky, my child," he said, "don't worry, I am happy this has happened. It's as if I had taught a brilliant student: there's no room for regret. I shall have you sent to your husband as soon as the hermits are ready."

ANASUYA. Who told him?

PRIYAMVADA. He knew. He guessed it as soon as he returned. And then. . .well, he heard a voice.

ANASUYA, *surprised*. A voice? What did it say?

PRIYAMVADA. "Your daughter is blessed, O Brahmin:
    The fruit she carries is the gift of Dushyanta.
    She is a *sami* tree, carrying flame."

ANASUYA, *embracing her*. Oh, I'm so terribly happy, Priyamvada! But I'll feel so lonely with her gone.

PRIYAMVADA. Let's perform some sacrificial ceremony for her sake.

ANASUYA. That basket there, on the mango branch—I have a garland in it, *vakula* flowers, they'll last a few days. Bring it here. I'll get the holy clay and grass ready.

*ANASUYA leaves and PRIYAMVADA plucks flowers.*

VOICE, *offstage*. Mother Gautami, let Sarngarava and a few others escort Shakuntala.

PRIYAMVADA, *listening*. Hurry, Anasuya—they're ready to go to Hastinapur.

ANASUYA, *entering with clay and grass*. Come on.

*They walk a few steps and pause, looking ahead.*

PRIYAMVADA. Do you see her, Anasuya, where the sun's rising? All those hermit women blessing her with gifts of grain. Oh, how wonderful!

*SHAKUNTALA enters, followed by three HERMIT WOMEN, GAUTAMI and others. The women address her in ritual phrases.*

FIRST HERMIT WOMAN. May you become the chief queen, child.

SECOND HERMIT WOMAN. May your son be brave.

THIRD HERMIT WOMAN. May your husband love you deeply and forever.

*Except for GAUTAMI, the HERMIT WOMEN leave. ANASUYA approaches SHAKUNTALA.*

ANASUYA. May this day be auspicious.

SHAKUNTALA. I'm happy to see you, Anasuya. And you, Priyamvada. Sit down.

PRIYAMVADA. We've come to bless you and say good-bye.

SHAKUNTALA. I'll never forget you. I won't have friends like you where I'm going. *She cries a little.*

ANASUYA. This is no time for crying, Shakuntala. *She wipes away* SHAKUNTALA's *tears and makes up her face.*

PRIYAMVADA. You deserve diamonds and golden bracelets. Clay's not good enough for you.

*Two* HERMIT BOYS *enter with jewels and golden ornaments. They are greeted with astonishment.*

FIRST HERMIT BOY. For Shakuntala.

GAUTAMI. Good heavens, Narada, where did you get these from?

FIRST HERMIT BOY. Father Kashyapa.

GAUTAMI. And where did he get them from?

SECOND HERMIT BOY. He asked us to pick flowers for Shakuntala, but when we went out we found a fairyland. Some trees were made of lengths of silk, some gave out nail polish, and some were full of ornaments— clinging to the branches, as if the fairies held them up.

PRIYAMVADA, looking at SHAKUNTALA. A good omen. This means you will be happy in the palace.

SHAKUNTALA *appears embarrassed.*

FIRST HERMIT BOY. Let us go, Mother Gautami, and tell Father Kashyapa about the fairy trees. By now he must have finished his bath.

SHAKUNTALA *bids them depart, and they do so.*

ANASUYA. We have no taste in ornaments, Shakuntala: we'll dress you the way we've seen in paintings—

SHAKUNTALA. You don't have to pretend in front of me.

*The girls adorn* SHAKUNTALA *with the jewels.* KASHYAPA *enters, his bath finished.*

KASHYAPA. There is so much pain in my heart, Shakuntala, since you

must go today. I can hardly speak; tears choke my voice. Now I realize
how deeply I love you. And I a hermit! You can imagine the condition of
ordinary parents when their daughters leave them to marry.

ANASUYA. There, we're finished, Shakuntala. Put on this silk shawl
and you're perfect.

SHAKUNTALA *does so, hesitantly.*

GAUTAMI, *gently.* Your father's here, my child. He wants to bless you.

SHAKUNTALA, *very embarrassed, falling at* KASHYAPA's *feet.* I shall need
your blessings, Father.

KASHYAPA. May he love you with all his heart, my child.
    May you bear him a son brave as Puru.

GAUTAMI. This is more than a blessing. It is a gift.

KASHYAPA. Go round this fire, child. We have offered prayers here. Keep
to the right.

*They circle the fire.*

KASHYAPA, *ceremoniously.* May these fires purify you, the fires made
with sacred sticks and the fires with sacred grass at the sides. May your
sins dissolve in the fragrance of these sacred offerings.

*As he chants,* SHAKUNTALA *moves around the fire.*

KASHYAPA, *speaking in more matter-of-fact tones.* That will do. Where
are Sarngarava and the others?

SARNGARAVA, *entering.* We are ready, Father.

KASHYAPA. See that your sister is safely escorted.

SARNGARAVA. We will, Father.

KASHYAPA, *chanting again.* O trees of the ashrama!
    She loved you, and would not drink till she had given you water.
    O trees of the ashrama!
    She loved you, and would not pluck the young leaves from you.
    O trees of the ashrama!
    She loved you, your flowers were a festival for her.

Bless her, O trees of the forest: she must go to her husband.

*He ends his chant.*

The trees bless you, Shakuntala. *He pauses to listen.* I think I hear the faint song of the kokila.

VOICE OF THE TREES, *offstage.* May her journey be safe.
May she see lotus ponds on the way.
May she find shady trees.
Like lotus pollen her feet, like the south wind her journey.

*They all listen with amazement.*

GAUTAMI. An auspicious start. If the trees bless you, you have nothing to fear. They are your friends.

SHAKUNTALA *bows. Then she speaks aside to* PRIYAMVADA.

SHAKUNTALA. I don't want to go, Priyamvada. But I must.

PRIYAMVADA. You aren't the only one to feel sad, Shakuntala. Look around you—you'd think the forest felt it too. The deer leave the grass and the peacocks cease to dance; dew falls from the branches in drops, like tears.

SHAKUNTALA, *remembering.* Let me say good-bye to the *vanajyotsna.* I loved her most of all.

KASHYAPA. I know. There, on the right.

SHAKUNTALA, *embracing the creeper.* Bless me, light-of-the-forest. I don't know when I will see you again.

KASHYAPA. I like the union of this creeper with the sturdy mango tree. You'll be safe, my child. Come.

SHAKUNTALA, *to her friends.* I leave her in your care.

ANASUYA *and* PRIYAMVADA, *sobbing.* What about us?

KASHYAPA. Please, Anasuya, you must think of Shakuntala.

SHAKUNTALA. And, Father, when this deer conceives, send me word please.

KASHYAPA. Certainly.

SHAKUNTALA, *pausing.* Someone's following me. *She turns around.*

KASHYAPA. It's only the fawn you adopted, it doesn't want to leave you.

SHAKUNTALA, *kneeling.* Go back, little one. You were an orphan, I'm not your mother. You're lucky you have a father. . . . Look after him, Father Kashyapa. *She rises.*

KASHYAPA. You must not cry, child. It doesn't help at all. . . . Here's the road; control yourself and everything will turn out all right.

SARNGARAVA. You have kept us company to the lake's edge, Father, and have observed the custom. Now we will go on by ourselves.

KASHYAPA. I'll watch you from the fig tree. But wait a minute.

*They pause.*

KASHYAPA *continues thoughtfully.* Let me see. I should send a message to the king.

SHAKUNTALA, *aside to* ANASUYA. Did you hear the *chakravaka* shriek? That means she cannot find her mate.

ANASUYA. It's the same with us. How long are the nights without the person one loves! Yet we live on hope.

KASHYAPA. Tell him this, Sarngarava, when you take Shakuntala to him:
    Honor her, O king,
    For her love is pure, and you are noble.
    Treat her with the same respect you accord the ladies of the palace.
    More than this I dare not ask:
    It is in the hands of fate.

SARNGARAVA. I will do so, Father.

KASHYAPA. Now you, Shakuntala. We may be hermits, my child, but we know something of the world. We are expected to know it. . . .
    Respect your superiors, Shakuntala;
    Be friendly toward the ladies of the palace.
    Never be angry with your husband, no matter what happens.
    Be polite with the maids;

In everything be humble.

These qualities make a woman; those without them are black sheep in their families.

What is your opinion, Gautami?

GAUTAMI. A bride needs nothing more. Remember his advice, Shakuntala.

KASHYAPA. And now, my child, you may embrace me.

SHAKUNTALA. Aren't Priyamvada and Anasuya coming with me, Father?

KASHYAPA. I'm afraid not. I must think of getting them married too. But Gautami will accompany you.

SHAKUNTALA. How will I ever manage in the palace? I feel so lost. I belong here, Father.

KASHYAPA. Don't worry, my child; you are privileged.

You will be his chief wife;

He is noble and great.

You will give him a son, as the East gives us light.

The pain of separation will then pass.

SHAKUNTALA *touches his feet.*

All this will happen: I wish it.

SHAKUNTALA, *approaching* PRIYAMVADA *and* ANASUYA. Good-bye, Anasuya.

ANASUYA. Good-bye, Shakuntala. Don't forget this ring. Show it to him in case anything happens.

SHAKUNTALA. Why should anything happen? You frighten me.

ANASUYA. Just in case. Love is a very complicated feeling. Sometimes it makes people suspicious.

SARNGARAVA. We must go. It is late.

SHAKUNTALA, *facing the ashrama.* Shall I ever return here, Father?

KASHYAPA. You will, my child—but that's a long time from now. Your husband will come with you.

GAUTAMI. She will never stop talking. It's getting very late. We really must leave, Father.

KASHYAPA. Good-bye, Shakuntala.

SHAKUNTALA, *embracing him.* You fast too much, Father. Do not weaken yourself over me.

KASHYAPA, *sighing.* There are some sorrows that never fade.

SHAKUNTALA *and the escorting party leave.*

ANASUYA, *watching.* They're out of sight.

KASHYAPA, *sighing again.* Let's go back, Anasuya.

ANASUYA. It's all so empty now.

KASHYAPA. That's one of the tricks of affection. But I feel relieved, Anasuya. A daughter never really belongs to her father. I'm glad she has gone to her husband. It is where she belongs.

C U R T A I N

# ACT V

## PRELUDE

*On the fore-stage, the* KING *and the* JESTER *are seated on cushions. They are in the palace garden.*

JESTER, *listening.* Such lovely music!
    It's the queen practicing, I think.

KING, *aside.* Hansavati!

*A song is heard from offstage.*

Thirsty bee, remembering
    The mango's kiss of fire,
Can the simple lotus
    Placate your desire?

KING. What a touching snatch of song!

JESTER. Do you know what it means?

KING, *smiling*. I've a pretty good guess. It's her way of saying she doesn't like me showing my love to the other queens the way I do. Shrewd, jealous girl—tell her she has hit the nail on the head.

JESTER. I will, sire. *He gets up.*

KING. And don't be so damned serious about it.

JESTER. No, sire. *He leaves.*

KING. Her song moves me deeply. I wonder why. I don't miss anyone.
It may be that I recall the lovely thoughts of a past birth:
Memory has a funny way of tapping a person on the shoulder
When sweet scenes or sweet sounds drive away happiness.

*The* CHAMBERLAIN *enters on another part of the stage.*

CHAMBERLAIN. Why must this happen to me? I have been here since I don't know when, in the service of the king. Visitors all the time—and now hermits! I don't like the idea of disturbing the king, but I can't keep Kanva's hermits waiting either. The sun is lucky; he stays where he is. The wind has only twenty-four hours to blow about in. Only I am awakened at all odd hours! Perish the thought—duty is duty. . . . .His Majesty is in the garden, relaxing after the strain of the morning's work. *He approaches the* KING. Good morning, sire. There are some hermits from Father Kashyapa's ashrama in the Himalayas to see you. They say they carry a private message. There are some ladies with them too, sire.

KING. Ladies? With hermits?

CHAMBERLAIN. Yes, sire.

KING. That's strange. Tell Somarata to receive them. And see that they are made comfortable. I'll meet them in a quieter spot.

*The* CHAMBERLAIN *leaves.*

KING, *calling*. Guard!

*The* FEMALE GUARD *enters.*

KING. Lead me to the holy chambers.

GUARD. This way, sire.

*The* KING *follows, showing a worried expression. He speaks in soliloquy.*

KING. Most people are happy getting what they want.
  But a king's different: he must guard what he gets.
  And that creates so many worries.
  Being a king is like holding an open parasol:
  It provides shelter from the sun, but wearies the arm.

*The* VOICES *of the court poets are heard within.*

FIRST VOICE. You work unselfishly for your subjects:
  Like a tree that takes the sun full blast
  And shelters the bushes beneath it.

SECOND VOICE. You dispense justice, and banish strife.
  You are a friend and guardian when all else fails.

KING. It's good to know that. I feel so much better.

GUARD. Here is the gate, sire. I cleaned it recently. The holy cow stands nearby.

*The* KING *ascends the steps, his right hand on the* FEMALE GUARD's *shoulder.*

KING. I wonder why Father Kashyapa sends these hermits, guard. Are there demons loose? Or has a careless hunter harmed the sacred beasts?

GUARD. Very likely they have come to offer their blessings, sire.

*The hermits,* SARNGARAVA *and* SARADVATA, *enter, bringing* GAUTAMI *and* SHAKUNTALA *with them. The* CHAMBERLAIN *and a* PRIEST *attached to the royal household follow.* GAUTAMI *places* SHAKUNTALA *in front of her. At first the group stands at some distance from the* KING.

SARNGARAVA. This king is a fine man, Saradvata, and very gifted. The meanest of his subjects are well behaved. But I feel like a fish out of water with so many people around.

SARADVATA. All hermits do in a city. I'm not very happy here myself. I've a trick though: I look on the people as the pure look on the impure, the waking on the sleeping, the free on the enslaved.

SHAKUNTALA. I have a feeling it's not going to turn out right, Mother Gautami.

GAUTAMI. There's nothing to worry about, Shakuntala.

PRIEST. The king is ready to receive you, O hermits. He will hear you standing.

SARNGARAVA. You honor us, sire. We are grateful to you, but your courtesy doesn't surprise us. Trees bend with fruits, the clouds with rain, and wealth brings humility to a good man.

GUARD. You look happy, hermits. I hope your news is pleasant.

*The* KING *looks at* SHAKUNTALA *and speaks in an aside to the* FEMALE GUARD.

KING. Who is that veiled lady? She stands out like a glistening bud among brown leaves.

GUARD, *aside.* I couldn't say, sire. But she is very lovely.

KING, *aside.* Hold your tongue. She may be married.

SHAKUNTALA, *aside.* I must keep calm. I know he loves me.

PRIEST, *advancing toward the* KING. They carry a message from their father, sire.

KING. I am ready.

SARNGARAVA, *raising his right hand.* We bless you, O king.

KING. Thank you.

SARNGARAVA. May you receive all you wish for.

KING. Are the ashrama rites undisturbed?

SARNGARAVA. They are, sire. You have helped us greatly.
    When the sun shines, we don't fear darkness.

KING. Thank you. And how is Father Kashyapa? Doing well?

SARNGARAVA. Perfectly well, sire. He is never out of sorts. He inquires after you. He sends a message.

KING. What can I do for him?

SARNGARAVA. "You fell in love with my daughter and married her," he says. "I approve of it, for you are known to be a man of honor, and she is devoted to you. When two excellent persons are brought together, there can be no blame. Take her now, for she is with child."

GAUTAMI. I can add nothing to the message, sire. You are aware of the exceptional circumstances of the case. She kept her love to herself; you didn't tell us either. It's difficult for a third person to interfere with a private arrangement.

SHAKUNTALA, *aside*. What can he possibly say to that?

KING. I don't understand.

SHAKUNTALA, *aside*. There is anger in his voice.

SARNGARAVA. We don't either. You know the custom, sire. We cannot keep her in the ashrama. We know she is pure, but what will people say? A wife must stay with her husband.

KING. Are you implying that I'm married to her?

SHAKUNTALA, *aside*. I was afraid of this.

SARNGARAVA. You may have made a mistake, but duty comes first to a king.

KING. You're presumptuous.

SARNGARAVA. I do not like the tone of your voice, sire. You speak like one drunk with power.

KING. You insult me.

GAUTAMI, *to* SHAKUNTALA. Come here, child—take off the veil. That may jog your husband's memory.

SHAKUNTALA *removes her veil. The* KING *looks at her fixedly.*

KING, *aside*. I can't remember a thing. Until I do I can neither take nor leave her, for she is very beautiful.

*The* KING *continues to stare at* SHAKUNTALA *without speaking.*

SARNGARAVA. Why are you silent, sire?

KING. I am sorry, but I remember nothing, certainly not the marriage you speak of. You must excuse me if I refuse to think of myself as an adulterer.

SHAKUNTALA, *aside.* I am lost. He can't even remember what happened.

SARNGARAVA. Of course not, sire. You are no adulterer; it's Father Kashyapa who's to blame for giving his daughter in honor to the robber who stole her.

SARADVATA. Stop it, Sarngarava. We have said what we could. . . . Shakuntala, it is your turn now.

SHAKUNTALA, *aside.* What can I possibly say that will change his mind? *She speaks aloud, hesitantly.* My husband. . .*She falters and speaks to herself.* But he says he never married me. *Again she summons her courage.* It is not right, O Puru, to reject so soon the girl you loved in the ashrama. . .

KING, *covering his ears.* This is impossible! Why must you drag my ancestral name into it?

SHAKUNTALA. If you think I am someone else's wife, this gift may remind you that I'm not.

KING. Gift?

SHAKUNTALA, *touching her finger.* Oh, no! Oh, no! The ring. . . .it's gone! *Terrified, she looks at* GAUTAMI.

GAUTAMI. It must have slipped from your finger while you were bathing in the Ganges.

KING, *smiling.* A fertile imagination—women are famous for it.

SHAKUNTALA. Fate has intervened. But I can tell you some of the things we did. Then you will remember.

KING. From rings to incidents!

SHAKUNTALA. You remember the day you brought a lotus leaf filled with water. . .

KING. Go on.

SHAKUNTALA. And you offered it to Dhirgapangha, my adopted fawn, but he wouldn't drink it, for you were strange to the place; and when I gave him the water, he drank it immediately; and you said, "He trusts you, you both belong to the forest"?

KING. Very pretty. That's the way painted girls trap a man.

GAUTAMI. You're unfair, sire. You know she belongs to an ashrama and knows nothing of deceit.

KING. I am not so sure, Mother. I find even the innocent birds very cunning. The cuckoo, for instance—she has her eggs hatched by others.

SHAKUNTALA, *in anger*. Must you judge everyone by your own small selfish heart? You are like a well that grass has grown over. Who will respect only a mask of virtue?

KING, *aside*. Her anger seems genuine. Her eyes are red, and these are hard quick words. She looks straight into my eyes: her lip quivers and her eyebrows curve like bows. *Aloud*. Dushyanta's acts are all public. Such a thing is unheard of among my subjects.

SHAKUNTALA. So I am unchaste! You tricked me—you, a Puru!—honey-mouthed and poison-hearted! *She covers her face and weeps*.

SARNGARAVA. This is the inevitable result of rashness. Those who marry in secret should know each other well before doing so.

KING. Why do you accuse me of these crimes? Have you no evidence beyond her word?

SARNGARAVA, *scornfully*. Remarkable! The words of a clean girl are suspect and the words of a man who practices professional deceit sacred!

KING. Sarcasm won't help. My mind's made up.

SARADVATA. Let us go, Sarngarava. We have done what Father Kashyapa asked us to do. *To the* KING. She is your wife, sire. Take her or leave her. . . . Lead the way, Gautami.

*They start to leave.*

SHAKUNTALA. And leave me behind? Rejected by him, and now by you? *She follows.*

GAUTAMI, *stopping.* Let us take Shakuntala with us, Sarngarava. It's not her fault he won't accept her.

SARNGARAVA, *turning in sudden anger.* Never! Stay where you are! SHAKUNTALA *shrinks back.* If what he says is true, Father Kashyapa won't have you back. If your heart's pure, you might as well stay here.

KING. She can stay if she likes. As far as I'm concerned, she is another man's wife—I'm not going to molest her.

SARADVATA. If she is your wife, why don't you accept her? If she isn't, why do you let her stay?

KING. It's very simple. I may be forgetful, or she may be lying. If I am forgetful, should I not let her stay and wait till my memory comes back? If she is lying, time will tell.

PRIEST. A good suggestion, sire.

KING. I think so.

PRIEST. She will stay until the child is born.

KING. That's a strange provision. . . .

PRIEST. No, sire. The sages have predicted your first son will be blessed with a circle in his palm. If her child has this sign, take her as your queen. If not, send her back to the ashrama.

KING. Yes, I think that's a good plan.

PRIEST. Come, Shakuntala.

SHAKUNTALA. If only the earth could open up and swallow me!

*Sobbing, she goes out with the* PRIEST. *The others also leave. The* KING *sits down, remaining silent and thoughtful. Suddenly there are shouts offstage.*

KING. What's that?

*The* PRIEST *enters, running and waving his arms in bewilderment.*

PRIEST. The strangest thing has happened, sire. As the hermits were going out, the girl went toward them, weeping and clutching her breast in despair—

KING. Well, what happened?

PRIEST. Suddenly a white light in a woman's form swooped out of nowhere and picked her up and took her into the sky!

KING. Rest your mind, holy one. It doesn't matter. We had already given her up for lost, hadn't we?

PRIEST, *staring vacantly*. Yes. . .My blessings, sire. *He leaves.*

KING. I'm terribly worried. Guard, take me to my bedroom.

GUARD. Yes, sire.

KING, *aside*. It's true I don't remember her; but something in my heart tells me she's speaking the truth.

C U R T A I N

# ACT VI

### PRELUDE

*An* OFFICER *of the city police, the* KING's *brother-in-law, enters with two* CONSTABLES—JANUKA *and* SUCHAKA—*and a* PRISONER *in bonds.*

JANUKA, *hitting the prisoner*. You rascal! Tell us where you got the royal ring.

PRISONER, *trembling*. I didn't steal it, sir.

JANUKA. His Majesty made you a present of it, did he? Took you for a ruddy Brahmin?

PRISONER. I am only a fisherman, sir.

JANUKA. Shut your mouth, you swine. Who asked you what you are?

OFFICER. Let him have his say, constable. There's no point in interrupting him.

JANUKA, *politely.* Yes, sir. *He pushes the* PRISONER *and speaks gruffly.* Go on.

PRISONER. We're very poor, sir, and it's a hard scrape making ends meet, sir. I fish for a living, sir.

OFFICER, *ironically.* A very noble profession.

PRISONER. No, sir. But to each his own, sir—I was born into it. I plug along as best I can, sir.

OFFICER. Come to the point, come to the point.

PRISONER. One day, sir, I landed a *rohita,* and when I cut it open, sir, I found the ring in its belly. They nabbed me when I took it to market to sell it, sir. That's the whole story, sir. Yes, sir.

OFFICER. You smell like a fisherman, all right. But we'll have to look into this affair. *He speaks to the constable.* Let's check at the palace to see if they're missing a ring, Januka.

JANUKA. Immediately, sir.

*They walk a few steps.*

OFFICER. Here we are. *He turns to the second constable.* Suchaka, wait here. I'll tell His Majesty how we came by the ring, and get instructions on our next move. *He goes out.*

SUCHAKA. He's taking a long time.

JANUKA, *shrugging.* Red tape.

SUCHAKA. I can hardly wait to chop off this swine's head. *He points to the prisoner.*

PRISONER. That would be murder, you know.

JANUKA. Ah, there he is—with a scroll in his hand. It's the vultures for you, my fine fishing friend. Or the dogs.

OFFICER, *entering.* Release him. His Majesty says everything's in order.

SUCHAKA. Lucky swine. Gets off by the skin of his teeth! *He unties the prisoner.*

PRISONER, *bowing.* How will I manage for today, sir? I can't catch fish at this late hour.

OFFICER. Here. This will come in handy no doubt—a gift from His Majesty. *He tosses a bag of gold to the* PRISONER.

PRISONER, *bowing frantically.* Thank you, oh, thank you very much, sir. Thank you. . .

SUCHAKA. Look at him! From the gallows to an elephant's back!

JANUKA. That ring must be worth a tidy bit.

OFFICER. Not so much in gold as in sentiment. It reminds His Majesty of someone very dear to him. He tried not to show it, but I saw tears in his eyes when he examined it.

SUCHAKA. So we hit the mark, eh?

JANUKA. Not *us!* *He points to the fisherman, eying him enviously.*

PRISONER. Take half of this, sir. You did your bit, sir.

JANUKA. This man's a decent fellow, Suchaka.

OFFICER. Oh, excellent, excellent!—you're all right, fisherman. We're friends forever. But now—a celebration! What do you all say to a drop of wine? Off to the wine shop, off to the wine shop! Lead on, fisherman!

*They leave.*

END OF PRELUDE

*The curtain opens, disclosing* SANUMATI, *a nymph, as she flies toward the palace garden.*

SANUMATI. My duty in the celestial regions is over; the hermits have finished bathing; and it's time I investigated the facts of this new case.

Shakuntala is Menaka's daughter: one of the family! And Menaka once before asked me to look after her. *She looks around.* Why is the palace silent when it's time for the spring festival? Of course if I wanted to I could find out by a bit of concentration: but one must respect others' privacy! Lucky I'm invisible. I'll keep moving and see what I stumble on.

*Two* MAIDSERVANTS *enter, and stand looking at the mango blossoms.*

FIRST MAIDSERVANT. Copper and green and yellow: the first fruits of the season! Oh, spring, spring! I bless you, mango blossoms.

SECOND MAIDSERVANT. What's that you're mumbling, Parabhritika?

FIRST MAIDSERVANT, *turning.* These mango blossoms, Madhukarika. I lose my head each time I see them.

SECOND MAIDSERVANT, *catching her meaning.* Spring? Already?

FIRST MAIDSERVANT. Already spring. And songs and love and—love, love, love!

SECOND MAIDSERVANT. Give me a hand, Parabhritika. Let me pluck a branch of the blossoms; I'll honor the god of love.

FIRST MAIDSERVANT. Not unless I get half of what he gives you.

SECOND MAIDSERVANT. Of course, silly. We're in it together, aren't we? *She winks, and pulls down a branch of mango blossom.* Such fragrance! And not even in full flower yet. *She joins her hands in prayer.* Be an arrow in the bow of the god of love, O mango blossom, and remember me when the time comes. *She tosses away the branch.*

*The* CHAMBERLAIN *enters, showing exasperation.*

CHAMBERLAIN. You must be mad, you idiots. Don't you know the king forbids these silly games?

BOTH MAIDSERVANTS, *cowering.* We had no idea, sir.

CHAMBERLAIN. "No idea, sir"! Why, you fools, do you realize you are the only two she-donkeys in the whole of the kingdom who don't know the king's command? Even the trees know it—and the birds too! Look at the mango trees: where's the pollen gone? Where are the flowers of spring?

And have you heard the kokila yet? Even the god of hunting stays at home.

SANUMATI. This noble king has a few tricks up his sleeve!

FIRST MAIDSERVANT. We only began to work here a few days ago, sir—taking care of the palace gardens. We are completely new to this place, sir.

CHAMBERLAIN. Well, get used to it. The sooner the better!

FIRST MAIDSERVANT. Yes, sir. But tell us—if it isn't asking too much, sir—what made His Majesty ban the festival of spring?

SANUMATI, *aside*. People are mad about festivals. So there must be some serious reason.

CHAMBERLAIN. There's no harm in telling you. The kingdom's buzzing with the story anyway. Haven't you heard about Shakuntala?

FIRST MAIDSERVANT. We have, sir—at least up to the ring part. The head gardener told us.

CHAMBERLAIN. Then you know most of it. When His Majesty saw the ring, it all came back to him in a flash—his marriage, his absentmindedness, his harsh denial. He's stricken with remorse. He refuses to look at lovely things, his ministers are asked not to wait on him, he passes sleepless nights, and—what's worse—he can hardly remember names, not even the palace ladies! Why, he slips up often in their presence. And his jokes fall flat.

SANUMATI, *aside*. Nothing could be better!

CHAMBERLAIN. Now you know why the spring festival's been canceled.

FIRST MAIDSERVANT. Yes, sir. And a good thing too, sir.

VOICE, *offstage*. This way, Your Majesty.

CHAMBERLAIN, *listening*. It's the king. All right, all right—get on with your work, you two.

*The* MAIDSERVANTS *leave. The* KING *enters, wearing black, followed by the* JESTER *and a* GUARD.

CHAMBERLAIN, *aside.* How noble he looks in spite of his sorrow! Only one bracelet on his left wrist, dark circles under his eyes, and drooping lips—but these can't disguise his dignity. It is like a diamond: scratches don't hurt it.

SANUMATI, *aside, seeing the* KING. No wonder Shakuntala loves him still, even though he's been so rough with her.

KING, *speaking to himself as he paces to and fro.* I was asleep then, insensible to her lovely eyes. Now my heart wakens, stirred by remorse.

CHAMBERLAIN, *aside.* Crying over spilt milk.

JESTER, *aside.* Damn this Shakuntala sickness. There seems to be no cure for it.

CHAMBERLAIN, *approaching the* KING. Good morning, sire. Such a lovely day; and I've seen to the gardens: they are ready to receive you.

KING. Come here, guard. Tell my minister that I'm a little indisposed this morning, and can't attend to state matters. Have him write up the reports and complaints and ask him to send them on to me. Pisuna will understand.

GUARD. Yes, sire. *He goes out.*

KING. And, chamberlain, please see I'm not disturbed here.

CHAMBERLAIN. Certainly, Your Majesty. *He leaves.*

JESTER. Good riddance! Gluey flies, the whole lot of them. Now you can relax to your heart's content. A lovely season this, sire, neither summer nor winter. Ah, spring!

KING, *sighing.* I'm sandwiched all right—between two weathers! I'm so depressed, Mathavya. Sorrow has a hundred ways of getting in, each one better than the other. My memory's come back, but the god of love is after me now. Look, he is aiming at me from behind that mango tree.

JESTER. Not for long! *He raises his staff against the mango branches.*

KING, *smiling.* You don't have to, I know the power Brahmins have. Tell me where I should sit, and look at the creepers, and think of Shakuntala.

JESTER. You ordered Chaturika to bring a portrait of Shakuntala—here in the *madhavi* bower. She'll be along any minute.

KING. Foolish things begin to matter now. Ah, well. . .

JESTER. Sit down, sire, in the *madhavi* bower—here on this crystal rock.

*The* KING *seats himself.*

SANUMATI, *aside.* This is getting interesting. I'll take back good news for Shakuntala!

KING. You know something, Mathavya—it all comes back to me now. And I had told you everything after it happened! Pity you weren't there when I refused her at the palace gate. But wait. . .why didn't you tell me before? Is your memory as bad as mine?

JESTER. Oh, I knew everything. But you said once it was just a little game you were playing, and I believed you. Fate thinks of everything.

SANUMATI, *aside.* Yes, indeed.

KING. Help me out, Mathavya—I can't stand it any longer. . . .

JESTER. Please, sire—this is most unexpected. A good man is like a mountain, sire: steady even in a strong wind.

KING. But I think of her all the time. How I must have hurt her!
She turned to join them.
But the hermit said, "Stay where you are."
And she turned, and her eyes were on me—
Oh, it goes through me like a knife.

SANUMATI, *aside.* That's sensible. Now he's thinking of others, not himself. All to the good.

JESTER. I have it! It must be a goddess or a nymph that carried her off. . . .

KING. Who else could have done it? She was my wife. I am told that the nymph Menaka is her mother. Menaka's friends must have carried her away.

JESTER. In that case, everything's all right. You'll find her.

KING. How?

JESTER. No mother likes to see her daughter unhappy.

KING. True. But I don't deserve her. She was a dream, an incantation, a breath of lovely air. Such things don't come back.

JESTER. They do sometimes. Why, the ring's an indication. . . .

KING, *taking out the ring*. Forget the ring: it fell from a heaven I have little hope of reaching. *He addresses the ring*. How foolish you were, to forsake such a lovely hand!

SANUMATI, *aside*. It would have looked even more foolish if it had wound up on someone else's finger!

JESTER. Why did you give her the ring?

KING. She was crying when I left her at the ashrama. "When will you return?" she asked. And I gave her the ring and showed her my name on it, and said, "Count one letter a day. When you've spelled out my name, a messenger will appear to take you to the palace." But it didn't work out that way, for I had less of a heart than I imagined.

JESTER. Fate steps in at awkward moments. . . . How did the carp get it?

KING. It slipped from her finger. She was bathing in the Ganges, on pilgrimage at Sachi.

JESTER. A tall story. But strange things happen.

SANUMATI, *aside*. And that's where his doubts began. What a queer man—as if love needs a sign!

KING. Damn the ring!

JESTER, *aside*. He's half out of his head.

KING, *examining the ring*. Why did you have to leave her soft sweet fingers? Lifeless fool—you don't know what's good for you. My fault too, though. Why did I go away? . . . Please come back, Shakuntala.

CHATURIKA *enters, carrying a portrait*.

CHAMBERLAIN. The portrait, sire.

JESTER, *looking at it*. Exquisite! Such delicacy of line! I like art; but I'd prefer the original, thank you, any time, thank you.

SANUMATI, *aside*. It is well painted. I almost see her before me.

KING. This doesn't do her justice at all. I must brush it up.

SANUMATI, *aside*. He loves her. Humility's a sure sign. Deeply, too.

JESTER. I see three figures here, all very easy on the eyes. But which one is Shakuntala?

KING. Which one do you think?

JESTER, *examining the portrait closely*. The one near the mango tree—a little tired, graceful arms, flowers in her flowing hair, drops of perspiration on her face. The other two are her friends.

KING. Brilliant! I couldn't have done better. Look at the corner here, where my wet finger has smudged the picture, and here, where a tear has fallen on her cheek. Chaturika, get me a brush—this is badly painted.

CHAMBERLAIN, *to the* JESTER. Hold this in the meantime.

KING. It's all right. I'll take it. *He takes the painting as the* CHAMBERLAIN *goes out*. I left her when she was near me. Now, in love with her portrait, I love a mirage, I—who once had the reality before me!

JESTER, *aside*. After the real river, the mirage! *Aloud*. What do you intend to add, sire?

SANUMATI, *aside*. The places she loved.

KING. First, the Malini: swans on its sandy banks; in the distance, the Himalayas; stags in the forest; next, a fawn nuzzling a black doe under a tree; then the hermits; and clothes hanging on a tree.

JESTER, *aside*. This is getting too religious for me—hermits all over the place!

KING. Next, something she loved deeply. It nearly slipped my mind.

SANUMATI, *aside*. Something gentle and holy.

KING. The *sirisha* flower, hanging in her hair, its petals brushing her cheek; and the lotus buds next to her breasts.

JESTER. Why does she cover her face with her hands? *He looks closely.* It's a bee, the thief, rushing at her!

KING. Stop him.

JESTER. Not me. You're the man for rough work, sire.

KING. Very well. Why do you bother yourself here, O guest of the flowers? Your thirsty mistress waits for you in the cup of a flower and will not drink till you come.

SANUMATI, *aside.* Excellent rhetoric!

JESTER. No effect at all.

KING. Ignoring a royal command! One more warning: if you touch my beloved's lips—leafy lips, lips I have kissed—I shall imprison you in a lotus.

JESTER, *aside.* A stiff sentence! . . . He's daft, mad as they come. And I'm afraid I'll go off the track myself if this keeps on much longer. *He speaks aloud.* It's only a painting, sire.

KING. Is it?

SANUMATI, *aside.* It fooled me too. Why shouldn't it fool the painter?

KING. Yes, just a painting. You needn't have told me, though. I had her in front of me until you jogged my memory.

SANUMATI, *aside.* Love is a strange sickness.

KING. My nerves are letting me down, Mathavya. If I stay awake, I forfeit my dreams of her; if I paint her, the tears come to my eyes.

SANUMATI, *aside.* He's suffered enough.

CHAMBERLAIN, *entering.* I was coming this way with the brush, sire, when Queen Vasumati stopped me. The queen says she will bring it to you herself.

JESTER. Good. You're let off!

CHAMBERLAIN. I came away to warn you, sire.

KING. This is serious, Mathavya. I've been paying her all the attention I could, but Hansavati's very touchy. See if you can save the painting.

JESTER. Save yourself, you mean. *He takes the painting and stands up.* I'll see you in the palace. *He goes out.*

SANUMATI, *aside.* The king's heart belongs to Shakuntala. But he respects his first love.

FEMALE GUARD, *entering with a scroll.* Good morning, sire.

KING. Did you see the queen, guard?

GUARD. I did, sir, coming this way. But she turned back when she saw me with the scroll.

KING. Very thoughtful of her not to interrupt matters of state.

GUARD. Your minister reports that he has been able to finish only one case so far. He says a number of receipts had to be gone through first. *She offers the scroll to the* KING.

KING, *reading it.* Very sad, this. A merchant called Chanamitra has died in a shipwreck, and now his wealth is to be taken over by the state, as he had no son. A terrible thing to have no son, guard. Find out if one of his wives is with child.

GUARD. I was told that one of them recently passed through the ceremony of the would-be mother.

KING. Girl or boy, the inheritance shall go to the baby. Tell that to my minister.

GUARD. Yes, sire. *She turns to go.*

KING. Just a minute, guard. With child or without child doesn't matter. Have it proclaimed that henceforth I personally shall look after any person affected by the death of a relative.

GUARD. Yes, sire. The people will welcome it. *She goes out but soon returns.*

KING, *sighing deeply.* This is the way it is: wealth finds its way into the hands of a stranger if one has no child. That is what stares me in the face too.

VOICES. Better luck will come, sire.

KING. It came, and I sent it packing.

SANUMATI, *aside*. He means Shakuntala.

KING. I made her my wife,
   Giving birth to myself in the process.
   She would have sat by me at sacrifice and reared my children.
   And then I left her:
   Like a field sown, watered—and abandoned at harvest.

SANUMATI, *aside*. You need not fear. Your line will carry on.

CHAMBERLAIN, *aside*. The merchant's story has added fuel to the fire. *He speaks to the* GUARD. Send Mathavya from the palace immediately; the king needs him.

*The* GUARD *goes to do as she is bid*.

KING. And the rites after death are useless without a son. When I offer water to my ancestors, they will take it with tears, knowing there is no one after me to offer it. *He falls into a faint*.

CHAMBERLAIN, *supporting him*. Sire! Sire!

SANUMATI, *aside*. Oh, how terrible! His mind has gone. I'll cure him. . . . Yet I shouldn't; Mahendra's mother said it would come out all right at the proper time—the gods will see to it. It isn't proper to interfere with destiny. . . . But I'll go and tell Shakuntala. *She departs, dancing*.

JESTER'S VOICE, *offstage and above*. I am a Brahmin! You can't do this to me—I'm a Brahmin!

KING, *recovering*. That's Mathavya's voice. Where is he? Bring him here.

GUARD, *entering in alarm*. Oh, sire, save Mathavya!

KING. What's happened?

GUARD. Very curious, sire. Some invisible power has raised him up in the air and placed him on the dome of the palace.

KING, *getting up.* Demons in the palace! . . . Or am I getting careless?

VOICES, *offstage.* Help! Help!

KING, *walking briskly to the right and calling offstage.* Keep calm, Mathavya, I'm here.

JESTER'S VOICE, *offstage.* Help! He's at me. He's got me by the neck. He's bent me in three places. Help!

KING. My bow. Quickly!

GUARD. Here it is, sire.

A DEMON'S VOICE, *offstage.* I've got you now! Blood, fresh blood— the tiger and the prey. Shout for Dushyanta; see if he can help you.

KING, *angrily.* He mocks me! Guard, lead me to the staircase.

GUARD. This way, sire.

DEMON'S VOICE, *offstage.* You can't. I see you, but you can't see me. I'm invisible—the cat and the mouse—

KING. My arrow will find you and save the Brahmin. The swan and the milk!

*The* KING *aims his arrow, but before he can release the bowstring* MATALI *enters, carrying the* JESTER. *The* KING *hastily removes his arrow from the bow.*

KING. Matali! How are you, O charioteer of Mahendra?

JESTER. This fellow nearly gobbled me up. How are you indeed!

MATALI, *smiling.* Hari sends me, Dushyanta.

KING. Can I do anything for him?

MATALI. You know the demon race called Durjaya?

KING. Yes, Narada told me of them.

MATALI. Your friend Sataketu finds them too much of a job for him. Could you help him? The moon destroys what the sun cannot. Indra has sent for you; the chariot is waiting.

KING. Indra flatters me. But why did you have to play this prank on Mathavya?

MATALI. You seemed all done in. I thought this might restore your spirits. Touch the snake, up goes his hood; stir the ashes, you'll get a new fire. It takes encouragement to make people realize what they're made of.

KING, *to the* JESTER. I can't disobey a divine command. Give this bow to my minister and tell him he'll have to rule by his wits for the time being.

JESTER. Yes, sire. *He goes out.*

MATALI. This way, Dushyanta. The chariot's waiting.

*They both go out.*

C U R T A I N

# ACT VII

MATALI *and the* KING *are seen in a flying chariot.*

KING. I have done my duty, Matali, but I can't say I feel happy about it. Indra has showered such honor on me. . . .

MATALI, *smiling.* Neither one of you is happy. You take too lightly the honor that you have done Indra: he is surprised at your feat and doesn't want to acknowledge the honor he has done you. *He looks below.* But your fame has spread. Look, the dwellers in the heavens—there, all painted up and dressed in *kalpa* creepers—are singing your praise and already planning a drama on your exploits.

KING. I didn't notice this region yesterday. I was too busy chopping down demons. Where are the winds taking us?

MATALI. This is Hari's region, sanctified by his footsteps.
The region of Pravaha,
The region of the three-forked river that flows in heaven
And makes the planets revolve.

KING. It must be, I'm so sweetly at peace, my mind and body relaxing. *He looks downward over the side of the chariot.* I think we've come to the region of the clouds.

MATALI. How can you tell?

KING. The wheels are wet with spray.
   Thirsty birds dart through the spokes,
   And the horses are fleshed with lightning.
   We're in the region of the clouds.

MATALI. And soon we shall be over your kingdom.

KING, *still looking down.* How strange it looks, Matali, the world of men!
   The land seems to slide off the backs of the mountains.
   The trees stand up, shaking off clouds of leaves.
   You would think someone were throwing the world up at me!

MATALI. You have keen eyes. How lovely the earth looks!

KING. What is that mountain, Matali, slipping into the eastern and western seas, from whose side liquid gold pours like sun-shot clouds?

MATALI. That is Hemakuta, the mountain of the Kimpurushas, O long-lived one. It is the resort of ascetics. There the lord of creation does penance with his wife.

KING. We must have his blessing then.

MATALI. A good idea, O long-lived one.

*The chariot stops and they both alight.*

KING, *in surprise.* This is queer: the wheels aren't touching the ground:
   No dust rises: there was no lurch as the chariot stopped.

MATALI. A small thing; it is Indra's doing.

KING. Where is Maricha's hermitage?

MATALI, *pointing.* There he is, still as a tree trunk, facing the sun,
   His body half-buried in that anthill,
   On his chest a snakeskin, around his neck withered creepers,
   On his shoulders clotted hair filled with birds' nests.

KING. I bow to you, great hermit.

MATALI. This is the ashrama of the lord of creation, the ashrama of *mandra* trees.

KING. This is heaven! I'm immersed in nectar.

*They step away from the chariot.*

MATALI. We'll visit a few of the ashramas.

KING. And stand in wonder before them.
   Here the *kalpa* trees breathe out air to sustain the hermits.
   The bathing water is golden with the pollen of lotuses.
   Meditation is practiced on heaps of gems,
   Here there is self-discipline near bewitching girls.
   Other sages practice austerity for gain:
   Here they scorn it.

MATALI. The greatest aspire to the purest. *He turns.* Vriddha-sakalya, what is holy Maricha doing? Is he explaining to Dakshayani the duties of a wife while the wives of the other sages listen?

KING. This is the chance of a lifetime. *He listens.*

MATALI. Stay near the asoka tree, sir. I'll announce you to Indra's father. *He leaves.*

KING. Why does my arm throb? I desire no one.
   I am alone and sad: my joys have left me.

VOICES, *offstage.* No, no, now don't be naughty.

KING. Who could be naughty in such a place? *He goes forward and looks in the direction of the voices.* A little boy with two girl hermits. The child is playing with a lion cub that has been taken from a lioness!

*The children enter.*

BOY. Open your mouth, I'll count your teeth.

FIRST GIRL. Naughty, naughty! Why do you tease the cub? Isn't he a baby, the same as we all were once? No wonder they call you Sarvadamana!

KING. Having no son makes me unduly tender.

Why is my heart drawn toward this boy?

SECOND GIRL. Now, you bad boy, leave the beast alone, or he'll bite you.

BOY. Hee, hee, he'll bite me. I'm so frightened. Hee, hee! *He makes a face at the girl.*

FIRST GIRL. Let him be, child. I'll give you something else to play with.

BOY. Give it to me then.

KING. Look at his hand:
Opened for the object, the fingers touching,
Like a lotus touched by early dawn,
The soft red light hardly slipping between petals.
The sure sign of royal birth.

SECOND GIRL. Words won't help, Suvrata. You can go. Get the clay peacock that belongs to Markandeya. It's in my cottage. Perhaps he'll like it.

*The first hermit girl leaves.*

BOY. Tell them I'll play with the lion.

KING. I love this naughty little fellow.

SECOND GIRL. You won't listen? Who can help us? *She sees the* KING. Good sir, help us get him away from the beast. He's teasing the animal for no reason, and his fists are so tightly clenched I can't get them loose.

KING, *approaching and smiling.* Why are you up to monkeyshines, small one? Your father a noble sage—and you behave in this fashion!

SECOND GIRL. I'm sorry, sir, but he isn't a sage's child.

KING. He certainly doesn't act like one. I was only guessing, I feel so elated in his presence. Lucky father, who can boast such a son!

SECOND GIRL. Now, isn't that strange. . .

KING. What's strange?

SECOND GIRL. Why, he's the very image of you, sir! No wonder he didn't mind your taking him to task—

KING, *patting the boy.* If he isn't a sage's son, what race does he belong to?

SECOND GIRL. He belongs to the line of Puru.

KING, *aside.* My race! That's why she thinks he resembles me. *Aloud.* Then how is he in this place?

SECOND GIRL. His mother gave birth to him here. She is related to the heavenly nymphs.

KING, *aside.* I feed on hope. *Aloud.* And which royal sage is her husband?

SECOND GIRL. Sh-h—don't ask me his name. He deserted her. . . .

KING, *aside.* It must be me then. Suppose I asked her the name of the boy's mother—but that's not proper.

FIRST GIRL, *entering with a toy peacock.* Sarvadamana, see this Shakuntalavanya, this lovely bird.

BOY. Where's Mother?

BOTH GIRLS. He's confused by "Shakuntalavanya."

SECOND GIRL. No, my child, she wants you to see the beautiful bird.

KING, *aside.* Is Shakuntala her name? But there must be many Shakuntalas.

BOY. I like this peacock. *He takes the toy.*

FIRST GIRL. His amulet—it's missing!

KING. Here it is. It slipped from his wrist while he was playing with the cub.

BOTH GIRLS. Don't, sir, don't! Oh, he's picked it up! *They stare at each other in horror.*

KING. Why, what's wrong?

FIRST GIRL. The amulet contains a rare herb called *aparajita* given by Sage Maricha to the child at the time of his birth. Only his mother and father may safely touch it.

KING. And if someone else touches it?

FIRST GIRL. It becomes a poisonous snake.

KING. Have you seen that happen?

BOTH GIRLS. Oh, many times, sir.

KING, *unable to contain himself, embracing the child*. So is my desire fulfilled.

SECOND GIRL. Come with me, Suvrata, we must report this to Shakuntala.

*The two girls leave.*

BOY. Let me go. I want to go to my mother.

KING. We'll both go to your mother.

BOY. You're not my father, Dushyanta's my father.

SHAKUNTALA *enters, her hair tied in a hermit's knot.*

KING. There she is, the pure-minded one,
    Wearing saffron, her face thin with penance,
    Forced to separate from a heartless husband.

SHAKUNTALA. A stranger being so familiar with my son. . .

BOY, *running to her*. Mother, he calls me his son.

KING. I have been cruel to you, my dearest.
    It does not matter. You recognize me.

SHAKUNTALA, *aside*. Be still, my heart.
    My fate pities me, having done its worst.
    This is my husband.

KING. My dearest, my beautiful wife,
    My eyes see clearly once more.
    The fates have been kind.

SHAKUNTALA. My husband. *She sobs.*

KING. Having seen you, I am happy.
    Having seen your face, and your pale-red lips.

BOY. Who is he, Mother?

SHAKUNTALA. My son, a star is dancing. *She weeps.*

KING. Forget the sad past of separation, my beautiful wife.
Delusion filmed my mind.
To a blind man a garland is a snake.

*He falls at her feet.*

SHAKUNTALA. No, my husband, no.

*The KING rises.*

Did you remember me?

KING. Let the sorrow pass: there is time enough.
O my dearest, let me dry your eyes.
*He does so.*

SHAKUNTALA, *noticing the royal signet.* This is the ring.

KING. This is the ring that brought me to my senses.

MATALI, *entering.* So he has found his joy—at last!

KING. I do not think Indra knows of this.

MATALI. There is very little he does not know. Come with me. Maricha
the perfect grants you an audience.

KING. Shakuntala, take the child's hand.

MARICHA, *entering.* My son, live long. And do not let self-pity overpower you. Durvasas was responsible for the curse that brought you to your
error. I learned this in deep meditation.

KING. Now I know why I feel so free.

MARICHA. And this is your son.

KING. And heir, O perfect one.

MARICHA. And so—this is the end. Go to the capital with your wife and
son. Indra will send you and your subjects blessings and prosperity. . . .
See that you do the necessary acts of worship.
And all will be well. . .
What more can I do for you?

KING. There is no greater favor, O perfect one.
  Yet perhaps there is. . .
  May the lord of the earth seek the good of my subjects.
  May the wise be honored.
  And may I be released from further lives.

C  U  R  T  A  I  N

# THE TOY CART

by

## KING SHUDRAKA

# Preface

On a Friday evening, December 5, 1924, *The Toy Cart,* a "Hindu drama, attributed to King Shudraka," was staged at the New York Neighborhood Playhouse, the first play of the eleventh season, presented by the National Theatre Conference. It was directed by Agnes Morgan and Irene Lewisohn, with settings and costumes by Aline Bernstein; the cast consisted entirely of Americans, though the background music—to "take care that the mood, at least, should be truly Eastern, and that no obvious occidentalisms should mar the calm sweetness of the atmosphere of the original drama"—was by Arjuna Govind, playing the sitar, and Sarit Lahiri, the esraj.

The version used for the production, abridged from Ryder's *The Little Clay Cart* in the Harvard Oriental Series, is not an altogether satisfactory one for stage purposes, but the play apparently did well and attracted the notice of discerning critics. *The Toy Cart* has never failed in that respect; it has always impressed non-Indian audiences with an immediate impact. It is, by the strictest standards of the *Natyashastra,* not a very *Indian* play, by which I mean that it is the most secular of the great Sanskrit plays, and can be appreciated on a level that does not require elaborate knowledge of the Indian cultural milieu; the other plays do. The story is partly historical and partly invented, with no mythological ingredients; it has ten acts, not seven; only five of its characters speak elite Sanskrit, the rest use various vernaculars, such as Shauraseni, Avanti, Prachya, Magadhi, Sakàri, Chandali, and Dakka; the horseplay exceeds Bharatan limits; the idea of a courtesan as a heroine is already a departure from the tradition; Sansthanaka, described by Dr. Keith as the "lisping villain," is in many ways a character out of Elizabethan or Restoration drama ("his vices are egregious; he is coldly and cruelly malicious, and yet he is so frivolous as scarcely to excite our indignation"); "the minor characters among the twenty-seven in all who appear have each an individuality rare in Indian drama"; and the plot is given a class-conflict twist at the end that makes the play dearly beloved of left-wing drama enthusiasts.

"From farce to tragedy, from satire to pathos, runs the story"—and the *santa rasa* tends to get lost on the way.

Dr. Keith feels that the "real Indian character of the drama reveals itself in the demand for the conventional happy ending. . . If fate plays with men like buckets at the well, one rising as another falls, Shudraka is not inclined to seek realism sufficiently to permit of his introducing even a tinge of sorrow into the close of his drama." Professor Jagirdar goes further and explains how *The Toy Cart* continues the "realistic" trend initiated by Kalidasa: the gamblers in Act II; the cartmen driving on crowded roads in Acts VI, VII, VIII; the thief breaking in in Act IV; Sansthanaka and his courtier chasing Vasantasena on a dark road, and the quarreling guards in Act VI. Unlike symbol, legend, and myth, this type of realism is quickly comprehensible because it is, in the superficial sense of the word, "universal."

Which means, of course, that appreciation of this play is more a matter of knowing the elementary stage conventions of Sanskrit drama than involving oneself in a world-view. The conventions are simple enough and neatly listed by the anonymous preface writer in the Neighborhood Playhouse edition: "when a character must cover a considerable distance in going from place to place, he circles the stage several times before arriving; when pitch darkness cloaks the scene and the characters are invisible to one another, enough light is always left for the audience to see what is happening; the open space in the center of the stage may be many places in rapid succession—a street, a market place, a park; a low wall is considered too high to look over whenever that is desirable; many things which are handled and many passers-by are purely imaginary—the seeds which are scattered as an offering, flowers which are plucked, a wild animal in the bushes, piles of dead leaves in the park, the horse which the messenger mounts and rides away, squads of policemen, and always the crowds in the streets"; and the illusion of motion is conveyed by appropriate handling of the reins. The presence of bullocks on an off-Broadway stage would necessarily present problems, and this was cleverly resolved by the directors of the 1924 production by getting each "bullock" manipulated "by two boys within the hide—one as the forelegs, one as the hindlegs."

*The Toy Cart* really needs no preface; it is modern in the most significant sense of the word—it is divorced from the pious and the religious. Therefore, it presents an interplay of manners and mannerisms in place of the miraculous play of life called *lila*; therefore it is enormously entertaining but only incidentally illuminating.

SHUDRAKA

*Birthplace*: Probably Andhra, in south India. Shudraka is "a mythical character," according to Professor R. V. Jagirdar, and very likely a king who was patron to the actual writer of *The Toy Cart*.

*Date of birth*: Unknown, varying between the first century B.C. (H. H. Wilson), first century A.D. (Monier-Williams), and the utter uncertainty of Keith ("We are left with no more than impressions, and these are quite insufficient to assign any date to the clever hand which. . . made one of the great plays of the Indian drama"). The historical events described in *The Toy Cart* belong to 485 B.C.

# Characters

Maitreya, *Brahmin friend of Charudatta*

Charudatta, *penurious Brahmin*

Radanika, *slave girl to Charudatta*

Courtier, *to Sansthanaka*

Sansthanaka, *brother-in-law to King Palaka*

Servant, *to Sansthanaka*

Vasantasena, *courtesan of Ujjain*

Maid, *to Vasantasena*

Madanika, *slave girl attendant to Vasantasena*

Mathura, *owner of a gambling den*

Gambler

Masseur, *later a Buddhist monk*

Darduraka, *friend of Sharvilaka*

Karnapuraka, *slave to Vasantasena*

Vardhamanaka, *servant to Charudatta*

Sharvilaka, *Brahmin thief and lover of Madanika; follower of Aryaka*

Charudatta's Wife

Servant to Vasantasena

Coachman

Kumbhilaka, *servant to Vasantasena*

Courtier, *to Vasantasena*

Rohasena, *Charudatta's son*

Sthavaraka, *Sansthanaka's servant*

Aryaka, *exiled prince whose father abdicated in favor of Aryaka's uncle, Palaka*

Viraka, *captain of the guard*

Chandanaka, *captain of the guard and Sharvilaka's friend*

Clerk in Court of Justice; Judge; Recorder; Vasantasena's Mother; Two Executioners (Ahinta and Goha); etc.

# ACT I

*The scene is a city street with* CHARUDATTA's *house at the left of the stage. The two sides of the stage are alternately lighted and dimmed out as the action requires.* MAITREYA *enters, carrying a cloak.*

MAITREYA, *reading.* "I am sorry, but I suggest you try some other Brahmin. . . ." *He looks up.* What an awful mess you are in, Maitreya. There was a time—ah, those were the days!—when Charudatta had money in his pockets, and I could go to his house and stuff myself with scented sweets. I could sit by that door and poke my finger into a thousand delicious cakes. . .shove these aside, touch those, and eat the others, like a painter dipping his fingers in his colors. If I wished, I could stand in a corner of the market, like a well-fed bull, chewing away without a care in the world. But now he is poor; poverty has fallen on Charudatta! So I knock about from door to door, picking up whatever crumbs I can find, poor pet pigeon that I am. Just an odd-job man! Here I am, bringing a cloak for Charudatta from his friend Jurnavriddha—a jasmine-scented cloak that he has been asked to wear after he finishes his morning prayers. *He looks around.* Ah, here he is.

CHARUDATTA *enters with an offering for the divinity of the house. He is accompanied by* RADANIKA.

CHARUDATTA, *sighing and looking up.* Once the graceful swans and cranes would fly off with my offering. Now grass grows here, and the seeds I scatter are eaten by the hungry worms. *He walks around sadly a while, then sits down.*

MAITREYA, *approaching him.* My greetings to you, sir.

CHARUDATTA. Ah, my friend Maitreya. It's very good to see you, Maitreya. Sit down.

MAITREYA. Thank you. *He sits down.* Jurnavriddha sends you this cloak, fragrant with jasmine, and asks you please to wear it after prayers. *He hands the cloak to* CHARUDATTA, *who takes it absent-mindedly.* Sir, you look very serious today.

CHARUDATTA. Happiness hard on the heels of sorrow
  Is wonderful: a glowing lamp that scatters darkness.
  But a man who falls from riches to poverty,
  Though the face he wears is human, wears it on a spiritless body.

MAITREYA. Would you rather be dead than poor?

CHARUDATTA. I'd rather be dead, my friend. Death is only an instant of suffering; but being poor drags on and on.

MAITREYA. That well may be, but there is more than that. The money you spent on your friends has increased their respect for you in their hearts. You are like the moon: when three-quarters of her beauty has been drunk by the gods, the quarter that remains seems all the lovelier.

CHARUDATTA. You misunderstand me.
  It is not that I mind the wealth that's lost,
  But that my friends desert me, now I'm poor—
  That is my sorrow.
  Like bees that suck the fragrant exhalation
  Of juices on an elephant's shoulders,
  And then, the mating season done, ungratefully disappear.

MAITREYA. Damn them and double-damn them! They're cattle herders who feed their herds in the greenest pastures. Guests are like that—birds of passage.

CHARUDATTA. I mean it. It's not the loss of wealth that hurts.
  Money comes, money goes.
  But that the love of friends should come and go—
  That hurts.
  A man poor is a man ashamed;
  A man ashamed is a man without dignity.
  Frustration follows insult, despair follows frustration,
  Indecision follows despair.
  From this small root, all man's evils grow.

MAITREYA. That's the way it is. But let's change the subject.

CHARUDATTA. There's more. A poor man is laid bare to gossip,
  A dogging shame, a crown of thorns.

It brings the scorn of friends, and hate of strangers.
I tell you, Maitreya, if his wife turn against him,
Let him leave her, live in the forest, and
Be sad. Sorrow at most will bring fire down on his soul,
But it will not destroy him.
My friend Maitreya, I have offered prayer to the gods of my house.
Go where the four roads meet and offer better prayers on my behalf.

MAITREYA. Not me, sir.

CHARUDATTA. No?

MAITREYA. If the gods don't favor you here, they won't at the four roads either.

CHARUDATTA. Don't refuse, Maitreya. We do our duty, that is all. I have no doubt that the gods are pleased with whatever is offered to them in humility and piety, in thought and deed. Go.

MAITREYA. No, sir, not me. I might mess things up. Send someone else. I'm a useless Brahmin and as muddle-headed as a mirror—right side left, and left side right. Besides, what's worse, evening is the time when courtesans, thugs, and courtiers stalk the main road. And I'm just the man they'd see a prize catch. No, sir, I'm no guinea pig; I won't be the mouse that gets gobbled up by the snake who's out frog-hunting!

CHARUDATTA. Very well then, stay here. I'll go in and finish my prayers. *He and* RADANIKA *leave.*

VOICE, *offstage.* Vasantasena, stop! Stop, Vasantasena!

MAITREYA *hastily follows* CHARUDATTA. VASANTASENA *enters, running in the darkness, pursued by the king's brother-in-law* SANSTHANAKA, *his personal courtier, and his servant.*

COURTIER. Stop, Vasantasena! Why do you forget your modesty in your fear and run so fast? Your feet should dance—dance, not run. Why do you run like a frightened deer, looking at the hunters from the corners of your eyes?

SANSTHANAKA. Stop, Vasantasena! Why do you run like this, stumbling at each step? You need not fear. My heart overflows with love for you. It is burned to a cinder, sweet girl, like meat on blazing coals.

SERVANT. Stop, lady, stop! Why do you run like a peahen in summer? My lord can run faster, like a hound chasing a bird in the woods.

COURTIER. Stop, Vasantasena! You are trembling like a plantain tree; the hem of your dress is fluttering in the wind.

SANSTHANAKA. Stop, Vasantasena! Why run away from a love that you create? My nights are a ruin; by day you avoid me.

COURTIER. Like a bird from a snake, you flee from me. Why, Vasantasena? How far will you go? I could outstrip the wind if I liked.

SANSTHANAKA. Sir, I have loved her by ten different names. I called her the whip of the god of love. I called her fisheater, flatnose, angel, witch. I called her love's juiciest dish, baggage, bad girl, culture-vulture. All those wonderful sweet names. But, sir, she can't spare a word to throw at me.

COURTIER. Why run from us, Vasantasena?

SANSTHANAKA. Sweet girl, sweet Vasantasena, your jewels jingle as you fly from me. I shall catch you, my sweetheart, and kiss you, my sweetheart, as Rama kissed Draupadi.

SERVANT. Do as he says, lady. He's the king's brother-in-law. Take the flesh and the fish.

COURTIER. A hundred stars flash from your waist; your face is marvelous with fear. O goddess, O guardian of our city!

VASANTASENA. Pallavaka! Parabhritika!

SANSTHANAKA. Men, eh?

COURTIER. I know how to deal with *them*.

VASANTASENA. Madhavika, Madhavika!

COURTIER. The fool, she's calling her servants.

SANSTHANAKA. You mean women?

COURTIER. Yes.

SANSTHANAKA. Women, eh? Who's afraid? I can fight a hundred of them at once.

VASANTASENA, *getting no reply*. Not one to help! I'll have to use my wits.

COURTIER. Keep searching! She's here somewhere.

SANSTHANAKA. Scream away, Vasantasena, scream for your *pallava* flower and your *madhavika* creeper. Your screams won't help you, the whole month of April won't help you, when I catch you. Call Bhimasena! My sword's out. . .slurrp!—there goes your head. Call the son of Kunti, call Ravana himself, the ten-headed demon! Where can you run, my little pet? Your life's in my hands.

VASANTASENA. Sir, I am a woman, a weak woman.

COURTIER. One reason you're not dead already.

SANSTHANAKA, *laughing*. Not finished off already!

VASANTASENA, *aside*. How terribly kind! *Aloud*. Sir, why are you chasing me? What do you want? My jewels?

COURTIER. Heavens, no! Why pluck the blossoms from a beautiful creeper? No, no, not the jewels.

VASANTASENA. What do you want, then?

SANSTHANAKA. Your love. Vasantasena, love me. I'm a splendid lover, I promise you.

VASANTASENA, *angrily*. You insult me, sir. Leave me alone. I'm sick of you.

SANSTHANAKA, *laughing and clapping his hands*. Now what do you say to that, courtier? This pretty girl is gone, far gone, on me. "You're sick for me," she says. "You're sick. . ." That's a good one. Yes, my pretty little chick, I'm sick for you. I'm sick, and not because I've been running from village to town looking for you. . . . By your pretty feet and your pretty head, I'm sick for your love. . . . Oh, love me, Vasantasena!

COURTIER, *aside*. But what she said was, "I'm sick of you." The fool! *Aloud*. That's a strange way for a courtesan to talk, Vasantasena. You know how it is: the doors of a courtesan's house are open to all young men. She is a flower by the roadside. Money will buy her love. She gives the same greeting to the man she likes and to the man she loathes. Come,

Vasantasena, the genius and the fool, the Brahmin and the outcast—the same stream gives a cleansing bath to both. The crow and the peacock perch on the same glittering tree. The soldier and the merchant and the scholar—the same boat takes them all across the river, doesn't it? It's a courtesan's business to be. . .er. . .friendly to all.

VASANTASENA. I've never heard of love being forced, sir. It has to be deserved.

SANSTHANAKA. Is that so? The real trouble, sir, is that this slut is in love with a nobody, a wretch by the name of Charudatta, whom she met in the garden of Kama's temple. So she won't give me a second look. His house is near, on our left. See that she doesn't slip out of our fingers into it.

COURTIER, *aside*. This utter idiot: he has to say the wrong thing every time! So she's in love with Charudatta. You don't say. Well, pearl matches pearl. But this moron. . .*Aloud*. Did you say that Charudatta's house is on our left? Did you?

SANSTHANAKA. Yes, on our left. I did. I did.

VASANTASENA, *aside*. Oh, what a relief! On my left. Just by trying to hurt me, he's helped me. The house of the man I love.

SANSTHANAKA. It's dark, dark! I can't see a thing. Now you see her, now you don't. It's like hunting for a bottle of ink in a coal mine.

COURTIER. It *is* dark. The darkness closes down over my eyes so I can't see even the road. It's all over my body, as if it were raining darkness. My eyes are worthless, like a friend who's played one a dirty trick.

SANSTHANAKA. I *must* find her.

COURTIER. How? Have you anything to go by?

SANSTHANAKA. Go by? What do you mean?

COURTIER. The tinkling of her jewelry, the perfume of her garland. . .

SANSTHANAKA. Yes, sir, I hear the fragrance of her garland, but I cannot see the tinkling of her jewels—there's too much darkness here.

COURTIER. Listen, Vasantasena.
   Though the darkness hides you, as clouds hide the lightning,

> The fragrance of your garland will give you away;
> The music of your anklets will give you away.
> Where are you, Vasantasena?

VASANTASENA, *aside.* Thanks for the warning. *She takes off her garland and anklets, and feels her way.* This is the way, I think. I can feel it with my fingers. And here's the back door. Oh dear, it's shut!

CHARUDATTA, *in his house.* My prayers are finished. Now, Maitreya, it's time for yours. Pray for me at the four roads.

MAITREYA. Not me!

CHARUDATTA. This too!

> Who listens to a poor man?
> His friends? Once they loved him, now they say good-bye.
> His sorrow grows and grows.
> The crimes of others are loaded on his shoulders.
> No one cares a whit for his once resplendent character.
> No one talks to him.
> Greetings are formal—politeness without respect.
> At a party or a festival the rich men scatter,
> Withdraw to a corner, size him up scornfully.
> On the street, suddenly conscious of his poor clothing,
> He slinks to one side, ashamed.
> Are the deadly sins five in number?
> No, let us add a sixth: that is, to be poor.
> Why do you cling to me, Poverty?
> You will get nothing from me.
> What will you do when I die? Where will you go then?

MAITREYA, *embarrassed.* All right, I'll go. But I should like Radanika to come with me.

CHARUDATTA. Radanika, go with him.

RADANIKA. Yes, sir.

MAITREYA. Do you mind holding this offering a minute, Radanika, while I open the back door?

VASANTASENA. I'm lucky: the door has opened by itself! *She starts to enter.* Oh! a candle! *She snuffs the candle out with a fold of her dress, and goes in.*

CHARUDATTA. What was that, Maitreya?

MAITREYA. Something blew out the candle—the wind, I think, sir. Never mind. You go first, Radanika. I'll light another candle and follow you.

SANSTHANAKA. Where the devil has she disappeared to?

COURTIER. She's here. She can't go far.

SANSTHANAKA. I have her! I have her!

COURTIER. You fool, let go of me!

SANSTHANAKA. Oh-ho, oh-ho, beat about, look around. . .I have her! I have her!

SERVANT. You have *me,* sir.

SANSTHANAKA. Me, sir? Oh-ho, oh-ho, master and servant, servant and master. Stay where you are, stay where you are, don't move! Look about, search! Search! *He catches hold of Radanika by the hair.* Oh-ho, I have her. This time I really have her! I can tell her by the scent of the garland. Oh-ho, I have her now!

COURTIER. A pretty hide-and-seek we played, didn't we, my sweet girl? That's a nice head of hair, all scented with flowers.

SANSTHANAKA. I have her by the hair. Oh-ho! I have you, my girl! Scream away, yell, call your friends, curse your God!

RADANIKA. Sir! Sir! What is all this?

COURTIER. Hey, that isn't her voice.

SANSTHANAKA. I know these cats, sir. When they want milk, they have a different mew. Don't believe her.

COURTIER. I'm not sure. . . . Still, why not? She must know the tricks of her trade.

MAITREYA, *entering.* How queerly the candle flickers. . .like the fluttering heart of a goat that can't escape. *He sees* RADANIKA *and the others.* Radanika!

SANSTHANAKA. Ho, sir, sir! A man, a man!

MAITREYA. He may be poor, but this is still his house. You are going too far, sir.

RADANIKA. He laid hands on me, Maitreya. He insulted me.

MAITREYA. Insulted you? You insult *us,* sir.

RADANIKA. He laid hands on me, Maitreya.

MAITREYA. Who? This one?

RADANIKA. Yes.

MAITREYA, *lifting his staff in anger.* Sir, even a worm will turn—and I, I am a Brahmin! This stick of mine is crooked, sir, but it's still good enough to crack a skull or two!

COURTIER. O great Brahmin, please, please. . .

MAITREYA. This can't be the one. *He turns to* SANSTHANAKA. You are the man. Ha! The king's own brother-in-law! Ha! Sansthanaka, you coward! You damned sex fiend! Don't you know that Charudatta is the finest citizen of Ujjain? And you break into his house! And you lay hands on his servants! You idiot, don't you know that poverty isn't a crime—not yet, at least—that there are still plenty of rich rascals around?

COURTIER, *considerably embarrassed.* Sir, we had no idea. . . . We're sorry. It's a case of mistaken identity. We were looking for a girl—

MAITREYA, *angrily.* And you found her?

COURTIER. Oh, no. No. It was a girl that can take care of herself that we were looking for, and now it seems that we have insulted her in the process. *He points to* RADANIKA. We didn't mean to. Believe us, we're terribly sorry. *He drops his sword and falls at* MAITREYA'*s feet.*

MAITREYA. I see that *you* at least have sense. It's all right—you may rise. I did not know you when I abused you. I too am sorry.

COURTIER. We have more reason to be sorry. I will rise, but on one condition.

MAITREYA. Yes?

COURTIER. Charudatta must never know what happened here.

MAITREYA. You have my word.

COURTIER. There speaks a Brahmin! No sword can harm a man so well grounded in virtue.

SANSTHANAKA. This is intolerable! Why should you slobber in front of this cardboard man and join your palms and fall at his feet?

COURTIER. Fear.

SANSTHANAKA. Of what?

COURTIER. Of Charudatta's virtue.

SANSTHANAKA. Fine virtue, that! Why, you can't find a crumb to eat in his house!

COURTIER. You do not understand.
   It was his virtue brought him poverty.
   When rich, he overflowed with kindness.
   The summer lake has dried; there were too many thirsty travelers.

SANSTHANAKA, *stamping his foot*. Son of a slave, and a slave himself! Who is he, anyway? Rama's son? Radha's son? Pandu's son?

COURTIER. Hold your tongue!
   He is Charudatta:
   A tree of bounty to the poor when he was heavy with fruit,
   A patron of good men, a mirror of learning,
   The essence of holiness—
   In short, a man of character,
   Humble, courteous, in every way admirable.
   We exist; he *lives*—so rich is the wealth of his virtues.
   Come, let us go.

SANSTHANAKA. Without Vasantasena?

COURTIER. She isn't here.

SANSTHANAKA. I'm not budging without her.

COURTIER. May I remind you of a wise saying? Hold an elephant with a chain, a horse with horsemanship, a woman with love. Let's go.

SANSTHANAKA. You may go, but I'm not budging.

COURTIER. Very well. *He leaves.*

SANSTHANAKA. Good riddance! *He speaks to* MAITREYA. Now, you hairless lump of holiness, let's see you bow, let's see you bow to us.

MAITREYA. We are bowed down already.

SANSTHANAKA. And who has been bowing you down?

MAITREYA. Fate.

SANSTHANAKA. All right, then, stand up, stand up.

MAITREYA. We will.

SANSTHANAKA. When?

MAITREYA. When Fate is kind enough.

SANSTHANAKA. What a crybaby!

MAITREYA. We are crying.

SANSTHANAKA. Why?

MAITREYA. We are poor.

SANSTHANAKA. Then laugh, you fool, laugh.

MAITREYA. We will.

SANSTHANAKA. When?

MAITREYA. When Charudatta is rich again.

SANSTHANAKA. In the meantime, then, take this message from me to Charudatta. Tell him this: "A slip, a fool of a girl, common trash, by the name of Vasantasena, with a heap of golden things on her, a stage manageress, a female of the species who puts on cheap comedies—this woman saw you in the garden of the temple of Kamadeva. And she lost her heart to you, that is, she fell in love with you. When we tried to set her right, using a bit of persuasion, she slipped in and took shelter in your house. The point is this: if you give her up unconditionally, without my having to go to the police and take legal action, if you hand her over nicely to me, then you have my best regards. If you don't, you are my enemy, and God help you." See that you break this news to him politely but firmly—and *distinctly*; see that your voice carries as far as the terrace of my splendid house. For, sir, if you swallow a word or two, I'll chew your head off with my own teeth—like this—like a nut cracked in a door hinge.

MAITREYA. He will get your message.

SANSTHANAKA, *to the* SERVANT. Has the courtier really left?

SERVANT. Yes, sir.

SANSTHANAKA. We must be off too.

SERVANT. Your sword, sir.

SANSTHANAKA. Oh, yes, my sword. You carry it.

SERVANT. Your sword, sir. Take it.

SANSTHANAKA, *taking the sword by the wrong end*. Radish pink, my sword sleeps in its sheath on my shoulder. The bitches yap at me from behind—and the dogs! I'm going home, the jackal is going home. *They both leave.*

MAITREYA. Radanika, there's no need to tell Charudatta about this incident. He's up to his neck in misery as it is; this will only make him feel worse.

RADANIKA. I won't say a word about it to him, sir.

MAITREYA. Good.

*They leave.*

CHARUDATTA, *to* VASANTASENA. Don't you think, Radanika, that it's time you brought the boy in? I know that Rohasena enjoys the cool evening, but it gets quite chilly at this hour. I suggest you go and bring him home. And here, cover him with this cloak. *He gives her his cloak.*

VASANTASENA, *aside.* He thinks I'm the servant girl. *She takes the cloak; its fragrance strikes her.* Such sweetness! He isn't a *complete* saint yet. *She puts the cloak on her shoulders.*

CHARUDATTA. So, Radanika, bring Rohasena home.

VASANTASENA, *aside.* If only I had the right to!

CHARUDATTA. Even you don't answer, Radanika? Well, that's the way the world is. And why not? Even my closest friends have left me since I became poor.

MAITREYA *and* RADANIKA *re-enter.*

MAITREYA. Did you call, sir? Here's Radanika.

CHARUDATTA. But. . .then who is this lady? How shameful of me to be so familiar. . .My shawl. . .

VASANTASENA, *aside.* How wonderful for me!

CHARUDATTA. She's half in shadow, a slice of moon among autumn clouds. No, I mustn't—how dare I speak like this? She must be someone's wife. . . .

MAITREYA. Not someone's wife, sir. She is Vasantasena, who fell in love with you when she saw you in the temple of Kamadeva.

CHARUDATTA. Vasantasena? *He continues to himself.*
    But what is the use of returning her love
    In my decrepit state? So let it die.
    Better a coward should kill his mounting anger.

MAITREYA. Sir, the king's brother-in-law sends a message.

CHARUDATTA. To *me?*

MAITREYA. He says: "A slip, a fool of a girl, common trash, by the name of Vasantasena, with a heap of golden things on her, a stage manageress, a female of the species who puts on cheap comedies—this woman saw you in the garden of the temple of Kamadeva. And she lost her heart to

you, that is, she fell in love with you. When we tried to set her right, using
a bit of persuasion—"

VASANTASENA, *aside*. "Set her right, using a bit of persuasion." Well put!

MAITREYA. "—she slipped in and took shelter in your house. The point
is this: if you give her up unconditionally, without my having to go to
the police and take legal action, if you hand her over nicely to me, then you
have my best regards. If you don't, you are my enemy, and God help you."

CHARUDATTA, *strongly*. He is a fool!
    What a remarkable woman she must be!
    Money has no fascination for her.
    She told him to be off; for me, she has gracious silence.
Let me say how sorry I am, mistaking you for my servant and speaking
so boorishly.

VASANTASENA. Oh, sir, it is I who should be sorry, walking in like this,
an uninvited guest.

MAITREYA. Now isn't that a pretty sight!—two civilized people nodding
away like a field of waving grass. Let me also bow my head, though stiffly,
like a knock-kneed camel. And let me ask you please to stop nodding—
we've had enough—and stand erect.

CHARUDATTA. Very well, then, no more formalities.

VASANTASENA, *aside*. He is gracious. He is good. But I mustn't take
advantage of his goodness—I have no right. Sir, I thank you deeply for
your kindness, and I hope you will not mind if I leave these jewels here. I
think they were trying to rob me when I ran in.

CHARUDATTA. This poor house does not deserve such a weighty trust.

VASANTASENA. Sir, it is not houses we trust, but men.

CHARUDATTA. Maitreya, take these jewels.

VASANTASENA. Thank you very much. *She hands over her jewels.*

MAITREYA, *taking them*. Thank *you*.

CHARUDATTA. They aren't for you!

MAITREYA, *aside.* They're for thieves, I suppose?

CHARUDATTA. Very soon—

MAITREYA, *aside.* What's in our hands is ours. That's logic.

CHARUDATTA, *to* VASANTASENA. You may have them again whenever you want them.

VASANTASENA. I should be grateful, sir, if you could send an escort with me.

CHARUDATTA. See her safely home, Maitreya.

MAITREYA. You are the best man for that, sir: a fine handsome escort for a graceful lady. I'm a miserable Brahmin, and a poor one; they'll yap at me in the market place, as dogs snap at bits of meat.

CHARUDATTA. Very well, I'll go with her. Have torches lighted; I don't want any trouble on the way.

MAITREYA. Hey, Vardhamanaka!

*A* SERVANT *enters.* Light the torches.

VARDHAMANAKA. Without oil, sir?

MAITREYA. You're right. Torches are like courtesans—they don't warm up unless you feed them.

CHARUDATTA. Never mind, we'll do without the torches.
    The moon is up, and her starry servants. too,
    Pale as first love on a young girl's cheeks.
    The moonlight will do.
    Look at its crystal light falling like milk on the marshes.

*They slowly cross the stage.*

Here you are, Vasantasena.

*His voice betrays feeling. She looks at him tenderly, and enters her house.*

Now, Maitreya, shall we turn back?
There's not a light on the road now,

Not a creature stirring. Only the watchman.

The night covers many sins.

Let's go home, Maitreya. See that you guard this gold box well at night;
Vardhamanaka will keep his eye on it during the day.

MAITREYA. Yes, sir. *They leave.*

C  U  R  T  A  I  N


## ACT II

*At the left side of the stage is the house of* VASANTASENA; *on the right,
an open field; in the background, a small deserted temple. A* MAID *enters
the house.*

MAID. Here is a message from your mother. But where is my mistress?
*She looks about her.* Oh, there! *She sees* VASANTASENA *seated, painting,
with* MADANIKA *beside her.* Painting a picture—and lost in her painting.

VASANTASENA. Well, my girl, did you—

MAID. Did I what? Why, mistress, you didn't ask me to do anything.

VASANTASENA. I didn't?

MAID. No. And now you ask, "Well, my girl, did you—?"

VASANTASENA, *confused.* I did? Yes, I guess I did.

MAID, *approaching.* Mistress, your mother would like to have you come
over today for worship.

VASANTASENA. Tell her, my girl, that today I can't. A Brahmin can
take my place.

MAID. Yes, mistress. *She leaves.*

MADANIKA. Please don't be offended—it isn't impertinence but affection
that makes me ask—but whatever did you mean just now?

VASANTASENA. Madanika, tell me frankly: how do I strike you?

MADANIKA. Well, you're certainly very absent-minded. I think you must be in love.

VASANTASENA. And so I am. You're a pretty good judge of feelings, I see.

MADANIKA. Oh, I'm so happy! The god of love spares no one—and he likes them young! Is it a king you worship? Or a courtier?

VASANTASENA. I do not worship, Madanika. I am in love.

MADANIKA. Is he a Brahmin—young, pious, brilliant?

VASANTASENA. A Brahmin should be worshiped, not loved.

MADANIKA. A merchant then—rich, well established, much traveled?

VASANTASENA. Tsk, tsk, Madanika. A merchant is always away, always doing business in foreign lands. Love a merchant? Why, I'd die of loneliness.

MADANIKA. Not a king. Not a courtier. Not a Brahmin. Not even a merchant. I give up.

VASANTASENA. Oh, Madanika, you went with me to the garden of the temple of Kamadeva.

MADANIKA. Yes.

VASANTASENA. Then why do you ask? As if you knew nothing!

MADANIKA. I have it! The man who later helped you when you were being pursued.

VASANTASENA. His name?

MADANIKA. Why, he lives just a stone's throw from here!

VASANTASENA. But his name, his name?

MADANIKA. A good name: Charudatta.

VASANTASENA, *happily.* Yes, you're right, Madanika.

MADANIKA. But they say he's poor.

VASANTASENA. I love him anyway. And now at least no one can say that it was for his money that I ran after him.

MADANIKA. But butterflies don't light on to empty flowers, mistress.

VASANTASENA. That's why they're called butterflies.

MADANIKA. If you love him, then why not at least visit him?

VASANTASENA. I will. All in good time. I have a plan. But if something happens. . . It's not easy at all. But we'll see. We'll manage.

MADANIKA. So that's why you left your jewels with him?

VASANTASENA. What a clever girl you are, Madanika!

VOICE, *offstage*. Hey! Hey! What about my ten pieces of gold, eh? Stop him! That dirty chiseling gambler! Stop, you! Stop!

*The* MASSEUR *runs in, panting.*

MASSEUR. Damn gamblers! And damn gambling! Aces and deuces and pocket flippers! Bastards! But did I give them the slip? The moment the keeper turned his back! Whew! So here I am, running like mad, but now what's the next stop? The keeper and his gambling friend are close behind. Aha, a deserted temple. Perhaps I could become a temple god, yes? *With comic gestures, he steps up into the niche reserved for the deity.*

MATHURA *and the* GAMBLER *enter.*

MATHURA. Ten pieces of gold that massage-man owes us—and he's skedaddled! Stop the bastard! There he goes.

GAMBLER. You may hide yourself in hell, friend, but we'll fish you out, never fear.

MATHURA. You two-timing crook, you double-crosser of honest Mathura! I can hear you—your frightened steps; you're trembling with fear; you're stumbling. Drop dead, you rascal, you blackener of your family's name!

GAMBLER, *examining the ground*. His footprints stop here.

MATHURA. *studying the ground*. Ha, they turn, they turn back, and— And this temple has no idol. *He reflects*. The swine, he walked backward into the temple, with his feet facing front.

GAMBLER. After him!

MATHURA. Ha!

*They enter the temple and look around, at first using just sign language. Then they speak.*

GAMBLER. Would you say this idol was made of wood?

MATHURA. No, stone, I think. *He gives the "idol" a push; it teeters comically.* Who cares? Well, the masseur's gone. Say, shall we have a little game?

*The* GAMBLER *nods, and they start throwing dice.*

MASSEUR, *fascinated, aside.* It's like the sound of a drum to a king without a kingdom, the rattle of dice to a man without a stake. Fascinating. I know it's bad. To gamble is to fall into ruin. But it's fascinating. The rattle of dice—ah, it's a koel's song.

GAMBLER. My turn!

MATHURA. No, mine.

MASSEUR, *jumping down out of the niche.* No, no, mine!

GAMBLER. We have him.

MATHURA, *seizing him.* My little pet! And what about those ten pieces of gold?

MASSEUR. I'll pay.

MATHURA. Cough up, cough up! Now!

MASSEUR. I'll pay. Give me a few days.

MATHURA. No! Now!

MASSEUR. Let go my head! *He falls to the ground. They beat him up.*

MATHURA. Ten pieces! Ten solid pieces of gold!

MASSEUR, *getting painfully to his feet.* Sir, sir! *He speaks worriedly.* I just haven't got the money. You must give me time. How can I pay this minute?

MATHURA. A pledge!

MASSEUR. Oh, all right, all right. *He draws the* GAMBLER *to him.* Let me off half, and I'll give you half. All right?

GAMBLER. Suits me.

MASSEUR, *drawing* MATHURA *to him*. I'll give you my word I'll pay you half. Let me off half, won't you?

MATHURA. Suits me.

MASSEUR, *to the* GAMBLER. You let me off five gold pieces?

GAMBLER. That's what I said.

MASSEUR, *to* MATHURA. And you let me off five?

MATHURA. Suits me.

MASSEUR. Well, that's that. Be seeing you. *He starts to leave.*

MATHURA. Hey, not so fast, friend! Where's my ten pieces?

MASSEUR. What's wrong? You let me off half, five pieces; and *you* let me off half, five pieces. That's ten pieces. And that's that.

MATHURA. Ve-ry funny! Look here, friend, my name's Mathura, and no free-and-easy tricks get by with me, see? I want my ten gold pieces, and I want them *now!*

MASSEUR. I haven't got ten.

MATHURA. Then sell your father for ten pieces.

MASSEUR. I have no father.

MATHURA. Sell your mother, then.

MASSEUR. I have no mother.

MATHURA. Sell yourself.

MASSEUR. Whatever you say. All right, take me to the main street.

MATHURA. You go in front.

*They walk a few steps.*

MASSEUR. Here we go. Hey! Hey! For sale! A bargain! Ten gold pieces for this excellent masseur! *He stops a passer-by.* Hey! What can I do? What *can't* I do? I'll keep house for you. *The passer-by brushes on.* No go. *He stops another.* Hey! Ten gold pieces for me. No? No. Bah! Ah, Charudatta is no longer my patron. He's poor, so I'm poor. And no one's interested.

MATHURA. Come on, cough up, cough up.

MASSEUR. But I haven't *got* ten pieces. *He is dragged down by* MATHURA. Help! Murder! Hey, help! Help! Hey!

DARDURAKA *enters.*

DARDURAKA. A gambler is a king without a crown. Nothing to lose, everything to spend: servants, money, wife, friends—won, kept, and lost at the gambling table. A throw of three took my money. . .the deuce took my health. . .the ace threw me out in the street. . .and the four—that did me in good and proper. Oh, there's Mathura. Well, this shawl should help to hide me. *He examines it.* No, it's threadbare stuff; too many holes— big ones. *He folds it up again and puts it under his arm.* But who cares, anyway? What can he do? He can't eat me.

MATHURA, *still addressing the* MASSEUR. Cough up!

MASSEUR. I told you: I haven't got the money.

DARDURAKA, *aside.* What's going on here? *He addresses an imaginary spectator.* What's that you said, sir?--"Mathura's beating up the masseur"? Well, let's see. *He steps forward.* Poor man, he's been beaten black and blue! Poor fellow, what has he to do with gambling? Oh, hello, Mathura.

MATHURA. Hello yourself.

DARDURAKA. And what do I see here?

MATHURA. You see a swine who owes me ten gold pieces.

DARDURAKA. Only ten? Only ten pieces?

MATHURA, *pulling* DARDURAKA'*s tattered shawl from under his arm.* "Only ten? Only ten pieces?" Look who's talking! The man with the threadbare shawl!

DARDURAKA. Mathura, my foolish friend, haven't you seen me risk ten gold pieces a thousand times? If a man has money, should he lug it around in his pockets? But you, you foolish wretch, you're ready to knock out this poor fellow's five senses for ten pieces.

MATHURA. Ten pieces may be "only" ten pieces to you, but to me they're ten solid gold coins.

DARDURAKA. Good. Good. So why not give him ten solid gold coins, set him free, and let him gamble away?

MATHURA. Are you mad?

DARDURAKA. If he wins, he'll pay you back.

MATHURA. And if he loses?

DARDURAKA. Then he won't pay you back.

MATHURA. Bloody clever, aren't you? Why don't *you* give him ten pieces? Look, my name is Mathura and I'm a crook. I play a crooked game—I play it well—and everyone knows it. But you don't frighten me, you lily-livered bastard.

DARDURAKA. Who's a bastard?

MATHURA. *You* are!

DARDURAKA. Your father was a bigger bastard! *He makes signs to the* MASSEUR *to try to escape.*

MATHURA. Why, you son-of-a-bitch, aren't you a gambler yourself?

DARDURAKA. Me? a gambler?

MATHURA, *turning to the* MASSEUR, *and starting to drag him by the hair.* Come on, cough up.

DARDURAKA. Stop! No one's going to lay hands on him while I'm here!

MATHURA, *regardless, punches the* MASSEUR *on the nose, which starts bleeding. The* MASSEUR *collapses.* DARDURAKA *steps in, and there is a scuffle between* DARDURAKA *and* MATHURA.

MATHURA. You damned son-of-a-bitch! I'll get you for this!

DARDURAKA. You fool! Suppose I say you beat me up on the road as I was quietly passing by? You'll see in court tomorrow if they let you off so easily.

MATHURA. All right, we shall see, we shall see.

DARDURAKA. You will? And how will you see?

MATHURA, *thrusting his face in* DARDURAKA's *and opening his eyes wide.* Like this. Does that satisfy you?

DARDURAKA *throws a handful of dust in his eyes;* MATHURA *flinches and falls back;* DARDURAKA *makes signs to the* MASSEUR *to escape. The* MASSEUR *scrambles up and runs off.*

DARDURAKA. This fellow has a lot of influence around here; I'd better scoot too. My friend Sharvilaka tells me he heard a prophecy that a cowherd named Aryaka is going to be king. He'd be the best leader for such as us. I'll hunt him up. *He hastens off.*

MASSEUR, *running and stumbling toward* VASANTASENA's *house.* This house is open. *He enters and sees* VASANTASENA. Please help me. Please help me.

VASANTASENA. Don't be afraid—you are safe here. Madanika, shut the door. *The maid does so.* What are you afraid of?

MASSEUR. I owe a man some money.

VASANTASENA. Madanika, open the door.

MASSEUR, *aside.* She isn't afraid of creditors. Little does she know. But it's a good proverb that says a man must face the music—meaning that I'll have to face it.

MATHURA, *to the* GAMBLER, *rubbing his eyes.* Cough up, cough up!

GAMBLER. He isn't here. While you two were scuffling, the swine scuttled off.

MATHURA. I gave him a punch on the nose, though, and he's bleeding. He won't get far. We'll track him down. Look, here's blood. *They follow the trail of blood.*

GAMBLER. He's in here. *He stops at* VASANTASENA's *door.*

MATHURA. Good-bye, ten pieces. My ten gold pieces, good-bye.

GAMBLER. Let's go file a complaint in court.

MATHURA. And have the bird fly away while we're gone? Not me! I'm sitting tight till the bastard coughs up.

*Inside,* VASANTASENA *makes a sign to* MADANIKA.

MADANIKA. Sir, my mistress wishes to know where you come from, who you are, why you are here, and what you are really afraid of.

MASSEUR. Well, I was born in Pataliputra, the son of a householder. I'm a masseur.

VASANTASENA. A delicate, pleasant art, sir.

MASSEUR. I learned it very well, madam, so now it's just routine work.

MADANIKA. I see. Go on.

MASSEUR. While with my father, madam, I used to hear visitors tell stories of other lands and I wanted to see things for myself. So I came to Ujjain and became masseur to a first-class gentleman, a model of good manners and handsomer than I can say. He was quick to give away money and bore insults in silence, forgiving his worst enemy—in short, such a fine man that he seemed to be caring for the whole world.

MADANIKA. Is there such a man in Ujjain?

VASANTASENA. I know him. My heart tells me.

MADANIKA. Go on.

MASSEUR. He gave so freely, so liberally, that—

VASANTASENA. —he hasn't anything left.

MASSEUR. How did you guess? Did I—?

VASANTASENA. I only had to put two and two together. Goodness and money go together very seldom. But you can't call a good man *poor*; such a man is richer than anyone else.

MADANIKA. And his name?

MASSEUR. Who hasn't heard of him? Who hasn't heard of the moon? His name is Charudatta. He lives very near here.

VASANTASENA, *standing up, looking very happy*. A fan, Madanika. Can't you see he's tired? Sit down, sir. There's no need to be formal.

MASSEUR, *aside*. All this at the mere mention of his name! God bless you, Charudatta! You really live; others merely pass time in the world. *He falls at* VASANTASENA's *feet*. Thank you, madam. Please sit down. I'm all right like this.

VASANTASENA. But go on with your story.

MASSEUR. Well, as I said, I was his masseur, but when he had no more money left I took to gambling. And my luck was against me and I lost ten gold pieces.

MATHURA, *outside*. I've been cheated! I've been robbed!

MASSEUR. That's him, madam. Him and the other one. What shall I do?

VASANTASENA, *removing her bracelet and giving it to* MADANIKA. Give them this, Madanika, and say this gentleman sends it.

MADANIKA. Yes, mistress.

MATHURA, *outside*. I've been robbed!

MADANIKA *emerges unobserved by a side door*.

MADANIKA, *aside*. Such shouting and crying! Such muttering and anxiety! And the way their eyes are pinned to the front door! These must be the ones. *Aloud*. Good morning, sir.

MATHURA. And good morning to you.

MADANIKA. Which of you gentlemen is the chief gambler?

MATHURA. Me, my pretty one. But it won't do. No pouting lips at me, no sweet words. Don't give me the come-hither, my girl. I have no money.

MADANIKA. Gamblers don't talk like that. Is there someone who owes you money?

MATHURA. Yes, ten gold pieces. Why?

MADANIKA. My mistress sends this—no, *he* sends this, by way of payment.

MATHURA, *grabbing the bracelet*. Aha! Tell him we're quits. And tell him to drop in again whenever he wants some fun.

MATHURA *and the* GAMBLER *leave*.

MADANIKA, *returning to* VASANTASENA. They've gone, looking very pleased.

VASANTASENA. Now, sir, you may go safely.

MASSEUR. If I can be of any help to you, madam. . .

VASANTASENA. You can be of more help to the man for whom you were working and thanks to whom you learned your art.

MASSEUR, *aside*. A neat way of saying, "No, thanks." *Aloud*. Madam, my work brings me only disgrace. I'm going to become a Buddhist monk.

VASANTASENA. Don't do anything rash.

MASSEUR. My mind's made up. *He starts to leave*. When I gambled everyone looked down on me. Now I can hold my head high and walk freely in the streets. *Loud shouts are heard offstage*. What's up now? *He looks around*. What! Vasantasena's hunting elephant has broken loose? Ha! What fun! I must go see the mad beast! Oops!—I nearly forgot. I'd decided to become a monk. It won't do. *He leaves*.

KARNAPURAKA, *splendidly dressed, rushes in, in high elation*. Where is she? Where is my lady?

MADANIKA. What's the matter with you? Are you out of your senses? She's right there in front of you.

KARNAPURAKA. Your humble servant, my lady.

VASANTASENA. You look very happy, Karnapuraka. What is it?

KARNAPURAKA, *beaming*. Oh, what a pity you were not there to see the bravery of your servant!

VASANTASENA. Why, what did you do?

KARNAPURAKA. Well. . .your elephant—the one called "Gate-Smasher"—well, he killed his keeper, broke his chain, and banged out onto the main road. Oh, what a ruckus! Men shrieking all over the place: "Get the babies out of here! Climb up the tree! Get up on the roof! The elephant's broken loose!" Snip went the girdles, snap went the anklets; snip went the pearls, snap went the diamonds. Oh, what a glorious rain of jewels! And then came the elephant, barging into Ujjain as if it were a lotus pond, with his trunk flailing, his feet and tusks ripping things apart! Along came a holy man—a beggar. Swoosh went the water from the mad beast's trunk; the begging bowl was smashed, the beggar's staff broken in two—and there he was, caught up between the animal's tusks. The men gathered round, shrieking, "He'll be killed! He'll be killed!"

VASANTASENA. Oh, how horrible, how horrible!

KARNAPURAKA. No, don't worry. Just listen. There was the poor beggar right between his tusks, when I saw him—I mean, when I, your humble servant, saw him. And I grabbed an iron rod from a shop, tripped but kept running, dashed in from one corner and stood in front of the beast. . . .

VASANTASENA. Go on, go on.

KARNAPURAKA. And I plunged the rod into him—he was a great mountain of a beast—with all my strength. And he fell, and I saved the holy man.

VASANTASENA. Isn't that wonderful! How brave of you!

KARNAPURAKA. And all the people in the city were suddenly all over me, showering me with praise, there near the beast lying like a boat tipped over on its side. One of them looked at me, sighed, and threw this shawl over me.

VASANTASENA. Does it smell of perfume? Jasmine?

KARNAPURAKA. I can't tell, my lady; my nose is full of elephant smell.

VASANTASENA. Is there a name on it?

KARNAPURAKA. A few letters. Read them, my lady. *He hands her the shawl.*

VASANTASENA, *reading*. Charudatta. *She folds the shawl around her.*

MADANIKA. It looks nice on her, doesn't it?

KARNAPURAKA. I think so.

VASANTASENA. This is for you, Karnapuraka. *She gives him a jewel.*

KARNAPURAKA, *taking it and bowing.* Nice? I'll say it does!

VASANTASENA. And where is Charudatta now?

KARNAPURAKA. Well, my lady, he was going home. He'll be passing by this road.

VASANTASENA. Quick, Madanika, to the balcony. Perhaps we'll catch a glimpse of him as he walks by.

*They leave.*

C  U  R  T  A  I  N


# ACT III

*Outside* CHARUDATTA'S *house.* VARDHAMANAKA, CHARUDATTA'S *servant, enters.*

VARDHAMANAKA. A good kind master is the man for me. Who cares if he is poor? A sullen snob's the very devil even if he has all the money in the world. That's the way it is. You can't keep a hungry bull out of a wheat field; you can't stop a gay blade from chasing another man's wife; you can't stop a gambler from gambling; and you can't stop a fool from making a fool of himself. My master is still at the concert, and it's not quite midnight yet, so there's still time before he returns. I think I'll take a little snooze in the hall. *He goes inside.*

CHARUDATTA *and* MAITREYA *enter and walk toward the house.*

CHARUDATTA. Rebhila sang exquisitely, don't you think? And the vina is a pearl of an instrument. It soothes the waiting lover; it consoles lovers who are separated. It adds a sad sweetness to sweet sadness.

MAITREYA, *impatiently*. Yes, yes, yes. It's time we were home.

CHARUDATTA. Oh, but he sang exquisitely, didn't he?

MAITREYA. Well, if you must know, there are two things I can't stand: one is a woman reading Sanskrit aloud, and the other is a man trying to sing in a soft key. When a woman reads Sanskrit, all you get is "moosh, moosh, moosh," as if a calf were sneezing. And when a man tries singing softly, he's like a priest chanting through his nose. I tell you, it's not pleasant at all.

CHARUDATTA. You are hard to please. But Rebhila sang exquisitely this evening.
> Melody, warmth, a smoothness, peacefulness.
> Oh, I could feel it.
> Almost as if the lyrical voice of a girl
> Were singing—such sweetness!
> It seemed that my own love was singing.
> I can hear it even as I walk with you now—
> I'll never forget it—
> The trembling on a theme,
> The dying fall.

MAITREYA. Fine, fine. But let's get home. Even the street dogs are fast asleep. And there's the moon stepping down through the clouds, leaving the world to pitch-darkness.

CHARUDATTA. Yes, only his tusks are visible,
> Two sharp eyes above the surrounding darkness,
> Like an elephant browsing in a forest pool.

MAITREYA. Well, here we are. Vardhamanaka, wake up! Open the door!

VARDHAMANAKA. That's Maitreya's voice. They're back. *He opens the door*. Sir, the couch is ready.

MAITREYA. Call Radanika; we need water for our feet.

CHARUDATTA. Let her sleep. Why disturb her now?

VARDHAMANAKA. I'll get the water, Maitreya, and you can wash his feet.

MAITREYA, *losing his temper*. The impertinent son of a slave! He will bring the water; and I—a Brahmin—must wash the feet!

CHARUDATTA. Oh, come, Maitreya, you get the water and he'll wash my feet, if that suits you better.

VARDHAMANAKA. Gladly. Yes, Maitreya, you bring the water.

MAITREYA *brings water;* VARDHAMANAKA *washes* CHARUDATTA's *feet, then starts to move away*.

CHARUDATTA. And now, Vardhamanaka, what about washing the Brahmin's feet?

MAITREYA. Don't bother. It's water wasted, because I shall be going out again, trudging along like a dirty donkey.

VARDHAMANAKA. But you are a Brahmin, Maitreya.

MAITREYA. Yes, sir. I am a Brahmin. I am a Brahmin among Brahmins, like a boa constrictor among snakes.

VARDHAMANAKA. Then I must wash your feet. *He does so.* And here's the golden box, which I look after during the day. It's night now, so it's your turn. *He gives* MAITREYA *the box, and leaves*.

MAITREYA. The golden box! Isn't there a single thief in the city of Ujjain who'll steal this stealer of my sleep? Let me just put it away inside.

CHARUDATTA. Of course not. It has been left in our care. Look after it, as a good Brahmin should. It must be returned safely to its owner. *He lies down*.
  Such sweetness!
  It seemed that my own love was singing. . . .

MAITREYA. Going off to sleep?

CHARUDATTA. Yes, I hope so. Sleep comes over me like old age, nibbling away at my powers of resistance. So let us sleep.

*They both fall asleep.*

SHARVILAKA *enters the garden stealthily*.

SHARVILAKA. How I skinned myself crawling on the ground, like a snake

wriggling out of its skin! But I've managed to slip through. *He looks up.*
The moon has set. Night's a good mother to people like me who work in
the dark and slink off when the guards come. I've scaled the garden wall
all right and got in; now for the house. They call it a crime, this slinking
in under cover of darkness, making hay while others sleep. We're crooks,
they say. All right, I'd sooner be a crook than an exploited slave. Besides,
I'm in good company: didn't Drona's son himself prowl and strike by
night? But now, how do I get in? On which side is the wall dampest—that
will make the least noise. Where can I make a hole that I can cover up
later? Where is the brickwork old and crumbling? How do I get in so
that no woman spots me? And where's the swag? That's what the textbook
says. *He feels the wall.* This spot seems a bit weak: it's been exposed to the
sun and rotted away. And here's a convenient rathole. Wonderful! O god
of thieves, blessed sir! A thousand thanks! Sir, you advise four ways of
breaking in. First for baked bricks—pull them out. Second for unbaked
bricks—cut through them. Third for clay—soften it up by wetting. Fourth
for wood—saw through it. Here we have baked bricks. So pull them out.
Here goes! *He starts to work.* Next, what shape shall I make the hole?
Lotus, lake, half-moon, sun? Swastika, waterpot? The book says take your
choice. The waterpot: that will look nice in this wall. Last night they
complained I wasn't artistic: my breaches, they said, should have been
made with better taste. O god of thieves, blessed sir, thanks again. O giver
of good, O god of the golden spear, a thousand thanks. And thanks to
my teacher, who taught me the whole bag of tricks. No one sees me, no
sword finds me. . . . Damn, I've forgotten my tape. I hope this will do
instead. *He unties the cord from round his neck.* The sacred thread's a
useful thing to a Brahmin, especially a Brahmin like me. It's just the thing
to measure walls; it's handy to pull up jewelry, to pick locks; and if a
snake bites, it's first-class for first aid. But let's get going. First, measure
the wall. Then out with the bricks. *He works.* One still left. Damn it, a
snake! *He quickly pulls out his hand and ties the sacred thread round one
finger.* That should do for now. *He peeps through the hole.* I see a light, a
candle. The light floods the darkness like pure gold. *He completes the
breach in the wall.* Now in I go. No, wait; first, the "feeler." That's what
the book says. *He puts his hand through and gropes about.* All clear. A
thousand thanks, blessed sir. *He crawls through.* Two men sleeping. I'd
better open the front door: it helps in an emergency. *He starts to open it.*
How it creaks! Everything's rusty here. A little water. *He sees the jug,*

*takes it, and sprinkles water on the door.* Not too much—it might make a splash on the floor. *He puts his back against the door and carefully eases it open.* That's done. Now, are these two really out or just faking? *He passes the candle close over their faces.* Fast asleep. *He looks around.* What's this? A drum. . .a lute. . .pipes. . .books. Hell, have I got into the house of a poet? A dancer? I thought he was a big shot. I don't steal from beggars. Is he really poor or is he just hiding his money? Afraid of thieves? Afraid of the king? Well, if he's got it buried around here, these will tell. *He scatters special seeds.* Nothing. Poor fellow. What am I doing here, then?

MAITREYA, *talking in his sleep to* CHARUDATTA. I see a hole in the wall. I see a thief. Here, you'd better keep the golden box.

SHARVILAKA. Has he seen me? Is he making fun of me? Then he dies, the swine! *He comes close to* MAITREYA *and studies him.* No, he's just babbling in his sleep. What's this? Something wrapped in a towel. How about taking it? No, it wouldn't be right. He's a poor man; why make him even poorer? *He starts to move away.*

MAITREYA. Take it, take it away, for the sake of a sacred cow, for the sake of a Brahmin!

SHARVILAKA. Well, if it's come to cows and Brahmins, then it's all right for me to take it. But that light! My pretty flame snuffers will take care of that. *He extracts a moth from his kit.* Just the right time and the right place. Dear friend, flutter round the wick; pretty moth, snuff out the light with your wings. *The moth does so.* There, now it's dark. But the greater darkness is the one that's fallen on me—me, Sharvilaka, a Brahmin and the son of a Brahmin who knew the scriptures by heart—me, doing this. And for whom? For a common courtesan like Madanika! But it's too late for tears now. Let's get on with it. Thanks, Brahmin, I'll take the box. *He stretches out his hand toward the casket.*

MAITREYA. Oh, how cold your fingers are!

SHARVILAKA. Idiot of a thief that I am! That water chilled them. I'll warm them. *He rubs them on his thigh; then takes the casket.*

MAITREYA. You have it safe?

SHARVILAKA. Yes, Brahmin, I have it.

MAITREYA. Good. Now, like a vendor who's sold all his goods, I can sleep in peace.

SHARVILAKA. Sleep, sir, sleep a thousand years. Oh, what a shameful thing to do—and all for the sake of love. To ruin this good Brahmin for the sake of Madanika! I hate it, but I do it. And now to Vasantasena's house, to buy Madanika's freedom! *He listens.* Footsteps! Who can it be? Shall I stand motionless and let him pass? Bah, what do I care about watchmen? I crawl like a cat, run like a deer, pounce like a hawk, twist like a snake and yowl like a dog! I'm a lamp, a horse, a boat, a snake, a rock. I'm a wolf, a lion, the king of birds, the prince of hares.

RADANIKA, *entering.* Where is Vardhamanaka? He was sleeping outside, I know, but he isn't there now. I must find Maitreya.

SHARVILAKA, *he starts to stab her, then stops.* Just a girl! I'm safe. *He slips to the door.*

RADANIKA, *frightened.* Help! A thief! Stop, thief! He's cut through the wall. There he goes! Maitreya, wake up! Where are you? A thief! A thief! There he goes, out the door!

MAITREYA. What thief? What's all this nonsense?

RADANIKA. Don't be silly. Help! Thief! Can't you see? There!

MAITREYA. What? The door's open! Help! Charudatta, wake up! A thief broke in and he's escaped! Wake up!

CHARUDATTA. I'm in no mood for jokes, Maitreya.

MAITREYA. This is no joke. Look!

CHARUDATTA. Where? How did he get in?

MAITREYA. There.

CHARUDATTA, *seeing the breach in the wall.* But that's well done! A very neat bit of work. Just look: a few bricks from the top, more below. Why, this fellow is a genius.

MAITREYA. Either the man's new to this city and doesn't know how poor we are—for everyone in Ujjain knows there's nothing to steal in this house —or else he was a beginner just practicing.

CHARUDATTA. Very likely a stranger to this city. He probably didn't know about my poverty and thought that the house looked promising from the outside. How disappointed he must have been when he ran away. Poor fellow! He'll have to go round admitting to his friends, "I broke into a merchant's house—and found nothing!"

MAITREYA. Yes. He must have entered with high hopes—for a jewel box at least. *He remembers his dream.* A golden box! Thank goodness! You always call me a fool, don't you? "Maitreya, you know nothing! Maitreya, you're a baby!" Well, wasn't it brilliant of me to hand the golden box over to you in the middle of the night? If not, the thief would have walked off with it.

CHARUDATTA. The box? What are you talking about?

MAITREYA. No, no, I'm serious. I may be a fool, but I know when to joke and when not to.

CHARUDATTA. When did you give me the box?

MAITREYA. Don't you remember? When I said your fingers were cold?

CHARUDATTA. I don't know. You might have. *He searches; then speaks in a cheerful tone.* Well, thank you, Maitreya.

MAITREYA. Whatever for?

CHARUDATTA. The box *has* been stolen. At least, it isn't here.

MAITREYA. But why should I be thanked?

CHARUDATTA. Because at least the poor fellow didn't go away empty-handed.

MAITREYA. But it's the box that we were supposed to keep in safe custody.

CHARUDATTA. *That* box! *He faints.*

MAITREYA. Oh, I'm sorry. But it isn't *your* fault that a thief ran off with a box left in your care.

CHARUDATTA, *recovering.* Maitreya, who will believe us? The poor man is always suspected—that's the way it is. Till now Fate was unkind only to my riches; now she is unkind to my good name.

MAITREYA. What's to prevent us from saying that she never gave us the box? She never gave it; we never took it. There was no witness.

CHARUDATTA. Tell a lie like that? Never. I will beg in the streets and pay off the entire amount of the box. It's a blot on my soul. *He leaves, followed by* MAITREYA.

RADANIKA. I must go tell his wife. *She goes out and returns immediately with* CHARUDATTA's *wife.*

WIFE. Is he safe? And is Maitreya safe?

RADANIKA. Both are safe, mistress. But the jewels of the courtesan have been stolen. Are you ill?

WIFE, *recovering from the shock*. Yes. Oh, I'm so happy he's safe! But what will people say? They'll suspect right away that he stole it himself because he's poor. *She sighs.* How strange Fate is! She plays with our fortunes and makes them as ephemeral as drops of water on a lotus leaf. There's always this necklace that my mother gave me—all I have left. But my husband has his pride: he would never accept it. *She reflects.* Radanika, call Maitreya here.

RADANIKA *goes out, then comes back with* MAITREYA.

MAITREYA. You honor me by calling me.

WIFE. You honor me, too. You will honor me even more by facing me and looking squarely into my eyes.

MAITREYA. That's easily done.

WIFE. Here, Maitreya, take this. *She offers the necklace.*

MAITREYA. Why?

WIFE. I observed the jewel ceremony this morning—and the customary present has to be made to a Brahmin. You are the first Brahmin I have met since this morning. So take it—the necklace is yours.

MAITREYA, *taking the necklace*. I must go tell Charudatta.

WIFE. Do it tactfully, Maitreya. See you don't embarrass me. *She leaves.*

MAITREYA. What a marvelous woman!

CHARUDATTA *enters, unseen by* MAITREYA.

CHARUDATTA. What's the matter with Maitreya? I hope his distress doesn't lead him to do anything rash. Maitreya!

MAITREYA. Here I am. This is for you. *He shows the necklace.*

CHARUDATTA. Where did you get this?

MAITREYA. This comes of having an excellent wife.

CHARUDATTA. Excellent, indeed! But oh, that I should fall so low as to have to depend on a woman's jewels! That comes of being poor; a man becomes helpless, and a woman takes his place. But no, I shouldn't call myself poor. I have a wife who loves me in spite of my poverty; I have a friend who stands by me, come fair wind, come foul. And, thank goodness, I have a few principles left. Take this necklace to Vasantasena, Maitreya. Tell her we gambled away the golden box, forgetting it was hers, and that I send this necklace instead.

MAITREYA. No, I can't. Are we going to give away this priceless sacred ornament for a silly box that a thief has decamped with? What did we get out of the box?

CHARUDATTA. What does that matter? The box was left in our trust. She trusted us—is there anything nobler than that? Listen to me. By this hand I place on my breast, you shall not return till you have given this necklace into her hands. *He calls.* Vardhamanaka, put those bricks back in place again. I don't want tongues wagging over this new scandal. Come, come, Maitreya, you're being stubborn.

MAITREYA. What's the use? Beggars can't be choosers.

CHARUDATTA. Who says I am a beggar? I have a wife who loves me in spite of my poverty. I have a friend who stands by me, come fair wind, come foul. And, thank goodness, I have a few principles left. You go ahead and do as I say. And I must go about my morning prayers.

*They all leave.*

C U R T A I N

## ACT IV

VASANTASENA's *house. A* MAID *enters the reception court.*

MAID. Another message from her mother. *She looks up.* Ah, there comes my mistress, looking at a picture and talking to Madanika.

VASANTASENA *and* MADANIKA *enter.*

VASANTASENA. You think this resembles Charudatta? You really do?

MADANIKA. Oh, yes.

VASANTASENA. How can you tell?

MADANIKA. From the way you look at it with so much love in your eyes.

VASANTASENA. You're just being polite, as all we courtesans are.

MADANIKA. But politeness can be true too, sometimes.

VASANTASENA. Not with us, I'm afraid. We meet so many kinds of men that mostly we're reduced just to saying pretty things.

MADANIKA. But you needn't have asked. The way you looked at the picture, it was obvious. . . .

VASANTASENA. Tell me, Madanika, do I behave strangely these days? I don't want to have my friends giggling at me behind my back.

MADANIKA. You're all right, mistress. Women understand one another pretty well.

MAID, *approaching.* A carriage is waiting for you at the side door, mistress; but your mother also wishes you would come.

VASANTASENA. Was it Charudatta who sent the carriage?

MAID. No, mistress. But the man who sent it has sent ten thousand gold pieces with it.

VASANTASENA. Who is it?

MAID. Sansthanaka, the king's brother-in-law.

VASANTASENA, *angrily.* No. Go tell him I'm busy. And don't bother me again!

MAID. Forgive me, mistress. I was only bringing the message.

VASANTASENA. I'm not angry with you; I'm angry with the message.

MAID. But what news shall I take back to your mother?

VASANTASENA. Tell her, if she doesn't want me dead, to stop sending such messages. *She goes into the house, followed by* MADANIKA.

MAID. Yes, mistress. *She leaves.*

SHARVILAKA *enters the house.*

SHARVILAKA. I am like the moon, brightest at night, killed by the light of day. Last night I worked wonders: I defied sleep and baffled the watchmen. But this morning I'm just a bundle of nerves. Who was that following me out there? Why was he chasing me? I didn't like the looks of him. Damn it, a man's worst enemy is his own conscience. At least I did it for Madanika —that's some consolation. But it was a close shave all the way. I made it a point to talk to no servants, and *no* woman; and when the guards passed by, I stood as still as a doorpost. I had a busy time last night—a hundred little tricks.

VASANTASENA, *inside the house.* Put this painting on the couch, and bring me my fan.

SHARVILAKA. Vasantasena's house! *He sees* MADANIKA *emerge and start toward another door into the house.* Graceful as Love's own bride! Though my heart is aflame, she cools my eyes. *He calls.* Madanika!

MADANIKA, *turning, startled.* Oh, it's you, Sharvilaka! How nice to see you. Where have you been all this time?

SHARVILAKA. I'll tell you later.

*They gaze long and lovingly at each other.*

VASANTASENA, *inside.* Where has she gone? She *does* take her time. *She opens a window and looks out.* There she is, talking to a man. She looks completely lost in him. That must be the man who wants to buy her freedom. Good. No one should interfere with true love. She'll come when she's through.

MADANIKA. Sharvilaka, tell me—*He keeps looking around him in a worried way.* Why do you look like that, Sharvilaka? What's wrong?

SHARVILAKA. Can you keep a secret? Are you sure we're alone?

MADANIKA. Absolutely alone.

VASANTASENA, *aside.* A secret? I shouldn't be listening.

SHARVILAKA. Tell me, Madanika, if I ask Vasantasena to set you free, what price will she demand?

VASANTASENA, *aside.* If it concerns me, there's no harm in listening.

MADANIKA. She's often said that if she had her way she'd free all of us without asking anything. But where have you managed to lay hands on so much money that you can buy my freedom?

SHARVILAKA. I was poor. I was in love. So last night I did something I shouldn't have done. I sinned.

VASANTASENA, *aside.* He looks too happy to have a crime on his conscience.

MADANIKA. Sharvilaka, you did it for *me*? You risked both for *me*?

SHARVILAKA. Both what?

MADANIKA. Your life and your good name.

SHARVILAKA. Oh, it was nothing. Fortune favors the brave.

MADANIKA. I know you, Sharvilaka: you are a good man. I know you couldn't have done anything very bad—even for my sake—could you?

SHARVILAKA. Well, I didn't steal from a woman. After all, jewels are to make women beautiful, as flowers do a plant. I didn't steal a Brahmin's money, if that's what you mean. Brahmins collect money for holy purposes, I know that. I didn't kidnap a baby from his nurse. I may be a thief, but I know the difference between right and wrong. Tell Vasantasena these jewels are for her, but no one should see them. They aren't meant to be worn by women.

MADANIKA. Jewels? And not to be worn by women? Let me see them.

SHARVILAKA. Here. *He brings them out and shows them uneasily.*

MADANIKA. Haven't I seen these before somewhere? Where did you get them?

SHARVILAKA. That's my business. Ask me no questions and I'll tell you no lies.

MADANIKA, *angrily.* If you love me, why are you afraid to tell me?

SHARVILAKA. All right, if you must know. . . . Last night a little bird told me that in the business quarter of the city a man called Charudatta—

VASANTASENA *and* MADANIKA *both faint.*

SHARVILAKA. Madanika! What's the matter? Can't you hear me? Have I done wrong?

MADANIKA, *recovering.* You fool! Tell me, did you hurt anyone? Did you kill anyone in the house where you stole these?

SHARVILAKA. I'm not a scoundrel: I don't kill sleeping men. I harmed no one.

MADANIKA. Is that true? You're sure?

SHARVILAKA. Of course, I'm sure.

VASANTASENA, *recovering.* Thank God!

MADANIKA. Thank God!

SHARVILAKA, *jealously.* What's going on here anyway, Madanika? I did it because I love you. You know my family commands respect: my virtue is of some worth. Is this all I get for the love and devotion I've shown for you—that you should love another man? Oh, I know all the tricks: a good man duped by a cunning courtesan, like a fruit tree pecked bare by greedy birds. Lust is all. Our beauty—money, love—bah! The fire of lust devours them all.

VASANTASENA, *smiling.* Poor man, he's a little worked up.

SHARVILAKA. Bah! I should know better. We're fools, fools, all of us who believe in women and in money! A woman's a snake—don't trust her—and so's money. Never love a woman—no, no! Let her love you. Let her bring you sweet words and soft lips, encourage her, and then jilt her. It's a wise man who said: a woman will laugh and cry for money and make use of a man's trust as long as it suits her. Run, young man, if you value your purse and your good name. A woman is a flower that grows in a graveyard. You can trust the changing ocean, the fickle colors of sunset, but not a woman. All she's after is your money: once you're empty as a powder box, off she goes. What fun she has: one man she loves, another she flirts with and a third she takes to bed with her. But what else could you expect? No lotus grows on a mountain; no damn ass bears a horse's harness; you don't get rice from barley seed; and you don't get honesty from a woman. Oh, what a fool I've been! Charudatta, this time you shall die!

MADANIKA, *catching hold of him.* What's come over you? You're behaving like a fool! *She moves away from him.*

SHARVILAKA. Who's a fool?

MADANIKA. These jewels belong to Vasantasena.

SHARVILAKA. They do?

MADANIKA. And she had left them with Charudatta.

SHARVILAKA. She had?

MADANIKA. And here's why. *She whispers in his ear.*

SHARVILAKA, *looking silly.* Damn it, I didn't mean to rob *him* in order to free you.

VASANTASENA, *aside.* I'm glad he's sorry. He acted foolishly.

SHARVILAKA. So what now, Madanika?

MADANIKA. You should know.

SHARVILAKA. I wish I did. Man learns only from books, but a woman is born with common sense.

MADANIKA. Well, I think you should give these jewels back to Charudatta.

SHARVILAKA. And go to jail?

MADANIKA. Did you ever hear of heat coming from the moon?

VASANTASENA, *aside.* Thank you, Madanika.

SHARVILAKA. I'm not so much afraid of him, Madanika, as of myself. What made me do such a shameful thing? I'd feel so small having to face him. Can't you think of anything else?

MADANIKA. Well. . .

VASANTASENA, *aside.* I should like to know, too.

MADANIKA. You can always say to my mistress that you're Charudatta's servant and return the jewels to her.

SHARVILAKA. How will that help?

MADANIKA. Then you're not a thief. Charudatta has lost nothing, for my mistress has her jewels.

SHARVILAKA. What! You rob me, a robber?

MADANIKA. And if you don't do as I say, you'll be a real robber, with the guards searching for you everywhere.

VASANTASENA, *aside.* I do admire you, Madanika. You're a good friend.

SHARVILAKA. Thanks for that advice. I was lost in darkness, and you came like the moon.

MADANIKA. Wait here. I'll go tell my mistress.

SHARVILAKA. Right.

MADANIKA *enters the house and speaks to* VASANTASENA. A Brahmin from Charudatta has come to see you.

VASANTASENA. How do you know he comes from Charudatta?

MADANIKA. I have my own ways of knowing, mistress.

VASANTASENA, *smiling.* Naturally. Let him come in.

MADANIKA, *emerging to the court.* Come in, Sharvilaka. *She escorts him in to* VASANTASENA.

SHARVILAKA, *embarrassed*. Charudatta sends greetings.

VASANTASENA. I am glad to receive them. You may sit.

SHARVILAKA. He says his house is insecure. So he returns this box, and hopes you will not mind. *He gives it to* MADANIKA, *and starts to leave.*

VASANTASENA. That was very thoughtful of him. Wait: I have something for him.

SHARVILAKA, *aside*. I didn't think of that. *Aloud*. What message shall I take?

VASANTASENA. No message. Take Madanika.

SHARVILAKA. I don't understand.

VASANTASENA. You see, we had an agreement that the person who returned the box would get Madanika as a present from me on Charudatta's behalf. So take her, and thank Charudatta for his kindness.

SHARVILAKA, *aside*. She's seen through the game. Thank you, Charudatta. *Aloud*. Thank you.

VASANTASENA, *calling*. Is my carriage here?

*A* SERVANT *enters.*

SERVANT. Your carriage is ready, mistress.

VASANTASENA. You may go, Madanika. Use my carriage. Look at me, my girl—and smile. That's better. And think of me now and then.

MADANIKA, *sobbing*. What shall I do? *She falls at* VASANTASENA'*s feet.*

VASANTASENA. Don't be silly, my girl. Stand up. *I* should honor *you* now. Go. Everything's ready. But think of me.

SHARVILAKA. How can I thank you, sweet lady? Bow to her, Madanika. She has given you the dignity of a wife. Smile, Madanika.

*All three emerge into the courtyard.* SHARVILAKA *and* MADANIKA *salute* VASANTASENA *and step into the carriage, which has been waiting in the courtyard.*

VOICE, *from the street*. A proclamation by the governor! A proclamation by the governor! "To all citizens." Hear ye! "An astrologer has declared that the son of a cowherd, by the name of Aryaka, will be king. Therefore King Palaka has thought fit to arrest him and put him in solitary confinement. There is nothing to fear. There is nothing to fear. This is a warning."

SHARVILAKA. Aryaka, my friend, arrested! And I, married and about to live happily ever after! No. Two things are dear in this world: a friend and a mistress. But a friend is worth a hundred mistresses any day. I must go. *He gets down from the carriage.*

MADANIKA. Don't leave me now, my lord. At least take me first to the house of one of your friends, where I can stay safely.

SHARVILAKA. And so I will, my love. *To the* COACHMAN. Hey you, have you any idea where the singer Rebhila lives?

COACHMAN. Yes, sir.

SHARVILAKA. Take my wife there.

COACHMAN. Yes, sir.

MADANIKA. Take care of yourself, dearest. I'll be waiting for you.

*The carriage drives her away.*

SHARVILAKA, *aside.* Now to work. First I must get in touch with Aryaka's friends—all of us who have suffered at the hands of this king and are ready to fight back. This is most illegal, most treacherous—the act of a spineless king. But we'll have you out, Aryaka, in no time. How long can they eclipse the moon? *He leaves.*

*A* MAID *enters.*

MAID, *seeing* VASANTASENA. Oh, what a lucky morning! A Brahmin from Charudatta brings you a message, mistress.

VASANTASENA. Yes, isn't it lucky? Receive him respectfully: call the chamberlain to escort him, and show them in to me.

*The* MAID *and* VASANTASENA *enter the house by separate entrances. The* MAID *re-emerges with the* CHAMBERLAIN; *they cross to the street gate and bow ceremoniously to* MAITREYA.

MAITREYA, *entering.* What do you know! Ravana, the lord of the demons, used to ride around in a magnificent chariot; and it cost him tons and tons of special prayers. I am a simple Brahmin and I don't pray much but I go around with the prettiest ladies in town.

MAID. Sir, this is the front door.

MAITREYA, *admiringly*. You don't say! All spick and span, well watered; flowers on the threshold. You look up and you're in the softness of clouds; and, as you look downward, you see the jasmine creeper floating down, swaying in the winds of heaven. The arch is of ivory, I see; and small glittering flags flirt with the newcomer. "Come," their fingers beckon, "come in, you're welcome." On either side there are crystal flowerpots, with young mango shoots springing up. The door itself is gold-plated, diamond-studded. "Go," it tells a poor man, "go away, what are you doing here?" But it fascinates the lover of beautiful things, even if he doesn't like them expensive.

MAID. This is the first court, sir.

MAITREYA. You don't say! Balconies white as the moon, as lilies, as sea shells; the floor of precious mosaic; golden stairs, dotted with gems; the stairs lead up to pearly windows, and the windows look down on Ujjain, like round moon-faced girls. And there's the porter, snoring in an armchair, as comfortable as a Brahmin chanting mantras. Lead on, girl.

MAID. This is the second court, sir.

MAITREYA. You don't say! Here fat carriage oxen, their horns glistening with oil, are having a delightful time on lumps of grass and pulse. And there's a prize specimen: a buffalo, snorting like an indignant Brahmin. And here's a ram, being massaged like a wrestler. And there are horses being groomed; and there's a monkey tied to a post like a thief; and over there an elephant breakfasting on huge balls of rice and ghee. Lead on, girl.

MAID. This is the third court, sir.

MAITREYA. You don't say! Here are seats for Ujjain's gay blades; a half-read book on a gambling table; dice made of gems. And there are hangers-on, the courtesans skilled in the hot and cold techniques of love. I see them lazing with pictures in their hands. Next, girl.

MAID. This is the fourth court, sir.

MAITREYA. You don't say! Drums here, for feminine fingers to make a noise like murmuring clouds; and the music of the cymbals, like stars falling through space; the voice of the flute, like a humming of bees. Here is a girl plucking the vina, with excitable fingers, like a jealous flirt scratching her lover's face; and a group of girls singing—a song like a swarm of honey-drunk bees. Here some are dancing; there others are rehearsing; there still others are reciting. Grass fans swinging to send down the cool breeze. What next, girl?

MAID. This is the fifth court, sir.

MAITREYA. You don't say! How my mouth waters! Such an overpowering odor of oil and spices! Out of the kitchen emerge puffs of steam, sighs from the half-open mouths of ovens kept lighted twenty-four hours a day. Delicious! Incomparable! Here the kitchen boy skins the meat, shapeless as used linen; there the pastry cook is at his magic: sweets and cakes and sauces. *Aside*. Oh, if I could just wash my feet and fall to! *Aloud*. And there are courtesans and young boys. God, but isn't this heaven! And those young men—what might be their work here?

MAID. They have no fathers or mothers, sir. They live in a strange house, they earn their money from strangers, they eat strange food. But they have a nice time of it; they're as happy as baby elephants.

MAITREYA. Next, girl.

MAID. This is the sixth court, sir.

MAITREYA. You don't say! The gate is of gold and diamonds, the rest of sapphires; it all sparkles like a rainbow. They seem very busy here. Jewelers at work, I see: with pearls, topazes, sapphires, emeralds, rubies, coral, and lapis lazuli. Some are setting rubies in gold; some are threading gold jewelry; some are stringing pearls; some are polishing lapis lazuli, some coral; some are piercing shells. Wet bundles of saffron are being dried, sandalwood ground, perfumes mixed. Betel leaves are being served to courtesans and their lovers—flirting and laughter and drinking and merriment. And there are the scum: those who have left wife and children and fortune, and hang about for pleasure. They stand and drink—and drink. Lead on, girl.

MAID. This is the seventh court, sir.

MAITREYA. Doves billing and cooing; parrots croaking like overfed Brahmins; a housemaid of a mynah ordering the servants about; a koel, throat crammed with sweet syrups, gurgling like a water carrier. Quail fighting; partridges wailing; pigeons being teased. A peacock fans the heated walls with a glittering tail. And on this side are swans, balls of moonlight, chasing pretty girls, swinging as they go; and cranes here, like eunuchs guarding a palace. A whole zoo here, I see. Well, what next?

MAID. We shall now go to the eighth court, sir.

MAITREYA. Who is that, that overdressed man in silk, stumbling as he wanders about, his body covered with superfluous ornaments?

MAID. The brother of my mistress, sir.

MAITREYA. He must have done a lot of penance in his last birth to be so lucky in this! Yet he's not too happy, after all, poor fellow: a champak tree in a burial ground—fragrant but off limits. And who is that lady on that throne, with shoes on her oiled feet and wearing expensive muslin?

MAID. My mistress's mother.

MAITREYA. Talk about witches having a gay time! God, what a mighty belly she has! How did she get in? Or did you first put her on the throne and then build the house around her?

MAID. Don't be impertinent. Can't you see that she is suffering from a trouble that makes her that way?

MAITREYA. Oh, blessed trouble that makes her that way! Come, fall on this poor Brahmin, O blessed trouble! Favor me, favor me!

MAID. What impudence! You should die of shame before speaking like that.

MAITREYA. Me die? Let the fat one die instead, let her die first, swollen with wine and age. She'll supply dinner for a thousand jackals. I had heard a lot of praise for Vasantasena's palace, but now I can hardly believe my eyes. Is this the house of a courtesan or the palace of the god of wealth? Where's your mistress?

MAID. In the garden, sir. Here.

MAITREYA, *looking around.* Ah, heavenly! Trees bent under fruit, trees rich with flowers. Silk swings under the trees, just the size for a young sweet girl. Jasmine, *malati,* full-blown *mallika, sephalika* blossoms on the ground. And the pool is white as dawn, its lotuses red as suns. The asoka tree is spattered with fiery blossoms like a warrior bloodstained from battle. Perfect! Where is your mistress?

MAID. If you lowered your eyes, sir, you would see her.

MAITREYA. Ah, there! *He approaches* VASANTASENA. I bring you greetings, lady.

VASANTASENA, *speaking in Sanskrit.* Ah, Maitreya. Please make yourself comfortable. You are very welcome here.

MAITREYA, *remaining standing.* Thank you. *He sits down only after she has done so.*

VASANTASENA. I hope Charudatta is well.

MAITREYA. Very well, thank you.

VASANTASENA. Maitreya, do birds still find shelter under the gentle boughs of that excellent tree, whose leaves are virtues, whose roots are courage, whose flowers are honor, and whose fruit is goodness?

MAITREYA, *aside.* A pretty sentence, that! *Aloud.* They do.

VASANTASENA. And what brings you here, Maitreya?

MAITREYA. This: Charudatta sends his greetings—*He joins his palms.*—and wishes—

VASANTASENA, *joining her palms.*—commands—

MAITREYA. He wishes me to report that he has lost the golden box. He lost it at the gambling table, and the keeper has gone away on royal business.

VASANTASENA, *aside.* He is too proud to admit that a thief stole it. I love him all the more for that.

MAITREYA. And he asks you to accept this pearl necklace in lieu of the lost box.

VASANTASENA, *aside*. Shall I tell him the truth? *She reflects; then speaks half aloud.* No. Not now.

MAITREYA, *hopefully, thinking she has spoken to him.* You will not accept the necklace?

VASANTASENA. Why not, Maitreya? *She takes it and presses it to her heart, speaking aside.* The mango tree is dry, yet drops of honey fall from its branches. *Aloud.* Sir, tell Charudatta, who is a noble gambler, that I shall call on him this evening.

MAITREYA, *aside.* What for? What more does she want? *Aloud.* I will, my lady. *Aside.* And I hope that will be the end of our acquaintance! *He leaves, escorted by the chamberlain.*

VASANTASENA. Take this necklace; and come with me to Charudatta's.

MAID. But a storm is coming up: look how dark the sky is.

VASANTASENA. Let it come. Let it rain till the world ends. How does it touch me? I am going to meet the man I love. Take this necklace, and come with me.

*They both leave.*

C U R T A I N

## ACT V

CHARUDATTA *is seen seated under a shelter in his garden.*

CHARUDATTA, *looking up.* It is going to storm. The peacocks and the swans are disturbed; so is the lover far from home. As the clouds climb, the lightning flashes briefly, and the rain spatters down, prelude to silver cascades. And the clouds keep gathering—a shoal of dolphins, a soaring of swans, a crowd of warriors, driven by the wind, cluttering the sky. *He reflects.* Maitreya should be back by now.

MAITREYA, *entering by the grillwork gate.* Scheming selfish woman! Not a word, not one civil word; she just pockets the necklace. And she isn't exactly the nadir of poverty, is she? She could have said, "Maitreya, my good friend Maitreya, sit down; here are sweets for you, and a cool drink." But no, not even a miserly glass of water. Damn her! What they say is right: "There's no such thing as a lotus without a root, a goldsmith without a swindle, a village meeting without a quarrel or a courtesan without selfishness." I must tell Charudatta to keep a safe distance away from such women. *He sees* CHARUDATTA. Ah, he's out here in the garden. *He approaches.* Looks like a storm blowing up.

CHARUDATTA, *rising and coming forward to greet him.* So it does. It is good to see you back, Maitreya. Come in here and sit down.

MAITREYA. Thanks.

CHARUDATTA. What news, my friend?

MAITREYA. It's over, finished.

CHARUDATTA. Why—did she refuse to take the necklace?

MAITREYA. No such luck! She greeted me with her lotus-soft palms joined very respectfully—and took the necklace.

CHARUDATTA. Then what did you mean by saying, "It's over, finished"?

MAITREYA. A damned pretty bargain, wasn't it, giving away a fabulous necklace for a shiny gold box that a thief ran off with? What did we get out of it?

CHARUDATTA. Don't be silly. She trusted us. That's reward enough.

MAITREYA. That isn't all. She'd tipped off her maids, and they were giggling behind my back, veiling their faces. Giggling at a Brahmin! Please, I beg of you, keep away from her. She will destroy you. A courtesan's like a thorn in the foot: you'll have a hell of a painful time getting it out. It's a good warning that says, "Keep away from a courtesan, an elephant, an accountant, a begging monk, a snooper, a swindler, and an ass. If you don't, you're asking for trouble."

CHARUDATTA. What nonsense, Maitreya! I am poor—isn't that protection enough? What can she want of me? I have nothing to give her. Such women are gold diggers: no money, no love.

MAITREYA, *aside*. You can't argue with a man in love. I warned him to keep clear; but, from the way he sighs and moans, that seems only to encourage him. *Aloud*. She said she would drop in this evening. She's probably looking for more than a necklace.

CHARUDATTA. Let her come. She will not go away unsatisfied.

KUMBHILAKA, VASANTASENA's *servant, is seen at the gate.*

KUMBHILAKA, *to himself*. What a downpour! The more it rains, the wetter I get; the wetter I get, the more I shiver. Brrr, it's a cold night outside. *He laughs suddenly*. A nice day for a genius like me, who plays the flute and sings like a god! All I do is carry messages from Vasantasena to Charudatta. *He sees* CHARUDATTA. He's here in the garden—and that blithering fool Maitreya is with him. The garden gate's closed. I'll prod him. *He throws mud pellets at* MAITREYA.

MAITREYA. What's this? Lumps of mud? What am I, a man or an apple tree?

CHARUDATTA. Oh, it's very likely the pigeons.

MAITREYA. Dirty-minded pigeons! This stick will show you! I'll bring you down, nests and all. *He starts to run at them with his staff*.

CHARUDATTA, *holding him back by the sacred thread*. Calm down, Maitreya. Poor little pigeons. Leave them alone.

KUMBHILAKA. The blithering fool! He sees the pigeons but can't see me. Here goes another. *He throws another mud pellet*.

MAITREYA, *looking up*. Another! *Seeing no pigeon overhead, he looks around him*. Oh, it's you, Kumbhilaka. Wait. *He goes and opens the gate*. Come in, come in. What brings you here?

KUMBHILAKA, *entering*. Thank you, sir.

MAITREYA. Well, what brings you here, in spite of the wind and rain?

KUMBHILAKA. She sent me.

MAITREYA. She? Who? Who?

KUMBHILAKA. She. See? She.

MAITREYA. What's all this she-she-she-ing about, you clod, you wheezy beggar? Who? Who? Who?

KUMBHILAKA. What's all this who-who-who-ing about, you frightened owl of a fool?

MAITREYA. Come, man, let's talk sense.

KUMBHILAKA. First, a riddle for you.

MAITREYA. And a box on the ears for you.

KUMBHILAKA. If you solve it. Here it is. In what season does the mango tree blossom?

MAITREYA. That's easy. In summer.

KUMBHILAKA, *grinning.* Wrong.

MAITREYA, *reflecting.* Wait. I'll ask Charudatta. *He goes over to* CHARU-DATTA. Sir, when does the mango tree blossom?

CHARUDATTA. In spring, of course, in *vasanta.*

MAITREYA, *returning to* KUMBHILAKA. In spring, of course, in *vasanta.*

KUMBHILAKA. That's it. Now another. Who protects the cities?

MAITREYA. The town guard, of course.

KUMBHILAKA, *grinning.* Wrong.

MAITREYA, *calling to* CHARUDATTA. Sir, who guards the cities?

CHARUDATTA. The army, of course, the *sena.*

MAITREYA, *to* KUMBHILAKA. The army, of course, the *sena.*

KUMBHILAKA. That's it. Now, quick, quick, put the two together.

MAITREYA. *Sena,* army. *Vasanta,* spring. Sena-vasanta!

KUMBHILAKA. No, no, the other way round.

MAITREYA, *pivoting around.* Sena-vasanta.

KUMBHILAKA. Idiot! Clod! Moron! Turn the stems around!

MAITREYA, *turning his feet in*. Sena-vasanta!

KUMBHILAKA. No! The words! Turn the *words* around!

MAITREYA, *after deep reflection*. Vasanta-sena.

KUMBHILAKA. Right. She's here.

MAITREYA. I must tell Charudatta. *He goes to* CHARUDATTA. Sir, a creditor's here.

CHARUDATTA. A creditor? In my house?

MAITREYA. Not in the house—at the door. Vasantasena is here.

CHARUDATTA. No!

MAITREYA. Kumbhilaka says so. Hey, Kumbhilaka! Come here.

KUMBHILAKA, *approaching*. Sir, I bring you greetings.

CHARUDATTA. Is Vasantasena really here?

KUMBHILAKA. Yes, sir.

CHARUDATTA, *joyfully*. You are a bringer of good news. Take this: it's my gift to you. *He gives* KUMBHILAKA *his shawl*.

KUMBHILAKA. Yes sir. *He goes out to inform* VASANTASENA.

MAITREYA. There you are. There's only one reason why she comes out on a foul night like this.

CHARUDATTA. What's that?

MAITREYA. Oh, I can tell. She thinks the necklace isn't worth the price of the casket and she wants more. Take my word for it.

CHARUDATTA, *aside*. She will get what she comes for.

VASANTASENA *enters, beautifully dressed as a woman who goes to meet her lover. She is accompanied by a courtier and a maid with an umbrella.*

CHARUDATTA. Welcome her in.

MAITREYA, *approaching Vasantasena respectfully*. We are honored to receive you.

VASANTASENA. You flatter me. Thank you. *To the* COURTIER. Sir, the maid will attend you with the umbrella.

COURTIER, *aside.* I can take a hint. *Aloud.* No, thank you. *He leaves.*

VASANTASENA. Now, Maitreya, where is the good gambler?

MAITREYA, *aside.* "Good gambler"! A nice way to begin. *Aloud.* Over there, madam, in the dry garden.

VASANTASENA. Dry? How is that?

MAITREYA. Nothing to eat or drink. VASANTASENA *smiles.* Please come in.

VASANTASENA, *aside to the* MAID. What shall I say? How shall I begin?

MAID, *aside to* VASANTASENA. "Good evening, Sir Gambler."

VASANTASENA, *aside.* I can't. I shouldn't dare.

MAID, *aside.* Don't worry. You will at the right time.

MAITREYA. Please come in. This way.

VASANTASENA, *entering and playfully throwing a flower at* CHARUDATTA. Good evening, Sir Gambler.

CHARUDATTA, *rising.* Vasantasena! It is so good to see you. Believe me, I have been most unhappy. Please sit down. No, here.

MAITREYA. Here.

VASANTASENA *sits down; then the others.*

CHARUDATTA. But you are dripping wet, Vasantasena. I can see the drops trickling down from the flower in your ear. Maitreya, bring her a new dress: she should change into something dry.

MAITREYA *looks at one of* CHARUDATTA'S *maids.*

MAID. No, wait, Maitreya. I'll go. *She goes to get the dress.*

MAITREYA, *aside to* CHARUDATTA. May I ask her a question?

CHARUDATTA. Of course.

MAITREYA. Why do you come here, madam, at this time of night—a night so dark, moonless, windy, and raining?

MAID, *aside*. The cheek of him!

VASANTASENA, *aside*. No, he's just being careful.

MAID. My mistress has come to inquire the value of the pearl necklace given to her.

MAITREYA, *aside to* CHARUDATTA. Didn't I say so? She wants something better.

MAID. You see, she gambled it away. And now the keeper of the gambling house has left on royal business, so she can't find out what it's really worth.

MAITREYA, *aside*. Tit for tat. I've heard that before.

MAID. In the meantime, while we're searching for him, my mistress asks you please to accept this gold box. *She shows the box.* MAITREYA *looks at it sharply.* Sir, you are examining it very closely. Have you seen it before?

MAITREYA. No, but it's a real work of art. Very pretty.

MAID. You aren't very sharp. It's the same gold box.

MAITREYA, *joyfully*. It is! Charudatta, here's the gold box that the thief carried away from our house.

CHARUDATTA. The trick we played on her is now being played back on us. I can't believe it. The box may look the same, but it can't be.

MAITREYA. But it is. As I am a Brahmin, it is the very same box.

CHARUDATTA. If true, this is splendid news.

MAITREYA, *aside to* CHARUDATTA. Shall I ask where they found it?

CHARUDATTA, *aside to* MAITREYA. A reasonable question. Do.

MAITREYA, *whispering in the* MAID'*s ear*. So. . .pss. . .pss. . .

MAID, *whispering in* MAITREYA'*s ear*. So. . .pss. . .pss. . .

CHARUDATTA. What is it? Why not tell us?

MAITREYA, *whispering in* CHARUDATTA'*s ear*. So. . .pss. . .pss. . .

CHARUDATTA, *to the* MAID. So this is the same gold box.

MAID. Yes, sir.

CHARUDATTA. That is good news. Here, take this ring from me: it's for you. *He feels his finger, finds there is no ring, and is extremely embarrassed.*

VASANTASENA, *aside.* How lovable he is.

CHARUDATTA, *aside to* MAITREYA. What's the use of living, Maitreya, if a man has no money at all? His anger is futile; his love is futile. Birds without wings, pools without water, trees without leaves, snakes without venom—such are the poor.

MAITREYA, *aside to* CHARUDATTA. But you mustn't take it so seriously. *Aloud, laughingly.* And I should like, madam, to get back my towel in which the box was wrapped when the thief took it.

VASANTASENA, *ignoring him.* It was not right of you, Charudatta, to send this pearl necklace in place of the stolen box. You think very poorly of me to have done so.

CHARUDATTA. Who would have believed the truth? The world is merciless to the poor.

MAITREYA, *to the* MAID. And you—are you going to spend the night here?

MAID. That's not very polite, sir.

MAITREYA, *to* CHARUDATTA. The storm has started again, and the rain is simply tumbling down.

CHARUDATTA. How well you put it.
  The rains pierce through the clouds, as lotus roots
  Pierce the soil, softly, as if
  Weeping for the absent moon.
  My dearest, look at the sky, black-haired, scented with wind.
  The lightning scoops her into his arms,
  Tenderly but fiercely, as lover does lover.

VASANTASENA, *unable to control her feelings, embraces him.* CHARUDATTA *puts his arms around her.*

  Let the clouds alone, Maitreya.
  Let it rain a hundred years,

A hundred years of thunder, a hundred of lightning.
They are my friends:
They have given me my love.
My love is in my arms.
Happy is he who embraces his love in the rain.
Vasantasena, dearest, the door creaks,
The walls are miserably wet;
The mortar is cracked, the roof will leak—
Nothing will last.
Oh, see the tongue of lightning licking the yawning sky!

But now look, look at the rainbow!
See how its arms rise in holy prayer!
Now it is time to sleep.
Sleep will come sweeter with these pebbly drops
Splattering on palm leaves, falling on brooks;
Like a lute, and a voice singing,
Like a lute—the rain, and the music of the rain.

C U R T A I N

## ACT VI

*A room in* CHARUDATTA'S *house.* VASANTASENA'S MAID *enters.*

MAID. Not awake yet? It's time she was up. I must wake her. *She sees* VASANTASENA *coming, rubbing her eyes.* It's morning, mistress.

VASANTASENA. So soon? Is the sun up?

MAID. It's certainly up for us.

VASANTASENA. And where is our excellent gambler?

MAID. He rose, gave Vardhamanaka his orders and went to the Push-pakaranda flower garden.

VASANTASENA. Did he leave any message?

MAID. He told Vardhamanaka to have the carriage ready before dawn. He said to take you—

VASANTASENA. Where?

MAID. To join him in the garden.

VASANTASENA, *embracing her*. Last night I hardly got a good look at his face. Now I shall see him to my heart's content. Tell me, did I enter the inner court last night?

MAID. Not only the inner court but into everyone's heart.

VASANTASENA. His people must be worried.

MAID. They will be.

VASANTASENA. When?

MAID. When you leave.

VASANTASENA. Then my worries will begin. *She speaks sweetly*. Here, take this pearl necklace and give it to my good sister, his wife. Tell her from me: "I admire Charudatta, therefore I admire you too. I send you these pearls: they are yours; they look prettier on you."

MAID. But Charudatta won't like that.

VASANTASENA. That isn't your worry. Do as I tell you.

*The* MAID *goes inside and returns promptly*.

MAID. She says: "My husband gave the necklace to you. It is yours. It is not proper for me to take it back. Besides, the only ornament I value is my husband."

RADANIKA *enters, with* CHARUDATTA'*s son,* ROHASENA.

RADANIKA. Won't you give me a ride on your toy cart?

ROHASENA, *irritably*. No. I don't want this toy cart. I don't want a clay cart. I want a gold cart.

RADANIKA, *exasperated*. Gold at your age! When we have plenty of money, we'll buy you a gold cart. Meanwhile, isn't this a sweet cart? Oh, look, there's Vasantasena. Say good morning.

VASANTASENA. Radanika. How nice to see you. Oh, what a sweet child. Who is he? *Is*n't he sweet? But he's so badly dressed.

RADANIKA. This is Rohasena, Charudatta's son.

VASANTASENA. Oh, how nice! Come, young man, put your arms around me. *She takes him on her lap; he begins to cry quietly.* Why, he's just like his father!

RADANIKA. And *good*, like his father. Charudatta loves him more than anything in the world.

VASANTASENA. But why is he crying?

RADANIKA. Well, the neighbor's son was given a gold toy cart; and Rohasena liked it and wanted it. I made him this clay one; but he says he doesn't like it, he wants one made of gold.

VASANTASENA, *aside*. How sad, that a little boy should suffer because others are rich. *She represses a sob.* Don't cry, young man: you shall have a gold cart.

ROHASENA. Who are you?

VASANTASENA. I came to see your father.

RADANIKA. She is a friend of your mother, Rohasena.

ROHASENA. She can't be: she wears so many gold things. Mother doesn't.

VASANTASENA, *sobbing and removing her ornaments*. There. Now I'm your mother's friend. Take these and buy a gold cart for yourself.

ROHASENA. No, I won't. Because you're crying.

VASANTASENA, *wiping her eyes*. No, I'm not. See? *She fills the clay cart with her ornaments.* There, go get a gold cart.

RADANIKA *and* ROHASENA *leave by the street gate, and meet* VARDHAMANAKA, *pulling up in an ox-carriage.*

VARDHAMANAKA. Radanika, tell her the carriage is ready.

RADANIKA, *re-entering the house*. Vardhamanaka is here and says the carriage is ready.

VASANTASENA. Tell him I'll be coming in a minute.

RADANIKA, *shouting to* VARDHAMANAKA. Wait a little, Vardhamanaka.

VARDHAMANAKA, *looking into the back of the carriage.* Damn, I've left the cushions behind! I'll have to go back and get them. But these beasts are too jumpy to be left alone. Oh, I'll be back in a jiffy. *He drives away.*

VASANTASENA, *to her own maid.* Just get me my outer things; I'll put them on myself.

STHAVARAKA, SANSTHANAKA's *servant, drives his carriage into the square outside.*

STHAVARAKA. What a jam! And Sansthanaka has ordered me to take the carriage to the Pushpakaranda flower garden and to be quick about it! Giddap! Giddap! *The carriage advances a little, and he stands up to look around.* A real traffic jam: village carts everywhere. What now? *He shouts.* Hey, you! Make room! Move over, move over! Who am *I?* Me? Sir, it may interest you to know that I am the driver of Sansthanaka, the king's own brother-in-law. Move *over,* move! Make room, there! Pull to the left, you! *He looks up ahead.* Why, there's someone running as if the devil was at his heels. Probably a welshing gambler. Who can he be? There, he's lost in the crowd. It's none of my business anyway. Hey, you village louts, get a move on! I don't care if you're bogged down. What, give you a hand? *Me,* give you a hand? The driver of Sansthanaka give *you* a hand? All right, all right, just one little push. I'll stop here, in front of Charudatta's garden gate. *He jumps down and goes to help, leaving the carriage at the door.*

MAID. That must have been the carriage driving up: I heard the wheels.

VASANTASENA. I feel nervous. See me to the gate.

MAID. This way, mistress.

VASANTASENA. That will do. Now go and rest.

MAID. Thank you. *She leaves.*

VASANTASENA, *passing through the gate and getting into* SANSTHA-NAKA'S *carriage.* Why should my right eye twitch? It's a bad omen. But what does it matter? Meeting Charudatta will cancel all bad omens.

STHAVARAKA, *returning.* There, the road's clear now. Off I go. *He climbs up and drives off, speaking to himself.* Why does the carriage feel heavier?

Or am I just tired from helping them with the bogged wheels? Giddap! Giddap! Move on, my beauties!

VOICE, *offstage*. Police! Police! The traitor is loose! The jailer is killed! All guards at their posts! The traitor is loose!

ARYAKA *dashes frantically out of the crowd, dragging the chains on his feet, and concealing his face with his hands.*

STHAVARAKA. There's going to be trouble here. I'd better clear out while there's time. *He drives the carriage rapidly off.*

ARYAKA, *to himself*. It's behind me, that terrible sea of jail and suffering —all on account of the tyrannous Palaka. Thank God. It's worth it, even if I must drag these broken ankle chains along wherever I go. Thanks, Sharvilaka: you're the one who got me out. What shame! Snatched away from my house, shoved into a dingy cell, left to die—all because a trembling king is afraid of an astrologer's words! *He raises his voice.* What did I do? What did I do to deserve this, to be treated as a wild beast? If the stars said something, is that my fault? Can I fight fate? Can I change fate? *He looks around.* Here's a gate left ajar. Some kind man doesn't believe in locks. The hinges are rusted; fate's not been kind to this man either. I'll slip in.

VARDHAMANAKA'S VOICE, *offstage*. Giddap! Giddap!

ARYAKA, *pausing at the gate*. A carriage! If it's a rich man's carriage returning empty from town, or some noble lady's, or even a bunch of villagers—this is the thing for me!

VARDHAMANAKA *re-enters, driving* CHARUDATTA's *ox-carriage.*

VARDHAMANAKA. There, now I have the cushions. *He calls.* Radanika, tell Vasantasena the carriage is waiting to take her to the Pushpakaranda flower garden.

ARYAKA. A courtesan's carriage going out of the city! I'm lucky. *He approaches slowly.*

VARDHAMANAKA, *hearing the sound of* ARYAKA's *broken ankle chains*. The tinkling of anklets! That must be her. I have to manage these oxen, mistress: please get in at the back. ARYAKA *climbs in*. There, the carriage slumps to the right with more weight. Giddap, you lazy lumps, giddap! *He starts to drive off.*

VIRAKA, *a captain of the guard, enters, with guards.*

VIRAKA. Here, all of you! You, Jaya, you, Jayamana, Mangala, Pushpabhadra! Jump to it, my fine fellows—there's no time to waste. The traitor cowherd is loose: the king can't sleep any more. You, take the east gate; you, the west; you, the south; you, the north. I'll climb this old wall here and look around. *He calls.* Chandanaka, follow me!

CHANDANAKA, *another captain, enters, with more guards.*

CHANDANAKA. Viraka, Vishalya, come on! Dandalaka, Dandashura, Bhimangada, come on! Hop to it!—or the old king will be out and a new king in. Search the streets, the roads, the gardens, the houses, the markets, the shops—leave not one stone unturned! Where will he escape as long as Chandanaka lives?

VIRAKA. Well, the bird's been flown since dawn. And he has many friends outside.

VARDHAMANAKA. Giddap! Giddap!

CHANDANAKA, *seeing the carriage.* What's this doing here? A covered carriage—mighty suspicious! Search it.

VIRAKA. Stop, you! Whose carriage is this? Who's inside? Where are you going?

VARDHAMANAKA. Charudatta's carriage, sir. I am taking mistress Vasantasena, who is inside, to meet Charudatta in the Pushpakaranda flower garden.

VIRAKA, *to* CHANDANAKA. He says it belongs to Charudatta; Vasantasena is inside it, and he's taking her to Pushpakaranda.

CHANDANAKA. He may pass.

VIRAKA. You mean without a search?

CHANDANAKA. Without a search.

VIRAKA. Why?

CHANDANAKA. It's Charudatta's.

VIRAKA. And who is Charudatta, who is Vasantasena, that this carriage shall pass without being searched?

CHANDANAKA. You haven't heard of Charudatta? Not even of Vasantasena? My poor man, haven't you heard of the moon, of moonlight? They are the finest citizens in our noble Ujjain.

VIRAKA. That's all very well, but I have my duty to do. My own father can't pass here without a proper search.

CHANDANAKA. If that's the way you feel, go ahead.

VIRAKA. Oh, you look in.

CHANDANAKA *climbs up the back of the carriage, peers in, and finds* ARYAKA.

ARYAKA. Please, don't give me away.

CHANDANAKA. You have my word, Aryaka. *Aside.* Trapped like a poor bird. But I know he isn't guilty. Besides he's Sharvilaka's friend, and Sharvilaka saved my life once. I'll die for them—and happily too—if I have to. *He gets down; then speaks to* VIRAKA. I'm afraid that he—I mean, she, Vasantasena—thinks it highly improper to insult her in this fashion on the royal road.

VIRAKA. He—she—does, eh?

CHANDANAKA. That's what I said.

VIRAKA. I don't like this "he-she" shuffling, my friend.

CHANDANAKA. Are you mad? Can't a man make a slip of the tongue, like any honest person?

VIRAKA. Can't a second honest person take a look too? The king has ordered it. I obey the king.

CHANDANAKA. You mean I don't obey the king?

VIRAKA. The king has ordered a general search.

CHANDANAKA, *aside.* If the king is told that Aryaka was hiding in Charudatta's carriage, Charudatta will have quite a job of explaining to do. I'll give Viraka a dose of South Indian rhetoric. *Aloud.* Viraka, I have searched the carriage, and now you tell me you're going to search it again? As my name is Chandanaka, and as I stand here, what the devil does this mean? Who are you, sir, to challenge my competence?

VIRAKA. Damn and blast! And who are *you,* sir, may I ask?

CHANDANAKA. A person of eminence, worthy of your respect. You are low-caste.

VIRAKA. Low-caste? *My* family, low-caste!

CHANDANAKA. The less said about it, the better.

VIRAKA. Say it!

CHANDANAKA. Oh, what's the use? It wouldn't help. You can't restore a rotten apple.

VIRAKA. Go on, say it!

CHANDANAKA *makes a gesture to show that* VIRAKA *is a leather-stitcher.*

CHANDANAKA. Didn't you deal in dead skins? Stitch flesh and bones? Cut tough skins—*He gestures.*—like this, and this, and this? And now you're a captain! A captain of the king!

VIRAKA. A nice caste you come from, Chandanaka! Or have you forgotten?

CHANDANAKA. Forgotten what? I'm as pure as the moon.

VIRAKA. Let's forget such things, shall we?

CHANDANAKA. Go on, say it! What?

VIRAKA. Pure as the moon! Your father was a drum, your mother was a kettledrum, your brother is a tambourine. You—a captain, a captain of the king! Bah!

CHANDANAKA, *losing his temper.* I, a tanner? Chandanaka, a tanner? All right, go on, go on and search the carriage!

VIRAKA. Hey, you! Driver! Wait! I *will* search it!

*As* VIRAKA *starts to climb into the carriage,* CHANDANAKA *grabs him by the hair, pulls him down and kicks him.*

VIRAKA, *rising; speaking violently.* You bloody swine! What does this mean? I was only doing my duty. Why, I'll have you dragged into court and whipped. My name's not Viraka if I don't; Viraka doesn't forget so easily. You'll see. *He leaves.*

CHANDANAKA, *shouting after him.* Run to the palace, run to the court, you dog. Run with your tail between your legs. Who cares? *To* VARDHAMANAKA. Drive on, quick. If anyone stops you, say that Viraka and Chandanaka have already searched the carriage. *To* ARYAKA. My lady Vasantasena, a passport for you. *He hands over his sword to* ARYAKA.

ARYAKA. Thanks, friend. This brings my courage back. I'm safe now.

CHANDANAKA. Remember me, sir—my name is Chandanaka. I speak from love, not selfishness.

ARYAKA. I shall indeed. Fate sent you to me, my friend. If everything turns out right, I'll remember you very specially.

CHANDANAKA. God give you courage and luck, sir. VARDHAMANAKA *drives the carriage off;* CHANDANAKA *stands gazing after it, his back to the audience.* I see my friend Sharvilaka following at a discreet distance. Good! I had better tell my family to join him, too: Viraka is no doubt up to mischief behind my back.

*He leaves.*

C U R T A I N

# ACT VII

CHARUDATTA *and* MAITREYA *are seen walking in the Pushpakaranda flower garden.*

MAITREYA. Such a lovely garden.

CHARUDATTA. Yes, pretty as a market: here are the trees, small shop-keepers with glittering things; and the bees, like the king's officers, busily collecting taxes.

MAITREYA. This is a nice stone seat. *He motions* CHARUDATTA *to sit on it.*

CHARUDATTA, *sitting down.* Vardhamanaka takes his own time, doesn't he?

MAITREYA. I told him to hurry.

CHARUDATTA. Why does he take so long then? Is the carriage too heavy for the oxen? Did a wheel break? A tree fall across the road? Did he lose his way?

VARDHAMANAKA *enters, driving the carriage in which* ARYAKA *is hiding.*

VARDHAMANAKA. Giddap, you!

ARYAKA, *aside.* Safe for the time being. But what next? Here I am, in a stranger's carriage, like a koel's eggs in a crow's nest. But the chains are still on my legs, and the king's spies are everywhere. At least I'm far outside the city. Shall I hide here in this garden? Or shall I wait till the owner of the carriage comes and appeal to him? They say Charudatta is a fine man and always ready to help. I'll wait till he comes. It will help me to meet him and talk to him.

VARDHAMANAKA. Here we are. Ho, Maitreya!

MAITREYA. That's the voice of our friend Vardhamanaka. Vasantasena is here.

CHARUDATTA. Welcome her to the garden.

MAITREYA, *going to the gate.* And why are you so filthy late, Vardhamanaka?

VARDHAMANAKA. Now don't lose your temper, Maitreya. I had to go back for the cushions that I'd left behind.

CHARUDATTA. It's all right. Maitreya, help her down.

MAITREYA, *aside.* Does she have chains on her feet so that she can't get down by herself? *He lifts the curtain of the carriage door.* This isn't mistress

Vasantasena! It's mister Vasantasena!

CHARUDATTA. What a time to choose for joking, Maitreya! Here, let me help her. *He rises and approaches.*

ARYAKA, *aside.* That's the man. He not only is noble; he looks every inch a good man. I'm safe.

CHARUDATTA, *seeing* ARYAKA. A man! Strong, brawny, fierce-eyed. Why that chain on his feet? Sir, who are you?

ARYAKA. Aryaka, a herdsman. I need your help.

CHARUDATTA. The same Aryaka whom the king arrested out of fear?

ARYAKA. Yes.

CHARUDATTA. You are welcome to my help. Fate has brought you here, so I cannot refuse you. Vardhamanaka, remove that chain.

VARDHAMANAKA, *doing so.* It's quickly done, sir.

ARYAKA. Now I am bound to you by a stronger chain.

MAITREYA. And now, away with you! Now he's free, our work is over. Shall we go?

CHARUDATTA. You should be ashamed of yourself, Maitreya.

ARYAKA. Charudatta, you must forgive me: I made use of your carriage without your permission.

CHARUDATTA. I am glad you behaved informally.

ARYAKA. I thank you for your kindness, and, with your permission, I should like to leave.

CHARUDATTA. You have my permission. *He watches* ARYAKA *get down from the carriage.* But you can't go on foot, sir: you're cramped and tired. Besides, if you go in the carriage, you need not fear: no one will suspect you. You had better keep the carriage.

ARYAKA. Thank you.

CHARUDATTA. And you have my best wishes for the journey to your friends.

ARYAKA. I am leaving a good friend behind.

CHARUDATTA. If you need me again, you are welcome.

ARYAKA. I'll keep that in mind.

CHARUDATTA. And God be with you.

ARYAKA. As you were with me.

CHARUDATTA. It was nothing. Forget it. Fate stepped in.

ARYAKA. And chose you as an agent.

CHARUDATTA. Don't waste time. There are spies and soldiers everywhere. You must hurry to your friends.

ARYAKA, *getting in again*. We shall meet again. Until then, good-bye.

VARDHAMANAKA *drives him off in the carriage*.

CHARUDATTA. Now *I*'m not safe from the king's anger, either. Even walls have eyes. Throw this chain in the well, Maitreya. MAITREYA *goes to do so;* CHARUDATTA's *left eye twitches; he speaks aside*. A twitching eye's a bad omen. I did want to see her. But it won't be today, I fear. *To* MAITREYA, *returning*. Let's go, Maitreya. *He stops*. Oh, a Buddhist monk coming this way. Another bad omen! *He turns to* MAITREYA. Let's take this other path, Maitreya; I want to avoid him.

*They leave.*

C  U  R  T  A  I  N

## ACT VIII

*A Buddhist monk (the ex-masseur) enters Sansthanaka's garden, carrying a wet robe.*

MONK. Collect virtue, my friends.
   Be moderate, be frugal. Meditate.
   The five senses are thieves.

> Keep an eye on the senses,
> Beware of the senses,
> Stealers of virtue, stealers of faith.
> For all things pass. Only virtue remains.
>
> Kill the five senses.
> Knock out the ego, cast off ignorance.
> Make the flesh pure,
> And heaven is yours.
> For all things pass. Only virtue remains.
>
> Some shave the head, some the chin.
> But the cancer's in the mind: the knife must turn inward.
> Be cleansed of lust and cleansed of pride;
> Leave head alone, leave chin alone.
> Collect virtue, my friends.
> For all things pass. Only virtue remains.

I have dyed this robe saffron. Now to rinse it in the pool. It's the garden of the king's brother-in-law; but I shan't take long. *He begins to rinse the robe.*

VOICE, *offstage.* Stop, you rascal! What are you doing there?

MONK, *fearfully.* Here he comes—Sansthanaka himself! God help me! He hates all monks just because one rubbed him the wrong way once. So he seizes them, pierces their noses like bullocks', and sends them packing. What shall I do? The Lord Buddha is my refuge.

*A* COURTIER *enters, brandishing a sword, followed by* SANSTHANAKA.

SANSTHANAKA. You bastardly monk, stop it! Stop it before I make radish jelly out of you! *He strikes the monk.*

COURTIER. Don't be a fool. Can't you see his yellow robe? He's a monk. Forget him. Look at the garden: it opens out like a feast before our eyes.

MONK. Oh, thank you, my lord, my savior.

SANSTHANAKA. The rascal! He's insulting me.

COURTIER. Why, what has he done?

SANSTHANAKA. He called me a "shaver."

COURTIER. No, he was praising you. He said "savior."

SANSTHANAKA. Praise me more, monk, praise me more. But why are you here?

MONK. I was rinsing this robe, sir.

SANSTHANAKA. Was this pool meant for washing clothes, you rascal? My sister's husband gave it to me. But who comes here? Just dogs and jackals and monks washing robes! I don't even dare to have a bath here. One good clout should finish you off.

COURTIER. Leave him alone. He seems to be a neophyte: he's just joined the monks.

SANSTHANAKA. I don't think so.

COURTIER. Look at his head: it's freshly shaven. He's hardly worn that rough robe: no scars on his body. It fits him loosely, too; you can see he doesn't feel at home in it.

MONK. Yes, I have only recently joined.

SANSTHANAKA. And why? Why not all your life, you poseur, you fraud? *He strikes the monk repeatedly.*

MONK. Glory to the Buddha!

COURTIER. Stop it. Let him be. Let him go.

SANSTHANAKA. Wait. I must consult—

COURTIER. Who's here to consult?

SANSTHANAKA. Me. I must consult myself. My heart.

COURTIER, *aside*. Why doesn't the silly fool run away?

SANSTHANAKA. Let's see. Dear heart, sweet palpitating heart, little chit of a heart, shall I let him go? *To himself*. Neither. *Aloud*. I have consulted my heart, and my heart says—

COURTIER. At last!

SANSTHANAKA. My heart says: he must not be allowed to go, and he must not be allowed to remain here. He shall neither breathe in nor breathe out. He shall fall on his face here—and die. Expire.

MONK. Glory to the Buddha! Mercy, my lord!

COURTIER. Let him go.

SANSTHANAKA. On one condition.

COURTIER. What?

SANSTHANAKA. Let him throw mud in the pool without spoiling the water. Or, let him take mud from the bottom of the pool without spoiling the water. That's good, eh?

COURTIER, *aside.* The world's packed with fools. *Aloud.* How can he do that? It's impossible.

*The* MONK *makes faces at* SANSTHANAKA.

SANSTHANAKA. What's he doing?

COURTIER. He's praising you. That's a Buddhist blessing.

SANSTHANAKA. Praise me more, monk. Praise me more.

*The monk gesticulates and hurries off.*

COURTIER, *quickly.* Just look at the lovely garden now, so well guarded by watchmen. Those creepers around those trees, so lovingly embracing them—like a wife meeting her husband.

SANSTHANAKA. And the ground is full of flowers, the trees heavy with fruit, the creepers busily climbing and the monkeys bobbing like jack fruit.

COURTIER. Sit here on this stone seat.

SANSTHANAKA. I will. *They sit down and relax.* You know something? I can't forget Vasantasena. It's like when a man abuses you; you can't forget it, can you?

COURTIER, *aside. You* can't, of course. A sex fiend can't take no from a woman; a normal man is hurt, but once it's over, it's over.

SANSTHANAKA. Why does that devil of a driver of mine take so long? I told him to get here in record time. The sun's up, at high noon, and splutters like an angry ape. I'm footsore and hungry, and I can't walk in this heat.

COURTIER. It *is* hot. The cows are keeping to the shadows; here and there a deer is looking for a pool—even if it's only hot water that he'll find. There's not a man out on the streets. The driver must have taken a longer but cooler route.

SANSTHANAKA. That's very kind of him, while the sun here is roasting me brown. The birds are hidden in the cool leaves, but we pant here like furnaces. I bet you he's taking his time. Well, how about a song to make the time pass? *He sings.* Wasn't that brilliant?

COURTIER. Wasn't it? You sing like an angel.

SANSTHANAKA. Naturally. Pepper and powder, oil and ghee—that's my daily recipe for a sweet voice. Damn it, the man's still not here!

COURTIER. He'll be here soon.

STHAVARAKA *drives up before the gate with the carriage containing* VASANTASENA.

STHAVARAKA. Giddap, you two! I'm late; it's past noon. I hope he doesn't blow up.

VASANTASENA, *within.* That isn't Vardhamanaka's voice. Did Charudatta send another driver? My right eye twitches. I suddenly feel faint. Where am I? I can't see clearly.

SANSTHANAKA, *approaching.* So, you are here at last!

COURTIER, *approaching.* About time, too!

SANSTHANAKA. I heard the wheels squeal like pigs. Hello, Sthavaraka. Good to see you.

STHAVARAKA. Sir?

SANSTHANAKA. Good to see the carriage, too.

STHAVARAKA. Sir.

SANSTHANAKA. And these two beasts.

STHAVARAKA. Sir?

SANSTHANAKA. And you.

STHAVARAKA. Sir?

SANSTHANAKA. Drive in, man, drive in!

STHAVARAKA. Sir?

SANSTHANAKA. This way, you fool, where the wall's broken down.

STHAVARAKA. It can't be done: the opening's too narrow. The carriage will be smashed, the oxen will be killed. I'll be killed.

SANSTHANAKA. If the carriage is smashed, I'll get another one made. If the oxen are killed, I'll buy two more. And if you die, I'll get another driver.

STHAVARAKA. Yes, sir. You will have another driver, but I shall be dead.

SANSTHANAKA. No back talk, you idiot! Drive! Drive! Let the whole thing crash!

STHAVARAKA. As you say, sir. Here goes. Drive in, my carriage, my friend—it's your funeral—and mine. *He drives through the narrow opening.* We made it! We're lucky, sir.

SANSTHANAKA. Nothing wrong? The oxen all right? The ropes all right? You all right?

STHAVARAKA. Yes, sir.

SANSTHANAKA. Good! I like you, you know, and admire you. *To the* COURTIER. Let's get in and see if the inside of the carriage is all right too.

COURTIER. Yes. *He starts to get in.*

SANSTHANAKA, *pulling him back.* Me first, my friend. This isn't your father's carriage. I am the owner. I get in first.

COURTIER. But you asked me to do so.

SANSTHANAKA. So what? Haven't you the politeness to say, "Sir, after you"?

COURTIER. After you, sir.

SANSTHANAKA. That's a good boy. *He gets up and looks in, backs out in a great fright, and falls on the* COURTIER. Help, thief! Help, witch! A thief in the carriage! A witch in the carriage!

COURTIER. Don't be silly. What would a witch be doing in a carriage? You've had a touch of the sun. It was just Sthavaraka's shadow that gave you the jimjams.

SANSTHANAKA. Sthavaraka, Sthavaraka, are you still alive?

STHAVARAKA. Yes, sir.

SANSTHANAKA. Take a look in the carriage. I tell you there's a woman inside!

COURTIER. A woman!

VASANTASENA, *frightened, to herself.* It's Sansthanaka. What shall I do? Fate has deceived me.

SANSTHANAKA. Hey, you rascal, didn't I tell you to look in? *To the* COURTIER. Come.

COURTIER. A woman can do no harm. *He puts his head inside the carriage.* Vasantasena? No! The deer follows the tiger. The swan runs after the crow. *To* VASANTASENA. That you should do this, Vasantasena! I should never have believed it. First your pride says no, and now, for the sake of money, because your mother tells you—

VASANTASENA, *shaking her head violently.* No!

COURTIER. You are a courtesan, after all.

VASANTASENA. It's all a mistake. This is not the carriage—please help me, please—

COURTIER. Since you ask me. Leave everything to me. *He withdraws his head and turns to* SANSTHANAKA. Yes, there's a witch inside.

SANSTHANAKA. Why didn't she eat you up?

COURTIER. Thank God, she spared me. How about a nice pleasant walk back to Ujjain under the shady roadside trees?

SANSTHANAKA. Well. . .

COURTIER. It's good exercise. And the oxen could do with a bit of rest.

SANSTHANAKA. Let's go. You, Sthavaraka, follow us with the carriage. Wait, let's see. . .I go on foot only before gods and Brahmins. The carriage suits me best. People will see me from afar and say, "There he is, the king's brother-in-law."

COURTIER, *aside*. That does it. What now? I hope this helps. *Aloud*. There wasn't any witch: I was joking. It's Vasantasena. She has come to see you.

VASANTASENA, *to herself*. Oh, no!

SANSTHANAKA. And why shouldn't she? I'm a first-class nobleman, am I not?

COURTIER. Yes.

SANSTHANAKA. What luck! What wonderful luck! The last time, I made her angry. This time, I'll fall down before her and ask her forgiveness.

COURTIER. An excellent idea.

SANSTHANAKA. Watch me. *He approaches and kneels before* VASANTA- SENA. Listen to me, my mother, dear mother. My lotus hands supplicate you in prayer. Please forgive the mistakes I made in the past. Yours sincerely, your lover, your slave.

VASANTASENA, *angrily*. Go away. You insult me. *She spurns him with her foot*.

SANSTHANAKA, *rising*. What! Kick this head? Sansthanaka's head that does not bow even to gods? And you kick it the way jackals kick rotting flesh? Hey, Sthavaraka, where did you pick this woman up?

STHAVARAKA. The road was blocked, sir. I stopped near Charudatta's garden gate while the traffic cleared. I was helping to get a villager's cart unmired. I think she must have got in then, thinking it was her carriage.

SANSTHANAKA. I see! She *wasn't* coming to meet me. Get out, you!

This is my carriage. You were going to meet that beggar Brahmin, weren't you? Not in my carriage, you don't! Get out, get out!

VASANTASENA. Yes, I was going to meet Charudatta. And I am proud of it.

SANSTHANAKA. How I always wanted to lay hands on your lovely body. Now I'll drag you down by the hair, my sweet beauty.

COURTIER. This is no time to insult a lady. Come down, Vasantasena. *He helps her to alight. She stands at a little distance from them.*

SANSTHANAKA, *aside.* First she refused me. Now she kicks me. Fire is in my heart! She'll die for this! *Aloud, to the* COURTIER. And you now, what would you like? A brilliant gold mantle with a hundred tassels? A taste of most delicious bit of bird's meat you ever had in your life? Tell me, what do you want most?

COURTIER. Why?

SANSTHANAKA. Do me a favor.

COURTIER. I'll do anything for you—within reason.

SANSTHANAKA. Oh, wonderfully reasonable, most wonderfully reasonable, I promise you!

COURTIER. What?

SANSTHANAKA. Kill Vasantasena.

COURTIER, *shocked.* The finest lady in Ujjain, a most blameless courtesan, refined, beautiful—kill her? My soul would forever rot in hell.

SANSTHANAKA. I'll take care of your soul. If you kill her in this lonely garden, who will ever know?

COURTIER. The sky, the gods, the wind, the moon, the big-eyed sun, my heart, my conscience. The whole world will know. *I* shall know.

SANSTHANAKA. That's too bad. Hide her, then, and kill her.

COURTIER. You mad fool!

SANSTHANAKA. You're afraid of the gods. You're a poor jackal. Sthavaraka will do it. *He calls him over.* Sthavaraka, my man, do you want gold bracelets?

STHAVARAKA. I'll wear gold bracelets.

SANSTHANAKA. Sthavaraka, my man, do you want a golden couch?

STHAVARAKA. I'll sit on a golden couch.

SANSTHANAKA. Sthavaraka, my man, do you want delicious dishes?

STHAVARAKA. I'll eat delicious dishes.

SANSTHANAKA. Sthavaraka, my man, do you want to boss my slaves?

STHAVARAKA. I'll be boss over the slaves.

SANSTHANAKA. But first, you'll have to do as I say.

STHAVARAKA. Say it, and it shall be done.

SANSTHANAKA. It's a small thing, a very small thing.

STHAVARAKA. Say it.

SANSTHANAKA. Kill Vasantasena.

STHAVARAKA. No, sir! Please, sir! I didn't mean anything. I only brought her here. She got into the wrong carriage, sir.

SANSTHANAKA. Why, you're my slave, aren't you? What are you afraid of?

STHAVARAKA. Of the future, sir.

SANSTHANAKA. What is this future? Bah!

STHAVARAKA. It brings good and bad.

SANSTHANAKA. What good, damn you?

STHAVARAKA. Well, sir, if I'm a good man now, later I'll be rich and powerful like you.

SANSTHANAKA. And what bad, damn you?

STHAVARAKA. Sir, if I do evil, I'll remain as I am, a slave. I won't do evil, sir.

SANSTHANAKA. You mean you won't kill her? *He knocks him down.*

STHAVARAKA. Beat me. Kill me. But I won't do evil. I was born a slave, I'll die a slave. But I don't want to be born a slave again.

VASANTASENA. I throw myself on your mercy. Let him alone.

COURTIER. He's had enough: let him go. That was brave of you, Sthavaraka!

SANSTHANAKA, *aside.* The first is a fool: he's afraid of his conscience. The second is a bigger fool: he's afraid of the future. But I'm afraid of nothing, for I am the king's brother-in-law. *To* STHAVARAKA. Very well, you may go. Go, and never show your face to me again.

STHAVARAKA. Yes, sir. *To* VASANTASENA. I had no hand in this, lady. *He leaves.*

SANSTHANAKA. Get ready to die, Vasantasena. *He starts to seize her.*

COURTIER, *catching him roughly by the neck.* Not while I'm here.

SANSTHANAKA, *falling backward.* You would kill me? Me, your lord? *He loses consciousness, but quickly recovers.* So, the dog turns against his master? *Rising, speaking aside.* I have a trick to take care of you, my friend. I have seen the signs you've been making. First you shall go; then we'll attend to her. *Aloud.* How could you suspect me? I who come from the noblest family in the kingdom. I just wanted to frighten her into saying yes.

COURTIER. A noble family does not always produce noble characters. Weeds as well as flowers grow in fertile soil.

SANSTHANAKA. Look, why don't you leave us alone? She can't make up her mind so long as you stay here. I am sure Sthavaraka has taken to his heels. Catch him and bring him back. In the meantime, this proud lady will say yes to me.

COURTIER, *aside.* Perhaps he'll come to his senses when she pleads with him in private. *Aloud.* All right, I'll go.

VASANTASENA, *clutching at his garments.* Please don't leave me with him. Please! You gave me your word.

COURTIER. It's all right, Vasantasena. *To* SANSTHANAKA. It is as a pledge that I leave her in your hands, and I will come back for her.

SANSTHANAKA. Very good—as long as you leave her in my hands.

COURTIER. I want your word of honor.

SANSTHANAKA. You have my word.

COURTIER, *aside.* He might trick me. I know him well. I'll hide myself here for a minute and see what he does. *He hides.*

SANSTHANAKA, *aside.* Now to kill her. No, wait! Who knows, that foxy Brahmin may have slipped in somewhere to see what I do. But he won't catch me. *He picks flowers and adorns himself, then addresses* VASANTASENA. Vasantasena, my dearest, sweet of my heart, come to me!

COURTIER, *aside.* I see that he just wants to make love to her, as he said. Fine. *He leaves.*

SANSTHANAKA. You'll have gold, sweet words, my head, my turban at your feet. Love me, my dearest. Take me to your heart.

VASANTASENA. Gold? Take it away! Do the bees leave the lotus because it grows in filthy ponds? I am in love with a good man. His love has given me honor. Shall I leave the mango tree and love a withered thornbush?

SANSTHANAKA. Charudatta a mango tree? And I just a thornbush, not even a hedge creeper? Is this how you revile me and praise Charudatta?

VASANTASENA. What can I do? He lives in my heart. I must praise him.

SANSTHANAKA. I'll show you! I'll cut him apart, and you too. You filthy mistress of Charudatta!

VASANTASENA. Say his name again: it's like a song in my ears.

SANSTHANAKA. Call him! Call his name! See if he saves you now.

VASANTASENA. He would help me, if only he knew.

SANSTHANAKA. Help you? What is he? The monkey god? The chief of gods? The god of wind? The god of rain? A vulture? A demon? Let him be all these, and he cannot help you now. You are going to die, as Sita died, as Draupadi died. *He lifts his arm to strike her.*

VASANTASENA. Help me, Mother! Help me, Charudatta! Die? I shall scream! No, why should Vasantasena be afraid? Charudatta, I died loving you. God bless you.

SANSTHANAKA. That bastard's name again! *He strangles her.* Say his name again, say his name again!

VASANTASENA, *very faintly*. God bless you, Charudatta.

SANSTHANAKA. And you, Vasantasena, die, Vasantasena. *She collapses to the ground.* That's done. This dish of vice, this foul lump of no, no, no, she is dead. *He laughs.* She has met, not Charudatta, but Death. A lovely way she died. I did nothing: she just fell like a wet rag. I must hide her: the fox will be back soon. Bah! She should have struggled; I did nothing, really, I'll drag the body into this corner. *He does so.* And hide myself.

*The* COURTIER *and* STHAVARAKA *enter.*

COURTIER. I've persuaded Sthavaraka to return. Where's Sansthanaka?

SANSTHANAKA, *showing himself*. Here. And how are you, Sthavaraka, how are you?

COURTIER. Where is she?

SANSTHANAKA. Who?

COURTIER. Vasantasena.

SANSTHANAKA. The bird has flown.

COURTIER. Where?

SANSTHANAKA. I think she followed you.

COURTIER, *surprised*. No, she didn't.

SANSTHANAKA. No? Which way did you go?

COURTIER. East.

SANSTHANAKA. Ah, that's it. She went that way, south.

COURTIER. I turned south, too.

SANSTHANAKA. Then she must have gone north.

COURTIER. What rot! Tell me the truth.

SANSTHANAKA. If you must know. . .well, I killed her.

COURTIER, *desperately*. You what?

SANSTHANAKA. I killed her. I, Sansthanaka, say so. There's the body. *He points to the body. The* COURTIER *swoons*. What? You too? Out?

STHAVARAKA. Sir! Sir! It's my fault: I brought her here.

COURTIER, *recovering*. Vasantasena! All is over. *Aside*. He'll want to load this crime on me; I must get away from here, fast. *He starts moving away, but* SANSTHANAKA *catches hold of him*. Take your filthy hands off me! I'm leaving for good this time.

SANSTHANAKA. A pretty hope, my friend. First you kill Vasantasena, then you say I killed her, then you scoot off. And I'm left to face the music.

COURTIER. You swine!

SANSTHANAKA. Come, let's be sensible. I'll give you a hundred gold coins, money, clothes, anything you want. No one need know.

COURTIER. The guilt is on your head, you swine. It shall stay on your head. SANSTHANAKA *starts laughing hysterically*. From today on, let there be hate between us. May all friendship, all courtesy, be damned.

SANSTHANAKA. Easy, easy, man. Let's go have a bath in the pool.

COURTIER. How could I have been so blind? Wherever I go now, women will glance at me through half-closed eyes, saying: "He's the friend of the killer." Vasantasena, when you are born again, choose a good and virtuous house. Never be a courtesan again.

SANSTHANAKA. You aren't giving me the slip! No, sir! You killed Vasantasena and you'll have to answer for it in the court of the king. *He seizes the* COURTIER.

COURTIER. I warn you: take your hands off me! *He draws his sword.*

SANSTHANAKA, *recoiling in fear*. Oh, you're afraid, are you? Run off, then; I'll let you go.

COURTIER. This is no place for me. I'll join Sharvilaka, Charudatta and the others. *He leaves.*

SANSTHANAKA. Go to hell. And you, Sthavaraka, what do you think of this little business of mine?

STHAVARAKA. Sir, it's a terrible sin.

SANSTHÁNAKA. Sin? What sin? Let's put it this way. *He takes off his ornaments.* Take these: they're yours. When I want them, I'll take them. In the meantime, they're yours.

STHAVARAKA. They look nice on you, sir. What shall I do with them?

SANSTHANAKA. Take them because I give them to you. Drive these oxen to the palace. And wait for me there.

STHAVARAKA. Yes, sir.

SANSTHANAKA. My friend ran off to save his own skin. As for this foolish servant, I'll clap him into jail the moment I get to the palace. So the secret's safe. No, I must be sure. Is she dead? Or must I kill her again? *He looks at* VASANTASENA'*s body*. Stone-dead. This mantle should cover her. No, it has my name on it. These dry leaves are better: they'll hide her. *He scoops leaves over her*. Now to the court, where I'll file a charge against Charudatta for the murder of Vasantasena. Let's say he lured her into the Pushpakaranda flower garden and killed her for her money. That sounds good. Trapping Charudatta is the next step. But I must go about it cleverly. Too many puritans in this city; even the killing of a cow pinches their conscience. *He starts to leave, but suddenly halts*. Damn! Here's that fool monk again, with his yellow robe, coming my way. He won't forget the nose I slit once—and how I whipped him around. He hates me, and if he sees me and the body he'll run about saying I killed her. *He looks around*. Over the wall for me! Run, fly, like the monkey to Lanka—off I go, off I fly! *He scales the wall and disappears.*

*The Buddhist* MONK *(the ex-masseur) enters.*

MONK. My robe is rinsed. Shall I hang it to dry on this branch? No, too many monkeys here. And the ground's much too dusty. *He looks around.* This should do: a heap of dry leaves blown up here by the wind. *He spreads the wet robe over the leaves, chanting to himself.*

> Kill the five senses,
> Knock out the ego, cast off ignorance.
> Make the flesh pure,
> And heaven is yours.
> For all things pass. Only virtue remains.

Heaven is mine, but not until I have thanked Vasantasena. She put me on the right path by paying those ten gold pieces to the chief gambler. I am her slave forever. What's that? A sigh among the leaves? Maybe the heat and the wet robe are making the leaves curl up and crackle.

VASANTASENA, *recovering consciousness, slowly stretches out a hand.*

A hand from among the leaves! A woman's hand, with lovely pearl rings. Another hand! *He examines it carefully.* I know this hand. Of course. It's the hand that saved me. Let's look. *He throws the wet robe aside and recognizes* VASANTASENA. Vasantasena! Disciple of the Lord Buddha!

VASANTASENA *gasps for water.*

She needs water; but the pool's far away. I'll wring this wet robe over her. *He does so, passing the robe over her face and person.*

VASANTASENA, *reviving.* Who are you, sir?

MONK. Don't you remember? You paid ten gold pieces to buy me my freedom.

VASANTASENA. I remember you. I can't remember anything else. Oh, I could die. I have suffered.

MONK. What happened, good lady?

VASANTASENA. I deserved it.

MONK. Try to get up. Hold onto this creeper and pull yourself up. *He bends down the creeper; she grasps it and pulls herself to her feet.* There is a hermitage nearby where a holy sister lives. She'll nurse you till you are well. No, slowly, walk slowly. *He moves ahead.* This way, good lady, this way. *He leads her off.*

C U R T A I N

## ACT IX

*A Court of Justice. A* CLERK *enters.*

CLERK. What a job to arrange the seats! Well, I'll get it done. *He sweeps and tidies the courtroom, giving it finishing touches.* There, that's done. Now to report to the judge. *He stops.* Oh, here's that rascal, the king's brother-in-law, dashing in. I'll stand in a corner: I don't want to meet him. *He stands to one side.*

SANSTHANAKA, *magnificently dressed, hurries in.*

SANSTHANAKA. I've had a real bath, in cool, cool water. And a rest under shady trees in the company of soft lovely girls—angels, every one of them. They played with my hair—such soft fingers!—now a curl, now a knot, now a twist, now a braid. Oh, I'm a perfect gentleman. But there's a fear inside me, an empty nerve where the worm burrows. *He reflects.* But that's soon taken care of; Charudatta shall be the scapegoat. He's poor, so they'll swallow it when I say he murdered her by strangling. Well, here's the courtroom. The seats are ready. His Honor should be here any minute. I'll wait.

*The* JUDGE *enters, followed by a* WARDER, *a* RECORDER, *and others.*

JUDGE. Recorder.

RECORDER. Your Honor?

JUDGE. Note this down. The most difficult part of a trial is to discover the motives of those involved in it. Crimes are alleged that no one saw, and people work themselves up to such fantastic frenzies that they will continue to stick to allegations that are proved manifestly false by due process of law. Their supporters stick to falsehood, while their enemies broadcast the matter till the king himself is gradually implicated in one way or another. A judge is the worst sufferer; no one has a good word for him. This is natural, for he must be learned, sagacious, eloquent, impartial, and cool-headed; he must reserve judgment until all the evidence is presented and sifted; nothing may corrupt him; he must protect the innocent and punish the guilty, and be in all things honest and truth-loving. And he has to do all this without incurring the displeasure of the king.

WARDEN. Your Honor has no defect, as the moon has none.

JUDGE. Clerk, lead the petitioners into the courtroom.

CLERK. Yes, Your Honor. *He goes out and shouts.* The court is in session. All those who wish to present their cases should please come stand before the judge. *He re-enters.*

SANSTHANAKA, *stepping forward.* I demand justice; I have a case. Note also that I'm a famous man, I come of a noble family; I am the king's own brother-in-law.

CLERK. The king's brother-in-law. Please wait a minute, sir; I'll inform the judge. *He approaches the judge.* Your Honor, the king's brother-in-law has come with a case.

JUDGE. When important men come with complaints, noble men are ruined. I am afraid the court is very busy today. Tell him, clerk, that the court will admit his case any other day.

*The* CLERK *goes to* SANSTHANAKA.

CLERK. Sir, the judge says the court is very busy today; the court will admit your case any other day.

SANSTHANAKA, *angrily.* Is that so? And why not today? Tell the court that, if my case is not heard today, I'll go to the king, who is my sister's husband (and hence my brother-in-law). And tell the court that I shall go to my sister and my mother; and I'll bloody well have the judge dismissed and another put in his place—if my case is not heard today.

CLERK *returning to the* JUDGE. Your Honor, the king's brother-in-law says: *He repeats* SANSTHANAKA's *words.*

JUDGE. He is a fool; but he has all the connections. Well, bring him before us; we'll hear him today.

CLERK, *going to* SANSTHANAKA. Please come before the court, sir. Your case will be heard today.

SANSTHANAKA. It will, ha? And a minute ago it wasn't going to be, ha? Frightened pack of fools! They'll dance to my tune all right. *He steps up to the* JUDGE. I am very happy to see you, Judge. I hope you are happy to see me, for I have the power to make people sad or happy as I like.

JUDGE, *aside.* Just the language of an honest complainant! *To* SANS-THANAKA. You may be seated.

SANSTHANAKA. You bet I will. This place belongs to me, and I'll sit where I like and when I like. *To the* RECORDER. Here? *To the* CLERK. You think this is better? Well, let's try this. *He puts his hand on the seated* JUDGE'*s head to steady himself and sits on the floor.*

JUDGE. You wish to present a case?

SANSTHANAKA. You bet I do.

JUDGE. The court is ready to hear it.

SANSTHANAKA. But first let me remind you that I come of a noble family. My father is the king's father-in-law. The king is my father's son-in-law. I am the king's brother-in-law. And the king happens to be my sister's husband.

JUDGE. The court is aware of these facts. But we are here to listen to your case and judge it impartially, not to hear of your family connections. Proceed with your complaint.

SANSTHANAKA. All in good time, all in good time. There's no hurry: *I'*m not guilty. Well, you see, my sister's husband, that is, my brother-in-law, presented me with the garden they call Pushpakaranda, because he is fond of me. Now it just happens that it is a habit of mine to go there daily to see that it is watered and weeded and the pretty flowers kept flowering. And this morning, when I went there, I saw—I couldn't believe my eyes! —the body of a woman on the ground.

JUDGE. Do you know her?

SANSTHANAKA. Know her? Who doesn't know her? The pride of Ujjain, a pearl above price. It was Vasantasena, the courtesan. Some swinish fellow must have lured her into the garden and strangled her—for her jewels. I didn't—*He stops abruptly, putting his hand over his mouth.*

JUDGE. The police of our city are very careless. Recorder, make a note of that: the complainant said, "*I* didn't."

RECORDER. Yes, Your Honor.

SANSTHANAKA, *aside.* Damn! I've given the show away. Well, we'll see. *Aloud.* What's all the fuss about, dear judge? I was only saying "I didn't... see it happen." *He wipes out the record on the wax tablet with his foot.*

JUDGE. How can you tell that she was strangled, and that it was for her jewels?

SANSTHANAKA. I'm not a fool; her neck was exposed and swollen, and there were no ornaments left on the body.

CLERK. We can believe that.

SANSTHANAKA, *aside.* I've convinced them. Good!

CLERK. What next is necessary, Your Honor, in the conduct of this case?

JUDGE. Two factors are to be considered: the allegations on the one hand, and the evidence on the other. The plaintiff and the defendant are concerned with the investigation of the allegations. It is my business to sift the evidence and come to a conclusion.

CLERK. Then the presence of Vasantasena's mother is essential to the conduct of the case.

JUDGE. Precisely. Clerk, see that Vasantasena's mother is brought here; but do not upset her unduly.

CLERK. Yes, Your Honor. *He goes out and returns almost immediately with* VASANTASENA's *mother.* This way, please.

MOTHER. My daughter went to a friend's house. Now suddenly this news, and no sooner do I reach the courthouse than I am summoned into the court. I don't like any of this; I feel faint. Sir, where do I go?

CLERK. Come this way, please. *He leads her to the* JUDGE.

MOTHER. My blessings on you, good sirs.

JUDGE. You are very welcome. Please sit down.

MOTHER. Thank you. *She sits down.*

SANSTHANAKA. Ah, you mother of a common slut, so you are here!

JUDGE. Ignore him. You are the mother of Vasantasena?

MOTHER. Yes, sir.

JUDGE. Do you know where Vasantasena is now?

MOTHER. I thought she was at a friend's house.

JUDGE. Could you tell the court his name?

MOTHER, *aside.* This is so embarrassing. *Aloud.* Must I answer that question, sir?

JUDGE. I am sorry, but the court asks it, so you must answer it.

CLERK. You should answer it; it has to do with the conduct of the case.

MOTHER. Well, in that case, my daughter went to the house of a very proper man—the son of the noble Sagaradatta, the grandson of the merchant Vinayadatta. His name is Charudatta. He lives in the merchants' quarter. She went to see him.

SANSTHANAKA. That's him! Charudatta! I accuse him of the murder.

CLERK. He might be her friend, but that doesn't make him a murderer.

JUDGE. In that case, the court must have the evidence of Charudatta.

CLERK. Yes, Your Honor.

JUDGE. Recorder put this down: "Vasantasena went to meet Charudatta at his residence." His presence is therefore required. Couldn't we do without him? No, I'm afraid not. Clerk, bring him here; say that the court summons him. See that you do not inconvenience him in any way; just say, "The judge would like to see you."

CLERK. Yes, Your Honor. *He goes out, and returns quickly with* CHARU-DATTA. This way, sir.

CHARUDATTA, *aside.* The king knows me well, yet I am summoned into the court. Perhaps his spies have told him that it was in my carriage that Aryaka escaped; perhaps he thinks I am in the conspiracy.

CLERK. This way, sir.

CHARUDATTA, *aside*. I thought I heard a raven croak; that was a bad omen. And now my right eye is twitching ominously. I thought I saw the bird in a tree, fixing his baleful eyes on me. I saw a black snake on the road in front of me, his tongue flickering, fangs showing and eyes hating me. And now my left arm throbs again. All these things point to a terrible death. Give me courage, God, to endure what is coming.

CLERK. Across the courtroom, sir. Follow me.

CHARUDATTA, *aside*. A vast and sucking ocean, with the advisers lost fathoms below, deep in thought. The tossing waves are quarreling lawyers. The king's spies are sharks and crocodiles. The executioners are monstrous sea snakes. The scribes are slimy sea birds. Oh, how horrible. *He bumps against a pillar.* There goes my arm again, throbbing. And my eye twitches again. *He arrives in front of the* JUDGE.

JUDGE, *aside*. Here is Charudatta. Could a face like that—candid-eyed, with that honest nose—could that face hide guilt?

CHARUDATTA. My greetings to the court, and to you, Your Honor.

JUDGE, *disturbed*. You are welcome, sir. Clerk, see that he has a comfortable seat.

CLERK, *bringing a small seat*. Sir.

CHARUDATTA *sits down*.

SANSTHANAKA. You are here, I see, my fine strangler of women! Bah, call this a trial, where seats are given to women-killers? *He sneers.* Go ahead; you have the power.

JUDGE. Could you tell the court, Charudatta, if at any time there was attachment, affection or friendship of any kind between you and the daughter of this lady?

CHARUDATTA. Which lady?

JUDGE. This lady. *He indicates* VASANTASENA's *mother*.

CHARUDATTA, *rising*. My most respectful greetings.

MOTHER. May you live long, my son. *Aside*. So this is Charudatta. My daughter was a lucky girl.

JUDGE. Charudatta, how long have you known Vasantasena?

CHARUDATTA *is unable to conceal his embarrassment*.

SANSTHANAKA. He's shamming, you can see; it's a guilty mind that does that. He strangled her, and he stole her jewels, and I shall prove it.

CLERK. Speak up, Charudatta. The court asks you a question. You need not be afraid.

CHARUDATTA, *confusedly*. What can I say? How can I confess that a courtesan was my friend? All I can say is that my youth, not my character, was to blame.

JUDGE. I must ask you to be truthful. This is a court, and nothing must be hidden, however personal it is. There is a charge against you.

CHARUDATTA. Who has accused me?

SANSTHANAKA. I have.

CHARUDATTA. It must be a gruesome charge then.

SANSTHANAKA. Why, you woman-strangler, you kill a fine woman like Vasantasena for the sake of stealing her jewels, and now you try to cover it up by pretty lies!

CHARUDATTA. You must be mad.

JUDGE. Ignore him, Charudatta. Answer the question: was she your friend?

CHARUDATTA. Yes.

JUDGE. And can you tell us where she is now?

CHARUDATTA. I know only that she left my house.

CLERK. Where did she go? Did anyone go with her?

CHARUDATTA, *aside*. Shall I tell them that she went alone to meet me?

CLERK. Speak, sir.

CHARUDATTA. She left my home. That's all I know for certain.

SANSTHANAKA. Is that all? What about the way you lured her into my garden of Pushpakaranda, strangled her, and pinched her jewels? What about that?

CHARUDATTA. You are a liar. You must be crazy.

JUDGE, *aside.* You can weigh the Himalayas, catch the wind, and bridge the ocean, but you can't easily prove Charudatta guilty. *Aloud.* I'm afraid I do not see his guilt.

SANSTHANAKA. We don't want opinions; carry on with the case.

JUDGE, *losing his temper.* You utter fool! If you try to explain the Vedas, won't your tongue be cut out? If you look into the sun, won't it blind you? If you thrust your hand into fire, won't it get burned? And if you come with impossible charges against a noble man like Charudatta, won't the earth open up and swallow you? Whatever made you think that Charudatta strangled her? He gave away his whole wealth in charities, and do you think he would steal Vasantasena's jewels—and murder her on that account?

SANSTHANAKA. I repeat: it is not your business to speak in his defense. I want a fair trial.

MOTHER. It is false, the whole charge is false! I know she left a gold box in his care, and when a thief stole it he replaced it with a much more valuable necklace. How could such a man kill her for her jewels? Never! Oh, my daughter, my child, if only you were here! *She weeps.*

JUDGE. Could you tell us, Charudatta, if she left on foot or in a carriage?

CHARUDATTA. I did not see her leave. I cannot say.

VIRAKA *dashes in.*

VIRAKA. I'll go to court. I warned him! He abused me, he kicked me— *me,* a captain! For doing my duty, as was proper. Sirs, I greet you respectfully.

JUDGE. Ah, Viraka, a captain of the guard. What brings you here, Viraka?

VIRAKA. It's a long story, Your Honor. I was only doing my duty, as is proper, searching for Aryaka, who had broken out of jail. Well, Your Honor, I didn't like the looks of a carriage, so I stopped it. Chandanaka—he's the other captain—peeped in and told it to go on. "You've had a look," I said, "but now I'm going to search it properly." And then Chandanaka, Your Honor, stopped me, abused me, and *kicked* me! And I was just doing my duty, as is proper, Your Honor. That's all, Your Honor. I ask for justice.

JUDGE. Do you know who the owner of the carriage is?

VIRAKA. The driver said it was this gentleman here, Your Honor—Charudatta—and that Vasantasena was in it, going to meet him in the Pushpakaranda flower garden.

SANSTHANAKA. Didn't I say so?

JUDGE. A bad day for Charudatta. We shall look into your complaint later, Viraka. In the meantime, take one of the messenger's horses at the gate, go to Pushpakaranda and see if there is a dead woman's body in the garden. Report back here immediately.

VIRAKA. Yes, Your Honor. *He goes out and quickly returns.* There is a woman's body in the garden. The animals had been at it.

CLERK. Are you sure it was a woman's body?

VIRAKA. Yes, to judge from the long hair and the size of the hands and feet.

JUDGE. The more we investigate, the greater is my confusion. The law wants a straight case; but the heart refuses to admit plain facts.

CHARUDATTA. Like bees round an unfolding flower, so sorrows cluster round a poor man.

JUDGE. Charudatta, you must tell the court the whole truth, whatever you know.

CHARUDATTA. This is the truth. You all know me well. I—whom it hurts to pluck a creeper's flowers—how could *I* seize her by her bee-black hair and strangle her? But no one believes me. This too is the truth. A passion-torn man, half-crazed with hatred, plants a crime on another, whom he envies. But he is believed.

SANSTHANAKA. What nonsense is this! Why should this killer remain seated? This isn't law. Whom are you hoodwinking?

JUDGE. Clerk, take his seat away.

*The* CLERK *removes* CHARUDATTA'*s seat.*

CHARUDATTA. I shall obey, Your Honor, but I am innocent. *He squats on the floor.*

SANSTHANAKA, *aside.* Ha-ha! My sin is now on his head. I'll sit near him. *He edges closer to* CHARUDATTA. Come, Charudatta, be a sport about it. Look at me. Say, "I killed Vasantasena."

CHARUDATTA. You are foul and mean. Don't come near me. What will Maitreya think? What will my wife think, good noble woman? My son? Poor child, what does he know of his father's shame, busy as he is with his endless games? *Aside.* Why is Maitreya taking so long? I sent him to Vasantasena's house to return the jewels she gave Rohasena to buy a gold toy cart. He's very late.

MAITREYA *enters with the jewels in his girdle.*

MAITREYA, *aside.* Though Charudatta asked me to return these to her, saying, "It was good of you to give them to my son, but it would not be proper on my part to accept them," Rebhila met me on my way and told me that Charudatta had been summoned into the court. So I didn't go to Vasantasena's, but hurried here. *He comes forward.* I humbly greet the court. Where is my friend?

JUDGE. Charudatta? There.

MAITREYA. My friend Charudatta, may happiness—

CHARUDATTA. Happiness later, sorrow now.

MAITREYA. Be patient.

CHARUDATTA. I am.

MAITREYA. You look terribly worried. Why were you summoned?

CHARUDATTA. It seems I am a murderer. . .no hope for me. . .woman's love. . . . Instead, I killed her. . .they'll tell you the rest.

MAITREYA. What!

CHARUDATTA, *whispering in his ear.* That's the story.

MAITREYA. Who says so?

CHARUDATTA, *indicating* SANSTHANAKA. He is the man chosen by fate to accuse me.

MAITREYA, *aside to* CHARUDATTA. Why not tell them that we did not wait for her and she must have gone home alone.

CHARUDATTA. No one believes me. I am a poor man, you see.

MAITREYA. Gentlemen, what is this! The flower of Ujjain's manhood— a man who gave all his money to decorate this city with gardens, temples, wells, and fountains—would he kill a woman for a few measly jewels? *He speaks more and more angrily.* And you, you bastard, Sansthanaka, you king's brother-in-law, you stuffed monkey, you foul lying dunghill, you quadruple idiot, say it! Say it in front of *me!* Say that this man who never plucked a flower in his life for fear of hurting it, committed a bawdy stinking murder! You bloody bastard, say it and I'll crack your skull wide open with this crooked stick, you damned crooked villain!

SANSTHANAKA. Listen to that, gentlemen! I have accused Charudatta. My business is with Charudatta. And this swine, whom I've hardly met, wants to crack my skull. Go ahead, try it! Accursed swine!

MAITREYA *lifts his stick.* SANSTHANAKA *jumps up and hits him first. A scuffle ensues, and the jewels slip out of* MAITREYA'S *girdle.* SANSTHANAKA *picks them up and displays them triumphantly.*

SANSTHANAKA. Look, gentlemen, look! The woman's jewels! The reason he strangled her.

*The* JUDGE *and others favoring* CHARUDATTA *hang their heads.*

CHARUDATTA, *aside to* MAITREYA. My fate plays terrible tricks on me. With the falling jewels, I fall too.

MAITREYA. Why don't you tell them the whole truth and be done with it?

CHARUDATTA. I have, but the truth does not satisfy the court.

CLERK, *to* VASANTASENA's *mother*. Could you tell us, madam, if this gold box is your daughter's?

MOTHER, *examining it*. It looks the same, but it's a different box.

SANSTHANAKA. You old slut, you know it's the same. Why do you say it's not?

MOTHER. Shut up!

CLERK. Please be careful now: is it the same box or not?

MOTHER. It is an excellent imitation. But it is not my daughter's box.

JUDGE. And can you identify these jewels?

MOTHER. I have already said that they are excellent imitations, but these are not my daughter's jewels. Perhaps the same jeweler made them.

JUDGE. Examine them, clerk. It's true that jewelers are expert at duplicating ornaments.

CLERK. Are these jewels your property, Charudatta?

CHARUDATTA. No.

CLERK. Whose are they?

CHARUDATTA. They belong to the daughter of this lady.

CLERK. How did she lose them?

CHARUDATTA. It is true she lost them once.

CLERK. Speak the truth, Charudatta. The truth can bring you no harm. To hide truth is to lie.

CHARUDATTA. I cannot say how she lost them. I know they were taken from my house.

SANSTHANAKA. Liar! You lured her into the garden, killed her, and stole them. Don't give us your pretty mishmash.

JUDGE. Charudatta, speak the truth. Do not compel the court to sentence you to flogging.

CHARUDATTA. I am innocent. If others suspect me for no reason, I am prepared to suffer for it. *Aside.* What else is there in life but suffering, now that Vasantasena is dead? *Aloud.* I am called a murderer. Let him—*He points to* SANSTHANAKA.—call me what he will.

SANSTHANAKA. Why don't you admit it, you fool? Say, "I killed her."

CHARUDATTA. You have said it.

SANSTHANAKA. There! There! He confessed! He says he killed her! Sentence him!

JUDGE. The court has no other alternative. Clerk, arrest Charudatta.

*At the* CLERK's *gesture, guards move to each side of* CHARUDATTA.

MOTHER. Listen to me, sirs; gentlemen, kind sirs, be merciful. My daughter is dead, killed. Let him live. She was *my* daughter—yet *I* do not accuse Charudatta. Why should he be punished? Set him free.

SANSTHANAKA. Get out, you witch! This is none of your business now.

MOTHER. My son, my dear son. *She goes out, weeping.*

SANSTHANAKA, *aside.* A tidy bit of work I've done today. *He also leaves.*

JUDGE. Charudatta, our task is to sift the evidence. The king will pronounce sentence. Clerk, remind King Palaka that the culprit is a Brahmin, hence he cannot be sentenced to death; that the law lays down his maximum sentence as banishment from the kingdom with his wealth handed to him intact.

CLERK. Yes, Your Honor. *He goes out, and soon returns in tears.* I went to King Palaka, and His Majesty declares: "Since he killed Vasantasena for such a trifle, let the same jewels be hung from his neck, let him be led to the southern burial ground and there let him be executed. This punishment is a warning to all others who contemplate murder."

CHARUDATTA. A treacherous violation of the law. He has bad counselors, our king. But he shall reap the whirlwind of them if he is not careful. Evil ministers can kill thousands, and keep on doing so. It doesn't matter now. Maitreya, see that my wife is well cared for after I die. And look after my son, Rohasena, as if he were your own.

MAITREYA. How can I? When the root is cut, how can the tree survive?

CHARUDATTA. No, that is not true. When a man dies, he lives on in his son. Look after my son; give him the friendship you gave me.

MAITREYA. I will try. You have been the best friend I ever had.

CHARUDATTA. Bring Rohasena to me. I want to see my son before I go.

MAITREYA *hurries out.*

JUDGE. Clerk, take the prisoner away. Let the executioners receive their orders.

*The court leaves.*

CHARUDATTA, *as he goes.* What will Maitreya think? What will my wife think, good noble woman? My son? Poor child—his little games are endless. Test me by fire, by poison, on the rack—and if I fail the test, I will go smiling to my doom. But to trust a scoundrel's word above mine! Such a king! A Brahmin's curse on you! Your sons, and your sons' sons—may hell receive them! I am ready.

*He is marched out.*

C U R T A I N

# ACT X

*A street.* CHARUDATTA *enters, flanked by two executioners.*

FIRST EXECUTIONER. Don't worry, sir. It only takes a second. We'll have your head off in a jiffy. We're pretty good at it. Hey, make way, you!— this is the noble Charudatta, going to have his head chopped off.

CHARUDATTA, *sadly.* That raven again; I heard him. Red oleanders on my head, flowers of death. What a ghastly sacrifice!

SECOND EXECUTIONER. What's the big idea, there? Move on, move on! It isn't a pretty sight. He was a good tree once: that's what some birds tell me. But now it's the ax for him.

CHARUDATTA. Who can escape fate? A Brahmin dragged like a beast to the sacrifice!

FIRST EXECUTIONER. Here we are. Beat the drum and I'll announce the sentence. Gentlemen of the city, most worthy citizens! The king is pleased to proclaim that Charudatta, son of Sagaradatta, and grandson of the merchant Vinayadatta, having seduced the courtesan Vasantasena into the lonely Pushpakaranda flower garden, and there having strangled her and robbed her of her jewels, and having confessed his guilt in a court of law, is hereby sentenced to be executed. Let this serve as a warning to all others who contemplate crimes heinous both to this world and the next, for King Palaka will punish them in a similar manner.

CHARUDATTA, *aside*. As a Brahmin, performer of a hundred holy sacrifices, my name grew in prestige. Now it is spoken with shame, blackened in the black spots of our city by louts and loafers. *He looks up and puts his fingers in his ears.* Oh, Vasantasena! I who fed on the sweetness of your ruby-red lips, your teeth white as moons! I, with heaven in my heart—that I should live to pass through such filthy shame!

FIRST EXECUTIONER. Come, sir, let's move on.

CHARUDATTA. I had friends once. Where are they now? Hiding in their cloaks. An enemy will smile at you when you lose—but a friend!

FIRST EXECUTIONER. The street is cleared. Let's go.

VOICE, *calling offstage*. Father! Father!

CHARUDATTA. One favor I must ask you. . .

FIRST EXECUTIONER. A favor from *us*? But we are low-caste.

CHARUDATTA. But not so cruel as the king. Let me be happy once before I die; let me see my son's face.

FIRST EXECUTIONER. Let him come.

MAITREYA *and* ROHASENA *enter*.

ROHASENA. Father!

MAITREYA. My friend!

CHARUDATTA. My son. Maitreya. *He looks tenderly at his son.* What can I give you, my child? *He takes off his sacred thread.* Take this. No pearls and no gold. But it is sacred. *He gives the thread to* ROHASENA.

FIRST EXECUTIONER. Come, Charudatta.

ROHASENA. Where are you taking my father?

FIRST EXECUTIONER. We have orders from the king.

ROHASENA. Take me; let my father go.

FIRST EXECUTIONER. Why, what a brave boy!

MAITREYA. Why don't you set my friend free? Take me in his place.

CHARUDATTA, *to each.* No. No.

FIRST EXECUTIONER. Out of the way, gentlemen, out of the way! Let's announce the sentence again here. *He does so.*

STHAVARAKA, *from a high window in the palace jail overlooking the square, hears the announcement and cries out.* Charudatta sentenced to death? And me thrown in jail! Sirs, sirs, listen to me! I am the man who took Vasantasena to the Pushpakaranda flower garden; she entered my carriage by mistake. I swear it. There my lord Sansthanaka strangled her with his bare hands because she refused to love him. Listen! Can't you hear me? No, they're too far away. My voice doesn't reach them. Shall I jump down? That might save Charudatta. This window is so high that it's not barred; I can slip out of it. But shall I die? Oh, then let me die, let Charudatta live—that's all I want. Heaven is mine if I die so nobly. *He makes the leap.* Not hurt! And the jump snapped my ankle chains. Oh, where are you? Where are you! It's me, Sthavaraka! *He sees the executioners coming.* Stop! Listen to me! It's important. It was I who took Vasantasena to Pushpakaranda, where Sansthanaka strangled her because she refused to love him, and—

CHARUDATTA. Thank God, I am saved.

FIRST EXECUTIONER. Is all that true?

STHAVARAKA. Of course it is. And Sansthanaka threw me in jail and put me in chains, so that no one would know.

SANSTHANAKA *emerges from a palace gate into the square.*

SANSTHANAKA, *chuckling.* What a dinner I've had—meat, fish, sauce, and vegetables. Hm, I hear voices. . . . The drums and kettledrums that announce an execution. It's that swine Charudatta—what fun to watch an enemy's head chopped off! I must see the execution. They tell me that if a man watches his enemy die he gets better eyesight in his next birth. I'll climb to the first window in this palace tower. *He reappears at a window.* Oh, what a crowd to watch the fun! But when *I* die, I'll draw even bigger crowds. I'm a great man, the brother-in-law of the king. Well, there he is, dressed up like a prize cow. But why have they stopped so near the palace jail? And what is that rascal Sthavaraka doing there! Has he broken out of jail? Has he spilled the beans? This is getting serious! I must go down and see for myself. *He emerges from the bottom of the tower and wades into the crowd.* Make way for a lord!

FIRST EXECUTIONER. Make room, please, make room.

SANSTHANAKA. Sthavaraka, you'd better come along with me.

STHAVARAKA. No! Leave me alone! Isn't it enough that you strangled Vasantasena? Why do you want to murder Charudatta too?

SANSTHANAKA. What do you mean? I'm as honest as gold. I killed no woman.

VOICES FROM THE CROWD. He says you killed her. Charudatta did not kill her.

SANSTHANAKA. Who says that? Tell me, who says that?

*Members of the crowd point out* STHAVARAKA.

VOICES. *He.* And he's an honest man.

SANSTHANAKA, *frightened, aside.* The devil! I should have had him better chained. He's a witness to the crime. *Aloud.* A pack of lies, my friends. He's a no-good lout. I caught him redhanded stealing gold and had him put in chains. He's got a grudge against me; oh, yes, he has. He's invented this story. Isn't that so, you rascal? *He edges up to Sthavaraka and slips him a gold bracelet.* Here, take this, and keep your mouth shut.

STHAVARAKA, *taking the bracelet and showing it.* Sirs, sirs! He's trying to bribe me with this!

SANSTHANAKA, *snatching the bracelet from him.* That's it! That's the bracelet I caught him stealing! *To the* EXECUTIONERS. Look here, you!—I nabbed him redhanded and had him whipped. Look at his back if you don't believe me.

FIRST EXECUTIONER, *examining the welts.* Yes, sir, that's true; he has been whipped. No wonder he's making up stories.

STHAVARAKA. Oh, no one believes a slave. *He speaks sadly.* Charudatta, I did what I could. *He falls at* CHARUDATTA'*s feet.*

CHARUDATTA. Rise, Sthavaraka. It's not your fault. My fate is against me.

FIRST EXECUTIONER. Set him free now, sir. He has been whipped.

SANSTHANAKA. Run off, you! *He pushes* STHAVARAKA *away.* And now what's the delay? Kill him.

FIRST EXECUTIONER. Kill him yourself, sir, if you think we're too slow.

ROHASENA. Kill me; please don't kill my father.

SANSTHANAKA. Kill both. Kill father, kill son.

CHARUDATTA. Run off, son, to your mother. Don't waste another minute here. Go with your mother to an ashrama. They will kill you here. Maitreya, go; and take him to safety too.

MAITREYA. Do you think I can live without you?

CHARUDATTA. Your life is your life, Maitreya. You have no right to treat it so lightly.

MAITREYA, *aside.* Yes, but I cannot live without you. I'll go and lead the boy to safety; then I'll follow my friend's road to death. *Aloud.* I'll do as you say. *He embraces* CHARUDATTA *and falls at his feet.*

ROHASENA, *crying, also falls at his father's feet.*

SANSTHANAKA. Haven't I told you to finish father and son off?

FIRST EXECUTIONER. We have no orders from the king to kill the son. Go away, boy, go away. *They push the child out of sight, and move on a little.* Here's the third station. Beat the drum and announce the sentence.

*The sentence is again proclaimed.*

SANSTHANAKA, *aside*. This won't do. No one is listening. *Aloud*. Charudatta, open your mouth and speak the truth: "I killed Vasantasena." CHARUDATTA *is silent*. The swine won't speak. Make him speak! Give him a taste of the cane!

FIRST EXECUTIONER, *lifting the bamboo cane*. Speak up, Charudatta.

CHARUDATTA. I am afraid of nothing any more—save only this—that men should say I killed the thing I loved.

SANSTHANAKA. Speak up!

CHARUDATTA. Friends, citizens of Ujjain, my city—

SANSTHANAKA. Say, "I killed her."

CHARUDATTA. You have said it.

FIRST EXECUTIONER. It's your turn today, Ahinta.

SECOND EXECUTIONER. No, it's yours, Goha.

FIRST EXECUTIONER. Let's see. . . . Ah, yes. Well, let's wait a little. There's no hurry.

SECOND EXECUTIONER. Why?

FIRST EXECUTIONER. Well, my father once said to me, "Goha," he said to me, "you never know. Some kind man might come along and buy his freedom. You never know. A son might be born to the king, and a general pardon proclaimed. An elephant might break loose, and the lucky beggar might escape. You never know. There might even be a new king come to the throne, and all the prisoners set free." That's what he said.

SANSTHANAKA. A new king? What!

FIRST EXECUTIONER. That's why I never hurry.

SANSTHANAKA. Come on, come on, kill him. Finish it off. *He withdraws a little.*

FIRST EXECUTIONER. Forgive us, noble Charudatta. We are only carrying out the king's orders. Is there anything you would like to say before you are executed?

CHARUDATTA. I hope that whatever sins I have committed will be washed away by the virtue of the lady who is now in heaven.

FIRST EXECUTIONER, *pointing.* That's the southern burial ground. You can see the jackals and vultures.

CHARUDATTA, *covering his eyes.* Oh, horrible! *He sits down in sudden fear.*

SANSTHANAKA. I'll wait till he's killed good and proper. Why is he sitting down?

FIRST EXECUTIONER. Are you afraid, Charudatta?

CHARUDATTA, *standing up quickly again.* Yes, but only of what people will say, not of death.

FIRST EXECUTIONER. Sir, the moon changes, the sun changes; death is for us all. One man rises to fall; another falls and rises again. But when death comes, he *really* falls, and he throws his body aside, like a useless garment. Sir, that's what wise men say.

VASANTASENA, *very agitated, enters at the other side of the crowd, accompanied by the Buddhist* MONK.

MONK. It does look a little odd—me, a monk, in the company of a courtesan. Lady, where shall I take you?

VASANTASENA. Please, to Charudatta's house. When I see him, I know I shall live again, as a night lily lives on seeing the moon.

MONK. We'll go by this royal road. Come, follow me. But what are they shouting there?

VASANTASENA. What a great crowd of people! The whole city of Ujjain seems to have turned out here. What does it mean?

FIRST EXECUTIONER. This is the place for the final announcement. Announce the sentence. *There is a flourish of drums.* It won't be long now, Charudatta.

CHARUDATTA. I am ready.

*The sentence is again proclaimed.*

MONK, *fearfully.* Lady, the noble Charudatta is going to be executed for murdering *you!*

VASANTASENA, *in terror.* Take me there. Quickly.

MONK. Make room for us, please. Room for us, please.

VASANTASENA. Please, sirs. Please. . .

*They start to push their way through the crowd.*

FIRST EXECUTIONER. Once again, noble Charudatta, we ask your forgiveness. We are only carrying out orders.

CHARUDATTA. There is nothing in my heart against you. I only hope that whatever sins I may have committed will be washed away by the virtue of the lady who is now in heaven.

FIRST EXECUTIONER, *raising his sword.* Noble Charudatta, do not move. A single stroke will do it. *As he is about to strike, the sword suddenly drops from his hand.* Why did it fall? I held it tight. O goddess of the Sakya hills, hear me. It is your wish. Charudatta will escape. And the low-caste race will rise.

SECOND EXECUTIONER. We have our orders.

FIRST EXECUTIONER. Yes. We'll tie him to the stake first.

VASANTASENA *breaks through the crowd.*

VASANTASENA. Stop it! Stop it! I am Vasantasena. I am not dead. Oh, Charudatta! Charudatta, my love! *She falls on his breast.*

MONK, *breaking through the crowd.* Charudatta, noble sir! *He falls at* CHARUDATTA's *feet.*

FIRST EXECUTIONER, *worried.* Vasantasena! And we nearly killed an innocent man!

MONK, *rising*. Charudatta is alive. Glory to the Buddha!

VASANTASENA. And I too am alive at last.

FIRST EXECUTIONER. Let's go to the king with the news. He is at the place of sacrifice.

SANSTHANAKA, *seeing* VASANTASENA. A ghost? No, still alive! I'm ruined. I must run, I must fly! *He runs away*.

FIRST EXECUTIONER. Our orders were to behead the man who killed Vasantasena. Let's go after the king's brother-in-law; he must be the man.

*Both* EXECUTIONERS *go out*.

CHARUDATTA. Saved from the jaws of death, from eternal shame. Are you Vasantasena? Or a goddess from heaven? Am I mad? Are you alive? Am I seeing things dropped from heaven. . . ? No, someone else. . .a goddess. . . .

VASANTASENA, *falling at his feet*. I am Vasantasena, my love, a wretched woman, the cause of all your troubles.

VOICES. Vasantasena is alive! Alive!

CHARUDATTA, *blindly pulling her to her feet and embracing her with great feeling*. It is true, then. You are Vasantasena.

VASANTASENA. Unhappy Vasantasena.

CHARUDATTA. It is over.

VASANTASENA. What could you have done, my dearest?

CHARUDATTA. They said I killed you. Sansthanaka hates me. He wanted to have me killed too.

VASANTASENA, *clapping her hands to her ears*. No!

CHARUDATTA, *seeing the* MONK. And who is he?

VASANTASENA. A kind monk to whom I owe my life.

MONK. You may not remember me, sir. I was the man you engaged to be your masseur. But when I left you, I fell among gamblers and got into debt; then this good lady bought me my freedom with her jewels. I renounced gambling and became a Buddhist monk. And then many things happened. She got into the wrong carriage by mistake. I found her in the old Pushpakaranda garden, where she had been left for dead by Sansthanaka.

VOICES, *shouting offstage*. Aryaka has won! Glory to Aryaka!

SHARVILAKA *enters hurriedly*.

SHARVILAKA. Yes, I killed Palaka. This hand of mine slew the king, and this hand anointed Aryaka as the new king. Now to free Charudatta. Make way, you! *He sees* CHARUDATTA. Charudatta living? And Vasantasena! My king will be pleased to hear this. Can I go near him, I who played him false? I will; my honesty is my passport. Noble Charudatta, greetings!

CHARUDATTA. Who are you, sir?

SHARVILAKA. I am the thief who stole the gold box from your house. I throw myself on your mercy.

CHARUDATTA, *embracing him*. It has been a blessing in disguise, my friend.

SHARVILAKA. And I also bring the news that I killed King Palaka at the place of sacrifice, and that Aryaka is the new king.

CHARUDATTA. Aryaka!

SHARVILAKA. Yes, your carriage saved him, and now he is king.

CHARUDATTA. And you are the man who helped Aryaka escape from the palace prison?

SHARVILAKA. Yes, sir. A small thing, sir.

CHARUDATTA. I am happy to hear it.

SHARVILAKA. His Majesty King Aryaka bestows on you, as a token of gratitude and affection, the Kingdom of Kushavati, on the bank of the Vena, and hopes you will honor him by accepting it. *He turns*. And now bring in that swine.

SANSTHANAKA, *his hands tied behind his back, is dragged in*.

SANSTHANAKA. Well, I'm caught now; bound and dragged like an ass or a dog. But I still have a trick or two about me. *He appeals to* CHARUDATTA. Noble Charudatta, help me, help me.

VOICES FROM THE CROWD. Don't, Charudatta. We'll teach the swine. Leave him to us.

SANSTHANAKA. I am helpless, I am finished, Charudatta. Help me. Please help me.

CHARUDATTA. Yes, whoever seeks help shall not go without it.

SHARVILAKA. Damn him! Take him away from here. *To* CHARUDATTA. What shall we do to him, sir? Drag him till his flesh is torn off? Throw him to the dogs? Cut him up with a saw?

CHARUDATTA. Listen to me.

SHARVILAKA. Sir.

SANSTHANAKA. Charudatta, help me! Please help me! I promise I won't do it again. I come to you for help.

VOICES FROM THE CROWD. Kill him! Kill the swine!

VASANTASENA *takes the oleander garland from* CHARUDATTA's *neck and throws it around* SANSTHANAKA's.

SANSTHANAKA. Please, help me now, good courtesan. Have pity. I promise, I'll never kill you again. Never!

SHARVILAKA. Drag him away. Noble Charudatta, what punishment shall we give him?

CHARUDATTA. You will do as I say?

SHARVILAKA. I promise.

CHARUDATTA. Thank you. In that case. . .

SHARVILAKA. Kill him. But how?

CHARUDATTA. No, set him free.

SHARVILAKA. What!

CHARUDATTA. It is said that the sword should never be used on a man who begs for mercy.

SHARVILAKA. We won't use the sword; we'll throw him to the dogs.

CHARUDATTA. No. Let mercy be his punishment.

SHARVILAKA. I do not like it, but if you say so. . . .But what shall I do with him?

CHARUDATTA. Just untie him; let him go.

SHARVILAKA *does so.*

SANSTHANAKA. Ha-ha! I'm free! Free! *He runs out.*

SHARVILAKA. His Majesty has asked me, madam, to confer on you the title of Lady of the Court.

VASANTASENA. Please thank him for me.

SHARVILAKA, *placing a veil of honor on* VASANTASENA's *head; then turning to* CHARUDATTA. Sir, what does the monk desire?

CHARUDATTA. What do you want, holy sir?

MONK. All things pass. And nothing remains. I want nothing.

CHARUDATTA. In that case, you shall be the spiritual head of all Buddhist monasteries in the kingdom.

SHARVILAKA. That shall be done. Sthavaraka now remains.

CHARUDATTA. Give him his freedom. Let the executioners become chiefs of their profession. Chandanaka shall be chief of police; as for Sansthanaka. . .

SHARVILAKA. Leave him to me; I know how to deal with him.

CHARUDATTA. Sansthanaka shall remain as he was. Let him do as he likes.

SHARVILAKA. Anything else, noble Charudatta?

CHARUDATTA. Aryaka is king; Vasantasena, whom I love, shall be my second wife. You are my friend now. Our honor is intact. We have repaid cruelty with kindness. There is nothing else.

CURTAIN

# THE  SIGNET  RING  OF  RAKSHASA

by

## VISHAKADATTA

# Preface

"The Massinger of the Hindus" fits Vishakadatta well—he is a dramatist undeceived by prettiness and sentimentality. The idea of drama as a *loka-charita,* an art form portraying the social system, is certainly present in *The Signet Ring of Rakshasa,* and Vishakadatta puts high value on hierarchical obediences in such a system. At the same time, while holding the mirror up to nature, he conforms to the requirements of dramatic convention. Aware that the aspect of the social system which he will portray can often involve much that is crude, cunning, and complex, Vishakadatta tries to cushion the shock in many ways. First, by strictly delimiting the area of his action. Since there is going to be plenty of political intrigue in the play—an occupation eminently masculine—he has no heroine (there are female guards, however, but they merely usher people in and show them out, and could conveniently come under the category of court eunuchs, while the brief appearance of Chandanadasa's wife appears really to have been more an oversight than anything else). In any case, the rasa of *The Signet Ring* is one which the fair sex is not expected to be concerned with; this not only explains why female roles are excluded, but helps in understanding why the story is so sinuously developed, why so much "brainy" dialogue takes place, why poison girls, spies, and other scoundrels are given what looks like honorable mention. The important thing, says Chanakya in the first act, is that he mustn't lower his intellectual sights because the rational, cool man counts more than armies in the "cold war" he is waging to win the allegiance of Rakshasa, the incorruptible minister of the Nanda dynasty. This play does not in that sense "conform to the normal model"; it is indeed "a series of Machiavellian stratagems." But the outline of the plot itself is extremely simple.

Rakshasa, we learn from the play's long opening soliloquy, has to be reconciled to Chanakya and King Chandragupta, who have instigated the assassination of Nanda, in whose court Rakshasa was minister. Chanakya succeeds, by various means, all unfair, in making the prince who is sheltering Rakshasa believe that Rakshasa cannot be trusted. The disillusioned

Rakshasa surrenders when he finds that a close friend of his is about to be executed on orders from Chanakya. The audience knows, however, that this is a ruse, part of the grand plan of winning Rakshasa over to Chandragupta's camp, and the position of ministership is offered to Rakshasa as soon as he acknowledges defeat. He accepts the post, and the play ends on this note of reconciliation—another reminder of Vishakadatta's faithful application of the rules of the *Natyashastra*. And it is interesting to note that while the play embodies a political "morality not a whit superior to that of the Italian school"—why Wilson mentions this at all is difficult to understand, because even the Mahabharata speaks only of two kinds of political wisdom, straight and crooked, and both in the final analysis expedient—what is remarkable and "redeeming" is the "inviolable and devoted fidelity," such as we see in Bhagurayana, "which appears as the uniform characteristic of servants, emissaries, and friends: a singular feature in the Hindu character which it has not yet wholly lost." The orthodox *tika* on the play, by a Maithili Brahmin named Vatesvara Mishra, gives a double interpretation of *The Signet Ring,* stating that it teaches the nature of statecraft on one level, and is dramatic entertainment of an intellectual kind on the other. But there is surely a third approach possible: the play extols the ethics of loyalty, which survives the corroding effects of devious fraud and shabby conspiracy and can only be transferred to the service of another in the event of a moral change in the man who transfers it. Rakshasa is tricked into surrendering, but he did the pure act in surrendering—and this is what matters, not the right, or wrong, or absurd act—because he selflessly desired to save a friend from execution. As a result, we do not question his integrity when he does agree to be Chandragupta's minister—we can trust the man, we have been given a revealing glimpse of his moral fiber.

Personal advantage is never the point at issue, for that would spoil the rasa. Chanakya does what he does not for himself, but for his king, and when the task is accomplished—all cunning passion spent—he gladly retires to make room for the new minister. Rakshasa does what he does because he wishes to revenge the murder of his king, wanting neither "fame nor dignity" for himself.

*The Signet Ring of Rakshasa* is "one of the great Sanskrit dramas," says Dr. Keith, "although in India itself its merits have long been underrated." The plot, though complex in detail, subserves everything to one action—

the reconciliation of Rakshasa. The two chief characters, Chanakya and Rakshasa, are splendidly contrasted. "Chanakya is violent and inexorable; Rakshasa gentle and relenting. Chanakya's ruling principle is pride of caste; Rakshasa's, attachment to his friends and sovereign. Chanakya revenges wrongs done to himself; Rakshasa, those offered to them he loves. Chanakya with his impetuous passions combines deep design; Rakshasa, notwithstanding his greater temperance, is a bungler in contrivance, and a better soldier than plotter." The play, then, becomes a shrewd *mélange,* expertly blended. It has a complex unfolding of plot juxtaposed with an uncomplicated central task whose performance is the play's main concern; a subtle balancing of antithetical personalities and camps; and a repeated stress of the virtue of "word well given and well kept" within the framework of a political dharma. That should suffice; it is not necessary here to admire such technical points as the ease with which the signet ring episode and others like it are handled and fitted integrally into the cunning mosaic of the play itself.

VISHAKADATTA

*Birthplace:* Probably Pataliputra (the modern Patna), northeast India.
*Date of birth:* C. ninth century A.D. The mention of the lunar eclipse in the prelude to the play almost certainly alludes to the event of December 2, 860 A.D.

# Characters

Chanakya, *minister of Chandragupta*

Sarngarava, *servant to Chanakya*

Spy (Nipunaka), *in Chanakya's pay*

Female Guard, *named Sonottara*

Siddharthaka, *spy in Chanakya's pay*

Chandanadasa, *merchant friend of Rakshasa*

Snake Charmer, *Viradhagupta in disguise; spy in Chanakya's pay*

Rakshasa, *minister of Nanda*

Chamberlain

Priyamvadaka, *maid to Rakshasa*

Viradhagupta, *spy in Chanakya's pay*

Sakatadasa, *friend of Rakshasa*

Chamberlain, *for Chandragupta*

Chandragupta, *Emperor*

Attendant

Two Poets' Voices

Gatekeeper

Karabhaka, *spy in Rakshasa's pay*

Doorkeeper

A Man

Malayaketu, *son of King Parvataka (Parvateshvara) and ally of Rakshasa*

Chamberlain, *for Malayaketu*

Bhagurayana, *spy in Chanakya's pay*

Jivasiddhi, *spy in monk's disguise, in Chanakya's pay*

Bhasuraka, *Bhagurayana's servant*

Servant, *to Rakshasa*

Samiddhartaka, *spy in Chanakya's pay*

Vajraloman, *executioner*

Bilvapatra, *executioner*

Chandanadasa's Wife

Chandanadasa's Son

Doorkeeper (Female)

# ACT I

## HOW THE SIGNET RING WAS ACQUIRED

CHANAKYA *enters. He speaks angrily, rubbing his head with both fists.*

CHANAKYA. So! Who dares to challenge Chandragupta—while I live! What fool will thrust his hand into the bloodstained lion's jaws? The Nandas—do they dare? Will that foolish family play the singed moth to my angry fire? *He shouts.* Sarngarava!

SARNGARAVA, *entering.* Sir, you called?

CHANAKYA. I must relax, dear boy, I must relax.

SARNGARAVA. There's a cane chair in the hall, sir. I'll get it.

CHANAKYA. I'm worried. . .matters of state. Not angry with my students, no—though a teacher has a right to that. Thank you, Sarngarava. *He sits in the cane chair brought by* SARNGARAVA. Tell me, what's all this I hear about the people gossiping? Rakshasa has lost his head and signed a treaty with Malayaketu, and both are plotting against Chandragupta, is that it? Rakshasa's a Nanda, I know. And I've sworn to wipe out every last Nanda. So the matter is in my hands—that's what the people say. Well, we shall see. Anger cools off, like a forest fire—only it takes time. But if the person you're angry with is absent, it works faster. All right, I've scorched a good many young Nandas in my time, and the fire will abate, the fire will abate. The people have seen me in action: Nanda's family destroyed, an elephant mauled by a lion and sent toppling down a hillside. Nine Nandas uprooted —a good score! And all for a good cause, the glory of our great King Chandragupta. But Rakshasa is not yet taken care of. Rakshasa makes trouble. With Rakshasa still going strong, Chandragupta feels unsafe. Brilliant, brave Rakshasa, the finest of the Nandas—and it's well known that no Nanda bows to Chandragupta. We could neutralize this Nanda, but making him inactive isn't enough. You remember, Sarngarava, how poor Sarvarthasiddhi had to be killed in the ashrama—did that help? Still Rakshasa defies Chandragupta; and now, with Malayaketu for an ally, he'll stop at nothing. *He gazes intently into space, as if recognizing a face.*

Brilliant Rakshasa! You can teach us a trick or two. A genius of a minister, a devil! Bootlickers—we always have plenty of them, but when the hand-outs fail they disappear. Not Rakshasa. He remains loyal to the Nandas, even when he knows they're in trouble. The devil—he has something in him; but we'll get him on our side yet. No, Rakshasa, you won't escape us, we need devotion like yours. And you'll come gladly, *wanting* to come. A wise servant is all right, but greater than wisdom is honesty; and bravery is good, but we like loyalty better. Well, I won't lose sleep over this: the plan's in motion, and we can only wait to see how it works. First we removed Parvataka, by getting him to sleep with a poison girl, and the blame got put on Rakshasa. Next we packed off Parvataka's son Malayaketu, who had somehow got wind of the assassination; that was easy—Bhagurayana just whispered a few words in his ear, "Chanakya has murdered your father, get out of here while the going's good." Then we shut up Mala-yaketu's mouth by surrounding him with spies, making sure the news wouldn't leak out to Rakshasa. Yes, our spies are everywhere; they know a thousand languages, they have a thousand eyes, they travel in a thousand disguises. No friend of Rakshasa in the city of Pataliputra is safe, while Chandragupta is guarded day and night by a band of faithful servants, trained to detect assassins and poisoners. There is that excellent Brahmin—Indusarman—who knows the art of spying inside out. He's disguised as a Jain monk, Jivasiddhi, and by now should be getting friendly with the ministers of Rakshasa. Everything is arranged; the plan ripens. The only trouble is that Chandragupta doesn't take much interest in these activities. Men are like elephants: strong when strong, otherwise senile.

*A* SPY *enters, carrying a cloth woven with designs sacred to the god of death.*

SPY, *speaking in a chanting voice.* Salute Yama, god of death! Mocker of other gods, taker-away of life! Let us swear by the great god Yama.

SARNGARAVA. Who let you in?

SPY. Whose house is this, good Brahmin?

SARNGARAVA. Our guru, Chanakya's.

SPY, *laughing in a hard tone.* A friend's house, a soul-brother's. Let me in—I shall spread this cloth of Yama on the floor and instruct Chanakya on the nature of duty.

SARNGARAVA. You silly fool, what can you know about duty that our guru doesn't already know?

SPY. Now don't get worked up, good Brahmin. No man's omniscient, you know. Your guru knows *this*—so much. And men like me know *that*—so much.

SARNGARAVA. Bah!

SPY. You mean your guru's omniscient. Good. Then he can tell us, the moon being called Chandra, by whom is Chandra not liked?

SARNGARAVA. Precious bit of knowledge, that—isn't it?

SPY. Your guru will know how precious it is. Ask him. You of course know that Chandra is not liked by the lotuses that bloom in the day.

CHANAKYA, *overhearing*. So he knows the enemies of Chandragupta.

SARNGARAVA. Come to the point, man, come to the point. Where's all this getting us?

SPY. This is the point, but. . .

SARNGARAVA. But what?

SPY. You will have to listen to it carefully.

CHANAKYA. You there! I'll listen to you carefully. Come over here—you have nothing to be afraid of.

SPY. Greetings to you, sir.

CHANAKYA. And to you. *He looks at the* SPY *closely, then speaks to himself.* But this is Nipunaka, our good spy, who keeps an eye on the morale of the subjects. *Aloud.* Well, sir, what brings you here? Sit down, sit down. *The* SPY *sits on the floor.* Now then, let's get down to brass tacks. How do they feel toward His Majesty, Chandragupta?

SPY. Most loyally, sir. The causes of disaffection have been removed—by you—and His Majesty is popular. At the same time there are three people in the city who hate the king. Their hearts are given to Rakshasa: he has their affection and their faith.

CHANAKYA, *angrily*. The fools! They had better look after their hearts more carefully! Who are they? Do you know their names?

SPY. Sir, if I did not know them by name, how could I report them?

CHANAKYA. Then *who* are they?

SPY. There is the Jain monk, sir, who expresses loyal sentiments for Rakshasa.

CHANAKYA, *to himself*. The Jain monk.

SPY. Named Jivasiddhi. He was instructed by Rakshasa to use a poison girl against His Majesty, Chandragupta.

CHANAKYA, *to himself*. Jivasiddhi? He's *our* spy. *Aloud*. And the others?

SPY. A dear friend of Rakshasa's named Sakatadasa. No Brahmin, sir. A Kayastha.

CHANAKYA, *chuckling to himself*. Kayasthas are easily tackled. But we'll have to be careful. . . . However, Siddharthaka is already posing as his friend and keeping an eye on his movements. *Aloud*. The third?

SPY. The chief of the Jewelers' Guild, Chandanadasa. Rakshasa left his wife in Chandanadasa's house for protection when he fled the city.

CHANAKYA, *to himself*. Chandanadasa is a problem. And if Rakshasa leaves his wife with him, he must be quite something of a man. *Aloud*. And how do you know Rakshasa left his wife in Chandanadasa's house?

SPY. This ring, sir, will explain everything.

CHANAKYA *takes the ring and examines it closely. Upon finding* RAK-SHASA's *name on it, he mutters in pleased tones to himself*. The bird has flown into our net. What luck! *Aloud*. How did you get this ring? Tell me the whole story, in detail.

SPY. Well, sir, I was at my duties as usual—you had asked me to keep an eye on the people. I was carrying this sacred cloth of Yama with me, so no one would be too suspicious, and I chanced to enter Chandanadasa's house. He's the chief of the Jewelers' Guild, sir, as I said. So I entered, spread out the cloth, and began to chant shop like a regular priest. . . .

CHANAKYA. Go on.

SPY. I wasn't chanting long when a boy—couldn't have been more than five—a very good-looking boy, sir—he comes up and looks curiously at me. As any boy would, sir. But he had hardly stepped into the room when there was a hell of a hue and cry from the women inside, and one of them suddenly rushed in, scolded him, lifted him up, and took him away. In her nervousness this ring—you can see from the size it's a man's ring, sir—slipped off her finger, bounced on the floor, and came bowing (as it were, sir) close to my feet, suddenly hushed (as it were, sir) after so much excitement, like a shy bride in front of her elders. I noticed the name Rakshasa on it, and quickly made off with it. . . . That's the story, sir.

CHANAKYA. A good piece of work. You'll be rewarded for this. Now you may go.

*The* SPY *leaves.* SARNGARAVA *enters.*

SARNGARAVA. Sir?

CHANAKYA. Bring me ink and paper.

SARNGARAVA *does so, and* CHANAKYA *prepares to write.*

CHANAKYA, *to himself.* This needs thought. . .for this letter will finish off Rakshasa. *He looks up as a female* GUARD *enters.* What news, Sonottara?

GUARD. A message from His Majesty, sir. He would like to have your permission to perform the sacred rites, and wishes to give away his ornaments to deserving Brahmins.

CHANAKYA, *happily to himself.* Good! Just what I wanted. *Aloud.* Sonottara, tell His Majesty that he knows the best time for performing the rites, and that I appreciate his asking me for permission. About the gifts, please inform His Majesty that they are of special excellence and that I shall soon send some deserving Brahmins to receive them.

*The* GUARD *leaves.*

CHANAKYA. Sarngarava, tell the three Visvavasu brothers to receive the ornaments on our behalf.

SARNGARAVA. I shall do so immediately, sir. *He leaves.*

CHANAKYA. That will be the second part of the letter. But what do I write in the first? *He reflects.* Shall I. . .Yes! The spies tell me that among the Mlechha kings five have given their allegiance to Rakshasa: Chitravarman, king of Kaluta; Sinhananda, king of Malaya; Pushkaraksha of Kashmere; Sindhusena of Sindhu; and Meghanada, the lord of the Parasikas. These names go in; Death's accountant will erase them. Five birds with one stone—or shall I leave it happily vague? No names at all. . . that's better. *He writes.* Sarngarava!

SARNGARAVA *enters.*

A learned Brahmin's handwriting is always illegible. Ask Siddharthaka to give this to Sakatadasa, who will copy it out neatly. But see he doesn't know it's my letter. And let the cover remain blank.

SARNGARAVA *goes out with the letter.*

Malayaketu is now in our hands!

SIDDHARTHAKA, *entering.* Here is the letter, sir, written in Sakatadasa's hand.

CHANAKYA, *looking at the letter.* What a lovely hand he has! It's a pleasure to read it. *He reads the letter through.* Seal it with this signet ring.

CHANAKYA *gives* RAKSHASA's *signet ring to* SIDDHARTHAKA, *who uses it to seal the letter.*

SIDDHARTHAKA. Anything else, sir?

CHANAKYA. Yes, there is work for you, Siddharthaka. Very confidential work.

SIDDHARTHAKA. I am honored.

CHANAKYA. Let's see. First, a wink to the executioners—that's the secret sign. They will pretend to run about aimlessly in confusion. Then allow Sakatadasa to escape—*and see to it that he reaches Rakshasa safely.* This is most important. Naturally you will accept from Rakshasa a modest reward, his token of appreciation for the way in which you have saved his friend's life. Continue to serve Rakshasa diligently for some time. . . .

Then, when the enemies close in—*He whispers in* SIDDHARTHAKA's *ear.* You can do it. You are reliable.

SIDDHARTHAKA. It will be done, sir.

CHANAKYA. Sarngarava!

SARNGARAVA *enters.*

Have the following announcement proclaimed throughout the city by Kalapasika and Dandapasika: "In the name of His Majesty Chandragupta, the Jain monk Jivasiddhi, who on orders from Rakshasa murdered Parvataka with the help of a poison girl, is hereby disgraced and exiled from the city, after he has publicly confessed his crime."

SARNGARAVA. I will have it done, sir. *He takes a step toward the door.*

CHANAKYA. No, wait. "And it is further announced that, in the name of His Majesty Chandragupta, the conspirator Sakatadasa, who takes orders from Rakshasa, is to be impaled on the stake, after he has publicly confessed his crime, and all the members of his family are to be imprisoned."

SARNGARAVA *leaves.*

CHANAKYA, *anxiously.* If only the cunning Rakshasa can be roped in!

SIDDHARTHAKA. I am ready, sir. Are there any further orders?

CHANAKYA, *handing him the letter and signet ring.* None. You may go. And good luck!

SIDDHARTHAKA. Thank you, sir. *He leaves.*

SARNGARAVA, *entering.* Sir, Kalapasika and Dandapasika will soon make the announcements.

CHANAKYA. Good. And now, can you get me the chief of the Jewelers' Guild, Chandanadasa? I want a word with him.

SARNGARAVA. Yes, sir. *He leaves, and returns with* CHANDANADASA. This way, sir.

CHANDANADASA, *to himself.* Even an innocent man gets jittery when summoned by Chanakya. So I should be dying of fear—maybe being guilty gives me courage. Anyway I have arranged for the safety of Rakshasa's family. I asked Dhanasena and others to remove them to a safer place than my home, where I know the swine Chanakya would order a surprise search.

SARNGARAVA. This way, sir. *They approach* CHANAKYA. This gentleman is Chandanadasa, chief of the Jewelers' Guild.

CHANAKYA. I see. You are welcome, Chandanadasa. Please sit down. *He points to the cane seat.*

CHANDANADASA, *bowing*. Sir, undeserved courtesy pains more than insult. I shall sit on the ground.

CHANAKYA. You hurt me, Chandanadasa. I give you only elementary courtesy, which I am sure you deserve. No, do sit here.

CHANDANADASA, *to himself*. The rogue mocks me. *Aloud*. Thank you, sir. *He places himself in the cane chair.*

CHANAKYA. And how's business, Chandanadasa? Prospering?

CHANDANADASA, *to himself*. Such concern!—a dangerous sign. *Aloud*. Not bad, sir. You know how things are.

CHANAKYA. Don't Chandragupta's defects make the people think regretfully of the glories of past kings?

CHANDANADASA, *holding his hands to his ears in feigned horror*. Oh, sir! The subjects are as delighted with His Majesty as they are with the full moon on an autumn night.

CHANAKYA. That is pleasant news. But kings expect a return from happy subjects.

CHANDANADASA. In what way can I help, sir?

CHANAKYA. Chandanadasa, we are living in Chandragupta's reign, not Nanda's. Nanda loved wealth; he loved to be among merchants. Chandragupta loves only peace; he wants his subjects to be happy.

CHANDANADASA. I am glad to hear it, sir.

CHANAKYA. And the best way to make yourself happy is to make him happy. How can that be done?

CHANDANADASA. Tell me, sir.

CHANAKYA. I'll be blunt—by having a healthy attitude toward His Majesty.

CHANDANADASA. Who hasn't a healthy attitude toward His Majesty?

CHANAKYA. You, for instance—

CHANDANADASA, *in feigned horror*. Sir! Not me! How can a grass-blade fight fire?

CHANAKYA. You are sheltering Rakshasa's family in your house.

CHANDANADASA. A damned lie. There's no one in my house.

CHANAKYA. Don't lose your temper, Chandanadasa. The birds may have flown. I have had cases when that happened before. And sometimes the poor man has had no choice: the birds are thrust in his hands while the guilty escape, and he has to look after their safety.

CHANDANADASA. That's exactly what happened, sir. At one time I did have some of Rakshasa's family in my house.

CHANAKYA. First, a damned lie—and now this!

CHANDANADASA. A small quibble, sir. I'm sorry.

CHANAKYA. As long as Chandragupta is king, even small quibbles won't do. I want no more hocus-pocus. Where are they?

CHANDANADASA. But I told you, sir, they were with me once.

CHANAKYA. Where are they now?

CHANDANADASA. I don't know.

CHANAKYA, *smiling*. The clouds frown over your head, Chandanadasa. You had better know.

CHANDANADASA, *to himself*. He's right. But what can I do?

CHANAKYA. And make a note of this, Chandanadasa: Rakshasa won't destroy Chandragupta as Chandragupta destroyed Nanda.

*Shouts are heard offstage.*

CHANAKYA. Sarngarava, what's the matter?

SARNGARAVA *goes out and returns with the news.* It's the Jain monk Jivasiddhi, sir, being exiled from the city for plotting against His Majesty.

CHANAKYA. A monk! Well, the law favors no one. Let him pay the penalty. You heard, Chandanadasa? Chandragupta is in no mood to tolerate mischief against him. I warn you again—hand them over.

CHANDANADASA. They are not in my house.

*Further shouting is heard offstage.*

CHANAKYA. What now?

SARNGARAVA *again goes out and returns.* It's Sakatadasa, sir, being led to the stake for his impalement. . . .

CHANAKYA. For the last time, Chandanadasa, turn over Rakshasa's wife to us. You shelter her at risk to your own wife. I do not like jokes: your life is in danger.

CHANDANADASA. Why do you try to frighten me, sir? I would not hand her over to you if she *was* in my house. How can I hand her over if she isn't?

CHANAKYA. And, as far as you're concerned, that's that?

CHANDANADASA. That's that.

CHANAKYA, *to himself.* The man has courage—nothing will frighten him. . . . *Aloud.* That's that, eh?

CHANDANADASA. I've already answered that, sir.

CHANAKYA. You miserable traitor! *He shouts.* You'll find out what it means to defy Chandragupta!

CHANDANADASA. I am ready to pay whatever the penalty may be for the crime I have committed.

CHANAKYA. Sarngarava, tell Kalapasika and Dandapasika to throw him in prison. . . . No, wait—not that. Confiscate his property and tell the guard Vijayapala to tie him up and keep an eye on him and his wife and son until the matter is reported to His Majesty. The king will personally issue the order of execution.

SARNGARAVA. This way, sir. *He leads* CHANDANADASA *out.*

CHANDANADASA. I'm coming. *To himself.* I should count myself lucky that this is happening because of the kindness I did a friend and not because I committed any crime.

SARNGARAVA *and* CHANDANADASA *leave.*

CHANAKYA, *joyfully.* That settles Rakshasa! I don't think he'll be able to bear the misfortune of Chandanadasa, certainly not if he's the close friend he makes out to be.

*Shouts are heard offstage;* SARNGARAVA *enters.*

SARNGARAVA. Sir, Siddharthaka has escaped with Sakatadasa, who was about to be executed.

CHANAKYA, *to himself.* Well done, Chanakya—that's a good start. *Aloud.* What! Escaped with Sakatadasa? *He feigns anger.* What are you waiting for? Tell Bhagurayana to give chase and bring them back.

SARNGARAVA *goes out and returns.* Sir, Bhagurayana has escaped too.

CHANAKYA, *to himself.* He has, has he? Good. The plan takes shape. *Aloud.* Well, tell Bhadrabhata, tell Dingarata, tell Balagupta, Rajasina and Rohitaksha, tell Vijayarama to pursue the rascal and bring him here immediately.

SARNGARAVA *again goes out and returns. Speaking dejectedly.* Sir, I don't know what's gone wrong, but Bhadrabhata and the others are nowhere to be found. They too fled at dawn.

CHANAKYA, *to himself.* May good luck go with them. *Aloud.* What's the matter, Sarngarava? Don't look so sad. They were blackguards—it's good they've gone. *To himself.* I have you where I want you, Rakshasa. As a wild elephant is tamed, so shall you be tamed, and your strength and brilliance added to our side.

CHANAKYA *and* SARNGARAVA *both leave.*

C U R T A I N

## ACT II

### WHAT RAKSHASA THOUGHT

*A* SNAKE CHARMER *comes onto the fore-stage in front of the curtain and speaks, accompanying his words with pantomime.*

SNAKE CHARMER. A man who knows the arts of poisoning and politics will know how to deal with serpents and satraps. *He looks up at the sky.* Me? Who's *me?* Me's a snake charmer, my name is Jirnavisa. You want to play with my snakes? And who are you, sir? A servant of the king? You are? Then you play with a snake already, and have no need of mine. It's a wise man who said: amateur snake charmers, riders of mad elephants, and king's servants flirt with death. A very wise man. So you don't want to play with my snakes. Well... *He looks up at the sky again.* And you, sir, you are interested in my basket, what is in it? There are snakes in it. You want to see the snakes in it? This isn't the place to show snakes. Come to my house, and look for all you are worth. This is Rakshasa's house?—and men like me aren't wanted here? Sir, perhaps men like *you* aren't wanted here, but for men like me this is just the place. *To himself.* He's off too. . . . On the one hand, there's Chandragupta, helped by the brilliance of Chanakya; on the other, there's Malayaketu, helped by Rakshasa. And a ding-dong battle between them! I must see Rakshasa today.

*The curtain rises on* RAKSHASA's *camp, revealing* RAKSHASA *in a sad, anxious mood.*

RAKSHASA. I am a painter without canvas, my statecraft made useless by the destruction of the Nandas, for whom I worked so faithfully. Now I am a slave of Malayaketu; yet through him I shall still serve my dead master, the glorious Nanda. O goddess of fortune, fickle mistress! why did you desert the excellent Nanda and turn to Chandragupta? Why choose a lowborn when the finest families of the land importuned you? But women are like that, whimsical and strange, ignorant of the best qualities of the best men. But we shall see. The tables may still be turned. Keeping my wife in the safety of my friend Chandanadasa's house was a good idea—my followers in the city will not think I have deserted them and fled with my family. Sakatadasa has money to feed assassins and poisoners and spies. And Jivasiddhi is a whole fifth column by himself—a sharp man, Jivasiddhi. Why should I be apprehensive?

CHAMBERLAIN, *entering*. Greetings to you, sir.

RAKSHASA. Priyamvadaka, a seat for the honored Jajali.

PRIYAMVADAKA, *coming forward with a chair*. Sit here, sir.

CHAMBERLAIN, *seating himself*. Prince Malayaketu says he is sorry the noble Rakshasa does not pay proper attention to his dress these days, and sends these from his personal jewelry case as a gift. *He offers ornaments*.

RAKSHASA. I thank the prince for his kindness, and would like to say that I have decided not to decorate my body with ornaments until the day I am able to complete my mission by placing this throne of gold in the Suganga palace of Chandragupta.

CHAMBERLAIN. With you as our minister, that will be easy. Do not disappoint the prince.

RAKSHASA. I shall not. *He puts on the ornaments*.

CHAMBERLAIN. With your permission I leave.

RAKSHASA. I salute you, noble Jajali.

*The* CHAMBERLAIN *leaves*.

RAKSHASA. Priyamvadaka, isn't there someone at the gate?

PRIYAMVADAKA, *walking up to the* SNAKE CHARMER. Who are you, sir?

SNAKE CHARMER. Me? A poor snake charmer. My name is Jirnavisa. I'll do a show for the minister.

PRIYAMVADAKA. Wait. *He returns to* RAKSHASA. A snake charmer, sir, wishes to perform for you.

RAKSHASA. Snakes! Not now, Priyamvadaka. Pay him, and tell him to come again some other time.

PRIYAMVADAKA, *going back to the* SNAKE CHARMER. You are a lucky fellow, snake charmer. You'll get the money without doing the show.

SNAKE CHARMER. Yes, but tell the minister I am not only a snake charmer, but a pretty good poet in Prakrit, as this little leaf will prove.

PRIYAMVADAKA, *taking the leaf to* RAKSHASA. Sir, he says he's a poet in Prakrit, and sends you this leaflet as proof.

RAKSHASA, *reading aloud from the leaf.*
  The bee drinks juice,
  And sucks the flower dry,
  The bee's juice helps
  Others by and by.

*In a reflective mood* RAKSHASA *continues speaking*. This bee is a spy who has news to help me by and by. I had clean forgotten him in the press of state business. Send him in, Priyamvadaka. Not a bad rhymer. He must be Viradhagupta, disguised as a snake charmer.

PRIYAMVADAKA *ushers in the* SNAKE CHARMER.

SNAKE CHARMER. I salute you, sir.

RAKSHASA. Look, Viradha—*He checks himself*. Why, what a beard you have, sir! So you're a snake charmer and a poet. Priyamvadaka, have the hall cleared, and go about your work. I wish to relax with a snake show.

PRIYAMVADAKA *and others leave*.

RAKSHASA. Viradhagupta, my friend, sit here. . . . Poor Viradhagupta, who once served King Nanda, I am sorry for you—reduced to such a condition.

VIRADHAGUPTA. The good times will return.

RAKSHASA. Tell me, how are things in Pataliputra?

VIRADHAGUPTA. A bagful of news. I don't know where to begin.

RAKSHASA. Begin with the assassins and poisoners.

VIRADHAGUPTA. Pataliputra was besieged by Chandragupta, assisted by the Shakas, Yavanas, Kiratas, Kambojas, Parasikas, Balhikas, and others— all whipped into action by the schemes of Chanakya like furious waves breaking on a beach.

RAKSHASA, *drawing his sword excitedly*. Who attacks Pataliputra as long as I am alive? Praviraka, march the bowmen to the city walls! The elephants to the gates! Friends, fearless warriors, follow me—to the walls! Death to the enemy!

VIRADHAGUPTA. Sir, sir, all that's past. . . .

RAKSHASA. Yes . . . past. But just now it returned. *He throws down his sword and speaks in verse.*
   I remembered the good King Nanda,
   I remembered his kindness to me.
   I am sorry. Please go on.

VIRADHAGUPTA. So His Majesty, Sarvarthasiddhi, retreated, and escaped by the secret tunnel to an ashrama. And in the confusion Parvateshvara was killed by the poison girl you had employed to murder Chandragupta.

RAKSHASA. The poison girl killed Parvateshvara!

VIRADHAGUPTA. That's fate. What can a man do?

RAKSHASA. And then?

VIRADHAGUPTA. Prince Malayaketu, hearing news of his father's murder, fled, and Chanakya ordered the carpenters of Pataliputra to get busy decorating the eastern gate in honor of Chandragupta's victory. The expert artisan Daruvarman put the finishing touches on the golden arches, and they are now supposed to do up the inside of the palace. Chanakya was proud as a peacock, and promised a splendid reward to Daruvarman.

RAKSHASA. Daruvarman had no choice in the matter, poor fellow. Go on.

VIRADHAGUPTA. Chanakya had it announced publicly that Chandragupta would make his royal entry into the city at the stroke of midnight, and punctually, at the stroke of midnight, the king entered. Vairochaka, the brother of the poisoned Paravateshvara, sat beside Chandragupta on the throne.

RAKSHASA. Had a bribe been given to the treacherous Vairochaka?

VIRADHAGUPTA. Yes, sir. Half the kingdom, in exchange for his help.

RAKSHASA, *to himself*. The clever swine—this way he pacifies the people.

They'd never have endured the destruction of Paravateshvara otherwise.

VIRADHAGUPTA. And when Vairochaka had been put on the throne, Chanakya dressed him in the most glittering ornaments—flowers, flawless pearls, gem-studded crown—until you could hardly make out that it was Vairochaka. It was at Chanakya's insistence that Vairochaka mounted the elephant called Chandralekha, and entered the palace of the king of Nanda at the head of Chandragupta's allies. There Daruvarman, in a fit of mistaken folly, thinking Vairochaka to be Chandragupta, stood ready with the shooting weapon. And Varvaraka, Chandragupta's mahout, whom you had also paid, thinking Vairochaka to be Chandragupta, got ready with the dagger he had concealed in the golden staff.

RAKSHASA. I know what's coming.

VIRADHAGUPTA. The elephant of Vairochaka bolted. Daruvarman shot the weapon, his aim was wide, the bolt fell on poor Varvaraka, who died instantly. Daruvarman, fearful of his life, leaped from the platform on Vairochaka. That was the end of Vairochaka.

RAKSHASA. This would happen! Chandragupta, of course, escaped; and two of my finest assassins died. But what about Daruvarman?

VIRADHAGUPTA. The soldiers behind Vairochaka trampled him to death.

RAKSHASA. He was a good man, Daruvarman. I shall miss him. Do you know anything about the doctor Abhayadatta?

VIRADHAGUPTA. He did what he could.

RAKSHASA. You mean he—killed—Chandragupta.

VIRADHAGUPTA. No, Chandragupta escaped.

RAKSHASA. Then what do you mean, "He did what he could"?

VIRADHAGUPTA. Well, sir, he had the medicine ready, suitably mixed with poison. But the devilish Chanakya thought he saw the wine change color, and he whispered, "Your Majesty, don't drink from that cup."

RAKSHASA. What happened to Abhayadatta?

VIRADHAGUPTA. He was forced to drink out of the cup himself. He died. In great pain.

RAKSHASA, *sadly*. Another brilliant mind gone. What about Pramodaka, whom I paid to hide in Chandragupta's bedroom?

VIRADHAGUPTA. The same story.

RAKSHASA. What? What?

VIRADHAGUPTA. The fool began having a gay time with the money you had given him, squandered it right and left. When cross-examined, he couldn't explain himself; Chanakya tortured him to death.

RAKSHASA. Fate's against us! What about Bibhatsaka and his group? Weren't they supposed to enter the palace by the underground passage? I paid them to strike down Chandragupta in his sleep.

VIRADHAGUPTA. A terrible story.

RAKSHASA. Why? How could Chanakya find out?

VIRADHAGUPTA. He did find out. He noticed a row of ants in the bedroom carrying rice grains, and he scented hidden enemies. "Burn the room," he ordered. It was done; and Bibhatsaka and his friends, choked by smoke, groped toward the door, but they perished in the terrible fire.

RAKSHASA. That swine has all the luck! What I do turns against me.

VIRADHAGUPTA. We can't give up now, sir. The useless don't even start, they are so afraid of hitches cropping up later on. The chickenhearted give up midway. Only the very best carry on to the end.

RAKSHASA. I know. But go on, give me all the details.

VIRADHAGUPTA. Chanakya's next step was to round up all suspects—our friends—and clap them in jail.

RAKSHASA. Who?

VIRADHAGUPTA. The Jain monk Jivasiddhi is one, arrested and exiled from the city.

RAKSHASA, *to himself*. He's a monk. He hasn't much to lose. *Aloud.* Why was he exiled?

VIRADHAGUPTA. Chanakya accused him of killing Parvateshvara with the help of the poison girl you employed.

RAKSHASA. The rogue, he dumps the blame on us.

VIRADHAGUPTA. Sakatadasa was impaled on the stake, on the charge that he had incited Daruvarman and others to treason against Chandragupta.

RAKSHASA, *sadly*. Sakatadasa, my friend, you did not deserve such a fate. But you are a hero in a noble cause: you should not be mourned, for we are the ones who need pity—the living who have seen the downfall of Nanda and continue to live.

VIRADHAGUPTA. You did your best, sir.

RAKSHASA. And the best wasn't good enough, we couldn't save the king. It doesn't matter; carry on with your story. I am prepared for the worst.

VIRADHAGUPTA. But Chandanadasa got wind of what was coming, and secretly removed your wife to a safer place.

RAKSHASA. Thereby exposing himself to the wrath of Chanakya.

VIRADHAGUPTA. I should think, sir, better the wrath of Chanakya than betrayal of a friend.

RAKSHASA. Go on.

VIRADHAGUPTA. When he refused to tell Chanakya where he had sent her, Chanakya lost his temper and he was—

RAKSHASA. Killed—not *killed?*

VIRADHAGUPTA. No, sir, but his property confiscated, and he, his wife, and his son all clapped into jail.

RAKSHASA. What was the point in saying that my wife had escaped? His wife and son imprisoned—a terrible punishment.

PRIYAMVADAKA *enters and speaks to* RAKSHASA. Sir, Sakatadasa is at the gate, and wishes to see you.

RAKSHASA. What! Are you sure?

PRIYAMVADAKA. Why should I lie, sir?

RAKSHASA. What does this mean, Viradhagupta?

VIRADHAGUPTA. I don't know, sir. It seems luck's on our side.

RAKSHASA. What are you staring at, you? Hurry up! Show him in!

PRIYAMVADAKA *leaves and returns with* SAKATADASA, *who is followed by* SIDDHARTHAKA.

SAKATADASA, *to himself*. What a nightmare I've been through! The drums beating all sense out of my head, the death garland around my neck—oh. . .*He sees* RAKSHASA. The great Rakshasa, the most loyal of friends, what a relief to see him.

RAKSHASA. Friend Sakatadasa, I can hardly believe my eyes. Come close to me, let me embrace you. *They embrace.* Sit down, Sakatadasa. Tell me, how did you escape?

SAKATADASA. My good friend Siddharthaka here got me past the executioners.

RAKSHASA, *joyfully*. Siddharthaka, you are my friend too. Take these as a small token of my gratitude for your favor. *He takes off his ornaments and hands them to* SIDDHARTHAKA, *who takes them and falls at* RAKSHASA's *feet*.

SIDDHARTHAKA, *aside*. Now to do as Chanakya ordered. *Aloud.* Thank you, sir—your goodness overwhelms me. But I am new here, sir. I do not feel safe with so many ornaments. May I keep them in the treasure chamber till the time comes when I need them? And may I put this signet ring with them too, sir?

RAKSHASA. But of course. Sakatadasa, you'll see to that.

SAKATADASA. Yes, sir. *He examines the ring.* That's strange: this has your name on it.

RAKSHASA, *to himself*. I gave it to my wife when I left Pataliputra. How did this fellow get it? *Aloud.* Siddharthaka, pardon my curiosity, but how did you come across this ring?

SIDDHARTHAKA. In Pataliputra, in front of Chandanadasa's house. He's the chief of the Jewelers' Guild.

RAKSHASA. Hmm. Just as I thought.

SIDDHARTHAKA. Sir?

RAKSHASA. An expensive thing like this—where else but in front of the jeweler's house?

SAKATADASA. Siddharthaka, my friend, this ring has Rakshasa's name on it. I'm sure you won't mind giving it to him. He will pay you more than it's worth.

SIDDHARTHAKA. I will be honored if he accepts it as a gift.

RAKSHASA. Sakatadasa, keep this ring with you and use it for all official correspondence from now on.

SIDDHARTHAKA. I have a request to make, sir.

RAKSHASA. Make it, Siddharthaka.

SIDDHARTHAKA. May I stay here and serve you? I cannot return to Pataliputra after what I have done.

RAKSHASA. You may stay as long as you like. I would have asked you myself, but I didn't know your mind.

SIDDHARTHAKA. I am honored, sir.

RAKSHASA. Make him comfortable, Sakatadasa. See he lacks nothing.

SAKATADASA *and* SIDDHARTHAKA *leave.*

RAKSHASA. To resume, Viradhagupta. Do the subjects of Chandragupta appreciate our tactics?

VIRADHAGUPTA. They do, sir—at least what they see of them.

RAKSHASA. What do they see?

VIRADHAGUPTA. Well, sir, they see that Chandragupta is not too well pleased with Chanakya, because Malayaketu escaped. And they see that Chanakya thinks a lot of himself these days and disregards Chandragupta's orders. This has been my experience too.

RAKSHASA. That's refreshing news. Viradhagupta, disguise yourself as a snake charmer again and go to Pataliputra. Get in touch with a poet there, named Stavakalasha. He's one of us. Tell him to get busy with poems praising Chandragupta and working him up against Chanakya. Whatever news he wishes to send, he can send through Karabhaka. And make sure all this is kept secret.

VIRADHAGUPTA. Yes, sir.

VIRADHAGUPTA *leaves;* PRIYAMVADAKA *enters.*

PRIYAMVADAKA. Sakatadasa wishes to inform you, sir, that a set of three new ornaments is being offered for sale, and that he would like you to inspect them.

RAKSHASA. Tell him he can buy the lot from the jeweler in my name.

PRIYAMVADAKA *leaves.*

RAKSHASA. Now to send Karabhaka to Pataliputra. *He stands up.* Is there a chance of bad blood coming between Chanakya and Chandragupta? There is. I have hopes. One of them is obsessed with being king, and the other with wiping out the Nandas. The two will clash. *He leaves.*

C U R T A I N


# ACT III

### THE CONCOCTED QUARREL

*The* CHAMBERLAIN *enters before the curtain and speaks sorrowfully to himself.* Old age has gripped me; my eyes don't see, my hands and legs don't obey me. *He walks around, occasionally looking up into the sky.* Hoi! You up there—you guards of the palace!—His Majesty Chandragupta wants Pataliputra lit up for the Moonlight Festival. Decorate the terraces, brighten them up, my lads—the king wants it. *He looks up again.* Did you say the Moonlight Festival has been banned? Banned by whom? The king wants it, the king will have it. Whoever says it is banned does so at the risk of his life. Work away, my lads. Glittering chowries on the pillars, fragrant garlands everywhere. Sprinkle the grounds with sweet sandalwater, wake up the drowsy earth! You'll do it soon? Hoi, lads, do it *now!* His Majesty's here. Hurry up, hurry up!

VOICES, *calling, offstage.* Make way for the king!

CHANDRAGUPTA *and an* ATTENDANT *enter.*

CHANDRAGUPTA, *to himself.* Worry is the privilege of a good king. There's nothing to be done for himself, everything to be done for others. And they say a man who does everything for others is the best of men. Perhaps he is—but not the lord of men, not a king. For to do everything for others means to be influenced and persuaded by others; and a tool cannot be a weapon. A person who depends on others cannot really be happy, can he? What's worse, the goddess of fortune is more difficult than a courtesan. She loathes the fussy ones, flirts with the gentle, mocks the fools, rejects the learned, fears the brave, and spurns the timid. And now there's this directive from Chanakya—when the concocted quarrel is over, act like a despot. I don't like it, but it's safe to do as he says. No teacher is a hindrance as long as one does good. But when a man foolishly follows the wrong path, all teachers become a nuisance. Good men do good naturally; good men are not goaded by moral advice. *Aloud.* Chamberlain, take me to the Suganga palace.

CHAMBERLAIN. This way, Your Majesty. *They walk.* Here we are. *The king climbs the palace steps.*

CHANDRAGUPTA, *looking up.* The palace looks lovely, and autumn makes it lovelier. White strips of cloud and the autumn cranes flying, lotuses at night like a nosegay of constellations, peaceful rivers, a rich harvest, peacocks that forget to strut—a small world of perfect peace, a lesson to mankind. *He looks around him.* But why hasn't the Moonlight Festival begun? Chamberlain, what's the matter? Didn't I give orders for the Festival?

CHAMBERLAIN. Yes, Your Majesty.

CHANDRAGUPTA. Then why haven't my orders been carried out?

CHAMBERLAIN. Sire, Your Majesty's commands are obeyed by the entire world.

CHANDRAGUPTA. Where's the Festival? What's the matter with Pataliputra? Where are the ladies, their love talk murmuring lightly in the streets, their hips swaying? Where are the citizens, where are their wives? Why are they not celebrating the Festival?

CHAMBERLAIN. Sire—

CHANDRAGUPTA. What?

CHAMBERLAIN. Sire. . .

CHANDRAGUPTA. Don't "sire" me, you doddering idiot! Speak up.

CHAMBERLAIN. It's banned, sire.

CHANDRAGUPTA, *angrily*. Banned! Who banned it?

CHAMBERLAIN. I dare. . .I dare. . .not say, sire.

CHANDRAGUPTA. So! Chanakya will not even allow the citizens of Pataliputra their little pleasures? Was it Chanakya? Speak up! I'm the king!

CHAMBERLAIN. Who else would dare, sire?

CHANDRAGUPTA. Sonottara, bring me something to sit on.

ATTENDANT. Here's a lion-seat, Your Majesty.

CHANDRAGUPTA. And you, Chamberlain, tell Chanakya that I wish to see him immediately. *Now!*

CHAMBERLAIN. Yes, Your Majesty.

*The curtain rises, revealing* CHANAKYA *in his home, sitting in a mood of mixed anxiety and anger.*

CHANAKYA. So Rakshasa dares to challenge me! Give it up, Rakshasa, give it up while there's time. You're fighting against Chandragupta, not against a puffed-up, inefficient Nanda. You are not Chanakya, you are only Rakshasa. *He reflects.* Why should I worry? Our spies are ready, Siddharthaka has everything in hand, the fake quarrel is planned. . . .

CHAMBERLAIN, *entering, speaking to himself*. Above them all is His Majesty, the king. Then in order of importance come his minister, his favorite, and the receivers of his favors who stay in the palace. I neglect this at my peril. Ah, here's Chanakya's house. *He looks around.* Here's stone to break cowdung cakes with, here's the sacred grass gathered by his pupils, the clay roof says simplicity, and the walls have cracks in them. Good. Flatterers fatten on airy words. But a simple person commands respect, because he holds his head high and doesn't fear even the king. *He notices* CHANAKYA *and falls on his knees. He speaks aloud.* Sir, His Majesty sends a message—

CHANAKYA. Well, what is it?

CHAMBERLAIN, *still on his knees.* His illustrious Majesty sends you his greetings, sir, and says he would like a word with you in private, sir, if that is not inconvenient to you, sir.

CHANAKYA. So he wishes to see me. Does he know I've banned the Moonlight Festival?

CHAMBERLAIN, *trembling.* Y-y-yes, sir.

CHANAKYA, *angrily.* Who told him?

CHAMBERLAIN. S-s-sir, His M-m-majesty saw the city from the Su-su-suganga palace, and—

CHANAKYA. I see. So you've stirred him up!

*The* CHAMBERLAIN *trembles and looks at the ground, but makes no answer.*

CHANAKYA. How they gossip behind my back, these bootlickers of the king! Where's His Majesty?

CHAMBERLAIN. The Su-su-suganga palace, sir. He sent me here.

CHANAKYA. Well, lead on, lead on.

CHAMBERLAIN. This way, sir. *They walk a little.*—The Suganga palace, sir.

CHANAKYA. And His Majesty resplendent on the throne. *He approaches the* KING. My blessings on you, Your Majesty.

CHANDRAGUPTA, *rising.* Noble Chanakya, I salute you. *He prostrates himself at* CHANAKYA's *feet.*

CHANAKYA, *lifting him by the hand*. Rise, noble king.

CHANDRAGUPTA, *rising*. I thank you, noble Chanakya. Please sit down.

*Both sit down, according to protocol.*

CHANAKYA. You summoned me, sire?

CHANDRAGUPTA. It is so long since I last saw you. You are a balm to tired eyes.

CHANAKYA, *smiling*. I may be, sire; but a king does not summon a minister merely to have a look at his face.

CHANDRAGUPTA. Noble Chanakya, what good do you see in banning the Moonlight Festival?

CHANAKYA. Your Majesty has called me here to tweak my ears?

CHANDRAGUPTA. No, no. Just a point of information.

CHANAKYA. So. The pupil rises against the teacher.

CHANDRAGUPTA. No, the pupil wishes to know the purpose of the teacher's commands.

CHANAKYA. And it does him credit, for the teacher never acts without a purpose.

CHANDRAGUPTA. Precisely, noble Chanakya.

CHANAKYA. In that case, Your Majesty, it will pay the pupil to listen carefully to what the teacher has to say. The best writers on political science say that administration has three aspects: there's a sphere exclusively under the king, a second sphere exclusively under his minister, and a third that is jointly controlled. What help is it, Your Majesty, to inquire about the purpose of an act that comes under the sphere belonging exclusively to the minister? That is all there is to it.

CHANDRAGUPTA *turns his face away in feigned anger. Offstage two poets recite.*

FIRST POET'S VOICE. May Shiva bless you,
  As autumn blesses the flower-white sky,
  As swans of smiling beauty,

As a filigree of moonlight on the cloud-dark hide of an elephant.

May Vishnu bless you,
From the circle of his snake-hoods,
Eyes glittering like lamps, like jewels,
Saliva on their open fangs,
Sleep in their tired eyes.

SECOND POET'S VOICE. Rise, O lord!
Be a lion, great-gifted!
O my lord, rise!
Crush the unfaithful,
As lions do; as elephants, the self-respecting conquerors.
It is not jewels make a king:
A king makes and unmakes jewels.

CHANAKYA, *to himself.* The first is all right—an invocation to autumn, with Shiva as the presiding god. But the second is a trick—Rakshasa trying to catch me napping. It was a good try, my friend—but I'm wide awake.

CHANDRAGUPTA. Chamberlain, give a thousand gold pieces to the poets.

*The* CHAMBERLAIN *takes a few steps.*

CHANAKYA. Wait! Your Majesty, surely this is a needless waste of money.

CHANDRAGUPTA, *angrily.* Am I a king? Is this my kingdom? Who blocks me? I live in a prison, not a kingdom.

CHANAKYA. A kingdom, Your Majesty, becomes a prison to a king who is not sure of the art of ruling.

CHANDRAGUPTA. I think I know how to rule.

CHANAKYA. I did not say you didn't, Your Majesty. But I know my part of the job too.

CHANDRAGUPTA. Why did you ban the Moonlight Festival?

CHANAKYA. If you do not mind, Your Majesty, I should like to know why you ordered the Festival.

CHANDRAGUPTA. So that my orders would not be disobeyed.

CHANAKYA. And I banned it so that your orders *would* be disobeyed: humility becomes a king better than pride. But there was another reason. Sonottara, tell Achala to bring the Bhadrabhata document here.

GATEKEEPER. Yes, sir. *He leaves and returns with a sheet of paper, which he hands to* CHANAKYA.

CHANAKYA. Your Majesty—

CHANDRAGUPTA. I'm listening.

CHANAKYA. A list of the officials, Your Majesty, who rose in revolt against you and have joined your enemy Malayaketu. There is, first, Bhadrabhata, Officer-in-Charge of Elephants; then Purushadatta, Officer-in-Charge of Cavalry; Dingarata, son of Chandrabhanu, Head of the Gate-keepers; Maharaja Balagupta, Your Majesty's cousin; Rajasena, who served Your Majesty's boyhood; Bhagurayana, brother of the General of the Army; Rohitaksha, son of the king of Malava; and Vijayavarman, Chief of the Kshatra group.

CHANDRAGUPTA. And why did they desert me?

CHANAKYA. Bhadrabhata and Purushadatta are notorious whorers and drinkers; the first preferred women to elephants, the second liked wine more than horses; they were dismissed and given a subsistence allowance, which it seems they didn't appreciate. They are now in charge of Malayaketu's elephants and horses. Dingarata and Balagupta were after more money—and it seems Malayaketu would pay them better than Your Majesty. Your boyhood servant couldn't stand the strain of too many favors from you; he feared a slump, and Malayaketu seems to have assured him a more balanced regimen. Bhagurayana first frightened Malayaketu out of here by saying I had assassinated Malayaketu's father, then fell under the influence of Chandanadasa and his conspirators, then realized things were too hot for him here; he scuttled to safety with Malayaketu. Malayaketu made him his minister out of gratitude. Rohitaksha and Vijayavarman were jealous; they couldn't endure the granting of favors to Your Majesty's relatives, and they fled.

CHANDRAGUPTA. If you knew all this beforehand, why didn't you take appropriate measures?

CHANAKYA. No action was possible in the circumstances.

CHANDRAGUPTA. You mean you were either weak or had a deeper plan.

CHANAKYA. A minister cannot afford to be weak, Your Majesty.

CHANDRAGUPTA. What was the plan then?

CHANAKYA. A plan that must be not only heard but understood and appreciated. There are only two ways to deal with dissatisfied officials— humor them or punish them. Humoring Bhadrabhata and Purushadatta was out of the question: it would have meant reinstating them in positions of dangerous authority. If the elephants and horses fall into unreliable hands, the defense of the kingdom becomes shaky. Humoring Dingarata and Balagupta would have been an even bigger headache; their voluptuous greed is so great that giving them a whole kingdom wouldn't satisfy them. Rajasena and Bhagurayana were so fearful of losing all they had that there was no point in humoring *them*, and the same went for the jealous Rohitaksha and Vijayavarman. As for the other alternative—punishing them—I didn't think it advisable. We have just defeated the Nandas, the people are still uneasy—why stir up more trouble by punishing prominent men? Besides, Malayaketu, with Rakshasa's help, is poised to attack us; the Mleccha army is with him, he is infuriated by the assassination of his father. I thought it best, Your Majesty, to let these men escape. This is a time to consolidate our position, not to indulge in the pleasures of a Moonlight Festival. Our defenses need attention: will a Festival help with that?

CHANDRAGUPTA. You intrigue me. There are many questions in my head.

CHANAKYA. Ask them, Your Majesty. There are many answers in mine.

CHANDRAGUPTA. To begin with, why weren't effective measures taken to prevent Malayaketu from escaping and making trouble for us now?

CHANAKYA. There were two alternatives, Your Majesty. We could have put him in prison; or we could have honored our promise to give him half the kingdom. If we imprison him, think what the people would suspect —first we murder the father, then we imprison the son. We would look like barbarians. But if we give him half the kingdom, we destroy the very purpose of assassinating Parvataka, for the assassination of Parvataka was ordered with the aim of getting his kingdom. So I let Malayaketu escape.

CHANDRAGUPTA. It sounds logical. But why did you let Rakshasa escape?

CHANAKYA. The people respect him. They admire his loyalty and devotion to Nanda. Had he stayed in the city, in prison or out, plots galore would have cropped up, money would have poured in, cells and conspiracies would have festered. Now he can sting us only from the outside, and I can handle him more comfortably.

CHANDRAGUPTA. Couldn't a brave show of force have settled him?

CHANAKYA. Force against a demon like Rakshasa? Yes, and how many men would we lose before we secured him? Besides, there would be no certainty—he might prefer suicide to falling into our hands. And then the loss would be all ours, a first-class brain and a loyal heart gone forever. No, Your Majesty, he has to be tamed as a wild elephant is tamed—with gentle cunning.

CHANDRAGUPTA. Your words dazzle me, Chanakya, but I have a feeling Rakshasa has tricked us. He's the better man, after all.

CHANAKYA, *angrily*. Better? How?

CHANDRAGUPTA. Oddly enough, he continued to live in the city even after we had conquered it, and contemptuously remained as long as it pleased him to do so. Did not my prestige with the army suffer on that account? His strategy has so confused us that I can't trust even the most reliable officers.

CHANAKYA, *laughing*. I see. You surprised me, Your Majesty. I thought you thought he had done what I had done—made Malayaketu destroy you, as I made you destroy Nanda.

CHANDRAGUPTA. It flatters you to say *you* had done it.

CHANAKYA. Oh, the insult! Did I not take the vow to obliterate the Nandas from the face of the earth? Look at the burnt-out cities, the vultures, the desolate fires, the dead bodies of the Nandas carried in procession to the burial places! Who did that?

CHANDRAGUPTA. It pleases you to think you did it.

CHANAKYA. *Who* did it then?

CHANDRAGUPTA. Fate. An evil fate struck them down.

CHANAKYA. The ignorant thank fate.

CHANDRAGUPTA. And the wise preserve their honor by not boasting.

CHANAKYA, *fuming.* Am I a slave, Your Majesty? By this knot of hair on my head I swear—*He stamps his foot.*—I swear my anger gets the better of me. Take care, sire! If you think Rakshasa better, then give him this. *He unbuckles his sword.* Take it, and give it to him! *He stares vacantly, melodramatically.* This is your day, Rakshasa, you have won. You have severed Chanakya from his master. *He walks out.*

CHANDRAGUPTA. Chamberlain, have this announcement made: "Chanakya is disgraced, and from today forward Chandragupta alone will conduct the affairs of the kingdom."

CHAMBERLAIN, *to himself.* Chanakya, not "noble" Chanakya! But it's Chanakya's own fault. It's a minister's fault if a king does wrong, a driver's fault if the elephant misbehaves.

CHANDRAGUPTA. What are you waiting for?

CHAMBERLAIN. No, Your Majesty, nothing, Your Majesty. Yes, Your Majesty. *He leaves.*

CHANDRAGUPTA, *to himself.* I hope the plan comes off. *Aloud.* Sonottara, I have a splitting headache. Take me to the bedchamber.

ATTENDANT. This way, Your Majesty.

CHANDRAGUPTA, *to himself.* I hope I didn't overdo it. A concocted quarrel —but how it pains my head! How would a real quarrel between teacher and pupil feel! What shame and heartbreak would it not produce?

C U R T A I N

# ACT IV

### RAKSHASA'S ACTIVITIES

*A* MAN, *dressed as a traveler, enters before the curtain and speaks to himself. A* DOORKEEPER *is standing at the opposite side of the fore-stage.*

MAN. The command of a king does wonders. Who'd scurry here and there, as I do, if it wasn't for the command of the king? First I shall go to the house of Rakshasa. *He looks around him.* Ah, sir, you are a doorkeeper? Is that Rakshasa's house? Send in word, sir, that Karabhaka has returned and brings important news from Pataliputra.

DOORKEEPER. Shhh! Don't shout like that. Rakshasa's in bed with a headache. Couldn't sleep all night—he was so busy with matters of state. Wait here. I'll send in word soon.

MAN. Do so, handsome doorkeeper, please do.

*The curtain rises, revealing* RAKSHASA *in his bedchamber. He looks worried.* SAKATADASA *is with him.*

RAKSHASA, *to himself.* I can't get a wink of sleep. . . . Damn Chanakya and his crooked schemes, making me worry all the time, "Will this happen?"—"Will that happen?"—"Why not this?"—"Why not that?" I'm worse than a blasted playwright, putting this in, taking that out, developing this, soft-pedaling that, pushing here, retreating there—all because the plot demands it. If only Chanakya—

DOORKEEPER. Sir—

RAKSHASA, *to himself.* —could be baffled.

DOORKEEPER. My lord Rakshasa—

RAKSHASA, *to himself.* "Chanakya, sir" and "baffled, my lord Rakshasa"! Not a happy omen! But I must go through with my plan. *Aloud.* Well, what is it?

DOORKEEPER. Sir, a gentleman named Karabhaka is waiting at the door.

RAKSHASA. Show him in.

*The* DOORKEEPER *approaches* KARABHAKA *and gestures to him.* This way, sir.

KARABHAKA, *to* RAKSHASA. Greetings to you, sir.

RAKSHASA. Please sit down. *He speaks to himself as the visitor finds a seat on the floor.* Let me see—what job did I entrust to him?

*A* MAN *enters, carrying a staff.*

MAN. Make way for the prince! The Prince Malayaketu has come to inquire after Minister Rakshasa's headache.

MALAYAKETU *is seen outside, accompanied by* BHAGURAYANA *and a* CHAMBERLAIN.

MALAYAKETU, *to himself.* My father was assassinated ten months ago, and even holy water was not offered in his name. I will do so today. *Aloud.* Noble Jajali, tell the accompanying kings that I would like to pay a surprise visit to Minister Rakshasa, and would like to be alone.

CHAMBERLAIN. Yes, Your Majesty. *He goes out and is heard speaking in a low voice; then he returns.* They have left, Your Majesty.

MALAYAKETU. You may go with them, noble Jajali. Bhagurayana will accompany me. *As the* CHAMBERLAIN *and other members of the retinue leave,* MALAYAKETU *turns to* BHAGURAYANA. You see, Bhagurayana, I do not quite understand what Bhadrabhata and the others said to me when they came over. "We approach you for protection through General Sikharasena," they said, "for we have severed loyalty with Chandragupta and we may be persecuted by Chanakya."

BHAGURAYANA. It is the political custom, sire, to approach an ambitious king through the good offices of someone close to him.

MALAYAKETU. There is none closer and dearer to us than Rakshasa.

BHAGURAYANA. Yes, sire. But Rakshasa hates Chanakya, not Chandragupta. If Chanakya falls from favor, Rakshasa will have no objection to

making alliance with Chandragupta. Remember, Chandragupta does have
Nanda blood in him, and Rakshasa is loyal to the Nandas. Also, Rakshasa
would welcome such an alliance to save his imprisoned friends. That is
why, sire, Bhadrabhata approached you through General Sikharasena. For
if an alliance comes about between Rakshasa and Chandragupta, Rakshasa's
recommendation would stand against them in the eyes of Your Majesty.

MALAYAKETU. You're right. Take me to the minister.

BHAGURAYANA. This way, sire. *They walk a few steps.* Here we are, sire.

RAKSHASA, *to himself.* Now I remember. . . . *Aloud.* My good man, did
you get in touch with Stavakalasha in Pataliputra?

KARABHAKA. I did, sir.

MALAYAKETU, *overhearing.* They're talking about espionage in Pataliputra. Wait. Let's listen. Ministers speak more freely when kings are not
present.

MALAYAKETU *and* BHAGURAYANA *eavesdrop.*

RAKSHASA. And you were successful in your mission?

KARABHAKA. Yes, sir.

MALAYAKETU, *whispering to* BHAGURAYANA. What mission?

BHAGURAYANA, *whispering.* Some mysterious goings-on. We'd better
listen and find out. . . .

RAKSHASA. Tell me all. Start from the beginning.

KARABHAKA. Well, sir, you ordered me to tell the poet Stavakalasha to
write flattering poems that would stir up Chandragupta against Chanakya.

RAKSHASA. I did. Go on.

KARABHAKA. I gave the message as you said. In the meantime the king
had ordered the Autumn Moonlight Festival because the people were
looking forward to it, as a husband looks forward to a night of love with a
gracious wife.

RAKSHASA. Yes, Nanda's Festival—polluted now by vulgar celebrations.

KARABHAKA. But Chanakya banned it, in spite of the king's order. In the meantime, however, Stavakalasha had got busy with suitable verses to turn the king's head.

RAKSHASA. You remember the lines?

KARABHAKA. "Rise, O lord!
  Be a lion, great-gifted!
  O my lord, rise!
  Crush the unfaithful,
  As lions do; as elephants, the self-respecting conquerors.
  It is not jewels make a king:
  A king makes and unmakes jewels."

RAKSHASA. Good work, Stavakalasha! An ordinary man can't tolerate interference with his enjoyments—and he is the king! And then?

KARABHAKA. Then he praised you, sir, and said you wouldn't have done such a thing. Saying which, he dismissed Chanakya.

MALAYAKETU, *aside.* He praised Rakshasa. You heard?

BHAGURAYANA, *aside.* And dismissed Chanakya, which is greater praise.

RAKSHASA. Is he angry only because Chanakya banned the Festival, or is there another reason?

MALAYAKETU, *aside.* What does he see in asking such a question?

BHAGURAYANA, *aside.* Very significant. He's trying to see if there's a stronger basis for Chandragupta's anger than just a temperamental quarrel over a trivial matter.

KARABHAKA. There is another reason, sir. Chandragupta accuses Chanakya of allowing you and Prince Malayaketu to escape.

RAKSHASA, *expressing joy.* I have him in my hands now. Now Chandanadasa will be freed, and united with his wife and son.

MALAYAKETU, *aside.* What does he mean, Bhagurayana—"I have him in my hands now"?

BHAGURAYANA, *aside.* He means it's enough that Chanakya's left him—there's no point now in destroying Chandragupta.

RAKSHASA. Where is Chanakya?

KARABHAKA. In Pataliputra, sir.

RAKSHASA, *excitedly*. Not gone to an ashrama? Not protesting, not plotting?

KARABHAKA. They say he is leaving soon for an ashrama.

RAKSHASA. That's fishy. The fellow couldn't tolerate the insult when King Nanda dismissed him—how can he gulp down Chandragupta's insult now and mew in an ashrama?

MALAYAKETU, *aside*. How does it help Rakshasa to know if Chanakya is in an ashrama or is protesting?

BHAGURAYANA, *aside*. I'm not sure. But the greater the distance between Chanakya and Chandragupta, I suppose, the more it helps his plan.

SAKATADASA. It stands to reason, sir. Chandragupta is not a king who tolerates disobedience, and Chanakya doesn't try protesting this time because he failed the first time when he took the vow to destroy the Nandas.

RAKSHASA. I see. Karabhaka, you have done well, you may go now and rest. Make him comfortable, Sakatadasa. SAKATADASA *and* KARABHAKA *leave*. I could wish Prince Malayaketu were here.

MALAYAKETU. And he is here! *He approaches* RAKSHASA.

RAKSHASA. Sire, I was thinking of going to you. Please sit down, sire.

MALAYAKETU. You sit too, noble Rakshasa. *They seat themselves according to rank*. How is the headache?

RAKSHASA. So long as my plans don't work out my headache remains.

MALAYAKETU. Your plans will succeed. Why shouldn't they? Our armies are ready, itching to come to grips with the enemy. They wait for a sign of weakness.

RAKSHASA. Let them march. Victory is ours.

MALAYAKETU. The weakness?

RAKSHASA. I have found it.

MALAYAKETU. Where?

RAKSHASA. Chanakya. He has been dismissed by Chandragupta.

MALAYAKETU. But that's a weakness in Chanakya, not Chandragupta.

RAKSHASA. Not in this case, sire. Here Chanakya's weakness is Chandragupta's weakness.

MALAYAKETU. I wouldn't jump to conclusions, noble Rakshasa. Chanakya's faults spread suspicion and disaffection among the people of Pataliputra; with him gone, they'll rally around their king with greater loyalty than before.

RAKSHASA. Not quite, sire. The people of Pataliputra fall in two camps—the first are those who helped Chandragupta, the second those still loyal to Nanda. Chanakya's errors may spread disaffection among the first group, and bring them closer to Chandragupta, but those who are loyal to Nanda are on our side. They cannot be touched—they wait for our armies to march and they wait to welcome you to Pataliputra as the rightful king. Am I not myself one of them?

MALAYAKETU. I still don't see how we can dare to attack just because Chanakya has been dismissed by Chandragupta. Is there any other reason to march?

RAKSHASA. That is the most important reason, sire.

MALAYAKETU. Why? Is Chandragupta rendered impotent? Can't he withstand us now? Hasn't he another minister to put in Chanakya's place?

RAKSHASA. Without Chanakya he is nowhere. I know it. . . . Everything was always in Chanakya's hands, and when Chanakya goes, chaos comes. How can that baby of a king act when Chanakya isn't there to suckle him?

MALAYAKETU, *to himself.* Good thing I'm not a baby and you're not suckling me! *Aloud.* That may be, but I dare not take a risk. In these matters we have to be sure of results before we begin.

RAKSHASA. But we *are* sure. The people will rise and join us. Chanakya's absence will give us a confused Chandragupta to deal with—and crush! A word from you and the kingdom is yours.

MALAYAKETU. Good! Then let us attack. Words only waste time. Get the elephants from the river Sona, where they are playing games with the bees. Gather them like massive clouds and lay siege to Pataliputra. I have decided to march!

MALAYAKETU *and* BHAGURAYANA *leave.*

RAKSHASA. You there—Priyamvadaka!

PRIYAMVADAKA, *entering.* Sir?

RAKSHASA. Is there one of our astrologers nearby? Bring him in.

PRIYAMVADAKA. There is a Jain monk, sir, at the gate.

RAKSHASA, *to himself.* A naked monk! An evil omen. *Aloud.* Well, what's his name?

PRIYAMVADAKA. Jivasiddhi.

RAKSHASA. Show him in.

PRIYAMVADAKA *leaves and returns with* JIVASIDDHI.

JIVASIDDHI, *in a chanting tone.* Blessings on the faithful.

RAKSHASA. Holy one, we need an auspicious date for the army to march. Help us.

JIVASIDDHI. The day of the full moon is holy, from noon onward. At sunset on that day Mercury presides in the zodiac. Ketu has risen and set. The armies can march to victory.

RAKSHASA. The day of the full moon is not normally considered auspicious, holy one.

JIVASIDDHI. The day has one mark, the constellation has four, the zodiac sixty-four. When an auspicious planet presides in the zodiac, an inauspicious day becomes auspicious. The moon, the *Chandra,* is your guide: under *Chandra* you will prosper.

RAKSHASA. This is a gigantic undertaking, holy one. I shall have to consult other astrologers.

JIVASIDDHI. Do so. And give me leave to go.

RAKSHASA. You are not displeased, holy one?

JIVASIDDHI. Why should *I* be displeased when the fates are displeased with some and happy with others? *To* PRIYAMVADAKA. What time is it?

PRIYAMVADAKA. The sun is beginning to set.

RAKSHASA *rises and looks out the window, and then speaks to himself.*
Sunset, and the soft sunlight lovingly touches the trees. As the sun slips
behind the hills, the trees retreat in shadow—*He watches* PRIYAMVADAKA
*and* JIVASIDDHI *go out.*—like servants who leave their master when his
wealth is gone. . . .

*He leaves.*

C U R T A I N

## ACT V

### THE CUNNING LETTER

SIDDHARTHAKA *enters in front of the curtain, carrying a letter and a
sealed casket full of ornaments.*

SIDDHARTHAKA. As a creeper sucks up water and breaks into flower, so
Chanakya's policy will soon flower. I have with me this letter, written
under Chanakya's instructions, sealed with the signet ring of Rakshasa. I
have with me this casket, also sealed with the signet ring of Rakshasa. As
ordered, I shall pretend I'm on the road to Pataliputra. *He looks ahead.* A
Jain monk! Just what I wanted—an evil omen so that I can take my time
about reaching Pataliputra. Evil for others—good for me.

   *A monk (it is* JIVASIDDHI *in disguise) enters chanting.* Blessed are the
      saintly,
   The discoverers of happiness:
   Their paths are noble.

SIDDHARTHAKA. I salute you, holy monk!

JIVASIDDHI. Good man, may happiness go with you. *He peers at*
SIDDHARTHAKA. You are a traveler.

SIDDHARTHAKA. How did you know?

JIVASIDDHI. A letter and a casket—what else but travel?

SIDDHARTHAKA. I am indeed, sir. Please, holy monk, is today auspicious for messengers?

JIVASIDDHI, *laughing*. First you have a haircut, then you want to know if the day's auspicious for cutting hair!

SIDDHARTHAKA. But evil may still lurk around the corner. Tell me, sir—I can still turn back.

JIVASIDDHI. It is not safe to be here, in this camp of Malayaketu.

SIDDHARTHAKA. Why, sir?

JIVASIDDHI. Because Pataliputra is too near. Only those who have the seal of Rakshasa's signet ring are permitted to enter. And Bhagurayana gives the seal. If you have it, proceed; the day is auspicious. If you haven't, Malayaketu's officers will truss you up and drag you to the palace for cross-examination.

SIDDHARTHAKA. But I am one of those closest to Rakshasa. Who would stop me?

JIVASIDDHI. Close or far, my good man, do not try it without the seal of the signet ring.

SIDDHARTHAKA. Give me your blessings, sir.

JIVASIDDHI. May success go with you. I too will go to Bhagurayana for the seal.

*The curtain rises, revealing* BHAGURAYANA *and his servant* BHASURAKA.

BHAGURAYANA, *to himself*. The brilliance of Chanakya's cunning! The variety and suppleness of it! *Aloud*. Bhasūraka, Prince Malayaketu wants me to be here—I shall be needing this chair.

BHASURAKA. Here it is, sir.

BHAGURAYANA, *seating himself*. Wait at the gate, and send in anyone who needs the seal of the signet ring. BHASURAKA *leaves*. A pity that it

should be so, but it must be so. Prince Malayaketu loves me, trusts me, but
he must be deceived. It is too late now to think of right and wrong.

MALAYAKETU, *enters, followed by a* DOORKEEPER.

MALAYAKETU, *to himself.* I'm worried about Rakshasa—I can't make up
my mind. Will he deceive me and make a treaty with Chandragupta?
Chanakya is gone, and so he might. Or will he remain loyal? *Aloud.* Vijaya,
where is Bhagurayana?

DOORKEEPER. Inside, sir, giving seals to those who wish permission to
go out of the camp.

MALAYAKETU. I'll wait here for a while. Don't announce me yet.

BHASURAKA *enters and speaks to* BHAGURAYANA. A Jain monk, sir, desires
permission to receive the seal.

BHAGURAYANA. Show him in.

BHASURAKA *leaves, and* JIVASIDDHI *enters, still disguised.*

JIVASIDDHI. My blessings on you.

BHAGURAYANA, *to himself.* Rakshasa's friend Jivasiddhi. *Aloud.* Are you
not going on Rakshasa's mission?

JIVASIDDHI, *horrified.* I go on no missions. I go where there are no
Rakshasas and no missions.

BHAGURAYANA. Why, has he offended you?

JIVASIDDHI. He has offended no one. I have offended myself.

BHAGURAYANA. I see.

MALAYAKETU, *aside.* Very interesting.

JIVASIDDHI. It's nothing of great importance.

BHAGURAYANA. If you wish to keep it secret, you may. I have no great
desire to know.

JIVASIDDHI. Oh, no, it's not a secret. But it was very cruel.

BHAGURAYANA. If it is not a secret, you may as well tell it.

JIVASIDDHI. It is not a secret, but I shall not tell it.

BHAGURAYANA. In that case, good monk, I doubt whether I shall give you the seal.

JIVASIDDHI, *to himself*. Now is the time to tell him. He's eager enough to find out. *Aloud*. You force me to speak. Listen. When Rakshasa was in Pataliputra, I used to know him. And I know for certain that he secretly employed a poison girl to assassinate Parvateshvara.

MALAYAKETU, *shocked and speaking aside*. My father! Assassinated by Rakshasa! Not by Chanakya?

BHAGURAYANA. Go on.

JIVASIDDHI. Then Chanakya banished me from Pataliputra on the ground that I was Rakshasa's friend. And now Rakshasa is plotting to have me not just banished but liquidated. Fate has been unkind to me.

BHAGURAYANA. But we heard that Chanakya poisoned Parvateshvara to prevent him from claiming the half of the kingdom he had been promised as a reward for helping Chandragupta.

JIVASIDDHI, *horrified*. Chanakya! Absurd. That man? Never!

BHAGURAYANA. Well, here's your seal. You should tell your story to Prince Malayaketu. He'll be interested.

MALAYAKETU, *approaching*. I have heard it all. Jivasiddhi is Rakshasa's friend, isn't he? Oh, what chaos in my brain!

JIVASIDDHI, *to himself*. He heard—good! My work is over. *He leaves.*

MALAYAKETU, *staring fixedly ahead of him*. So, Rakshasa, you are found out. My father's killer! You were his best friend, he trusted you in everything.

BHAGURAYANA, *to himself*. But Chanakya's advice is to get Rakshasa alive. *Aloud*. May I say something, sire?

MALAYAKETU, *seating himself*. Yes, Bhagurayana.

BHAGURAYANA. It is well known, sire, that ministers and politicians do not treat men and women as people, but as pawns, always keeping in mind the final aim, not the immediate methods. Perhaps Rakshasa felt the majesty of your father to be overpoweringly obstructing and wished him out of the way so that you could come to power. Politics makes strange bedfellows. Keep him, sire, till the time when the kingdom of the Nandas is restored to you. Then you may do with him as you like.

MALAYAKETU. I will. If I order his execution now, the people might not like it, and our whole plan would fail.

BHASURAKA, *entering.* Captain Dirgaraksha is here, sire, to report that a man was arrested while trying to escape from the camp. He had the seal of the signet ring and a letter on his person.

BHAGURAYANA. Have him brought here.

BHASURAKA *leaves, and returns with* SIDDHARTHAKA, *who is in chains.*

BHASURAKA. This is the man, sire.

BHAGURAYANA. Are you a stranger, or one of Rakshasa's men?

SIDDHARTHAKA. An attendant of Rakshasa, sir.

BHAGURAYANA. Why were you trying to leave the camp with the seal?

SIDDHARTHAKA. A matter of great importance, sir.

MALAYAKETU. Show me the letter, Bhagurayana.

BHAGURAYANA, *taking the letter from* SIDDHARTHAKA. Here it is, sire. *He notices the seal.* Rakshasa's seal is on it, sire.

MALAYAKETU. Open it. Carefully. Don't break the seal. *He watches as* BHAGURAYANA *does so and hands him the letter; then he reads.* "Greetings. From one high-ranking person to another: The rival has been removed, the best course now is to effect an alliance by granting the reward as promised earlier. That would permit both to help their benefactor. And more. Some are after the wealth, others after elephants, and still others after land. And more. The set of three ornaments sent has been received. Something has been sent by me, so that the letter only may not appear insignificant. Accept it—it is yours. Siddharthaka will tell you the rest. You can trust him.". . .Bhagurayana, what sort of a letter is this?

BHAGURAYANA. Siddharthaka, whose letter is this?

SIDDHARTHAKA. I don't know, sir.

BHAGURAYANA. Why you rascal, you're carrying it and you don't know! Wait! To whom are you supposed to deliver the message?

SIDDHARTHAKA, *fearfully*. To you, sir.

BHAGURAYANA. To us? To *us*?

SIDDHARTHAKA. Sir, I am afraid. I don't know what I'm saying.

BHAGURAYANA, *angrily*. You'll know what you're saying soon, my pretty fellow. Bhasuraka, take him away. Beat the truth out of him.

BHASURAKA *drags* SIDDHARTHAKA *out, then returns and speaks to* BHAGURAYANA.

BHASURAKA. Sir, this casket with the seal was found on him.

BHAGURAYANA. This has Rakshasa's seal on it, sire.

MALAYAKETU. This must be the present referred to in the letter. Pry it open—but don't break the seal. *He waits until* BHAGURAYANA *hands him the opened casket*. But I gave these ornaments to Rakshasa myself! I took them off my body and gave them to him. This is a letter to Chandragupta.

BHAGURAYANA. We'll soon know. Bhasuraka, how is he? Still not talking?

BHASURAKA *goes out and returns with* SIDDHARTHAKA.

BHASURAKA. He says he will talk now, sir. But only to Prince Mala-yaketu.

MALAYAKETU. Well, here I am.

SIDDHARTHAKA, *falling at* MALAYAKETU's *feet*. Your mercy, sire!

MALAYAKETU. Your story first.

SIDDHARTHAKA. Sire, I was sent by Rakshasa to Chandragupta.

MALAYAKETU. The message?

SIDDHARTHAKA. This was the message, sire: "The following five kings, friends of mine, bear affection for you in their hearts: Chitravarman, lord of Kaluta; Sinhananda, ruler of Malaya; Pushkaraksha, lord of Kashmere; Sindhusena, king of Sindhu; and Meghanada of Parasika. The first three

want Malayaketu's lands; Sindhusena wants the elephants; and Meghanada covets the treasure. As it pleased you to remove Chanakya, may it
also please you to satisfy the five kings."

MALAYAKETU, *to himself.* Chitravarman and the others plotting behind
my back. . . . *Aloud.* Vijaya, I would like to speak to Rakshasa.

*The inner curtain rises.* RAKSHASA *is seen in a room of his house; his
mood is thoughtful.* PRIYAMVADAKA *waits on him.*

RAKSHASA, *to himself.* Again my doubts come to my mind. I can have
no peace as long as deserters from Chandragupta's ranks infiltrate our
camp. *Aloud.* Priyamvadaka, tell the kings, in our name, that Pataliputra
is not far off now—let the armies be ready for the final march. If they
want details, tell them the Khasa and Magadha clans will move first. The
Gandharvas, with the Yavana chiefs, shall remain in the center; the brave
Shakas, reinforced by the Chinese and the Hunas, will be in the rear; and
the remaining troops, headed by Kaluta, will form a protective guard
around Prince Malayaketu.

PRIYAMVADAKA *leaves and re-enters.* Sir, Prince Malayaketu would like
to see you.

RAKSHASA. Wait, Priyamvadaka—call the servant.

SERVANT, *entering in response to summons.* Sir?

RAKSHASA. Tell Sakatadasa I'm going to meet Prince Malayaketu and
would like to wear one of the three ornaments he bought under my orders.

*The* SERVANT *leaves and returns with the ornament.* Here it is, sir.

RAKSHASA, *pinning on the ornament.* Conduct me, Priyamvadaka.

PRIYAMVADAKA. This way, sir.

RAKSHASA, *to himself.* When kings call, even ministers tremble, even
innocent ministers tremble. Fear of the king, fear of the king's favorite,
fear of his flatterers. . .the high may fall without warning.

RAKSHASA *and* PRIYAMVADAKA *go out, the inner curtain falls, and they
enter downstage into the presence of* MALAYAKETU.

PRIYAMVADAKA. Prince Malayaketu, sir.

RAKSHASA. Greetings to you, sire.

MALAYAKETU. And greetings to you, noble Rakshasa. Sit down. We have not seen you for a long time.

RAKSHASA, *seating himself*. I was busy with the arrangements for the attack, sire. I deserve the rebuke.

MALAYAKETU. And how are the arrangements progressing, noble Rakshasa?

RAKSHASA. So far, sire, excellently. Khasa and Magadha spearheading, the Shakas, Chinese, and Hunas in the rear, Gandharvas in the center, Kaluta's troops for your guard, sire—that's the battle plan.

MALAYAKETU, *to himself*. Very considerate. Assassins for my guard. *Aloud*. And what news from Pataliputra? Is anyone coming or going?

RAKSHASA. None, sire. We shall be there ourselves in a few days.

MALAYAKETU, *to himself*. You mean *you* will. *Aloud*. In that case, why was this person going to Pataliputra and carrying this letter?

RAKSHASA, *catching sight of* SIDDHARTHAKA. My friend Siddharthaka! What's the matter?

SIDDHARTHAKA, *ashamed and tearful*. Sir, they beat me, sir—I told them everything.

RAKSHASA. Told them what?

SIDDHARTHAKA. They beat me, sir, I'm half dead. *He stands fearfully, his head lowered.*

MALAYAKETU. He's too afraid or ashamed. You better tell him, Bhagurayana.

BHAGURAYANA. Yes, sire. He says you sent him to Chandragupta with a letter and a verbal message.

RAKSHASA. Siddharthaka says so? *I* sent you, Siddharthaka?

SIDDHARTHAKA, *fearfully*. They beat it out of me.

RAKSHASA. A sickening lie. If you torture him, he'll say anything.

MALAYAKETU. Show him the letter.

BHAGURAYANA *hands the letter to* RAKSHASA, *who reads it.*

RAKSHASA. A devil's trick!

MALAYAKETU. With this letter went this ornament as a gift. Is that part of the trick?

RAKSHASA, *examining the ornament.* This is the same one you gave me. I remember I gave it to Siddharthaka.

BHAGURAYANA. It is not quite proper to give away an ornament presented by the prince. . . .

MALAYAKETU. There's a reference to the verbal message in the letter.

RAKSHASA. The letter's a fake. Why think of messages?

MALAYAKETU. And this seal? The seal of your signet ring?

RAKSHASA. A clever forgery.

BHAGURAYANA. You explain it well. Siddharthaka, who wrote the letter?

SIDDHARTHAKA *fumbles and looks uneasily at* RAKSHASA *before speaking. Finally he brings out the name of* SAKATADASA.

RAKSHASA. If Sakatadasa wrote it, I wrote it. It's impossible.

MALAYAKETU. Vijaya, send for Sakatadasa.

*The* FEMALE DOORKEEPER *prepares to leave.*

BHAGURAYANA, *to himself.* What can Chanakya be getting at? *Aloud.* Sire, Sakatadasa will never admit he wrote it if Rakshasa is present. Let us see a sample of his writing. We can compare and find out.

MALAYAKETU. Get a specimen of his writing, Vijaya.

BHAGURAYANA. Sire, she should get the signet ring too.

MALAYAKETU. And get the signet ring.

*The* DOORKEEPER *leaves and returns.* Here they are, sire—some writing in the hand of Sakatadasa and the signet ring.

MALAYAKETU, *comparing*. The same hand.

RAKSHASA. And I thought he was my friend. He is trapped—the signet ring never left his finger and he and Siddharthaka are together. He has duped me. He has gone over to the enemy.

MALAYAKETU, *noticing* RAKSHASA's *ornament*. Where did you get this ornament, noble Rakshasa?

RAKSHASA. I bought it, sire.

MALAYAKETU. Vijaya, do you recognize this?

DOORKEEPER, *looking at it*. His Majesty's. . .Yes, sire, it is the king, your father's.

MALAYAKETU, *touched*. My father's. . .

RAKSHASA, *to himself*. Strange. I can hardly believe it. *Aloud*. Chanakya's merchant spies have foisted these ornaments on us.

MALAYAKETU. I would like to believe that, noble Rakshasa. But I am led to suspect that you have sold us out to Chandragupta. And my father's ornaments were the price!

RAKSHASA, *to himself*. Chanakya has got me where he wants me. I can't say I didn't write the letter—the signet ring is mine. I can't say Sakatadasa betrayed me—no one would believe it. I can't say Chandragupta sold off those ornaments—Chandragupta doesn't need money. It all sounds so thin. . . .

MALAYAKETU. One question, noble Rakshasa.

RAKSHASA. Rakshasa, sire—I am not noble now.

MALAYAKETU. Isn't it true that Chandragupta is the son of a king who was once your master? And that I am the son of a king who was only your friend? Isn't it true that slavery under Chandragupta brings you more honor than lordship under me? Doesn't Chandragupta give *you* prestige, whereas in my service you can only say that you will restore *my* prestige?

RAKSHASA. These are hard words, sire, to which I have no reply.

MALAYAKETU, *pointing to the casket*. And how do you explain this?

RAKSHASA, *sadly*. My fate plays tricks with me.

MALAYAKETU, *flaring up*. You mean you won't tell! Fate's a very convenient alibi, my friend Rakshasa. Fate sent the poison girl who assassinated my father, I suppose! Fate made my father trust you! And now it's Fate that is selling us out to Chandragupta! *You* have done nothing!

RAKSHASA, *to himself*. Let it come then. I am ready. *Aloud*. I ordered no poison girl against your father, sire.

MALAYAKETU. How did he die?

RAKSHASA. Ask Fate, sire. I do not know.

MALAYAKETU. Fate again! Of course—but why not ask the monk Jivasiddhi?

RAKSHASA, *to himself*. Jivasiddhi too! Chanakya has ringed me with his spies.

MALAYAKETU, *fuming*. Bhasuraka, take this command to General Sikharasena. The five kings who have plotted treason against us—Chitravarman, Sinhananda, Pushkaraksha, Sindhusena, and Meghanada—the first three are to be buried alive, and the other two—one of them wanted elephants, didn't he?—let the elephants trample them to death.

BHASURAKA. Yes, sire. *He leaves*.

MALAYAKETU. I don't deceive people, noble Rakshasa. My murders are straightforward. You can go to Chandragupta—and lick his feet. If I could fight two, I can fight three.

BHAGURAYANA. Let us go, sire. The armies await your command.

MALAYAKETU *and his company leave*.

RAKSHASA. What a wretched fool I am! Instead of enemies, five friends— five good friends sent to their deaths! What now? Shall I follow them? Die? Or go to an ashrama? . . . But the enemy lives—and I must not run now. Yet I cannot endanger Chandanadasa's safety either. I must think. What a stupid fool I have been!

*He leaves*.

C U R T A I N

## ACT VI

### THE FAKE NOOSE

SIDDHARTHAKA *enters before the curtain, and speaks in a joyful mood.*

SIDDHARTHAKA. Chanakya's plans bear fruit—slowly, but they do bear fruit. Good, good. Now to wait for Samiddharthaka. Dear Samiddharthaka! *He looks around.* Here he comes.

SAMIDDHARTHAKA, *entering and speaking to himself.* So Siddharthaka, I hear, has arrived here in Pataliputra from the camp of Malayaketu. *He sees* SIDDHARTHAKA. Ah!

SIDDHARTHAKA. How are you, Samiddharthaka?

*The two embrace.*

SAMIDDHARTHAKA. How do you expect me to be, Siddharthaka, if you don't come over to dinner at my house?

SIDDHARTHAKA. Any time, my friend. But I've been busy as a beaver. First to Chanakya, who sends me to His Majesty, and then from the king I set out toward your—and whom do I meet on the way but you!

SAMIDDHARTHAKA. And what is this wonderful news that keeps friend from friend so long?

SIDDHARTHAKA. Nothing very secret. Listen. Chanakya maneuvered things in such a way that Malayaketu was forced to banish Rakshasa and order Chitravarman and the four other kings to be put to death. But the remaining kings got panicky and took off; and then Bhadrabhata, Purushadatta, Dingarata, Balagupta, Rajasena, Bhagurayana, Rohitaksha, Vijayavarman, and a few others—what do you think they have done?—they've risen and made Malayaketu their prisoner.

SAMIDDHARTHAKA. That's very good, that's very good, but I understood Bhadrabhata and his followers couldn't stand Chandragupta. Now they apparently can't stand Malayaketu. If you don't mind, this is all very much like a muddled-up play by a cockeyed poet, which begins with a *this* and ends with a *that*.

SIDDHARTHAKA. A pretty compliment to Chanakya's brains! He does make this into *that*.

SAMIDDHARTHAKA. And then?

SIDDHARTHAKA. Naturally Chanakya attacked at once with a select force—he routed the leaderless Mlecchas and captured them all.

SAMIDDHARTHAKA. But we heard that Chanakya had been dismissed by His Majesty.

SIDDHARTHAKA. And you fell for it like a ton of bricks. Why, my friend, my idiot—if Rakshasa couldn't see through the trick do you think you could?

SAMIDDHARTHAKA. Where is Rakshasa now?

SIDDHARTHAKA. No one knows. But it's reported he may be here in Pataliputra. They say he slipped away in the confusion, and that he's being tailed by a first-class spy, Udumbara.

SAMIDDHARTHAKA. What about his vow to help the Nandas? Has he forgotten that?

SIDDHARTHAKA. They say he's here to help his friend Chandanadasa.

SAMIDDHARTHAKA. I've got a feeling they'll release Chandanadasa.

SIDDHARTHAKA. Keep your fingers crossed then—it seems Chanakya has asked me to help you execute Chandanadasa.

SAMIDDHARTHAKA, *angrily*. Execute Chandanadasa! Haven't I better work to do? What does Chanakya think he's doing—making us responsible for his dirty work! Can't he find other executioners?

SIDDHARTHAKA. Easy, easy, Samiddharthaka. It isn't healthy to defy the orders of Chanakya. You know that. Come on. Let's do ourselves up as executioners and lead Chandanadasa out to his doom.

SIDDHARTHAKA *and* SAMIDDHARTHAKA *leave. The end of the prelude is signified by the rising of the curtain. A* MAN *is seen walking about with a rope in his hands.*

MAN. This rope's as supple and long as Chanakya's schemes. *He looks around*. This is the spot Udumbara reported. And here's where Chanakya ordered me to wait for Rakshasa. *He looks again*. There he comes, his head covered. I'll get behind these trees and watch his behavior.

*As* RAKSHASA *enters, the* MAN *conceals himself*.

RAKSHASA. The goddess of kings has abandoned the kings, like a harlot who runs after richer comforts. When the goddess abandons kings, mortal men can only wait. What can I do? I tried to help Nanda, and he was poisoned. I tried to help his son, and Fate—and the spies—stepped in. The fates are against us, we haven't a chance! The prince wouldn't trust me, but then it wasn't his fault—the fates are against us, the fates turned him against me. Rakshasa will be captured, Rakshasa will die. But in dishonor? —never! To say I was false, to say I betrayed. . .oh, what horror, what shame! *He looks around*. Here I am in front of the walls and gardens of Pataliputra, made precious by the footsteps of His Majesty, my master, King Nanda. Here he shot arrows, talked to his ambassadors, rode horses— holy ground, holy ground! The fates are against us. All is vanished. I rode from these gates like a king, thousands behind me, the citizens applauding —now I enter like a thief. The garden is dry, hope is dead. *He slumps down on a seat*.

MAN. Now to proceed with the orders of the great Chanakya.

*The* MAN *approaches* RAKSHASA *from behind, then slips the noose around his own neck*.

RAKSHASA, *startled*. What's this? What are you up to, man? *He rises and takes the noose*. What's the matter?

MAN. I've lost a friend.

RAKSHASA. I've lost one too. But why the rope?

MAN. I can't bear to be without my friend, I must die.

RAKSHASA. Well then, if you must—but first tell me about it. I've lost a friend too.

MAN. The sorrow, the pain! I will tell you. You are most kind, sir. . . . There's a jeweler in the city. His name is Vishnudasa.

RAKSHASA, *to himself*. A close friend of Chandanadasa. *Aloud*. Hmm.

MAN. Vishnudasa is my very dear, very dear, dear friend.

RAKSHASA, *to himself.* "Dear friend." Good.

MAN. And he has left the city and given all his wealth to charity, and renounced the world, and is ready to die. . . . So I too must die. I am sad, let me die—my friend is dying. Give me the noose.

RAKSHASA. But why does your friend want to die? Is he ill? What's wrong with him?

MAN. No, sir, he is not ill. No, kind sir.

RAKSHASA. Has he offended the king?

MAN. No, sir, the king is very good. We all like him, God bless His Majesty.

RAKSHASA. Love troubles, then? Another man's wife? She rejects him?

MAN. No, sir. That sort of thing, sir, doesn't happen in our city.

RAKSHASA. You must mean then that he has lost a friend too—just as you have?

MAN. Yes, sir.

RAKSHASA, *to himself.* It's Chandanadasa that he has lost, and he can't bear it. How my heart trembles. Such love is rare in friends. *Aloud.* Tell me what happened. I've heard of the man.

MAN. Sir, Chandanadasa—that's the name of my friend's friend—is head of the Jewelers' Guild in Pataliputra.

RAKSHASA, *to himself.* There, there, my heart. *Aloud.* I've heard of him. A loving man, a good man, isn't he?

MAN. A dear friend of Vishnudasa. This morning Vishnudasa went to His Majesty with a request.

RAKSHASA. What? What?

MAN. He said, "Your Majesty, take all the money in my house, but free Chandanadasa, if it please Your Majesty."

RAKSHASA, *to himself.* A noble gesture, Vishnudasa. Very noble. For a merchant to give up all his wealth is not easy. *Aloud.* And what did the king say?

MAN. His Majesty said, "We arrested Chandanadasa and imprisoned him because he sheltered Rakshasa's family. We have ordered his execution because he refuses to surrender them. He cannot be released unless he surrenders the family of our enemy to us." That is all, kind sir. So Vishnudasa turned gloomy and wants to end his life before they execute Chandanadasa. And I have become gloomy and I want to end *my* life before Vishnudasa ends his.

RAKSHASA. Then Chandanadasa is still alive!

MAN. But he will be dead today, sir. They keep pressing him to give up Rakshasa's family—but he's too stubborn. Now would you please, sir, let me have the rope?

RAKSHASA. You don't need the rope, my good fellow. Go to Vishnudasa. Stop him. I'll stop Chandanadasa's execution.

MAN. You will, sir? How?

RAKSHASA, *drawing his sword.* With this—if necessary. . . .

MAN, *impressed.* Sir, you must be Rakshasa! *He falls at* RAKSHASA's *feet.*

RAKSHASA. I am Rakshasa.

MAN. Sir. . .sir. . .*He gets up, and falls again at* RAKSHASA's *feet.*

RAKSHASA. Enough of this. Go to Vishnudasa, and intervene in his rash decision. *He walks about with his drawn sword.*

MAN. The executioners have orders to kill the prisoner if they see anyone approaching with a drawn sword. They're not taking any chances, sir.

RAKSHASA. Damn Chanakya and his orders! *He reflects.* However, the sword won't do. And Chandanadasa's life must be saved, not sacrificed. . . . I will give *myself* as ransom.

RAKSHASA *and the* MAN *depart separately.*

CURTAIN

## ACT VII

### THE RECONCILIATION

*The executioner* VAJRALOMAN *enters before the curtain.*

VAJRALOMAN. To the left, please, to the left. Make way on the left. His Majesty warns his enemies to keep a safe distance from his wrath. For here is Chandanadasa, head of the Jewelers' Guild, traitor and spy, who incurred His Majesty's displeasure and is therefore being led to his execution. What's that? Can he be released? Of course he can be released —if he surrenders the family of Rakshasa to His Majesty. And let this be a warning to all who harbor hatred for the king in their hearts!

CHANDANADASA *is brought in by* BILVAPATRA, *the second executioner. Following are his wife and son. He is dressed as a condemned criminal and carries the stake on his shoulder.*

CHANDANADASA. That the hunter should kill the soft-eyed deer, the lover of grass—this too is part of life. Cruelty knows no distinctions. I salute you, Death! And I salute you, my dear friend Vishnudasa, though you are absent. And I salute you too, my friends who follow me and who can do nothing but weep for the fate of an unfortunate man.

BILVAPATRA. This is the place, noble Chandanadasa. You can send them away now.

CHANDANADASA, *placing his hand on his son's head.* Take him home, my wife. I have come to the end of my journey.

WIFE, *in tears.* My husband calls death a journey.

CHANDANADASA. Don't cry. I die honorably.

WIFE. In that case I need not leave.

CHANDANADASA. What do you mean?

WIFE. If my husband can die honorably, I can die honorably too.

CHANDANADASA. But our little son, my wife. . .who will look after him?

WIFE. God will look after him. Honor your father, son, before he goes.

SON, *falling at* CHANDANADASA'S *feet*. Command me, father.

CHANDANADASA. When I am gone, son, go and live in a country where there is no Chanakya.

BILVAPATRA. The stake is planted, sir.

WIFE. Save him! Save my husband!

CHANDANADASA. You cry in vain, my wife. I die in honor. You should be happy, for the gods are happy.

VAJRALOMAN. Bring him here, Bilvapatra. *To the* WIFE. You had better go now.

CHANDANADASA. Wait till I embrace my little son. *He embraces his son and kisses him on his head*. You will soon know, my son, that death comes sooner or later to every living thing. But remember that I died honorably, having done my duty to a friend.

SON. I know, father. I shall keep the honor of the family.

VAJRALOMAN. Bring him here!

*As* CHANDANADASA *still hesitates, both* VAJRALOMAN *and* BILVAPATRA *take hold of him*.

WIFE, *lamenting, striking her breast*. Help! Help! My husband! My lord!

RAKSHASA, *entering, running*. Let him alone! I am the man. Kill me—put the garland of death round my neck. Do not weep, good lady.

CHANDANADASA. Rakshasa, my friend! You here?

RAKSHASA. I am here, dearest Chandanadasa—imitating poorly what you did nobly. You, sir, tell Chanakya that I am here.

VAJRALOMAN. What message shall I take, sir?

RAKSHASA. Tell Chanakya that Rakshasa is here. . . . Tell him Chandanadasa may go free now, Rakshasa has given himself up.

VAJRALOMAN. Keep an eye on Chandanadasa, Bilvapatra. Take him to wait under that tree in the cemetery while I deliver the message. I'll be back.

BILVAPATRA *leads* CHANDANADASA *and his* WIFE *and* SON *out.* VAJRALOMAN *walks off in the opposite direction. The curtain then rises.* CHANAKYA *is revealed wearing a large shawl; only his face is visible.* VAJRALOMAN *and* RAKSHASA *enter, the latter hanging back.*

CHANAKYA. Well, well—out with it, man. Out with it!

VAJRALOMAN. The plans of noble Chanakya have succeeded.

CHANAKYA. Not my plans. . . . Fate has been very helpful.

RAKSHASA, *to himself.* The man's honest—yet a devil. Who can say if he is evil or noble?

CHANAKYA, *seeing* RAKSHASA. Rakshasa! I, Chanakya, salute you, noble Rakshasa! *He removes his shawl and approaches* RAKSHASA.

RAKSHASA. Don't come near me. These filthy executioners have laid hands on me.

CHANAKYA. They are not *Chandalas,* noble Rakshasa, but officers of the king, spies in my service—Siddharthaka and Samiddharthaka. And poor Sakatadasa wrote the false letter for me without knowing he was being tricked.

RAKSHASA, *to himself.* I'm glad Sakatadasa's name has been cleared.

CHANAKYA. To cut a long story short, Bhadrabhata, the letter, the ornaments, the suicide in the garden, the execution of Chandanadasa— *He lowers his eyes.*—they were all little tricks, noble Rakshasa—small tricks of policy. I hope you will forgive them. They were ordered in a noble cause—to bring about a reunion between you and His Majesty. He wishes to see you.

RAKSHASA, *to himself.* I haven't much choice.

CHANDRAGUPTA, *enters, followed by his retinue.* I salute you, Chanakya!

CHANAKYA. The work is over, sire. Salute *him,* sire—the noble Rakshasa is with us.

CHANDRAGUPTA. Noble Rakshasa, Chandragupta salutes you.

RAKSHASA. May Your Majesty prosper!

CHANDRAGUPTA. If I have the illustrious Chanakya and the noble Rakshasa on my side, I lack nothing in this world.

CHANAKYA. You wish Chandanadasa to be released, noble Rakshasa?

RAKSHASA. Is there any doubt of that?

CHANAKYA. There is some doubt, for the noble Rakshasa has not yet accepted the sword of office from His Majesty. Sire, give him the sword.

RAKSHASA. No, I don't deserve it.

CHANAKYA. I deserve it and you don't? Is that possible? But you have no choice, noble Rakshasa, for Chandanadasa does not go free till you accept. . . . His life is in your hands.

RAKSHASA. I have, as you say, no choice. Give it to me.

CHANAKYA *joyfully presents the sword to* RAKSHASA, *and then turns to* CHANDRAGUPTA. Sire, the noble Rakshasa is now with us. My congratulations, Your Majesty.

CHANDRAGUPTA. And you, Chanakya, are with us too.

*An* ATTENDANT *enters and speaks to* CHANDRAGUPTA. Sire, Prince Malayaketu has been brought here in captivity by Bhadrabhata, Bhagurayana, and other generals. *To* CHANAKYA. Sir, they are waiting at the gate for further orders.

CHANAKYA. Refer the matter to the noble Rakshasa. He is in charge now.

RAKSHASA. Sire, I enjoyed Prince Malayaketu's hospitality for some time. I beg you to let him go free.

CHANDRAGUPTA *looks at* CHANAKYA.

CHANAKYA. What the noble Rakshasa says must be sound. *To the*

ATTENDANT. Tell Bhadrabhata and the others that Prince Malayaketu, at the request of his noble minister Rakshasa, is to receive back his kingdom by the grace of His Majesty, King Chandragupta. Go with them. Attend his coronation—and bring us the news. *The* ATTENDANT *prepares to leave.* Wait. Tell Vijayapala, the captain of the fort, that His Majesty, King Chandragupta, acting on the advice of his noble minister, Rakshasa, has appointed Chandanadasa to be Chief Merchant of all the cities of the empire. And recall the troops. With the noble Rakshasa to help us, we shall not have much need of them now.

*The* ATTENDANT *leaves.*

CHANAKYA. Sire, how else can I be of service to you?

CHANDRAGUPTA. You have served us well, noble Chanakya. Friendship with Rakshasa, the Nandas routed—what more could you do?

RAKSHASA. Nothing, sire, except to help make His Majesty's rule long and peaceful. The enemies are routed—and the crown is restored.

C U R T A I N

# THE  DREAM  OF  VASAVADATTA

by

BHASA

# Preface

In 1912 Pandit Ganapati Shastri edited and published a collection of thirteen plays which he claimed he had "unearthed" at Trivandrum and whose authorship he attributed to Bhasa. There was nothing in the manuscripts to indicate at first glance that they were Bhasa's, so Pandit Shastri launched on an elaborately argued *tika* to prove their authorship; the incredible thoroughness and close attention to textual (specially grammatical) detail with which genuine Sanskrit pandits are admirably armed led him, via a maze of complex argument, to posit the existence of two Bhasas in Sanskrit drama—a Dhavaka-Bhasa, of the seventh century A.D., probably the author of *Nagananda* and *Ratnavali* (both attributed to Harsha), and the real Bhasa (c. fourth century B.C.), who wrote the thirteen newly discovered plays.

This conclusion is arrived at through a wealth of analysis involving the difference between the benedictory verse as spoken by the Stage Manager in Bhasa's thirteen plays and as it is spoken in the plays of Kalidasa and other dramatists. (Basically it boils down to the fact that in Bhasa the Stage Manager speaks the lines, while in Kalidasa and the other dramatists no explicit stage direction is given.) Much attention, however, is devoted to the actual words of the verse: "May His majesty rule over this kingdom which extends from sea to sea and which has the Himalayas and the Vindhya range [in central India] as her earrings." That is all the verse says, but the pandits argue that since earrings hang parallel to the female body, the Vindhya and Himalaya ranges must run parallel to the kingdom mentioned by Bhasa. And since these mountains stretch from east to west, Bhasa's "kingdom" must also be east to west. Be it noted also that since one earring is worn on the right ear and one on the left, the kingdom in question can only be in northern India. The manuscripts were discovered in the South, but Bhasa was very likely born in the North some time between the fourth century B.C. and the first century A.D. Pandit Shastri suggests that Bhasa could not have lived very much earlier than the fourth century B.C., since Chanakya's *Artha-Shastra* quotes a verse from a Bhasa play called *Pratijnana-nataka*. If it were the other way around, Bhasa quoting from Chanakya (it does not appear so), we would be back again to the unsatisfactory chronology we began with.

Who is Bhasa, who is he that all the bards commend him? There is the famous passage in Kalidasa's *Malavika and Agnimitra*: "No, no! When plays by such an eminent poet as Bhasa are available, why bother to produce plays by living poets?" That is high praise, but it brings us to the problem of "dating" Kalidasa. A medallion discovered during the recent excavations at Bhita conducted by the Indian Archaeological Survey Department suggests that Kalidasa was born considerably before Christ. Dr. Keith puts him in the fourth century B.C., and K. M. Panikkar makes him a contemporary of King Agnimitra in the second century B.C. The chronology game goes on, but this much seems certain: Bhasa is the oldest Sanskrit dramatist we have; the thirteen plays are the work of one hand; they were written before the birth of Christ, but not earlier than 500 B.C.; and of these the finest is *The Dream of Vasavadatta*.

There is a triple pun in the title—it is dreaming of Vasavadatta in the Ocean Room in Act IV which shocks the king into realizing that the queen may still be living; but it is, after all, a *dream,* unreal ("You are right," he tells the jester, "I have been dreaming. . . . Let me dream forever, if it is a dream; let it stay with me forever."); and, finally, it is the dream, the wild hope, of Vasavadatta to be reunited with the king. Bhasa brings this out very well by compounding *svapna* (dream) and *Vasavadattam,* so that in Sanskrit the sense would roughly be "The Dream *and* Vasavadatta," and that would contain all the interpretations I have given to the title.

Bhasa is not without faults—he tends to repeat incidents, his lyricism can become sirupy (though never embarrassingly so, as in the case of Bhavabhuti), his characters are never entirely human beings, his stage directions create awkward situations. One annotator (S. Ray)—the *Dream* is a favorite textbook for Indian undergraduates doing Sanskrit; the *Gita* and Kalidasa take over for graduate studies—sweetly explains that "from this drama we learn that political and social interests were at that time given preference over self-interest. Hence for the sake of Udayana's kingdom Vasavadatta sacrificed her personal interest and happiness." This is true, but think of what it does to the characters of both Vasavadatta and Udayana. Far from being Sitaesque, Vasavadatta is merely wooden in her passive suffering and melodramatic in her fits of anger and jealousy, while

Udayana is wooden in his unbending majesty and pathetic in his protestations of love for both Vasavadatta and Padmavati. All this has to be so because of the plot. Nor is the scene at the end very expertly handled. "The stage directions assume that the queen appears on the stage with Vasavadatta as her attendant, but that the king either does not see, or does not recognize the latter, both obviously very improbable suggestions; possibly it is assumed that the presence of Vasavadatta, though obvious to the audience, is concealed from the king in some manner by the use of the curtain, but this is left to be imagined, and it would have been much simpler to invent some ground for securing the entry of Vasavadatta by herself later on." (Keith)

None the less, the *Dream* tells a pretty little story, which Bhasa picked up from the *Ramayana* legends current at the time. That he did not take it from the first century *Brihat-katha-sarit-sagara* (*Great Ocean of Rivery Stories*) seems certain; the Vasavadatta of Valmiki and the Vasavadatta of Bhasa have a self-sacrificing quality in common, which separates them sharply from the Vasavadatta of the *Ocean of Stories*. The legend, as modified by Bhasa, has a quaintly romantic never-never flavor. The Raja of Vatsa, Udayana, and the Raja of Magadha are neighbors and, as a result of royal proximity, enemies. Udayana's queen is Vasavadatta; he is ambitious (this is brought out very indirectly in Bhasa's play, and even more circuitously in Harsha's *Ratnavali*), and his minister Yaugandharayana employs hidden persuaders to win over the Raja of Magadha as an ally of Vatsa. He has a prophecy from the holy men to give him moral support: the prophecy says that Padmavati, daughter of the Raja of Magadha, will be Udayana's queen. Yaugandharayana informs Vasavadatta—without telling her that the plan entails marrying Padmavati to Udayana—that her disappearance from the capital is temporarily required for the sake of her husband's glory. The plan takes shape. Udayana's royal camp at Lavanaka, a village near Magadha, is set on fire by agents of Yaugandharayana while the king is out hunting, and rumors are spread that Vasavadatta perished in the fire, along with Yaugandharayana who was trying to rescue her. The king's general, Rumanvat, is instructed to take care of Udayana. In the meantime Yaugandharayana, disguised as a Brahmin, succeeds in getting Padmavati's promise to look after Vasavadatta (disguised as his sister) while he pretends to go away to search for her "lost" husband. Vasavadatta sees Padmavati married to her husband, Udayana.

From Ujjain (Avanti), the nurse of Vasavadatta and the chamberlain of Pradyota, her father, arrive with a portrait of Vasavadatta sent by her mother to solace Udayana in his "bereavement." Padmavati recognizes the painting as a portrait of the Brahmin girl left in her care. There is reunion and rejoicing; Udayana, lucky king, now has two lovely queens instead of one and, what is more important, has Padmavati's father as an ally at last to help him defend his capital Kausambi (by making Magadha a valuable buffer state).

Some readers may well wonder why all this heartache over mistaken and disguised identity was required at all, since the marriage of Padmavati to Udayana had been foretold and would take place in any case. Why is there such need to rush matters when the alliance would come about in any event? Such questioning is irrelevant to an appreciation of the play's rasa. It is futile to regret one's dream when one awakens; since we are the music while the music lasts, we do not ask why it is what it is.


BHASA

*Birthplace:* Unknown, but very likely in northern India.

*Date of birth:* Unknown, but probably between the fourth century B.C., and the first century A.D. Kokileswar Sastri suggests the second century B.C., but Dr. Keith and Ganapati Shastri put him in the fourth.

# THE DREAM OF VASAVADATTA

# Characters

Stage Manager

Two Guards, *of Princess Padmavati*

Yaugandharayana, *King Udayana's minister*

Vasavadatta (as Avantika), *princess of Ujjain, daughter of Pradyota, and wife of King Udayana*

Padmavati, *princess of Magadha*

Maid, *to Padmavati*

Hermit Woman

Chamberlain

Hermit

Nurse, *to Padmavati*

Jester (Vasantaka)

King Udayana, *ruler of Vatsa*

Padminika ⎰ *maids of*
Mudhukarika ⎱ *Padmavati*

Female Guard

Chamberlain of Raivya clan, *from Vasavadatta's father, king of Ujjain (Avanti)*

Vasundhara, *nurse of Vasavadatta (coming from Ujjain)*

# ACT I

*As the curtain rises the* STAGE MANAGER *enters.*

STAGE MANAGER. This is bad. The servants of the king turning out the people of the ashrama—I know their duty is to protect the princess, but—

*Two* GUARDS, *entering, interrupt him.* Make way, you. Make way.

YAUGANDHARAYANA *enters. With him is* VASAVADATTA *dressed as an Avanti lady.*

YAUGANDHARAYANA, *listening.* Here too people are being driven out! Why should these peaceful vegetarians be dispossessed? Why should there be panic among them? Who is this pride-bloated ruler who makes a market place out of a holy ashrama?

VASAVADATTA. Who is this highhanded man, sir?

YAUGANDHARAYANA. A man without grace.

VASAVADATTA. Will he drive me out too?

YAUGANDHARAYANA. He does not look like a respecter of anybody.

VASAVADATTA. The pain of his insult strikes deeper than the pain of a long and tiring journey on foot.

YAUGANDHARAYANA. You should not worry. You had power at one time to turn out people with a single word. And you gave it up. But you shall have it again when your husband is victorious. The world's a merry-go-round. . .fate turns like the spokes of a wheel.

CHAMBERLAIN, *entering.* Hey, Sambhasaka! What's going on here? Stop it! Can't you see it shames our king? Leave these ashrama people alone—poor folk, they've come to the forest to be away from the worries of the world.

YAUGANDHARAYANA. He sounds sensible. *He calls out.* Sir! . . . Sir, why are the ashrama inmates ordered about like this?

CHAMBERLAIN. Because, holy Father—

YAUGANDHARAYANA, *aside*. "Holy Father"—that's good, very good. But I'm far from being holy!

CHAMBERLAIN, *continuing*. Well, it's a simple matter really, holy Father. King Darsaka's sister, Princess Padmavati, is paying a visit to her mother, and she will spend the night here. She is very religious, and will interfere with nobody. But I suggest you tell the people to have wood, flowers, water, and sacred kusha grass ready. . .for she means to be religious.

YAUGANDHARAYANA, *aside*. I see. Magadha's princess, Padmavati. She's the one whom the astrologers predict as Udayana's future wife. That is good: it increases my regard for her.

PADMAVATI *enters with a* MAID *and other followers*.

MAID. This way, princess. This is the ashrama.

*A* HERMIT WOMAN *of the ashrama enters and welcomes* PADMAVATI.

VASAVADATTA, *aside*. Every inch a princess!

PADMAVATI. Thank you.

HERMIT WOMAN. Enter, my child. Guests are very welcome here.

PADMAVATI. I know. And your sweet words make the place even more pleasant.

VASAVADATTA, *aside*. Not only beautiful. Gracious.

HERMIT WOMAN. I am told there are arrangements for—

MAID. There are. The king of Ujjain wishes her to be united in marriage with his son.

VASAVADATTA, *aside*. The king of Ujjain is my father. I shall have a pretty sister-in-law.

HERMIT WOMAN. I am so happy. The two best families in the land!

PADMAVATI. Sir, is there any ascetic here who is in need of anything? Please make the announcement.

CHAMBERLAIN. To all the holy people of the ashrama, this message from the princess. Listen! The princess is religious and seeks the favors of your prayers, for which she humbly offers presents. Who needs a pitcher? A monk's robe? What young disciple needs something to give to his teacher? The princess requires your prayers, and she will grant presents to all today.

YAUGANDHARAYANA, *aside*. Just what I wanted! *Aloud*. I! I!

HERMIT WOMAN. He must be an outsider. All the hermits here are satisfied with what they have.

CHAMBERLAIN. What do you want, sir?

YAUGANDHARAYANA. This is my sister. Her husband has gone abroad, and I want Princess Padmavati to look after her in the meantime. I have no money, no means—this monk's robe doesn't bring me much worldly profit. I know the princess is wise and virtuous, and I know my sister could not be in better hands.

VASAVADATTA, *aside*. So! He wants to leave me here. But he must have good reason.

CHAMBERLAIN. It is difficult to give what you ask. Money, penance, even life itself may be given—and gladly. But to look after a trust. . .well—

PADMAVATI. In that case you should have limited your announcement.

CHAMBERLAIN. I am sorry.

HERMIT WOMAN. You speak very nobly, my princess.

CHAMBERLAIN. Sir, the princess accepts charge of your sister.

YAUGANDHARAYANA. I am deeply grateful to her. Vasavadatta, go to her.

VASAVADATTA, *aside*. If you say so, I will. But I hope everything turns out all right.

PADMAVATI. Now you are one of the family.

HERMIT WOMAN. You speak very nobly, my princess.

MAID. Yes, she must have seen happier times.

YAUGANDHARAYANA, *aside*. Good. That's half the work done—exactly the way I had planned it! When my king, Udayana, is restored to his kingdom, he will know Vasavadatta was in safe hands. Besides, haven't the astrologers said that Padmavati will be Udayana's queen? What could be better? Fate has an answer to everything.

*A young* HERMIT *enters the fore-stage; he looks up toward the sky and then speaks.* Noon. Am I tired! . . . But this looks like an ashrama. The deer wander about freely, breathing the harmless air. No cultivated fields nearby. The fat brown cows, the trees thick with fruit and flower, and of course the thin smoke from the huts climbing up into the sky. *He enters the ashrama.* A chamberlain. And ladies too! Have I come to the wrong place?

CHAMBERLAIN. Come in, sir. The ashrama is for everyone.

VASAVADATTA *turns aside and veils her face.*

PADMAVATI. Such modesty! I'll really have to look after her well.

CHAMBERLAIN. We were here first. So you are our guest. *He gives the young* HERMIT *a glass of water.*

HERMIT, *sipping.* Your kindness makes me forget my fatigue.

YAUGANDHARAYANA. Where do you come from, sir? Where are you going?

HERMIT. I come from Rajgriha. I had come to the village of Lavanaka to study the sacred books.

VASAVADATTA, *to herself.* Lavanaka! My grief comes to me again.

YAUGANDHARAYANA. Are your studies over?

HERMIT. No, sir.

YAUGANDHARAYANA. Yet you are here.

HERMIT. It's a sad story, sir.

YAUGANDHARAYANA. I see. . . .

HERMIT. King Udayana lives in Lavanaka.

YAUGANDHARAYANA. I have heard of him. A good king.

HERMIT. His queen is Vasavadatta, daughter of the king of Ujjain.

YAUGANDHARAYANA. I see. . . . Well?

HERMIT. He was out hunting one day, and in his absence—so the people say—the queen perished in a terrible fire that swept the village.

VASAVADATTA, *to herself*. But I am alive, more's the pity.

YAUGANDHARAYANA. Well, what happened then?

HERMIT. They say his chief minister, Yaugandharayana, jumped in to save her—

YAUGANDHARAYANA. Did he? Brave man! And then?

HERMIT. And perished too. The king on his return went mad with grief, and wanted to jump into the fire too and kill himself—but the ministers held him back.

VASAVADATTA, *to herself*. I know how much he loves me.

YAUGANDHARAYANA. Carry on—what happened next?

HERMIT. But the king wouldn't listen and pressed her burning jewels to his heart again and again. . .and fell to the ground unconscious.

ALL. Oh!

VASAVADATTA, *to herself*. I hope Yaugandharayana doesn't make a mistake now.

MAID. She is crying, my princess.

PADMAVATI, *looking at* VASAVADATTA. She has a gentle heart.

YAUGANDHARAYANA. Yes, my sister is very gentle indeed. Well, go on.

HERMIT. But the king recovered his senses—

PADMAVATI. I'm glad to hear that. My heart went numb for a second.

HERMIT, *continuing*.—and his body all brown with the dust, he suddenly stood up, and would not stop crying, and mumbled to himself: "O Vasavadatta, my queen, my wife! O Vasavadatta, my beloved!". . .What more can I say? I'm told the birds called *chakravakas* cry when separated from their mates—but not as he cried. A woman is lucky to have such a husband. She died in the fire, but lives forever in her husband's love.

YAUGANDHARAYANA. And you say there was no minister near him to give him consolation?

HERMIT. There was. Especially Rumanvat, who will not eat if the king doesn't and whose face is a valley of tears. He looks after the king day and night. If Udayana dies, he will die.

VASAVADATTA, *to herself.* That at least is good news.

YAUGANDHARAYANA, *to himself.* Rumanvat is a good man with a great burden. All depends on him, because the king depends on him. *Aloud.* Tell me, how is the king now?

HERMIT. I do not know. But I know he keeps on crying. "Here I joked with her. Here we passed the night together. Here we quarreled, here we slept. O Vasavadatta, my wife!" Then the ministers at last coaxed him to leave the village and go elsewhere. When he left the stars and moon left too. The village lay in darkness. I could not stay on there.

HERMIT WOMAN. He must be a wonderful king to receive such praise from a stranger.

MAID. Will he let anyone become his new queen?

PADMAVATI, *to herself.* I wonder.

HERMIT. Please, sir, may I have your permission to leave now?

YAUGANDHARAYANA. Our blessings go with you.

HERMIT. Thank you. *He departs.*

YAUGANDHARAYANA. If I could leave too, for my work is over. . . ?

CHAMBERLAIN. The holy Father wishes permission to leave.

PADMAVATI. Sir, your sister will miss you terribly.

YAUGANDHARAYANA. She is in safe hands. She will not miss me long. *He prepares to leave.*

CHAMBERLAIN. Please visit us whenever you can.

YAUGANDHARAYANA. I will. *He departs.*

CHAMBERLAIN. Let us go in.

PADMAVATI, *to the* HERMIT WOMAN. I am so grateful to you.

HERMIT WOMAN. My blessings on you, child. May you get the husband you deserve so well.

VASAVADATTA. I am grateful to you, Mother.

HERMIT WOMAN. Child, may you see your husband soon.

VASAVADATTA. Thank you.

CHAMBERLAIN. Let us go. This way, please. The birds are now in their nests, the hermits have gone to the pool. How brilliantly the sacred fire gleams! The wayworn sun turns his chariot into the mountain cave.

*All depart.*

C U R T A I N


## ACT II

*A* MAID *enters, and peers offstage.*

MAID. Kunjarika! Kunjarika! Where is princess Padmavati? *She appears to listen.* What's that? She's in the garden, playing with a ball? Thank you. I'll go to her. *She circles the stage.* There she is, looking tired and perspiring, playing with her ball. How graceful she looks. *She goes out.*

PADMAVATI *enters, with her attendants. She throws a ball to* VASAVADATTA, *who is still dressed as a lady of Avanti.*

VASAVADATTA, *catching the ball.* Your throw, my princess.

PADMAVATI. No, thank you. We have played long enough today.

VASAVADATTA. But you were just beginning to enjoy the game.

MAID. Oh, do let us play. We're only young once.

PADMAVATI, *to* VASAVADATTA. What do you mean?

VASAVADATTA. Just that you looked so charming when you were playing that we thought—

PADMAVATI. Oh, come now—

VASAVADATTA. I'm sorry. But you did look charming enough to be Pradyota's daughter-in-law.

PADMAVATI. And who, may I ask, is Pradyota?

VASAVADATTA. Pradyota is the king of Ujjain.

MAID. You don't know, Vasavadatta. The princess has a different desire. Have another guess.

VASAVADATTA. I don't know. You tell me.

MAID. The princess is in love with Udayana, king of Vatsa.

VASAVADATTA, *aside*. In love with my husband. *Aloud.* I see. And is there a special reason for loving him?

MAID. No, nothing special, except that he is a gentle man.

VASAVADATTA, *aside*. She tells me my husband is gentle. As if I did not know.

MAID. I don't know if he is good-looking, though.

VASAVADATTA. Of course he's good-looking.

PADMAVATI. How do *you* know?

VASAVADATTA, *aside*. There I go again. *Aloud.* Well, that's what I am told the citizens of Ujjain say.

PADMAVATI. They should know. Good looks don't go unnoticed.

*A* NURSE *enters and addresses herself immediately to* PADMAVATI. I bring happy news, princess. Your engagement has been announced.

VASAVADATTA. To whom?

NURSE. Udayana, king of Vatsa.

VASAVADATTA, *starting but checking herself.* Is he well then?

NURSE. He has arrived here safely, and agreed to marry our princess.

VASAVADATTA. Oh, how terrible!

NURSE. Why, what's terrible about it?

VASAVADATTA. I only meant that he was so sad a few days ago over the death of his wife—

NURSE. Great men don't stay sad too long. They are always thinking of greater and better opportunities.

VASAVADATTA. Did he propose himself?

NURSE. Oh, no. He came here on some royal business, and our king, impressed by his breeding and good looks, suggested the engagement.

VASAVADATTA, *to herself.* I knew he wasn't to blame.

*A* MAID *enters and speaks excitedly.* Hurry, hurry—the queen says today is an excellently auspicious day for the marriage ceremony.

VASAVADATTA, *to herself.* She hurries to her marriage, and darkness descends on my heart.

MAID. This way, princess.

CURTAIN

## ACT III

VASAVADATTA *enters, deep in thought.*

VASAVADATTA. This garden's the best place for me. The other ladies are busy with the marriage preparations in the inner palace rooms. *She walks about the stage disconsolately.* My husband is now another's. *She sits down on a bench.* Such is my fate. But I will live, I will cling to sad life, in the hope that I can see my husband again.

*A* MAID *enters, carrying a basket of flowers.*

MAID. Where is the lady of Avanti? *She notices* VASAVADATTA. Ah, under the creeper, sitting on a bench. So sweet and graceful. *To* VASAVADATTA. I have been looking for you everywhere. The princess Padmavati says, "The lady of Avanti is highborn, loving, and intelligent. Let her make a marriage garland."

VASAVADATTA. For whom?

MAID. For the princess Padmavati, of course.

VASAVADATTA, *aside.* The gods *are* cruel, making this a part of my duties.

MAID. The garland is needed soon. The king is getting ready for the ceremony.

VASAVADATTA. Have you seen him?

MAID. Yes. I was curious. I had a glimpse of him.

VASAVADATTA. How did he look?

MAID. Oh, words cannot describe him.

VASAVADATTA. But tell me, is he handsome?

MAID. He is the god of love in person—without the bow and arrows. VASAVADATTA *looks displeased.* Why, have I said anything wrong?

VASAVADATTA. It's not proper to discuss someone else's husband. Give me the flowers. I'll do the garland. *She empties the basket and examines the flowers one by one.* What is this one called?

MAID. That's *avidhava-karana,* the flower that prevents widowhood.

VASAVADATTA, *aside.* I shall put many of these in the garland, for her sake as well as mine. *Aloud.* And this?

MAID. That stops the arrival of another wife.

VASAVADATTA. None of this kind.

MAID. Why?

VASAVADATTA. His first wife is dead.

*Another* MAID *enters.*

SECOND MAID. Hurry, hurry! The king is in the inner palace room, led by the maids of the princess.

VASAVADATTA *hands her the finished garland. Both* MAIDS *leave.* VASAVADATTA *follows, sorrowfully.*

*The* JESTER *enters, chuckling.* What fun to be alive at wedding time! Who would have thought we'd survive the great calamity of the queen's death? But here I am, bathing in the pools of the harem, and gulping down sweets whose nature is goluptious. *Sadly.* So goluptious that my belly protests; the pangs of indigestion overpower me. Too much sweetness is a jaundice in the blood. What good are big fat sweets without fine fit flesh?

*A* MAID *enters.* Vasantaka, where have you been hiding?

JESTER. Sweet girl, why have you been searching?

MAID. The princess Padmavati wishes to know if His Majesty has finished the ritual bath.

JESTER. The answer to that shall be given if the reason for the question be known.

MAID. So that flowers and scents may be brought before His Majesty.

JESTER. In that case he has bathed. Bring the goodies, my good girl— but, I beg of you, do not bring food.

MAID. What's wrong with food?

JESTER. Nothing's wrong with food. Everything's wrong with my stomach. My bowels whirl round and round like the eyes of a cuckoo.

*Both leave.*

PADMAVATI *and* VASAVADATTA *enter, escorted by the* MAID. VASAVADATTA *is still dressed as a lady of Avanti.*

MAID. Why the pleasure garden, my princess?

PADMAVATI. To see the *sephalika* flowers in bloom.

MAID. They *are* in bloom, so red that they bring out the green of the other plants.

PADMAVATI. Let's sit here. Shall we sit, Vasavadatta?

MAID. I'll get some flowers. *She steps offstage and returns with flowers.* Look at these! My hands are full of their passionate color.

PADMAVATI, *looking at the flowers.* How lovely! Aren't they lovely, Vasavadatta?

VASAVADATTA. Very lovely.

MAID. Shall I get more?

PADMAVATI. No, no more now.

VASAVADATTA. Why not let her?

PADMAVATI. I want my husband to see their beauty on the trees. I'll be so proud.

VASAVADATTA. You love your husband so much?

PADMAVATI. Oh, I don't know. But I miss him terribly if he's not with me.

MAID. What a noble way of saying, "I love my husband!"

PADMAVATI. With one small misgiving that worries me all the time.

VASAVADATTA. What?

PADMAVATI. Did Vasavadatta love him as much as I do?

VASAVADATTA. She loved him more.

PADMAVATI. How do you know?

VASAVADATTA, *to herself.* There goes my tongue again! *Aloud.* She wouldn't have left her family the way she did if her love had been ordinary.

PADMAVATI. Yes.

MAID. He loves the lute. I am learning to play it.

PADMAVATI. I've already told him you are.

VASAVADATTA. Did he say anything?

PADMAVATI. He heaved a deep sigh, and kept silent.

VASAVADATTA. That's strange.

PADMAVATI. I think he remembered Vasavadatta's charms, but didn't dare say so openly. He wants to show he loves all his wives equally. He's so well-mannered.

VASAVADATTA, *to herself.* I am a lucky woman.

*The* KING *and the* JESTER *enter.*

JESTER. Bravo! Soft breezes in the garden, the scent of flowers plucked and strewn on the ground. This way, sire.

KING. When I was in Ujjain, my friend, a long time back, on a short visit, the god of love fired all his five arrows at me the moment I saw the beauty of Vasavadatta. Now he shoots at me again. Hasn't he only the five arrows, though? Where does he get the sixth?

JESTER. Where is Princess Padmavati? Has she come to the garden house, or the stone bench where *asana* flowers fall, or the grove of the seven-leafed trees? *He looks upward.* Look at the lovely cranes, sire, up in the autumn sky, flying in formation like the outstretched arms of a man.

KING. They *are* pretty. Now straight, now curving, swinging up and down like a massive constellation. The sky is like the belly of a serpent, and the cranes are the line that runs its length.

MAID. Look at the cranes, princess, like flying lotuses—oh, he's here!

PADMAVATI. My husband! *To* VASAVADATTA. I can't let him see me in these morning clothes. Let's hide behind this jasmine bush. Quick!

*The three women conceal themselves.*

JESTER. She must have come and left.

KING. How do you know?

JESTER. Someone's been plucking from the white *sephalika* there.

KING. Aren't they lovely, Vasantaka?

VASAVADATTA, *aside.* The way he says Vasantaka reminds me of Ujjain.

KING. Let's wait here for Padmavati.

JESTER. Yes, sire. *He sits down.* The heat's terrible! Let's go under the jasmine.

KING. Good.

*The* KING *and the* JESTER *walk toward the jasmine bush.*

PADMAVATI. Vasantaka has to spoil everything! What now?

MAID. This creeper will do the trick. I'll shake the bees on them.

PADMAVATI. I hope it works.

*The* MAID *shakes the creeper.*

JESTER, *in consternation.* Wait, sire, wait!

KING. What's the matter?

JESTER. Those blasted bees!

KING. Let them alone. After all, you disturbed them first. Let them make love to their honey in peace. We'll turn back. *Both return and sit on a stone bench.* Someone's been trampling on the flowers here. And this bench is still warm. Who could have been here? They left when they saw us coming.

MAID. We're caught.

PADMAVATI. I'm glad he's found a place to sit down.

VASAVADATTA, *aside.* I'm glad he's looking so well.

MAID. Vasavadatta is crying.

VASAVADATTA. No, it's nothing—just the pollen the bees flung into my eyes.

JESTER. I want to ask you something in private. This place looks deserted enough.

KING. Fire away.

JESTER. Tell me, did you love Vasavadatta more than you love Padmavati?

KING. What a funny question to ask!

PADMAVATI. What can he say?

VASAVADATTA, *aside*. I feel so lost.

JESTER. Frankly, now—no hocus-pocus. One is dead, the other's not listening.

KING. You are a curious jester. I refuse to answer.

PADMAVATI. That's a good answer.

JESTER. Oh, come, come—I won't tell anyone. My word for it!

KING. I don't feel like answering stupid questions.

PADMAVATI. The impudent fool! Doesn't he understand he's hurting my husband?

JESTER. You're my prisoner, sire. If you don't answer, I won't let you budge from here.

KING. You mean you won't let me get up?

JESTER. Yes.

KING. Very well, we'll see.

JESTER. I'm sorry, sire, I didn't mean anything. It's just that I know you so well.

KING. You are a fool. However, if you must have an answer. . .I think Padmavati is the finest lady in the world—for her beauty, her character, her grace. But she cannot take my heart away from Vasavadatta.

VASAVADATTA, *aside*. I have suffered, but now I suffer no more.

MAID. That's a strange thing to say, princess.

PADMAVATI. No. It's noble of him to remember Vasavadatta.

VASAVADATTA. And it's noble of you to say so.

KING. Does *that* satisfy you? Now, my friend, you must answer my question. Whom do *you* like better, Vasavadatta or Padmavati?

PADMAVATI. My husband turns the tables!

JESTER. Oh—ah—hmmm. . .Well, I like them both. Quite a lot!

KING. Shut up! I answered frankly, why don't you?

JESTER. You'll force me to answer?

KING. Indeed I will.

JESTER. Then you'll get nothing. . .

KING. O Brahmin, O Fool, please, please. . .tell me what you like—I won't force you.

JESTER. That's better. Listen. I was very fond of Queen Vasavadatta. But Princess Padmavati is young, smiling, gracious, kind—and beautiful! Besides, she has a special quality that I don't easily forget. She serves me the tastiest dishes of the palace, saying, "Where is Vasantaka? Where is Vasantaka?"

VASAVADATTA, *aside*. Just like you—you ingrate!

KING. I'll tell Vasavadatta this.

JESTER. Vasavadatta! . . . Where is Vasavadatta? She is dead.

KING, *sorrowfully*. Yes, she is dead. The words slipped out of my mouth. Vasavadatta is here no more. . . .

PADMAVATI. The fool!—he's spoiled the pretty talk.

VASAVADATTA, *aside*. How nice to hear sweet words unobserved!

JESTER. That's all right, sire. What can we do? Our fate plays tricks on us.

KING. You cannot understand, Vasantaka. Even if my grief departs, my love remains rooted in her. And so my memory brings back my grief. . . . This is the way with ordinary people: they get relief by shedding tears.

JESTER. I'll get you water to wash your face. *He departs.*

PADMAVATI. He is crying. Let us go to him.

VASAVADATTA. No, you go—he is disturbed.

PADMAVATI. Shall I go to him?

VASAVADATTA. You must.

PADMAVATI *approaches the* KING.

*The* JESTER *enters, carrying water in a lotus leaf.* Princess Padmavati is here.

PADMAVATI. Vasantaka, what's the matter?

JESTER. Er—I mean—it's—

PADMAVATI. Come to the point, sir. What's the matter?

JESTER. Dust got into his eyes; this water is for him to wash them with.

PADMAVATI, *aside.* A neat reply. *Aloud to the* KING. My lord, here is water for your eyes.

KING. Padmavati! *Aside.* Vasantaka, what's the meaning of this? *The* JESTER *whispers in his ear.* Good. *Aloud.* Sit down, Padmavati. *She sits, as he lightly washes his eyes with the water and continues speaking.* You see, it's dusty here, the pollen got into my eyes. *Aside.* No point in telling her the truth—she'll just be upset.

JESTER. This afternoon will be a busy one for you, sire, what with all the interviews that have been arranged. We should get ready.

KING. A good idea. *He rises.* It's a pleasure to meet men of quality, there are so few of them.

C U R T A I N

## ACT IV

PADMINIKA *enters hurriedly in front of the curtain. She is shouting.*

PADMINIKA. Madhukarika! Madhukarika! Quick! Come here!

MADHUKARIKA, *entering.* What's wrong? Here I am.

PADMINIKA. Don't you know Princess Padmavati has a splitting headache?

MADHUKARIKA. I didn't know.

PADMINIKA. Well, hurry. Tell Lady Avantika.

MADHUKARIKA. What can she do?

PADMINIKA. Her pleasant stories will help to soothe our princess.

MADHUKARIKA. Where is Princess Padmavati?

PADMINIKA. In the Ocean Room. Hurry, go. I'll try to find Vasantaka too, so that he can tell the king. Go now. *Madhukarika leaves.* Now where can Vasantaka be?

JESTER, *entering and speaking to himself.* Even on his marriage day the king cannot forget Vasavadatta. Such is love! *He sees* PADMINIKA. Padminika, what news?

PADMINIKA. Don't you know, Vasantaka, that Princess Padmavati has an awful, awful headache?

JESTER. Don't you know, Padminika, that I don't?

PADMINIKA. Hurry, go tell the king. In the meantime I'll get the medicine.

JESTER. Where is she?

PADMINIKA. In the Ocean Room—that way. *She points offstage.*

JESTER. It's done. In a jiffy. The king shall know of it.


PADMINIKA *and the* JESTER *depart. As the curtain rises, the* KING *enters the main stage, speaking to himself.*


KING. She lives in my memory—the tall and graceful daughter of the king of Ujjain, my wife whom the flames killed as frost kills the lotus. I am married again, but she lives in my memory.

JESTER, *dashing in, shouting.* Hurry, sire! Princess Padmavati is in bed with an awful headache.

KING. Who told you?

JESTER. Padminika.

KING. Bad news. Where is she?

JESTER. Padminika said in the Ocean Room.

KING. Take me there.

JESTER. This way, sire.

*They both walk a short distance.*

This is the Ocean Room, sire.

KING. You go in first.

JESTER, *entering the room*. Sire, stay back!

KING. What's the matter?

JESTER. A snake, sire—rolling on the ground. I see him in the light of the lamp.

*The* KING *enters and looks around*. No wonder they call you fool. It's a garland someone dropped, Vasantaka, quivering in the breeze. Can't you see?

JESTER, *shamefacedly*. Sire, it's not a snake. But there's no one here. Princess Padmavati seems to have gone away.

KING. Gone? She hasn't even come here yet. The bed sheets aren't rumpled. The pillow isn't soiled with the headache ointment. A sick person doesn't just get up and walk away. You know that.

JESTER. We could wait here for her.

KING. Now you're being sensible. *He sits on the bed*. I'm tired, Vasantaka. Tell me a story.

JESTER. You'll have a story. You "hmm" along with me. Like this—"hmm, hmm."

KING. We'll see.

JESTER. Well, once upon a time, in a city by the pleasant name of Ujjain, the finest swimming pools belonged to a man called—

KING. What!—Ujjain!

JESTER. If you don't like Ujjain, we'll tell you another story.

KING. No, I love Ujjain. But the memories, Vasantaka! The daughter
of the king of Ujjain! When she left her father to be my wife, her tears fell
burning on my breast. Such memories, Vasantaka. . .of her at her music
lesson, her fingers suddenly limp, strumming the soundless air. . . .

JESTER. We'll change the story. The city is Brahmadatta, where rules a
king named Kampilya—

KING. What?

JESTER. The city is Brahmadatta, where rules a king named Kampilya—

KING. You mean the king is Brahmadatta, the city is Kampilya.

JESTER. The king is Brahmadatta, the city is Kampilya?

KING. That's right.

JESTER. Wait. I must memorize that. The king is Brahmadatta, the
city is Kampilya. *He repeats it over and over again. The king has lain
down on the bed.* That's it. Now we can start the story—but he's sound
asleep! Whew, it's cold. . .cold. I'll go get my shawl. *He departs.*

VASAVADATTA *enters, dressed as a lady of Avanti. With her is a* MAID.

MAID. Hurry. She has a splitting headache.

VASAVADATTA. Where is she?

MAID. In the Ocean Room. Come with me. I'll take you there. . . . Here
it is. I'll be back with the medicine shortly. *She leaves.*

VASAVADATTA. Fate couldn't be more unkind. Padmavati is now ill—and
she the only person who could help my husband to forget his sorrow. *She
enters the Ocean Room and looks around.* How careless these girls are!
Padmavati is sleeping, with no one to look after her but this lonely lamp.
I'll sit by her side in the dark. *She does so.* The breathing is slow and easy.
She must be feeling better now. Did she beckon me? I'll lie by her side: it
will soothe her. *She lies down beside the king.*

KING, *dreaming.* Vasavadatta!

VASAVADATTA, *springing up*. Not Padmavati! My husband. . .has he recognized me? What will happen to Yaugandharayana's plans?

KING, *still dreaming*. Vasavadatta. . .daughter of the king of Avanti.

VASAVADATTA. He's talking in his sleep. How sweet to listen to him!

KING. My dearest, speak to me.

VASAVADATTA. I will, I will.

KING. Dearest, are you angry?

VASAVADATTA. No, not angry. Unhappy.

KING. Come to me, dearest. *He stretches out his arms.*

VASAVADATTA. I have stayed here too long. Someone might see me. But before I go. . .*She lifts his arm, which is hanging partly over the edge of the bed, and places it by his side. Then she leaves.*

KING, *wakening suddenly*. Vasavadatta, wait! Did I dream? Was she real?

JESTER, *entering*. You're awake.

KING. I have good news for you, Vasantaka. Vasavadatta is alive.

JESTER. Vasavadatta! She is dead.

KING. That's what everyone thinks. But she was here just now. She touched me, she woke me up—then she ran out. Rumanvat must not have known the whole truth when he told me she had been burned in the flames.

JESTER. What nonsense! You have been dreaming. And my story about the swimming pools of Ujjain has fired your imagination.

KING. You are right. I have been dreaming. . . . Let me dream forever, if it is a dream; let it stay with me forever.

JESTER. There's a nymph in the city called Avantika. You must have seen her.

KING. No, I saw Vasavadatta's face, her long hair, her dark eyes—I saw the lady of chastity. She touched me here: my arm still trembles with love of her.

JESTER. This is all very silly. Let's go in.

CHAMBERLAIN, *entering*. Great news, sire! King Darsaka sends you the message that your general, Rumanvat, has arrived with elephants, horses, chariots, and a vast army of soldiers to crush the enemy, Aruni. All preparations for the battle have been made. Only your presence now is needed. We are lucky: the enemy is a divided camp. The Ganga has already been crossed, and our forces are in sight of the kingdom of Vatsa.

KING. Brilliant. Aruni's end is near. Our arrows shall fall like waves on his ranks, and the elephants and horses shall march triumphantly on the ocean of his sins.

*They all depart.*

C U R T A I N

# ACT V

*The* CHAMBERLAIN *enters as the curtain rises, and addresses a* FEMALE GUARD.

CHAMBERLAIN. Who's on duty here at the golden gate?

FEMALE GUARD. I, sir. Vijaya.

CHAMBERLAIN. Listen carefully, Vijaya. Tell King Udayana, who has now won back his lost kingdom, that the chamberlain of the Raivya clan is at the gate and wishes to have audience with him. With the chamberlain is Vasundhara, the nurse of Vasavadatta, who also seeks audience.

FEMALE GUARD. This is not the time nor the place for such a message.

CHAMBERLAIN. Why, what's wrong?

FEMALE GUARD. Nothing's wrong, sir. But this morning when a man was playing the lute, our king heard him and said, "That's Ghoshavati, isn't it?" And the king went up to him and asked where the man had found the lute. "Near the banks of the river Narmada. Take it, sire, if you like it," said the man. The king took it, put it in his lap—and fainted! When he recovered, his face was in tears. "So you have come home, Ghoshavati, at last!" he cried. "But *she* hasn't." So you see, sir, I can't give him a message—in the condition he's in.

CHAMBERLAIN. I think you can. Our business has a lot to do with the story you have told us.

FEMALE GUARD. I can see him coming down from Princess Padmavati's palace. I shall give him the message.

*The* CHAMBERLAIN *and the* FEMALE GUARD *leave. The* KING *enters, carrying a lute and accompanied by the* JESTER.

KING, *addressing the lute.* Once you rested in the arms of my queen, Vasavadatta—how did you find your way into the lonely and musty forest? Ghoshavati, you are ungrateful. You don't remember the love she showered on you, how she embraced you when we were together, smiled at you and stroked you softly. . . .

JESTER. It is not good to be so sad, sire.

KING. I know. But this lute kindles my love again. Ghoshavati is here, but *she* is not here. Look. Take this and have it repaired as soon as you can. And bring it back to me.

JESTER. Yes, sire. *He takes the lute and departs.*

FEMALE GUARD, *entering.* Sire, a chamberlain of the Raivya clan and Vasavadatta's nurse Vasundhara wish to see you. They have been sent by Angaravati. They are waiting at the gate.

KING. Ask Padmavati to come here.

*The* FEMALE GUARD *leaves.*

News travels fast!

PADMAVATI *enters, accompanied by the* FEMALE GUARD.

PADMAVATI. My lord.

KING. Padmavati, the guard tells me that a chamberlain of the Raivya clan of Pradyota, together with Vasavadatta's nurse Vasundhara, has come to see me.

PADMAVATI. It is good news to hear from one's relatives.

KING. I am glad you say that. Sit down, Padmavati. It is good of you to treat Vasavadatta's relatives as your own.

PADMAVATI. You do not mind my sitting next to you when you speak to them?

KING. No. Why should I mind?

PADMAVATI. I am your second wife, my lord. It may look awkward.

KING. It looks more than awkward not to treat one's wife as one's own, especially in front of others.

PADMAVATI, *sitting down*. I wonder who sends the message, father or mother?

KING. I don't know, Padmavati. But my heart is full of apprehension. What will they say? After all, I eloped with her. And I couldn't even give her the protection she needed. I feel like a guilty son in front of a father. *To the* FEMALE GUARD. Show them in.

*The* FEMALE GUARD *goes out and returns with the* CHAMBERLAIN *and* VASUNDHARA.

CHAMBERLAIN. There is no greater joy than visiting an ally, but the death of Queen Vasavadatta hangs like a shadow over our happiness. I bring greetings from King Pradyota, sire.

KING. You are welcome here. How is he?

CHAMBERLAIN. In excellent health, sire, and hopes you are too.

KING, *rising*. What is his wish? His least desire is a command.

CHAMBERLAIN. Nobly spoken, sire. King Pradyota says he is happy that you have regained your lost kingdom. He says fortune was always on the side of the courageous and never smiles on the weak and the hesitant.

KING, *sitting down again*. He is kind to me. I remember he brought me up as his own son. Then I eloped with his daughter, and could not look after her well, as you know. Yet he has the same affection for me. Please take my gratitude back to him.

CHAMBERLAIN. This lady brings the message of our queen.

KING. How is she? I remember she wept when I left: how can I forget?

VASUNDHARA. She is all right, sire, and hopes all are well here.

KING. All well! All well! Well. . .

CHAMBERLAIN. The lady Vasavadatta can never die, sire, if you remember her so lovingly. Death comes to all, sire. The rope snaps, the pitcher falls. Trees, men—they rise and decay. Nothing detains death.

KING. You make a mistake, sir. She was my queen. I taught her to play the lute. She lives in me forever.

VASUNDHARA. My queen sends this message: "Vasavadatta is dead, but you are our son-in-law, as dear to us as our sons Gopalaka and Palaka. We wanted you to marry her. That is why we asked you to teach her to play the lute. But you were rash and ran away with her. In your absence we drew your portrait and hers on a plate and performed the wedding ceremony. This is the plate; it is yours now, and it carries our love for you with it."

KING. A hundred kingdoms couldn't give me the happiness I now feel. I was guilty—yet I am loved.

PADMAVATI. This is the plate?

VASUNDHARA. Yes. *She hands the plate to* PADMAVATI.

PADMAVATI, *looking at the portraits and speaking to herself.* The face is the face of the lady of Avanti. *Aloud.* Is this a good likeness, my lord?

KING. Better than a likeness, it is she herself. But where is she now?

PADMAVATI. And this is my husband's portrait?

VASUNDHARA. This one here.

PADMAVATI. What a marvelous resemblance! It must be she!

KING. You look worried. Is anything wrong?

PADMAVATI. There's a lady in the palace who is the exact double of this portrait.

KING. You mean this? Vasavadatta's portrait?

PADMAVATI. Yes, my lord.

KING. Send for her—immediately!

PADMAVATI. She was put in my trust by a Brahmin, who said she was his sister. Her husband has gone abroad, and she avoids strangers. We could let Vasundhara judge if there is a likeness or not.

KING. If she is the Brahmin's sister, then she can't be Vasavadatta. Many people look alike. It's quite common.

FEMALE GUARD, *entering.* A Brahmin from Ujjain waits at the gate. He has come to take back his sister, whom he placed in Princess Padmavati's charge.

KING. Send him in. And, Padmavati, bring the lady here too.

PADMAVATI *and the* FEMALE GUARD *leave.* YAUGANDHARAYANA, *disguised as a Brahmin and accompanied by the* FEMALE GUARD, *enters.*

YAUGANDHARAYANA, *to himself.* I did what I thought was best. I don't know how he will take it.

FEMALE GUARD. This way, sir. The king will see you here.

YAUGANDHARAYANA. My blessings, sire.

KING. The voice sounds familiar. You say you placed your sister in my wife's charge?

YAUGANDHARAYANA. Yes, sire.

KING, *to the* FEMALE GUARD. Bring his sister here.

*The* FEMALE GUARD *goes out, and in a moment returns, bringing* PADMA-VATI *and* VASAVADATTA, *who is veiled, with her.*

PADMAVATI. I have good news for you.

VASAVADATTA. What is it?

PADMAVATI. Your brother has come to take you back.

KING. Return her, Padmavati. In front of these witnesses, the noble chamberlain and the respected Vasundhara.

PADMAVATI. Here is your sister, sir.

VASUNDHARA, *looking closely at* VASAVADATTA. But this is Vasavadatta!

KING. What! *Quickly.* Padmavati, take her in.

YAUGANDHARAYANA. She is my sister.

KING. Sir, do you deny that she is Vasavadatta, the daughter of King Pradyota?

YAUGANDHARAYANA. You are wise and noble, sire. It does not suit your character to take my sister away from me by force.

KING. Remove the veil.

YAUGANDHARAYANA. My king!

VASAVADATTA. My husband!

KING. So it's Yaugandharayana. And you *are* Vasavadatta! Am I dreaming still? I saw you, but you were a dream then. . . .

YAUGANDHARAYANA, *falling at the* KING'S *feet.* Sire, it is all my fault. Forgive me.

KING. You are a shrewd man, Yaugandharayana. Rise. I am grateful to you. Your ruses have pulled us through many difficulties.

YAUGANDHARAYANA. I have always done what I thought would be best for you.

PADMAVATI. I treated you so carelessly, Vasavadatta! *She falls at* VASAVADATTA'S *feet.* I did not know.

VASAVADATTA, *lifting her.* Please. . .you embarrass me. It's perfectly all right.

PADMAVATI. I am grateful to you.

KING. And why did you do all this, Yaugandharayana?

YAUGANDHARAYANA. It was the best way of defending the kingdom of Kausambi—through the marriage alliance with Padmavati's father.

KING. Why did you leave her in Padmavati's hands?

YAUGANDHARAYANA. Astrologers had predicted Padmavati would be your queen one day.

KING. Did Rumanvat know of this?

YAUGANDHARAYANA. Sire, it was common knowledge.

KING. The rascal! He tricked me!

YAUGANDHARAYANA. Sire, let the Chamberlain and Vasundhara take the good news to King Pradyota.

KING. No. We'll all go together. Padmavati will come with us.

*All go out together.*

C U R T A I N

# THE LATER STORY OF RAMA

by

## BHAVABHUTI

# Preface

The latter part of Valmiki's epic, the *Ramayana,* forms the background of *The Later Story of Rama*, but Bhavabhuti also wrote another play, the *Vira Charitra (Portrait of a Hero)*, dealing with Rama's early years. Of Bhavabhuti's three plays, *The Later Story of Rama* is concerned with developing the *karuna* rasa, the sentiment of tenderness; *Portrait of a Hero* develops the *vira* rasa, the sentiment of heroism; and *Malati and Madhava,* like *Shakuntala,* concerns itself with nuances relating to the sentiment of love, or *sringara* rasa. That Bhavabhuti chose Rama as the hero of two of his plays is not a coincidence—his forte was not what Bharata, the theorist of Sanskrit drama, described as the "invented play"; he preferred to operate within the confines of an established plot and always succeeded in molding it with extreme delicacy.

There have been numerous translations and versions of the *Ramayana,* among them those by "Asiatic" Jones, Wilford, Ward and Faber, and the Serampore missionaries Carey and Marshman. Since then, a didactic retelling of the story of Rama by C. Rajagopalachari, somewhat Edwardian in tone, and an eminently irreverent spoof by Aubrey Menen called *Rama Retold* (in America *The Ramayana*) have been added to the list. The Ayodhya Canto of the Kamba *Ramayana* is also available in the UNESCO Representative Works series, and for the assiduous reader there is the excellent three-volume translation by H. P. Shastri. The summary of Valmiki's tale that follows is largely a condensation of Wilson's, combined with Swami Vivekananda's elaborate account in the fourth volume of his *Complete Works*.

From the sage Pulastya, one of the "will-born progeny of Brahma," are descended various demonic races known as the asuras, daityas, and rakshasas, all hostile to the stability of the natural moral order. Their ranks are increased by the spirits of the vicious and the condemned as well as those who lust for wealth. The ten-headed Ravana, half brother of Kuvera, god of wealth, usurps the kingdom of Lanka, and upsets the balance of the natural order by his tyrannical use of authority. Vishnu, the Preserver in the Hindu trinity, is incarnated as Rama in order to restore the balance. He is born in the palace of King Dasharatha of Ayodhya, to his wife Kaush-alya; Dasharatha has two other wives, Kaikeyi (whose son is Bharata) and Sumitra (whose sons are Lakshmana and Shatrughna).

In his childhood, Rama pleases the sage Vishvamitra by killing the female rakshasa Tadaka, in return for which he is given celestial weapons which make him invincible. Vishvamitra takes Rama to Mithila, the kingdom of Janaka; here Rama not only bends but breaks the Haridhanu, the bow of Shiva, and is rewarded by marriage to Sita, daughter of Janaka. Sita's sister Urmila, and her cousins Mandavi and Srutakirti, marry Lakshmana, Bharata, and Shatrughna, respectively.

The happy couples return to Ayodhya. When the time comes to install Rama as king, Dasharatha is reminded that he had promised two boons to Kaikeyi, redeemable whenever she wished, because she had nursed him when he had once been grievously wounded in battle. Kaikeyi is incited by her evil-minded maid, Manthara, to demand first that her son Bharata be crowned instead of Rama, and second, that Rama be banished for fourteen years. Dasharatha dies shortly thereafter, and Bharata rules on behalf of Rama, who goes into forest exile accompanied by Sita and Lakshmana.

In the Dandaka forest on the banks of the Godavari (there are numerous allusions to this river in *The Later Story of Rama*), Rama continues his killing rakshasas. He has Lakshmana cut off the nose and ears of Sur-panakha, Ravana's sister, when she makes amorous advances—his way of killing his interest in these advances!—and her brothers Khara and Dushana, to whom she appeals for revenge, are next slain. Surpanakha appeals to Ravana, who agrees to help and transforms his uncle Marichi into a golden deer whose role will be to distract Rama. Sita sends Laksh-mana to look for Rama who is chasing the deer for her; in the meantime Ravana, disguised as a holy beggar, lures her to step out of the magic circle Lakshmana had drawn around the ashrama for her protection, and abducts her. The king of birds, the eagle Jatayu, tries to intercept the flying chariot and is fatally struck down by Ravana.

Rama, returning, is able to get Ravana's name from the dying bird, but it is only after he helps the monkey king Sugriva to kill Sugriva's treacher-ous brother Vali that he succeeds, through Hanuman's efforts, in learning where Ravana has taken Sita. The giant monkey Hanuman leaps across the

Indian peninsula to Lanka (Ceylon), meets Sita, sets the city on fire, using his lighted tail as a huge matchstick, and returns to Rama with the exact details. Rama gathers an immense army; a bridge is constructed; Ravana's brother Vibhishana deserts Lanka and joins the forces of Rama. The city is invaded by the monkey army and Ravana is killed by Rama. Strangely for an incarnation of Vishnu, Rama passes Sita through the "fire test" in order to establish her purity before the restless soldiers. She emerges unscathed, seated on a throne carried by the god of fire, and the *Ramayana* ends with the traitor Vibhishana on the throne of Lanka and the return of Rama and his party to Ayodhya, where Bharata eagerly waits to hand over the kingdom to his elder brother. Homer often has our sympathies for the Trojans rather than the Greeks, and Valmiki, legendary author of the *Ramayana,* is not always kind to the tactics of Rama. The actual *Ramayana,* in fact, ends here; an *Uttara-Kanda,* or supplement, describes the later events.

Bhavabhuti takes up from here, and rounds off Valmiki's tale. Rama spends a few years happily ruling Ayodhya, but the citizens begin murmuring again. To please them, he banishes Sita; the poet Valmiki gives her shelter in his ashrama. When she gives birth to twins, Lava and Kusha, Valmiki hides their identity from them, but forces them to learn by heart the entire *Ramayana,* which he is said to have composed in a nonstop bout of inspiration.

The twins grow up; and it is now time for Rama to perform the Ashva-medha, or the ritual of the horse sacrifice. Since a Hindu must have his wife, or *sahadharmini* ("coreligionist"), by his side during the performance of any religious rite, Rama is implored by his subjects to marry again. He refuses—one of the few really manlike things he does—and has a life-size golden statue of Sita made for the sacred occasion. A play is also to be performed, and Valmiki has Lava and Kusha chant the entire *Ramayana* to the assembled concourse (the book has five hundred cantos and, at the rate of twenty a day, it must have taken a month to sing the epic). Rama is deeply disturbed by the narration of the story of his own life, and suffers a nervous breakdown when the scene of Sita's exile is presented in the play. Valmiki has Sita brought on the stage, but the audience again clamors for the fire test. Brokenhearted, she asks her mother Prithvi (earth; Sita means "furrow") to take her back. The earth opens and Sita is swallowed up, never again to return. A few days later, a messenger from the gods informs Rama that his days as a king are over; Rama jumps into the river Sarayu and joins Sita in the other world.

How Bhavabhuti modifies the legend reveals at once his defects and virtues as a dramatist; A. B. Keith's synopsis of the play is so good it is worth reproducing: "Janaka has departed; Sita *enceinte* is sad and Rama is consoling her. News is brought from Vashishtha; he bids the king meet every wish of his wife, but ranks first of all his duty to his people. Lakshmana reports that the painter, who has been depicting the scenes of their wanderings, has finished; they enter the gallery, and live over again their experiences, Rama consoling Sita for her cruel separation from her husband and friends; incidentally he prays the holy Ganga to protect her and that the magic arms he has may pass spontaneously to his sons. Sita, wearied, falls asleep. The Brahmin Durmukha, who has been sent to report on the feeling of the people, reveals that they doubt Sita's purity. Rama has already promised Sita to let her visit again the forest, scene of her wanderings; he now decides that, when she has gone, she must not return, and the command is obeyed. Act II shows an ascetic, Atreyi, in converse with the spirit of the woods, Vasanti; we learn that Rama is celebrating the horse sacrifice, and that Valmiki is bringing up two fine boys entrusted to him by a goddess. Rama enters, sword in hand, to slay an impious Shudra, Shambuka; slain, the latter, purified by this death, appears in spirit form and leads his benefactor to Agastya's hermitage. In Act III the two rivers Tamasa and Murala converse; they tell us that Sita abandoned would have killed herself but Ganga preserved her, and entrusted her two sons, born in her sorrow, to Valmiki to train. Then Sita in a spirit form appears, unseen by mortals; she is permitted by Ganga to revisit under Tamasa's care the scenes of her youth. Rama also appears. At the sight of the scene of their early love, both faint, but Sita, recovering, touches unseen Rama who recovers only to relapse and be revived again. Finally Sita departs, leaving Rama fainting.

"The scene changes in Act IV to the hermitage of Janaka, retired from kingly duties; Kaushalya, Rama's mother, meets him and both forget self in consoling each other. They are interrupted by the merry noises of the children in the hermitage; one especially is pre-eminent; questioned, he is Lava, who has a brother Kusha and who knows Rama only from Valmiki's work. The horse from Rama's sacrifice approaches, guarded by soldiers.

Lava joins his companions, but, unlike them, he is undaunted by the royal claim of sovereignty and decides to oppose it. Act V passes in an exchange of martial taunts between him and Chandraketu, who guards the horse for Rama, though each admires the other. In Act VI a Vidyadhara and his wife, flying in the air, describe the battle of the youthful heroes and the magic weapons they use. The arrival of Rama interrupts the conflict. He admires Lava's bravery, which Chandraketu extols; he questions him, but finds that the magic weapons came to him spontaneously. Kusha enters from Bharata's hermitage, whither he has carried Valmiki's poem to be dramatized. The father admires the two splendid youths, who are, though he knows it not, his own sons.

"In Act VII all take part in a supernatural spectacle devised by Bharata and played by the Apsaras. Sita's fortunes after her abandonment are depicted; she weeps and casts herself in the Bhagirathi; she reappears, supported by Prithvi, the earth goddess, and Ganga, each carrying a new-born infant. Prithvi declaims against the harshness of Rama, Ganga excuses his acts; both ask Sita to care for the children until they are old enough to hand over to Valmiki, when she can act as she pleases. Rama is carried away, he believes the scene real, now he intervenes in the dialogue, now he faints. Arundhati suddenly appears with Sita, who goes to her husband and brings him back to consciousness. The people acclaim the queen, and Valmiki presents to them Rama's sons, Kusha and Lava."

So the play ends. A major problem remains. How much of Rama is the shrewd, expedient villain-hero and how much is the morally impressive royal avatar of Vishnu has never been wholly clear in Valmiki's work. His killing of Vali is a shabby affair; he has an eye for Surpanakha's good looks; he suspects that Bharata might like to have the kingdom for himself. He protests overmuch, but none the less passes Sita through the ordeal of fire. In Bhavabhuti's play, Rama is prettified and sugared up so heavily that he is neither divine nor royal nor human; he is mostly cardboard. The *karuna* rasa becomes, in places, sentimentalized out of recognition. Where tenderness stops and sentimentality begins is always difficult to determine; for this reason *The Later Story of Rama* is a play only the subtlest Hindu can appreciate, for its frames of emotional reference are filtered through very fine cultural sieves and the situations maneuvered with such dexterity that, to a reader on the right wave length, they communicate unbelievably fine poignancies.

Yet Bhavabhuti couches his tender-sweetness, strangely enough, in a Sanskrit that is artificial, labored, even in places clumsy. "It appears that the language is heavy, often it is unmusical." Admirable effects are achieved, "at the sacrifice of clearness and propriety of diction," which is another way of saying that Bhavabhuti is the only *experimenting* Sanskrit dramatist we have. "Bhavabhuti was clearly a solitary soul"; the audience for whom he wrote was too average and mundane to appreciate the nuances he was attempting to create. He was seeking to communicate "a sense of the mystery of things." Chronology and other kinds of dramatic decorum interested him little. He was disturbed by the patent injustice of the *Ramayana* in permitting the abandonment of Sita, and he resolves it by dwelling on the "mystery" of the family relationship—indeed, he does it, I think, with greater subtlety than Kalidasa in the last reconciliation scene of *Shakuntala*. That splendid metaphor of the knot of marriage held together by the strands of children is one of the most memorable in Sanskrit drama, and is the key to the play. "There are some," Bhavabhuti remarks in *Malati and Madhava,* "who treat us with contempt." (He must have had in mind critics such as Govardhanacharya who states in one place, "Speech turned into rock when it met Bhavabhuti," though he wisely adds, "When Bhavabhuti's speech weeps, the rock itself weeps.") "Our plays aren't meant for them—they know nothing of drama. A time will come when someone our equal will be born. Time is endless and the world is a big place, and strange things do happen!"

Strange things happen in the play itself, which is full of inconsistencies. This should not be taken as a reflection on Bhavabhuti's skill in creating the proper rasa. There are so many jumbles in the Stage Manager's prelude that I have omitted it altogether rather than confuse the already tangled time scheme. Take the *Portrait of a Hero*: in it Bhavabhuti explains how, after killing Ravana, Rama leaves the same day for Ayodhya, where he arrives in the evening. Next day he is installed on the throne, Bharata abdicating in his favor. A fortnight of festivity follows. Yet Rama, in *The Later Story of Rama,* which begins as the festivities close, is asked to satisfy his wife's puerperal longings (a walk in the forest and a bath in the Bhagirathi was what Sita wanted) only a fortnight after he has been living with her. There is no indication, in Valmiki or Bhavabhuti, that Sita conceived *before* she was abducted by Ravana. Or take Act II, when Arundhati refuses to return to Ayodhya because Sita isn't there. Vashishtha asks her and the queen mothers, who approve of her decision, to spend their time in Valmiki's ashrama. Why should he suggest this? He has an ashrama of his own, more conveniently located. Again, in Act I, we are told that the attack on Lavana has started; in Act VII, twelve years later, Valmiki explains that Shatrughna returns from Madura after killing Lavana. Did the war against Lavana take twelve years? Sad commentary on Rama's abilities! And if it did, how could Rama go ahead with the horse sacrifice, since only the unchallenged conqueror of the world is entitled to perform the Ashvamedha?

BHAVABHUTI

*Birthplace:* Padmapura (in Vidarbha, central India).

*Date of birth:* C. eighth century A.D.; Bhavabhuti was a poet in the court of King Yashovarman.

# Characters

Rama, *son of Ayodhya's king Dasharatha*
Sita, *his wife, daughter of Janaka*
Chamberlain
Ashtavakra, *messenger from Vashishtha*
Lakshmana, *Rama's younger brother*
Attendant
Durmukha, *Rama's spy*
Atreyi, *an ascetic*
Vasanti, *a forest goddess*
Sambuka, *a demon*
Tamasa, *a river goddess*
Murala, *a river goddess*

Bhandayana, *a hermit*
Saudhataki, *a hermit*
Arundhati, *wife of Vashishtha*
Kaushalya, *queen of Dasharatha*
Attendant
Lava, *son of Rama and Sita*
Soldier
Chandraketu, *Lakshmana's son*
Sumantra, *charioteer of Lakshmana*
Kusha, *son of Rama and Sita*
Prithvi, *Earth personified*
Bhagirathi, *the river Ganges personified*
Goddess (of the Forest), Voices, Spirits of the Air, etc.

# ACT I

### THE MURAL

*As the curtain opens,* RAMA *and* SITA *are seen seated.*

RAMA. Smile a little, Sita. They won't leave us.

SITA. I know it, my husband. But they are my family, and I can't stop my tears. When ones who are so close to us leave—

RAMA. Yes. I know. It hurts. For which reason the sensible renounce such sorrows and go to the forest to meditate.

*A* CHAMBERLAIN *enters.*

CHAMBERLAIN. My lord Rama. . .*He pauses.* Your Majesty—

RAMA, *smiling.* "My lord Rama" is all right, noble sir. It sounds all right in the mouth of anyone who served my father. What is it?

CHAMBERLAIN. Ashtavakra is here, come from the ashrama of Rishyasringa.

SITA. Send him in.

RAMA. Yes, do.

*The* CHAMBERLAIN *leaves.* ASHTAVAKRA *enters.*

ASHTAVAKRA. My blessings on you.

RAMA. Thank you, sir. Please sit down.

SITA. I thank you too, sir. How are my elders? How is the noble Shanta?

RAMA. And my brother-in-law, the noble Rishyasringa, how is he?

SITA. I wonder if she remembers me.

ASHTAVAKRA, *sitting down.* Constantly. And the great Vashishtha sends you this message: "The earth is your mother; the best of Brahmins, Janaka, your father. You married into a house whose ancestors are the world's heroes. What can I wish you, for you will be the mother of heroes?"

RAMA. He is kind to us. The wise of this world speak from experience; but the wisest need no experience—their speech comes first, their deeds later.

ASHTAVAKRA. The good Arundhati and Shanta asked me to say that whatever the noble Sita desires before the birth of her child should be done.

RAMA. Whatever she says will be done.

ASHTAVAKRA. Rishyasringa adds that everyone thinks it better for the noble Sita to stay with her husband until the birth of the child.

RAMA, *joyfully*. Excellent! And what has the good Vashishtha asked me to do?

ASHTAVAKRA. He sent this message: "I could not come. I was needed at the sacrifice. You are young and a new king. Respect the people. There is no greater honor."

RAMA. I will remember his words. I could sacrifice love, happiness, sympathy, even the noble Sita, in the service of my people.

SITA. That is why you are the greatest of the Raghava kings, my lord.

RAMA. Who's that coming? No, don't get up, Ashtavakra. You're not leaving?

ASHTAVAKRA, *rising and walking to the right side of the stage*. Lakshmana is here.

ASHTAVAKRA *leaves and* LAKSHMANA *enters*.

LAKSHMANA. My dear brother Rama, the mural along the walk has been finished. You can see it now, the artist says.

RAMA. It was good of you, Lakshmana, to think of diverting Sita's mind in this pleasant way. How many scenes are there? And what is the last one?

LAKSHMANA. It shows her trial by fire.

RAMA. Don't say that! How could fire test her? She was born pure. Water isn't made purer; nor is fire. Forgive me, my wife—for if *you* don't, this sin will stick to me all my life. The words I spoke—how they must have hurt! The things I did just to humor the people! I took a sweet-scented flower and nearly crushed it underfoot. Forgive me.

SITA. It is all over, my husband; why think of it now? Let us see the mural.

*They rise and go to the left side of the stage, where a curtain is pulled, revealing the mural.*

LAKSHMANA. Here is the first scene.

SITA, *looking at the painting*. What are those shapes crowded together as if they are praising my husband?

LAKSHMANA. They are deadly weapons with secret magical powers which the great Krishasva gave to the sage Vishvamitra, who in turn handed them to Rama when my brother slew the demon Tadaka.

RAMA. Bow to them, Sita, for they are sacred. Brahman himself did penance for a thousand years before he had a glimpse of their power. SITA *bows*. They will serve our children now.

LAKSHMANA. This next scene takes place in Mithila.

SITA. I can see my husband, graceful and lotus-blue, and my father Janaka gazing with admiration.

LAKSHMANA. Look, here is your father again, at the marriage ceremony. And here is Satananda, the family priest of Janaka, paying his respects to Vashishtha, the family priest of Rama.

RAMA. A moving scene—the union of the dynasty of Janaka, the dynasty of the moon, with the dynasty of Dasharatha, the dynasty of the sun.

SITA. And here are all four brothers ready for the marriage ceremony. Oh, it makes me think I am there once again!

RAMA. Yes, it all comes back. Look, here—here is your hand, holding the sacred thread, resting on mine. What joy shot through me at the touch of your hand!

LAKSHMANA. Here is my sister-in-law, the noble Mandavi, wife of Bharata; and here the noble Srutakirti, wife of Shatrughna.

SITA, *mischievously*. And this most noble lady?

LAKSHMANA, *aside, embarrassed*. She means my wife Urmila. *Aloud*. Look, here—isn't this interesting? The great Bhargava! And there is my noble brother, Rama himself, in the act—

RAMA, *quickly*. There's a lot still left to see. Let's move on.

SITA, *looking at* RAMA *affectionately*. Modesty suits you so well, my husband.

LAKSHMANA. We are now in Ayodhya.

RAMA, *sadly*. Gone are those days! I still remember how our mothers heaped affection on us. Father was still alive and all four of us just married. I remember too how you, my dear wife, how lovely you were—your teeth like buds, your hair glistening and thick. How your moon-soft beauty charmed my mothers!

LAKSHMANA. And here's the scheming Manthara.

RAMA, *ignoring this scene and passing on to another*. This is the *ingudi* tree in the city of Sringavera where I met the king of the Nishadas.

LAKSHMANA, *chuckling to himself*. He won't look at the painting of our second mother.

SITA. There is the mighty river Bhagirathi, her waters clear and holy.

RAMA. I salute you, most sacred river of the dynasty of Dasharatha! Grant me a prayer—protect my wife, as the good Arundhati does.

LAKSHMANA. The fig tree Shyama, on the bank of the Lakindi, on the road leading to the Chitrakuta.

SITA. Does my husband remember?

RAMA. Can I forget? Here you rested, leaning against me, and fell asleep. Your body was soft as a lotus, languid and frail and lovely. My hands soothed you, your body embraced me.

LAKSHMANA. This picture shows our encounter with the demon Viradha at the edge of the Vindhya forest.

SITA. We shan't look at it. This next scene is pleasanter—the palm-leaf shade in the hands of my husband, and both of us entering the southern forest.

RAMA. We are now among hospitable holy men whose ashramas stand by the side of mountain streams. They are shut off from the world, content with handfuls of wild rice.

LAKSHMANA. Here is the massive hill of Prasravana, ringed with wet clouds, whose torrents give birth to the river Godavari—who rushes between blue forests, her lovers.

RAMA. Sita, you remember? We were here with Lakshmana. O my darling, how cool the river was! How lovely the evening walks! How night slipped by us, brushed away in kiss and caress!

LAKSHMANA. That is Surpanakha, Ravana's sister. SITA *is alarmed.*

RAMA. Don't be upset, my darling; this is only a painting.

SITA. She is evil. I do not like her.

LAKSHMANA. Here are scenes from Rama's life of exile—the demons, the golden deer. Oh, the rocks would weep, the stones cry out at the sufferings of Rama in the forest!

SITA, *to herself.* How he suffered! And all for me!

RAMA. We've had enough of suffering. Let's move on.

LAKSHMANA. The great Jatayu, the divine bird, friend of Dasharatha.

SITA. He died trying to save me.

RAMA. King of birds, great Jatayu, take my gratitude.

LAKSHMANA. The forest of Dandaka, where lived the headless monster Danu; the ashrama of Matanga; the low-caste Sramana, who was freed from her sins for helping Rama; and there is the lake of Pampa.

SITA. The lake of Pampa, where my husband's tears fell fast.

LAKSHMANA. Next the noble Hanuman, chief of the monkeys.

RAMA. What could we have done without his help?

SITA. And this peacock-proud hill, where my husband stands in a trance?

LAKSHMANA. It is the hill of Malyavat, where the first clouds of the monsoon gather and spring's arjun flowers scent the air. Here Rama—

RAMA. Don't! It hurts me. I lost Sita here.

LAKSHMANA. We're coming to the last of the scenes. But you are tired. We can stop here.

SITA. Could I ask you a favor, my husband?

RAMA. *Order* me a favor, my wife!

SITA. Oh, how it all comes back! How I wish I could once again take a cool, holy dip in the Bhagirathi, and walk with you in the blue woods of the south.

RAMA. There, Lakshmana, you see! She has told us her wish, and the elders have ordered me to grant it. Please have the most comfortable of the chariots prepared and brought here.

SITA. You will come with me, my lord?

RAMA. I would not go without you.

LAKSHMANA *leaves.*

SITA. I am tired; sleep drifts across my eyes.

RAMA. Come by the window here. Lie next to me. No, in my arms. Put your arms around me, like moonlight around me. Oh, what happiness, dearest, when you touch me—no, not happiness; and it is not sorrow. Not sleeping, not waking. Not poison, not wine. But a magic in your hands, that puts me into a sleep that is peace, peace, peace. . . .

SITA, *smiling.* You love me, that's all.

RAMA. And when you speak, a flower in my heart opens.

SITA. My husband, my flatterer! I think I'll lie down. *She looks around for a pillow.*

RAMA. Here, Sita, my arm is your pillow. Wasn't it your pillow when we married, and when we walked and rested in the forest?

SITA, *sleepily.* Yes. . .yes. . .my husband. *She falls asleep.*

RAMA, *gazing on her tenderly.* Asleep—and on my heart. A vision in my house, lady of light, a world of coolness to my eyes. Her presence is fragrant, an arm of pearl around my neck. Oh when she goes, pain comes into my heart. Sweet lady, sleep.

ATTENDANT, *entering.* Sire—*Seeing* SITA *asleep, he starts to leave.*

RAMA. Wait. What is it?

ATTENDANT. Durmukha wishes to see you, sire.

RAMA, *to himself.* Durmukha? He is the one who reports to me about my subjects. *Aloud.* He can enter.

*The* ATTENDANT *leaves.* DURMUKHA *enters.*

DURMUKHA, *to himself.* The things people say! How can I report them? Damn my duty. . .but I have to do it.

SITA, *in her sleep.* O my husband, where are you?

RAMA. The paintings upset her—she thinks I've left her. *He caresses her.* Call him lucky whom love follows till his last years. For good love mocks time and smiles at joy and sorrow both.

DURMUKHA. Sire.

RAMA. Durmukha, what is it?

DURMUKHA. There is evil talk in the mouths of the people, sire.

RAMA. What kind of talk?

DURMUKHA, *bending to whisper.* That sort of thing, sire.

RAMA. Like lightning these ugly words! *He goes on quickly.* The news spreads like rabies, from poisonous dog to dog, and happiness crackles like dust in the air. *He speaks sadly.* If that is the complaint, let it be so. I know my vow: the people's good above all. My father kept it; his son will keep it too. Have I not received from my father honor that is spotless—the king's word above all? And will foulness stain the honor, will the word die in the desert? Sita, my wife, my beloved, believe me that I believe it all— you are daughter of the earth, the daughter of Janaka, wife of Rama, you are the sweet-voiced lady whom fire could not touch! But slander touches you now. You who make the worlds holy are called unholy; you who protect the worlds are yourself defenseless. *He pauses.* Durmukha, go to Lakshmana. Tell him that Rama orders him to lead Sita into exile.

DURMUKHA. Sire, the sacred test of fire proved the queen's innocence. Must the vicious words of the people prevail?

RAMA. The *vicious* words of the people! Did they witness the test by fire? Why should they believe it? No, don't blame them. Fate must intend this. You have heard me.

DURMUKHA. Our good queen! *He leaves.*

RAMA. Durmukha is right. I am a butcher—and the bird dies, while the butcher lives. Oh, I pollute her, pure queen, pure wife. . . . *He withdraws his arm gently from under* SITA's *head.* No scented creeper, this; a poison tree, a filthy root. *He rises.* The world is now dead for Rama. Life's over, the song over; let us wait for the dark. But what can I do? What else could I do? Vashishtha insulted! The good Arundhati insulted! All of them—the earth, Janaka, Sugriva, and Vibhishana—all insulted by the noble Rama! *He bows, touching* SITA's *feet with his forehead.* For the last time, my wife, anoint me with your grace.

RAMA *is startled from his reverie by the sound of a commotion offstage and voices shouting.*

VOICES. Help! Help! Murder! The sages are being terrorized by the demon Lavana! Help, Rama, help!

RAMA. Voices! And calling my name!

VOICES. Save us from Lavana, O Rama! Save us!

RAMA. The demons again! *He starts to go, then turns to look at* SITA. And must I leave you like this, my wife? I must. O Earth, great mother, look after her, the holy Sita, the good Sita your daughter. *He goes out.*

SITA, *drowsily.* My husband, where are you? *She wakes up.* What a bad dream I had! *She looks around her.* He's left without telling me. Wait till he gets back—he'll get a piece of my mind he's not had before!

DURMUKHA, *entering.* The good Lakshmana has the chariot ready, my queen.

SITA. I'm coming. *She rises.* My baby kicked me just then. I shall walk carefully.

DURMUKHA. This way, please.

C U R T A I N

## ACT II

*The Dandaka forest. Twelve years later. A female* ASCETIC *enters, dressed as a traveller.*

ASCETIC. I see a goddess of the forest, carrying fruits and flowers and leaves.

GODDESS, *entering.* The forest lies open for you.
    Tree's shadow, cool water, cool fruit—
    None to deny them, all for the asking.
    And I, I am happy, holy lady,
    Knowing that good alone will bring good.

ASCETIC, *taking the gifts.* Thank you. Good words, good deeds, a good heart, good friendship—these are all that matter, in life and death.

*They both sit down.*

GODDESS. Who are you, holy lady?

ASCETIC. My name is Atreyi.

GODDESS. Noble Atreyi, what brings you to the forest of Dandaka?

ASCETIC. The great Agastya and his band of scholars. They live here, and I will learn the truths of the Vedanta from their lips. I come from Valmiki to learn from the great Agastya.

GODDESS. But the best sages go to Valmiki, holy lady. What is there that he does not know or cannot teach?

ASCETIC. I can no longer concentrate in Valmiki's ashrama. Things are not the same there since the day a goddess brought two beautiful babies, who have now charmed not only the hearts of the sages but the forest animals too.

GODDESS. Babies? Who were they?

ASCETIC. Kusha and Lava—and the goddess who brought them had interesting things to say about them. For instance, they have power over the divine weapons.

GODDESS. That's remarkable.

ASCETIC. So the good Valmiki became an even better nurse than the goddess and brought them up like a mother. He taught them all the sciences and arts; he put the sacred thread round their necks. Eleven years have passed, and I must confess they go far beyond me in learning. It's not the teachers' fault if I'm a lump of earth and no good at mastering the sacred books. . .but those two children are like hard-polished gems, reflecting cleanly everything that is brought near them.

GODDESS. That's what you meant then by saying you couldn't concentrate?

ASCETIC. Not just that.

GODDESS. What then?

ASCETIC. Well, you see, it happened like this. One day the good Valmiki had gone to the river Tamasa for a bath, and he saw a hunter knock down one of a pair of herons flying peacefully in the sky. Something happened inside him, and he cursed the hunter with the words, "All your years shall be homeless, O heartless hunter, for you have killed a bird whose heart was full of love."

GODDESS. Beautiful lines!

ASCETIC. Well, the words weren't even all out of his mouth, when the lord of creation, Brahma, appeared before him and said, "You, Valmiki, are now one with the light of Brahma. Speak! Tell the story of Rama in your sweet words. Let the world know that a poet has been born among men." Then the god vanished as suddenly as he had appeared, and since then the good Valmiki has busied himself with composing the *Ramayana*, the glorious story of Rama.

GODDESS. To which the world listens spellbound.

ASCETIC. And which is the reason I can't concentrate, for the good Valmiki does nothing but compose.

GODDESS. I see.

ASCETIC. I feel rested now. Which is the path to Agastya's ashrama?

GODDESS. Go through the forest of Panchavati and keep to this bank of the river Godavari.

ASCETIC, *awed*. This is the holy forest? This is Panchavati? And you are Vasanti, the goddess of the forest?

GODDESS. I am.

ASCETIC, *closing her eyes*. Oh, I am favored. But what sad memories crowd in! For it was here that the virtuous Sita was left to her fate. She who was so close to me. Where is she now?—only the whisper of a name in my ears.

GODDESS, *alarmed*. Why, what is wrong, holy lady? Has anything happened to the noble Sita?

ASCETIC. Happened? What *hasn't* happened!

GODDESS. Tell me. Tell me. *She comes closer.*

ASCETIC. Her good name has been blackened. . . .*She goes on in a whisper.*

GODDESS. What horror! What shame! *She faints. The* ASCETIC *revives her.* That this could happen to Sita, the flower of womanhood! Oh Rama, Rama, how could you have done this? Tell me, holy lady, does anyone know what happened to Sita after Lakshmana deserted her in this forest?

ASCETIC. Not a word; no one knows.

GODDESS. How could this happen? How could this be, with Arundhati and Vashishtha still living, the old queens living?

ASCETIC. It was just bad luck; they had all gone to Rishyasringa's ashrama for the twelve-year rites and heard nothing. When the rites were over, they returned home and found out what had happened. The noble Arundhati said she would not enter Ayodhya if Sita were not in the city. Rama's mother agreed and they both went to Valmiki's ashrama on the advice of the great Vashishtha. They are still there.

GODDESS. And Rama?

ASCETIC. Rama is busy with the horse sacrifice.

GODDESS. Is he out of his head? Who sits beside him? Has he married again?

ASCETIC. No.

GODDESS. Who will sit beside him at the sacrifice?

ASCETIC. A golden statue of Sita.

GODDESS. Who can tell what tenderness hides in the hardest hearts? Flowers and steel make a man of genius.

ASCETIC. The sacrificial horse is ready, and the guards in ritual attendance. Lakshmana's son Chandraketu—

GODDESS. Lakshmana has a son too!

ASCETIC. Yes—Chandraketu; he was trained in various weapons so that he could stand guard with the army over the ceremony. But when all was ready a Brahmin suddenly dashed in, laid his son's corpse on the ground, and asked for Rama's help to avenge the murder. The murderer was the demon Sambuka, he said. Sword in hand, Rama jumped in the aerial chariot Pushpaka and is now reconnoitering the land in search of Sambuka.

GODDESS. He will come here then, for this forest is Sambuka's hide-out.

ASCETIC. I must go.

GODDESS. Go, holy lady; evening is coming on. See, the tired pigeons and woodcocks are scratching fallen trunks by the riverbank for their last beakful of worms.

*They both leave. After a moment,* RAMA *enters, with his sword raised.*

RAMA. Well may this hand strike its sword on the demon Sambuka, for this hand knows no pity. This hand drove out the pregnant Sita. This hand knows no pity. *He strikes in the air.* No pity. *He strikes again.*

*The demon* SAMBUKA *enters; he is in the form of a celestial spirit.*

SAMBUKA. I am Sambuka, my lord. The Brahmin's son is alive again. I bow to you, for you are goodness, and goodness will bring me salvation.

RAMA. That the boy lives is news that makes me happy. And that you are saved makes me happy too. Your penance has brought you the liberation you were beginning to deserve.

SAMBUKA. Not my penance but your grace, my lord. For had you not come to the Dandaka forest, I could not have been saved.

RAMA. Is this the Dandaka forest? *He looks around.* Yes—the same glitter of lakes, the ashramas, the same waterfalls, the bright blue patches of sky, the deadly monotone of the sky. It's still the same.

SAMBUKA. The Dandaka forest, my lord, where you killed fourteen thousand demons, including Khara, Dushana, and Trisira.

RAMA. Yes, I remember Khara. *He looks around him.* Sita loved this forest of Dandaka. These trees were dear to her. "The sweet-scented forest," she called it. Her sweet-scented words! Wherever she walked was peace.

SAMBUKA. This side is pleasanter scenery, my lord.

RAMA. My good friend, take my chariot. And may your journey be safe.

SAMBUKA. Before I go, I will pay homage to the learned Agastya. *He leaves.*

RAMA. The forest comes back, the lovely forest where our early years passed in peace and love and duty. The peacocks, the deer, the *vanjula* creepers, they haven't changed at all. And from this hill, the river Godavari stretching away below as stately as a chain of cloud. The birds and the trees of the Godavari! Isn't this the forest where her friend Vasanti lives? The pain of her goes through me like a splintered arrow, like gushing poison in warm blood, like a boil opening on the healed heart. . . . But the land remains; the land is the same. . . . Is there a sand bed where once there was water? Have the trees of the forest changed? Is the land the same, or is what I see something I have not seen? This hill is the same. Oh, the hill calls me, for my love wandered in the hills. The terrible shame, the terrible shame!

SAMBUKA *returns.* The learned Agastya invites you, my lord, to his ashrama, where the sages will welcome you. He says the aerial chariot will take you back in time for the horse sacrifice.

RAMA. He honors me by the invitation. . . . I go now, beloved forest, but I shall return.

SAMBUKA, *getting into the chariot.* There is the crow-haunted hill of Kraunchavata, my lord, that glories in owls and peacocks and serpents, and deafening wind through bamboo clumps. . . . And there are the southern blue hills, cloud-capped, where holy waters meet amid sounding foam.

*They both leave.*

C U R T A I N


# ACT III

### THE INVISIBLE SITA

*Two river goddesses,* TAMASA *and* MURALA, *enter.*

TAMASA. Why are you in such a hurry, Murala?

MURALA. Lopamudra, the good wife of Agastya, sends me here with the message that Rama cannot hide his sorrow over the loss of Sita. It's become worse since he came here, for he remembers the happy days he passed with her in this forest. Who knows what he will do? Sorrow clouds his mind as heat clouds the inside of a baking pot. Good Godavari, look after him— send him the softest breezes from your waves; fill them with cool spray and lotus fragrance. Rama's mind is troubled; send him peace.

TAMASA. That's a kind thought. It just happens, however, that the sedative isn't needed when the real cure is at hand.

MURALA. What cure?

TAMASA. Open your ears and listen carefully. When Lakshmana deserted Sita near the ashrama of Valmiki, she threw herself madly into the waters of the Ganga, and there gave birth to twin sons. Ganga herself brought these boys to Valmiki, while Sita disappeared into other regions.

MURALA. Out of pain comes joy and glory!

TAMASA. But listen to the rest! Now Ganga, hearing that Rama is going out of his mind with grief and that Lopamudra fears for his sanity, has brought Sita back to the Godavari.

MURALA. I hope everything turns out all right.

TAMASA. Sita is near us here now, plucking flowers for the Sun, the destroyer of sin, and celebrating the twelfth birthday of her sons. The great Ganga has given her the power to be invisible. "Even the forest goddesses will not see you," she said. "How can human beings?" And to me Ganga said, "Look after her well, Tamasa. She loves you." That's the truth.

MURALA. In that case, I'd better run and carry the news to Lopamudra. Rama must be here by now.

TAMASA. There, can you see her?—the virtuous Sita, light-braided and gently wan, entering the wood like Pity looking for help.

MURALA. It *is* Sita!

*They both leave.*

VOICE, *offstage.* Be careful! Be careful!

SITA *enters, gathering flowers; she looks extremely sad and preoccupied.* That was Vasanti's voice.

VOICE. Sita's pet elephant is being attacked by a tusker! Be careful! Move out of the way!

SITA. O my husband, save him! *She continues in despair.* But where is my husband? My husband? Where is he? *She faints.*

TAMASA *enters and revives* SITA.

TAMASA. Please. . .you mustn't get excited.

RAMA'S VOICE. Charioteer, stop here.

SITA, *reviving.* That voice. . .it came like a cloud of rain!

TAMASA, *sadly.* Sita, you mustn't get nervous. It was only a voice.

SITA. I think it was my husband's voice.

TAMASA. They say he came here to punish the demon Sambuka.

SITA. My husband's voice—a king's voice.

RAMA'S VOICE. These slopes, this hill, this river, blessed with the steps of my darling wife. The deer were her friends, and the trees were her friends.

SITA. It *is* his voice! *She faints in* TAMASA's *arms.*

TAMASA. You must be calm, Sita.

RAMA'S VOICE. This hill, this forest. . . . My sorrow is a column of thin smoke. . . . Sita, my dearest, come to me.

TAMASA, *to herself.* This *would* happen.

SITA, *recovering.* Again. . .not again. . . .

RAMA *rushes in and collapses on the ground.*

SITA. Tamasa, help me! *She kneels beside* RAMA.

TAMASA. The touch of your hand will revive him.

SITA, *caressing* RAMA's *forehead.* He is waking.

RAMA, *reviving.* Nectar to my heart. . .moonlight to my eyes. . .I know this touch. . .Not sleeping, not waking. . .But hands that wake me and, waking, drown me in sleepy delight. RAMA *does not see* SITA, *who is invisible.*

SITA, *drawing back.* But I must not.

RAMA, *sitting up.* I thought Sita had come back again. Weren't those Sita's hands?

SITA. He is restless.

RAMA. She is here. . . . She must be here.

SITA. Tamasa, take me away. He mustn't see me. He'll be angry.

TAMASA. But he can't see you. Even we goddesses of the forest can't see you.

RAMA. Sita, where are you? Dearest Sita, come back to me.

SITA. He still loves me. I know it.

RAMA. No, there is no one here. No one, no one.

SITA. Tell me, Tamasa, what shall I do? What shall I do?

TAMASA. You love him, I know. He did you wrong but now he is good. His wrong has been melted in the depth of your love.

RAMA. I felt your hands, my wife, cool and moist. But where are you? *He gets up and looks about him.*

SITA. The sweetness of his words!

RAMA. I am imagining things. She is not here.

VOICE, *offstage*. Help, help! Sita's pet elephant is being attacked by a tusker!

RAMA. Where? Where is the scoundrel?

VASANTI, *running in and recognizing* RAMA. Sire!

SITA. My friend Vasanti!

VASANTI. My greetings, sire.

RAMA. Vasanti—my wife's friend.

VASANTI. There is no time to lose. The elephant must be saved. Go along the Godavari to the right of Jatayu's hill. He is there.

RAMA. What memories in those names!

VASANTI. Quick, sire, let us go. *They start walking.*

SITA. You are sure even the forest goddesses cannot see me, Tamasa?

TAMASA. The great Ganga gave you the boon. You needn't fear.

316 The Later Story of Rama

SITA. In that case, we'll follow them.

VASANTI, *looking ahead*. It's amazing—the tusker has been driven off!

RAMA. Look at him! Her pet elephant is now a hulking giant after so many years. We're lucky—what a magnificent beast! And see the gentle way he caresses his child with his trunk.

SITA. His child. . .My sons. . .How are they, Tamasa? Love for them suddenly shoots up in my breast.

TAMASA. They are well. Call no marriage happy that does not have the knot of children to tighten it.

RAMA. The way he plays in the water. . .I think I see my son.

VASANTI. Sit here, sire. Once you sat here with your wife, and the deer, you remember, would come and nibble grass from her fingers.

RAMA, *averting his face*. I cannot look.

SITA. What are you doing, Vasanti? Why do you torture him?

RAMA. Sit next to me, good Vasanti.

VASANTI, *sitting beside* RAMA. How is the good Lakshmana, sire?

RAMA, *not listening*. These waters. . .and these deer that fed from her lotus hands. . . . O my heart, do not break open, do not gush open, as water through rock!

VASANTI, *sadly*. How is the good Lakshmana, sire?

RAMA, *aside*. The "good" Lakshmana. She said it so coldly. . . . She knows. *Aloud*. Oh, well; he is well.

VASANTI. You say that as if you didn't mean it, sire. Is anything wrong?

SITA. Vasanti, my husband needs love, not hard words!

VASANTI. How could you do it? How did you have the heart to be so cruel? You loved her as your own second soul. Her presence was a cool moon, her hands all sweetness. . . . How were you able to do it?

SITA. Don't, Vasanti, don't! I forbid it.

RAMA. My hands were tied.

VASANTI. I shall never understand it.

RAMA. The people forced me.

TAMASA. The people were mad.

VASANTI. Fame, prestige, your own good name—is that all you cared for? What about your wife in the lonely forest? Did you ever think what would happen to her?

SITA. Please don't, Vasanti; don't, please don't. Do not add fire to the fire in his heart.

RAMA. I am guilty. It is over. She is dead—a soft lotus crushed, a moonbeam devoured by ravenous beasts.

SITA. I am alive! My husband, I am alive!

RAMA. She is dead.

SITA. My husband, I am here. *She sobs.*

TAMASA. Yes, cry. The pool overflows when full; why shouldn't the heart?

RAMA. My heart is cut in two, Vasanti. Look inside me and you will see. Fire swells in my body, but the flesh endures; fire, but no ashes; only the searing pain. Fate pierces like a sword in my stomach, but I'm still in love. I live in pain. My subjects, my good people, listen to Rama! You said she was impure and could not stay in the palace. I left her to die. Listen to me, for I weep. Listen to the tears of Rama, for the world swirls around me, and I cannot see what I see. . . . Oh forgive me!

TAMASA. Who can plumb the ocean of sorrow?

VASANTI. Have patience, sire.

RAMA. Patience? It is nice of you to talk of patience. Twelve years. . . twelve years. . .Sita dead, and Rama living. . .for twelve years!

SITA. My head is spinning. I feel faint.

RAMA. Listen, Vasanti: do you know what is in my heart? Glittering coals, and the snake's venom, and the arrow that cuts but will not kill.

SITA. Twelve years of pain. . .and *I* am again the giver of pain.

VASANTI. Aren't these forest scenes beautiful, sire?

RAMA. So they are, so they are. *He rises and looks around him.*

SITA. Beautiful she calls them—and they bring him pain.

VASANTI. There is the clump of creepers where you waited while she played with the swans of the Godavari.

SITA. Oh, how cruel your sweetness is, Vasanti!

RAMA. Sita, help me! I am alone. Darkness is all around me, a fury of despair. . .fire that burns without consuming. Help me, my wife, I can bear it no longer! *He faints.*

VASANTI. Help! He's fainted!

SITA *quickly places her hands over* RAMA's *heart and on his forehead.*

RAMA, *reviving.* The same touch. My friend Vasanti, you have magic in your hands.

VASANTI. I don't understand, sire.

RAMA. You have brought me back Sita.

VASANTI. Where is she?

RAMA. Here, close beside us. Can't you see her?

SITA. I must go. . .but the moisture of my hand seals me to him. I feel as if I couldn't move.

RAMA. Can't you see her? Her hand is here, on my head—like ice, like piercing sweetness. *He seizes it.*

SITA, *struggling to release her hand.* What a fool I've been!

RAMA. It is real! She is here. This is her hand. Feel it, Vasanti. Sita is here.

VASANTI, *aside.* He must be mad.

SITA *snatches her hand away from* RAMA.

RAMA. It's gone! But the moisture from it is still on my head. See, feel my forehead. She *is* here! Do not forsake me, Sita! Pitiless wife, come back to me!

VASANTI. Excuse me, sire, but this is all most ridiculous. How could Sita be here?

RAMA, *collecting himself*. Of course she can't be here or you would see her. But she follows me everywhere I go. I know it. You'd better leave me, Vasanti. I am only a madman now, not fit to be seen.

SITA, *agitated*. He's going, Tamasa!

TAMASA. Don't worry, Sita. We will follow him. The ritual birth knots of Kusha and Lava must be tied near the Ganga.

RAMA. I must go for the horse sacrifice. . . . Beside me will sit—

SITA, *fearfully*. Who?

RAMA.—a golden statue of Sita.

SITA. Lucky the woman who is married to my husband!

TAMASA, *smiling*. You mean that you yourself are lucky?

SITA, *embarrassed*. I was joking.

TAMASA. Come, let us go.

SITA, *sadly*. Must we?

TAMASA. Yes.

SITA. I bow to you, my husband. I saw you as a moon through clouds, briefly.

RAMA, *getting into the chariot*. Come, Vasanti.

*They all leave.*

C U R T A I N

## ACT IV

### THE MEETING OF KAUSHALYA AND JANAKA

*Two hermits,* BHANDAYANA *and* SAUDHATAKI, *enter.*

BHANDAYANA. Valmiki's ashrama has attracted many guests today, Saudhataki. Vegetables cooking, jujube and rice fragrance, the thick flavor of ghee—it's going to be a big show.

SAUDHATAKI. God bless festivals—they mean holidays for us. And bless the longbeards for coming.

BHANDAYANA, *laughing.* So that's all the respect you have for the sages?

SAUDHATAKI. And who could that rag bag be, the one at the head of the caravan of august beard-wallahs?

BHANDAYANA. One day your jokes will break your neck. That's the holy Vashishtha, come here from the ashrama of Rishyasringa, bringing Arundhati and the queens of King Dasharatha. Does that mean anything to you?

SAUDHATAKI. Vashishtha, you say?

BHANDAYANA. That's what I said.

SAUDHATAKI. Not a tiger or a wolf?

BHANDAYANA. Are you mad?

SAUDHATAKI. I thought I saw a poor heifer start in fear when he entered.

BHANDAYANA. You should know the scriptures. Isn't a heifer offered as sacrifice to a Brahmin guest?

SAUDHATAKI. That's what *you* think?

BHANDYANA. Why, what's wrong?

SAUDHATAKI. A heifer for Vashishtha, I grant you. But the great Janaka

—who's as noble a Brahmin visitor, I can assure you—he got only curds and honey.

BHANDAYANA. Janaka's a vegetarian. He gave up meat the day he heard what was done to Sita. He's doing penance.

SAUDHATAKI. Why come here, then?

BHANDAYANA. To meet his friend and counselor, Valmiki. Kaushalya has asked Arundhati to come and meet him, too.

SAUDHATAKI. Meetings and more meetings. . . . The beard-wallahs meet, the scholars meet, we, meaning you and I, meet—but *we* meet for a holiday.

BHANDAYANA. There's Janaka, coming out of Valmiki's hut. I saw him under a tree outside the ashrama, thinking no doubt of his daughter Sita.

*They both leave. After a moment,* JANAKA *enters.*

JANAKA. My grief grinds like a saw within me. Foodless, I do penance, but death is denied me. Sita, Sita my daughter, lotus-faced child, I cannot weep, I cannot mourn—the grief goes too deep. Why did you permit the shaming of my daughter, O Earth? The shaming of *your* daughter, for the fire knows, the sages know, Ganga knows she was pure.

VOICE, *offstage.* This way, my queen, this way.

JANAKA, *looking offstage.* Arundhati, and Dasharatha's wife Kaushalya. . .How wan she looks! I hardly recognize her. Grief sits heavy on her too.

ARUNDHATI, KAUSHALYA *and an* ATTENDANT *enter.*

ARUNDHATI. I don't see why you are afraid. Isn't Janaka here? You were told to meet him.

KAUSHALYA. His grief and my grief are one. How can I face him?

ARUNDHATI. That can't be helped. Meeting old friends, griefs gush out and flow again in a hundred different ways.

KAUSHALYA. But the shame of it! To face him without his daughter, my daughter-in-law!

ARUNDHATI. Here he is, the noble Janaka.

JANAKA. Holy Arundhati, I salute you. How is the mother of the noble Rama?

KAUSHALYA *faints*.

JANAKA. Did I say anything wrong?

ARUNDHATI. No, but the past returned to her when she saw you. The shock was too great.

JANAKA. Forgive me if I did anything unseemly. Dashartha was close to me, very close; the finest friend I had. That I should have been the cause of sorrow to my friend's wife. . . . I am sorry. *He sprinkles water on* KAUSHALYA's *face*.

KAUSHALYA, *reviving*. My child, Sita, where are you?

ARUNDHATI. Try to forget the past, Kaushalya. There are times too when one shouldn't cry. Don't you remember your guru telling you when you left Rishyasringa's ashrama that all would end well?

KAUSHALYA. The one I loved is here no more.

ARUNDHATI. But she will return. Would the guru lie to you? When God shines on them the Brahmins speak truth, and their words bring joy.

*The sound of voices, like a humming, is heard offstage; they listen.*

JANAKA. The young hermits are enjoying themselves. Today's a holiday for them.

KAUSHALYA, *looking offstage*. That one there—he looks almost like my Rama. Who is he?

ARUNDHATI, *aside*. He's one of the boys Ganga brought us. Could it be Kusha? Or Lava? We'll find out.

JANAKA. A lovely child. . .Soft-blue skin like a lotus's—and so graceful in his movements, it's a delight to watch him. Who is he?

ARUNDHATI. I'm afraid I'm new here.

JANAKA, *to an* ATTENDANT. Could you bring that lad to us? Tell him some visitors wish to see him.

KAUSHALYA. Will he come?

ARUNDHATI. He should have good manners, he looks so noble.

KAUSHALYA. He's left his friends and is coming this way. Such a well-bred young man!

LAVA *enters, carrying a bow.*

LAVA, *aside.* How shall I speak to them? They are so far above me. *He approaches humbly.* I salute my elders.

JANAKA. May long life be yours, my child.

KAUSHALYA. Live long, my son. Come here; come to me. *She studies the boy's face.* Isn't he the image of Sita?

JANAKA. Yes, there is a very strong resemblance.

KAUSHALYA. But it can't be. . .I'm so foolish. I'm seeing things.

JANAKA. The same features—the features of the race of the Raghavas, my dynasty.

KAUSHALYA. Tell me, my son, where is your mother? And where is your father?

LAVA. I don't know.

KAUSHALYA. Who is your father?

LAVA. The holy father Valmiki.

KAUSHALYA. No, I mean your *real* father.

LAVA. He is my holy father.

VOICE, *offstage.* Listen, all of you! Lakshmana's son Chandraketu has come here to guard the ashrama while the sacrifice is performed.

JANAKA. An auspicious day.

VOICE, *offstage.* Chandraketu commands that there be no disturbance in the ashrama!

KAUSHALYA. He *commands*—that is well spoken.

LAVA. Who is Chandraketu?

JANAKA. You have heard of Rama and Lakshmana, Dasharatha's sons?

LAVA. The noble heroes of the *Ramayana*!

JANAKA. Then you should know that Chandraketu is Lakshmana's son.

LAVA. Yes, that's right, the son of Urmila.

ARUNDHATI, *laughing.* You see—he does know.

KAUSHALYA. You have a brother, my boy?

LAVA. Yes, my brother is Kusha.

KAUSHALYA. Is he older than you?

LAVA. We're twins. But he was born first. *To* ARUNDHATI. Noble lady, please tell me with whom I have been speaking.

ARUNDHATI. They are Kaushalya and Janaka.

LAVA *looks at them respectfully. An* ATTENDANT *enters.*

ATTENDANT. The holy Valmiki wishes to inform you that it is time for the sacrifice.

JANAKA. Let us go.

JANAKA, KAUSHALYA *and* ARUNDHATI *leave. Some young* HERMITS *rush in; they are excited.*

HERMIT. We saw a strange animal—a big one, with a tail, a long neck and four legs; it eats grass. What is it? Come with us, good Lava. Tell us quickly before it runs off! *They leave, taking* LAVA *with them.*

LAVA. The books say it's a horse; it must be the horse for the sacrifice.

HERMIT. How do you know?

LAVA. Can't you see the guards near it? Armorbearers, mace-holders, quiver-carriers—three hundred of them. That's all written in the books you've read.

VOICE, *offstage.* Chandraketu has mounted the horse—Chandraketu, the hero of the seven worlds, the slayer of the ten-necked demon.

LAVA. What arrogance!

HERMIT. Why do you say that? It's the truth.

LAVA. The truth! Is he the only warrior left in the world? Are there no others?

VOICE, *offstage*. Where are the others? Chandraketu is the great hero.

LAVA. Is he? We shall see. Your flag will go down when my arrows fly! You'd better guard the ashrama for all you're worth! You there, don't stand gaping! Drive that horse off—let him nuzzle with the deer.

SOLDIER, *entering*. What's going on here, you young scamp! Bandy words with the king's men, will you? Scoot off, little fellow, before Prince Chandraketu arrives and tweaks your naughty ear. We are the king's soldiers—we don't stand for any nonsense.

LAVA, *laughing*. King's soldiers! *He draws his bowstring taut.* Look at this! My arrows have teeth, my bow growls; my bow opens like the mouth of death. My bow will swallow you all, king's soldiers!

C U R T A I N

## ACT V

### THE BRAVE YOUNG MEN

VOICE, *offstage*. Help is coming, soldiers! Prince Chandraketu is galloping to the rescue; his charioteer Sumantra is lashing the horses over the shaking earth.

CHANDRAKETU *and* SUMANTRA *enter in a chariot,* SUMANTRA *holding the reins and* CHANDRAKETU *his bow.*

CHANDRAKETU. I don't believe it! Sumantra, look—that slip of a five-tufted boy and his twanging bow, his face flushed in anger. Look how he rains his arrows on my soldiers—as if he were shooting a herd of charging elephants.

SUMANTRA. He shoots with the skill of the Raghavas!

CHANDRAKETU. So many against one! Disgraceful!

SUMANTRA. *He* doesn't seem to mind, sire.

CHANDRAKETU. So many against one! Disgraceful!

SUMANTRA, *to himself*. Single combat? Between Chandraketu and him? Never! Who knows what might happen?

CHANDRAKETU, *awe-struck*. They're falling back, the cowards!

SUMANTRA, *loosening the reins*. You may talk to him now, sire.

CHANDRAKETU. What did they say his name was?

SUMANTRA. Lava.

CHANDRAKETU. Lava! Listen! I am here! Fight *me*! The brave against the brave!

SUMANTRA. He has heard, sire. He's coming this way.

LAVA *comes strutting in*. Spoken like an Ikshvaku! I am ready. *There is shouting offstage*. The cowards want another fight. The fools! They'll get it. *He strides haughtily to the right side of the stage*.

CHANDRAKETU. Ignore them. Your courage bewilders me. I give you my soldiers. Take them. How can you fight your own soldiers?

LAVA, *hearing the shouting*. They are insulting me. I won't stand it!

CHANDRAKETU, *shouting to the soldiers*. My men, listen to me! Aren't you ashamed to fight against a single boy? Ten thousand against one? Elephants, horses, chariots, against one bow and a deerskin? Have you lost your senses?

LAVA, *angrily*. Pity! I didn't want pity. I will use the divine weapon Jrimbhika. *He adopts the posture of meditation*.

SUMANTRA. No more shouting! The soldiers have been enchanted into numbness.

LAVA. Now we can talk freely and to our heart's content.

SUMANTRA. He used the Jrimbhika weapon. I'm sure of it.

*There are flashes of lightning on the stage. Darkness and storm alternate.*

CHANDRAKETU. Gloom and lightning—and my men like a painted army!

You're right, he uses divine weapons: blasts of wind—the terrible Jrim-bhika weapon!

SUMANTRA. But how could *he* have power over divine weapons?

CHANDRAKETU. Perhaps Valmiki taught him.

SUMANTRA. The divine weapons came from Krishasva. Only Rama knows their use.

CHANDRAKETU. But when divine light shines in holy men, they know too.

SUMANTRA. Sire, be careful! He's coming toward us.

CHANDRAKETU. A most pleasing face!

LAVA. A pleasing face!

*Both gaze at each other admiringly.*

SUMANTRA. Call it love or friendship or delight, affection stitches two hearts into one.

CHANDRAKETU. Sumantra, let me down from the chariot.

SUMANTRA. Sire. . .

CHANDRAKETU. For a chariot rider does not fight a foot soldier. It is written in the science of war.

SUMANTRA. And blessed are they who abide by the rules that are written in the scriptures.

LAVA. Why does my arm feel faint now?

CHANDRAKETU, *getting down from the chariot.* Sir, Chandraketu the Ikshvaku salutes you.

SUMANTRA. May the blessings of Varaha give you victory, the valor of Indra and Vishnu, of Fire and Wind attend you, the spell of the bows of Rama and Lakshmana bring you success.

LAVA, *to* CHANDRAKETU. The chariot suits Your Majesty better than the ground.

CHANDRAKETU. You should mount a chariot too, in that case.

LAVA, *to* SUMANTRA. Sir, persuade him to get back into the chariot.

SUMANTRA. You will do as he says?

LAVA. What good are chariots for us? We are people of the ashrama.

SUMANTRA. Those are courteous and graceful words. If Rama could see and hear you, his heart would melt.

LAVA. I honor Rama too. That was the reason I felt insulted when the soldiers made that foolish boast that there was only one hero left in the world.

CHANDRAKETU, *smiling*. You couldn't bear to hear another hero being praised?

LAVA. I won't stand for a hero's being shamed.

CHANDRAKETU. But you know little of the great Rama.

LAVA. I know more than many. Let us not discuss him. He is great. He is our elder. His actions are not meant for our idle talk.

CHANDRAKETU, *angrily*. Pride swells in every word you speak. You presume a great deal, young man.

LAVA. Don't "presume" me, Chandraketu. I know what I'm saying.

SUMANTRA. Anger again. How it flames up!

BOTH. To combat! We'll fight.

CHANDRAKETU. Yes, we must fight!

LAVA. To the field to fight!

*They all leave.*

C U R T A I N

## ACT VI

### THE RECOGNITION OF THE PRINCES

*Two* SPIRITS OF THE AIR, *one male, one female, enter.*

MALE SPIRIT. What courage! Deeds which would amaze the gods and the demons! Two youths, descendants of the race of the sun, twanging their bowstrings and showering arrows at each other. Bells clanging, drums roaring with voices of thunder. . . . Throw flowers on them, the flowers of the celestial tree, jewel-fresh and lotus-thick flowers—for these youths are brave.

FEMALE SPIRIT. Why is the sky suddenly bright yellow, as if fleshed with lightning?

MALE SPIRIT. It is Chandraketu's weapon of fire, swooping through the flagstaffs of the army in an orgy of licking destruction, till the glowing heat suffocates. . . . Come to me; my cloak will save you from the heat.

FEMALE SPIRIT. And now the sky is dark with clouds, like a peacock's throat. Lightning again—streaks of it. What does it mean?

MALE SPIRIT. That is Lava's weapon of water. It gluts and chokes the fire. Confusion has come on the world—the wind, bellowing fiercely, is almost toppling the earth over. The fearful clouds are scattered, and nature itself hangs perilously in the yawning mouth of all-devouring time.

FEMALE SPIRIT. Who is that man with his hand lifted? Even from the distance his sweet words seem to have soothed the princes. . . . Now his chariot comes between them. Who is he?

MALE SPIRIT. It is Rama, the lord of the Raghavas, returning after killing Sambuka. Lava is calm now, and Chandraketu offers Rama obeisance. May there be peace between father and sons!

*They both leave. After a moment,* RAMA *enters, with* LAVA *and* CHANDRA-
KETU.

RAMA, *getting down from the aerial chariot, Pushpaka.* Chandraketu, embrace me. Your cool limbs bring peace to my heart. *He embraces him.* Is all well?

CHANDRAKETU. Yes, all is well, for I have made a brave and handsome friend. *He points to* LAVA.

RAMA, *looking at* LAVA. A remarkable and pleasing face. That is how a soldier should look.

LAVA, *aside.* What bends me down against my will and makes me a slave? I have seen greatness.

RAMA. Like a lotus that opens to the moon, my heart goes to this boy.

LAVA, *nudging* CHANDRAKETU. Who is he?

CHANDRAKETU. One who is like a father to me.

LAVA. My father too, then, if you call me your friend. *To* RAMA. Father, lord of the Raghavas, I, a pupil of Agastya, bow to you.

RAMA. Come to me, my child. *He embraces* LAVA. There is something in you that gives me delight.

LAVA. I was very stupid. Forgive me if I did wrong.

RAMA. Has he done wrong?

CHANDRAKETU. He only battled the whole army like a hero when he heard the bragging of the guards.

RAMA. A hero has his pride. Even stones burst into flame when the sun provokes them.

CHANDRAKETU. The army is still paralyzed by the divine weapon he used.

RAMA. Lava, my child, remove the spell. And you, Chandraketu, go to the soldiers and try to restore their morale.

CHANDRAKETU *leaves.*

LAVA, *after a moment of deep meditation.* They are freed now from the magic.

RAMA. These divine weapons, my child, have been handed down by tradition. The one you used was obtained by Brahman and the rishis after a thousand years of terrible penance. Then it went to Krishasva, who taught it to Vishvamitra, his pupil for a thousand years. Vishvamitra gave it to me—but I have given it to no one.

LAVA. Yet both of us have the power of the divine weapon.

RAMA. Both?

LAVA. My brother and I. We are twins.

RAMA. Where is he?

KUSHA'*s voice, offstage.* My brother fighting the whole army! Oh, he'll win!

RAMA. That voice. . . .

LAVA. It's my brother's. Kusha is here.

RAMA. Ask him to come to me.

LAVA *goes off and returns with* KUSHA. *They pause at the side of the stage.*

KUSHA, *patting his bow.* This bow is my strength. *He swaggers proudly.*

RAMA. He has the spirit of a fighter.

KUSHA, *to* LAVA. What's all this talk about you fighting the whole army?

LAVA. It's all over. Your help isn't necessary now. And stop strutting!

KUSHA. Why? What's wrong?

LAVA. The king, the lord of the Raghavas, is here. He wishes to talk to you.

KUSHA, *doubtfully.* The hero of the *Ramayana,* the guardian of the Vedas?

LAVA. Yes.

KUSHA. How shall I approach him? I feel nervous.

LAVA. Respectfully, as you would your father. *He takes* KUSHA *to* RAMA. This is Kusha; he bows to you.

RAMA. Come here, my child. *He embraces* KUSHA. Once again I feel that rush of joy.

LAVA. Let us sit in the shade, father.

*They sit down together.*

RAMA, *aside.* Their walk and their words mark them as princes. And they have the traits of the Raghavas—the dark-blue skin, necks firm as a bull's, heavy shoulders. Their eyes look coolly as a lion's, their voices boom like a drum's. What Raghava is their lucky father? They are quite like me, in fact. *He looks closely at them and ponders.* And quite like Sita, too—the same lotus-face, pearl-white teeth, the lovely ears, the blue eyes of Sita. *He pauses to think* This is the forest where she was abandoned; and the magic weapons. . .Could it be? . . . *He speaks sadly.* And now I must ask, and I don't know how. *Aloud.* Do you know the work of Valmiki? Could you recite me something?

KUSHA. We know it all by heart.

RAMA. I am listening.

KUSHA. "For Rama loved Sita: her virtues he loved. And Sita loved him dearer than life. Such were the words; but who knows the love in the hearts of lovers?"

RAMA, *aside.* Yes, so it was. In joy and sorrow. I had faith in her—and I lost her. Now I live; this heart beats, and like a fool will not stop beating, for I live without her.

KUSHA. And these are the words of Rama when he saw Sita in the forest of Chandraketu near the river Mandakini. "Flowers on both sides, Sita in the middle: the *vakula* tree is flattered."

RAMA, *aside.* The words of boys! Her face comes up like a dream: her cool, moonlike brow, dark hair, bright cheeks kissed by the breezes of the river. When the fire goes, the heat remains—and the heat bakes the heart in its wilderness of loss.

VOICE, *offstage.* Vashishtha and Arundhati; Valmiki; the queens of Raja Dasharatha; and Raja Janaka have come to the ashrama.

RAMA. The great Vashishtha and Arundhati here! My mothers and Janaka. How will I face them? Oh, I could die of shame!

*They all leave.*

C U R T A I N

# ACT VII

### THE REUNION

*A small stage has been erected at one side of the main stage.* LAKSHMANA *enters.*

LAKSHMANA. The Brahmins, the Kshatriyas, gods and demons and Nagas, birds and beasts—all are here today, summoned by Valmiki's power. And Rama has asked me to receive the audience on the banks of the Ganga, where Valmiki's play will be staged by celestial spirits. Here he is.

RAMA, *entering.* Is the audience seated, Lakshmana?

LAKSHMANA. Yes.

RAMA. But Lava and Kusha are to sit with Chandraketu.

LAKSHMANA. That is arranged too. I know you love them. This seat is for you. *He pauses while* RAMA *takes his seat.* Let the play begin.

*The* STAGE MANAGER *enters in front of the small stage.*

STAGE MANAGER. The holy Valmiki has had a vision, and we will present this sacred vision for your enjoyment and instruction today. Let the world listen. All movable and immovable things, listen! Listen, for the vision is holy and marvelous and pathetic.

RAMA. And well it should be. For the sages see into things. Passion is stilled, nothing is false; all is nectar.

SITA'S VOICE, *offstage.* O my husband! Do not leave me alone. Lakshmana, I fear the beasts of the forest! Where shall I go, what shall I do? Holy waters of the Bhagirathi, take me in your arms!

LAKSHMANA. I thought I heard. . .

STAGE MANAGER. Sita, daughter of Earth, wife of Rama, and carrying Rama's sons, throws herself into the Bhagirathi. Oh, listen to the wise Valmiki! *He leaves.*

RAMA. My wife! Lakshmana, where is she?

LAKSHMANA. This is a play, my brother.

RAMA. Beloved wife, never think that I have been happy.

LAKSHMANA. It's only a play!

SITA *enters, supported by* PRITHVI *and* BHAGIRATHI, *both personified as goddesses, and in the lap of each a baby boy.*

RAMA. Help me, Lakshmana. There is darkness around me—such darkness!

BOTH GODDESSES. Blessed Sita, these are your twin sons, born in the waters of the holy river.

SITA. My sons! *She smiles.* My husband! *She faints.*

LAKSHMANA. Twin sons, my noble brother. Heirs of the Raghavas! He isn't listening. *He fans* RAMA, *who is staring without expression, as if in a trance.*

PRITHVI. Do not worry, Sita.

SITA, *recovering.* Who are you, good lady? And who is she?

PRITHVI. She is Bhagirathi, the guardian goddess of your father-in-law's house.

SITA. I offer you homage, holy lady.

BHAGIRATHI. May your spotless character bring you joy in life. And this is your mother, Sita.

SITA. Mother!

PRITHVI. Come to me, Sita. *She embraces her.*

SITA, *sobbing*. You see me so helpless and lost.

BHAGIRATHI. Even Prithvi, the Earth, is crying. Love rolls through all things. Child, Sita, everything will be all right.

PRITHVI. What can I do for my daughter? That Rama should have treated her as he did—I didn't expect it.

SITA. My husband's name. . . .

PRITHVI. What did you say, my child?

SITA. His name. . . .

BHAGIRATHI. Don't be angry with him, Prithvi. He did what the people forced him to do. The people would not have believed in her innocence otherwise. I beg of you, with joined palms, forgive him.

PRITHVI. I cannot deny you anything. You know it. But a mother's grief! I know that he loves Sita, but. . .

SITA. Take me with you, Mother, let me be with you.

BHAGIRATHI. What are you saying, Sita?

PRITHVI. What about your sons? Who will look after them?

SITA. I am helpless, helpless without my husband. Without him, I do not want my sons. Let me die.

RAMA. O my heart, do not break.

BHAGIRATHI. But you *have* a husband.

SITA. A husband who does not want me.

BOTH GODDESSES. The whole world wants you. It sings your praise. You are pure and noble. When you touch us, we are made pure, O Sita.

RAMA. Let the people hear! Let the people hear!

VOICES, *shouting offstage*. The divine weapons! There is a glow in the sky.

LAKSHMANA. You remember, my brother, how you once said that the divine weapons would serve your children?

SITA. There is a glow in the sky.

BOTH GODDESSES. Be happy, Sita, for your children are now the equals of Rama.

BHAGIRATHI. The great Valmiki will look after them and bring them up in the proper manner. He will perform for them the rites of the Kshatriyas.

LAKSHMANA. Lava and Kusha are now twelve years old!

RAMA. I can't believe it!

PRITHVI, *to* SITA. Come, my child. When your sons have sucked milk from your breasts, you may do as you like.

SITA, BHAGIRATHI *and* PRITHVI *leave.*

RAMA. My wife, do not go! Oh, I beg you, stay with me, stay with me! *He faints.*

LAKSHMANA. A fine play, Valmiki! What next?

VOICE, *from offstage.* Look at the miracle! The marvelous scene in the play of Valmiki!

LAKSHMANA. I see the Ganga's waters frothing and churning. There are gods and sages in the vast sky, and Sita coming out of the waves—a wonderful sight!

VOICES, *offstage.* Arundhati, do what we ask of you. Bhagirathi and Prithvi ask it of you. Take Sita. Help her. She is now in your care.

LAKSHMANA. Look, my brother! She is coming.

RAMA *is still in a trance.* ARUNDHATI *and* SITA *enter.*

ARUNDHATI. Help him, my child. Don't be afraid. He needs you.

SITA, *touching* RAMA's *forehead.* My husband. . .

RAMA, *coming out of the trance.* Her hand! Who's here? Arundhati, Rishyasringa, Shanta. . .everyone. . .

BHAGIRATHI. You remember, Rama, how you asked me to take care of Sita. This I have done. I have kept my word.

PRITHVI. And you asked me to look after her. I have done so. I have kept my word.

RAMA, *bowing to the* GODDESSES. For your great goodness I can only give thanks. Oh, believe me, I am grateful.

ARUNDHATI. And you, citizens and villagers, here is the good Sita, now declared to be the purest of the pure by the goddesses Bhagirathi and Prithvi, who have put her in my care. Now I return her to her husband, the great Rama.

LAKSHMANA. She is rebuking the people for their stupidity.

ARUNDHATI. Rama, here is your wife, equal in honor and duty. Take her with you to the horse sacrifice and seat her beside you. Throw away the gold image.

LAKSHMANA. Sita, I know that I have been shameless, but let me say this— little good as it is now—that I am sorry for what I did. Forgive me. *He bows before* SITA.

SITA. It is all over, good Lakshmana.

ARUNDHATI. Kusha and Lava, Rama's sons, where are they?

SITA. Where are my sons?

VALMIKI *enters with* LAVA *and* KUSHA.

VALMIKI. Here is your father, Rama, lord of the Raghavas; your uncle Lakshmana; your mother Sita. And here is your grandfather, Raja Janaka.

SITA, *joyfully*. Father!

RAMA *embraces the boys*.

Come to your mother, Lava. . .Kusha. I am born again! *She embraces them*. Holy Father, I thank you. *She bows to Valmiki*.

VALMIKI. Be happy, my child. And what can I do for you, Rama?

RAMA. Is anything left undone? All is gratitude, and all is love.

C U R T A I N

# RATNAVALI

by

## HARSHA

# Preface

"The story is romantic," says H. H. Wilson in *The Theatre of the Hindus*, "the incidents are well contrived, the situations are eminently dramatic, and although the spectator is let into the secret of the plot from the beginning, the interest is very successfully maintained." He adds, though, that the play's poetry "is merely mechanical," and laments "the want of passion and the substitution of intrigue," suggesting that this makes the play devoid of "poetic spirit," "gleam of inspiration," devoid even of "a conceit in the ideas." All of which means that *Ratnavali* "may be taken as one of the connecting links between the old and new school; as a not unpleasing production of that middle school through which Hindu poetry passed from elevation to extravagance."

It is a charming conclusion, but one which assumes that the play is by King Harsha of Kashmir, who ascended the throne in 1113, and since there is insufficient textual evidence to warrant such an assumption and considerably more evidence that suggests that the play was written in the seventh century A.D. during the reign of the *other* Harsha (also known as Harshavardhana, or Shiladitya, who reigned in Kannauj, 606–647 A.D.), it is required to modify Wilson's extreme judgment of *Ratnavali* as a "bridging" play. Another intriguing bit of information puts everything in question. Dr. Saradaranjan Ray mentions in his notes on *Ratnavali* that a friend of his forwarded him some verses from the *Kavimimamsa* ascribed to the tenth-century Sanskrit poet Rajashekhara which, translated, read: "A poet's skill isn't the result of being born rich or elegant. Look at Bhasa, a poor washerman, considered the best of poets. His *Priyadarshika* delights people with open minds; his *Ratnavali* is a necklace glittering on the breasts of Drama. King Harshavikrama was so pleased with *Nagananda* that he appointed Bhasa his court poet." Though later in the passage Rajashekhara seems to confuse the Bhasa of *The Dream of Vasavadatta* with the Bhasa of *Ratnavali, Priyadarshika,* and *Nagananda,* there is reason to believe that the plays attributed to King Harsha are actually the work of Dhavaka-Bhasa, his court poet. The seventh-century Dhavaka-Bhasa, in fact, borrows the plot of *Ratnavali* not from the first-century *Ocean of Stories,* as was commonly supposed, but from his namesake Bhasa's *Dream of Vasa-vadatta,* written some time in the fourth century B.C. There are many echoes that suggest this. King Udayana questions Yaugandharayana in identical words in both plays when he wants to know Yaugandharayana's motive in devising the plan; and in his nervousness during the plan's earlier stages, Yaugandharayana expresses very similar doubts about its success.

The story, corresponding so closely in so many respects, differs in one fundamental. Bhasa disguises the queen Vasavadatta as Yaugandharayana's sister and places her in the care of the princess Padmavati; Dhavaka-Bhasa (or Harsha) has the princess Ratnavali living incognito in Vasava-datta's palace. To the reader uninitiated in the intricacies of Sanskrit plot-weaving, a summary of the background may prove useful. King Udayana of Vatsa is married to Vasavadatta, daughter of Pradyota, king of Avanti (for which reason she is sometimes addressed as "Lady of Avanti" or "Avantika"). Her maternal uncle, Vikramabahu of Simhala, or Ceylon, has a daughter named Ratnavali (which literally means "a necklace of gems" and refers in the play to the necklace Ratnavali will receive as part of her dowry when she marries). The minister of Udayana, Yaugandhara-yana, realizing that the holy men have predicted absolute control of India for the man who marries Ratnavali, devotes himself to bringing about the matrimonial alliance of Udayana and Ratnavali. This isn't easy, for obvious reasons. Vasavadatta may not like the idea of a co-queen; her uncle Vikramabahu wouldn't like to hurt his niece's feelings; and Udayana loves Vasavadatta too much to entertain thoughts of another marriage. (The feelings of Ratnavali are nowhere taken into consideration: she is the charming, dutiful, maneuverable princess who knows her father knows what's good for her.)

Yaugandharayana's first step is to convince Vasavadatta that Udayana's marrying Ratnavali would mean his glory as unchallenged ruler of India, and that she should subserve her own interests for the sake of her husband's majesty. This she does; Yaugandharayana immediately spreads rumors in Simhala that Vasavadatta has perished in a fire at the village of Lavanaka, and that the king has intentions of marrying again. The chamberlain Babhravya is sent with proposals of marriage to the court of Vikramabahu. Nothing of this reaches the ears of Udayana.

Since Vasavadatta and Ratnavali knew each other by name only, the best plan Yaugandharayana could think of was to have Bhabravya bring Ratnavali from Simhala straight to his house; he would then smuggle her into the harem disguised as an orphan girl, and let the revelry of the spring festival, the beauty of Ratnavali, the words of the prediction, and the amorousness of Udayana do the rest. The mischief is well co-ordinated; a royal marriage seems likely. But the boat in which Ratnavali is being escorted by Bhabravya and Vasubhuti (the minister of Vikramabahu) capsizes, and Ratnavali, separated from her guardians, clings to a plank and is rescued by a merchant of Kausambi, Udayana's capital, who recognizes her by the necklace she is wearing. She is brought to Yaugandharayana and he proceeds with the plan. Ratnavali is grateful to the kind gentleman who gets her a maid's position (she is now Sagarika) in Vasavadatta's palace, and complies with his request that she should not disclose her identity to any person in the strange country where she has been brought by the merchant. The curtain now opens on the love-and-fun game called *Ratnavali*.

Dr. Keith's terse comment sums up the play excellently: it has "found favor," he says, "in the text-books of the drama, and has served to illustrate the text-book rules." But that is a cruelly kind cut. The swift interplay of love and scolding in the quick succession of scenes of mistaken identity in Act III can, with proper direction, be made eminently dramatic. One virtue Dhavaka-Bhasa has, even in his excessive moments—a sure sense of the stage and its requirements. Slight though it may be from the serious viewpoint of rasa, *Ratnavali* is a perfectly wrought comedy, combining horseplay, slapstick and soap opera; and if the reader cannot detect a gentle and humane irony in the king's apostrophe in the garden:

> O dearest Sagarika, darling Sagarika,
> Moon-faced Sagarika, lotus-eyed Sagarika,
> Lotus-fingered Sagarika, lotus-armed Sagarika,
> O Sagarika, lovely-thighed Sagarika,
> Pleasure-giving Sagarika,
> Come to me, Sagarika, and love me with your lips!

then he has failed to see how the seventh-century poet of *Ratnavali* went about his business of entertaining the sophisticated *nagaraka*.

## HARSHA

*Birthplace:* Kannauj, central India.
*Date of birth:* 606 A.D. He died in 647 A.D.

# Characters

Yaugandharayana, *minister to King Udayana*

King Udayana, *ruler of Vatsa*

Jester (Vasantaka)

Madanika, *maid to the queen*

Chatulatika, *maid to the queen*

Vasavadatta, *wife to Udayana*

Kanchanamala, *maid to the queen*

Sagarika, *Ratnavali disguised as personal maid to Vasavadatta*

Susamgata, *maid, friend of Sagarika*

Nipunika, *maid*

Vasundhara, *maid*

Vijayavarman, *son of General Rumanvat*

Sambarasiddhi, *court magician and entertainer*

Vasubhuti, *minister to Vikrambahu (father of Ratnavali)*

Babhravya, *guard of Ratnavali*

# ACT I

## THE FESTIVAL OF LOVE

YAUGANDHARAYANA *enters in front of the curtain. He speaks reflectively.* It's true. That she should be miraculously saved by the trader from Kausambi and then recognized from her pearl necklace. . .that was the prophecy. That there would be a shipwreck, that she would be saved. . .the daughter of the king of Simhala would be saved. . .*He speaks joyfully.* Luck favors our king. *He speaks reflectively again.* And I did well, keeping her in the care of the queen. . . . And then there's more good news. Our chamberlain, the excellent Babhravya, and the king of Simhala's minister, Vasubhuti, have conferred with Rumanvat, who was on his way to conquer the Kosalas. All this indicates a bright future for our king, but. . .I'm far from satisfied. Fate's on our side, true—but I've got a hand in it as well, and human hands are none too sure. *There is a noise offstage.* The clapping citizens, the sweet-sounding drums. Now His Majesty is proceeding to the palace, where soon the celebrations for Madana, god of love, will begin. *He looks up.* Now he is in the palace. . . . And I must be home too, planning for the future. *He leaves.*

*The curtain rises, showing the* KING *seated with the* JESTER, *colorfully dressed, at his side.*

KING. Vasantaka. . .

JESTER. Sire?

KING, *happily.* Look, Vasantaka—what more could a king ask? The empire's enemies under control, an honest minister in charge, the subjects all happy, and then my wife, the springtime, you . . . This isn't Madana's festival, it's mine!

JESTER. Sire, it is so. But not yours, no. Not the god of love's, no. *Mine!* A brat of a Brahmin's, sire. . . . Ah, the festive spirit! *He looks out.* Dancing in the streets, women and song, the drums, the red powder, the water sprinklers, the songs like firecrackers!

KING, *also looking out.* This is the peak of the festival. What a sight! The scented red powder, the glowing jewels, the asoka flowers drenching the dancers in gold: it's like a second dawn breaking over the city. And on the veranda there, a river of vermilion churned by the blossoming fountains into a scarlet mud.

JESTER. The ludicrous water syringes aimed at the pretty girls!

KING. Brilliant! Like snakes squirting sweet venom.

JESTER. Here comes Madanika, very lovelorn, her feet full of the dance. And with her I think is Chutalatika.

MADANIKA *and* CHUTALATIKA, *attendants to the queen, enter singing.*

MADANIKA. Blow, south wind, blow us mango scent, flower scent,
   In all hearts blow liveliness,
   Waiting means pain and the girls are languishing
   For love and a lover's caress,
   Spring comes to melt our hearts, bringing beauty,
   Bringing loveliness. . .

KING. Lovely! Delicious!

JESTER. I think I'll join them.

KING, *smiling.* By all means. Lucky rascal.

JESTER. Your Majesty commands. I obey. *He rises and dances with the girls.* Madanika, teach me the song.

MADANIKA *and* CHUTALATIKA, *speaking together.* Sing it. *The* JESTER *sings.* Silly, it's meant to be chanted, not sung.

JESTER, *surprised.* Chanted? *He speaks sadly.* Chanting's not in my line. I must return to my friend. *He shuffles away.*

MADANIKA *and* CHUTALATIKA, *barring his way.* You don't like us?

JESTER, *snatching his hand free.* Dear girls, sweet girls, I have danced, I have sung. Enough, I must go! *He runs back to the* KING.

KING. Bravo!

CHUTALATIKA. Madanika, the queen's message. . .

MADANIKA. Oh, yes, I nearly forgot. *She and* CHUTALATIKA *approach the* KING.

MADANIKA *and* CHUTALATIKA. Sire, the queen commands—*They check themselves, shamefacedly.* The queen *says—*

KING. "Commands" is good, very good, Madanika. Today is the festival. So why shouldn't the queen command? Tell me, what is it?

JESTER, *aside.* When *didn't* she command?

MADANIKA *and* CHUTALATIKA. Sire, the queen says she will expect Your Majesty near the red asoka tree in the honeyflower gardens where she is going to perform the ritual worship of the god of love.

KING. Then you may tell Her Majesty that His Majesty will be there. What do you say, Vasantaka?

JESTER. Most assuredly, sire.

MADANIKA *and* CHUTALATIKA. We shall take your message to the queen, sire. *They depart.*

KING. Let's go, Vasantaka. *The* KING *and the* JESTER *descend the palace steps.* And now you lead the way, sir.

JESTER. This way, sire. *They walk a few steps.* The honeyflower gardens, sire. *They enter.* The giddy black bees, the sweet kokila, the south breeze wait in the canopy of the garden for you, sire, to bid you welcome.

KING. It's an exquisite spot. Look at those trees there, how the touch of spring intoxicates them till they sprout green leaves and coral flowers. The drunken hum of bees is in their heads and the south breeze shakes them into teetering tipsiness.

JESTER. The drowsy hum of bees. But I think I hear the jingling of anklets.

KING. You may be right.

VASAVADATTA, KANCHANAMALA, *and* SAGARIKA *enter, carrying implements for the ceremony.*

VASAVADATTA. Is this the way to the honeyflower gardens?

KANCHANAMALA. Yes, my mistress.

VASAVADATTA. And how far from here is the red asoka tree?

KANCHANAMALA. A few steps, my mistress. Just three—beyond the *madhavi* and *navamalika* vines.

VASAVADATTA. Let's hurry. *They walk a few steps.* Ah, here's the tree. Now where are the flowers and other offerings? SAGARIKA *hands her the ceremonial objects.* VASAVADATTA *muses aloud to herself.* The fools! Letting her step forward. Why, she might be seen by the very person who should be the last to see her. *She looks up.* Sagarika, what are you doing here? Get back to the palace birds at once. Don't you know the poor *sarikas* are all alone there? Give the flowers to Kanchanamala. She can manage.

SAGARIKA. Yes, my mistress. *She obeys and walks away, but then stops and speaks to herself.* But I did so want to see the ceremony. The *sarikas* aren't alone! I'll just hide myself here and gather flowers for the ceremony. *She hides herself and plucks some flowers.*

VASAVADATTA. The god's image should go at the foot of the tree, Kanchanamala.

KANCHANAMALA *places the image.*

JESTER. No more jingling. Her Majesty must have begun her worshiping.

KING. Yes, yes, she is near the tree. See, the god's image is under the branches. We'll go to her. *He approaches the queen.* Dearest Vasavadatta—

VASAVADATTA. My husband! Please sit here.

*The* KING *sits down.*

KANCHANAMALA. The flowers are ready, my mistress, the saffron, the sandalwood, and the cloth offerings.

VASAVADATTA *worships.*

KING. When you worship, dearest Vasavadatta, it is you who look divine, for then your clear skin, fresh from the bath, glows in the added holiness of the ritual. A pity the god's an image. Otherwise the touch of your hand might arouse sweet feelings in him.

KANCHANAMALA. The rites for the husband now, my mistress.

VASAVADATTA. Flowers and scents, Kanchanamala. *She worships the* KING.

SAGARIKA, *finishing her flower gathering.* Oh, it completely slipped my mind, the flowers were so enchanting. Here, let me look. *She peers through the creepers.* The god of love! In person, worshipped by my mistress! I too will worship him. *She turns and tosses the flowers in the direction of the god's image.* O god of love, I salute you: help me and guide me. *She bows.* So, I have seen what I wanted. But there is a difference: in my father's palace we worshipped a painting, here we worship the god of love in person. *She tries to slip away unseen.*

KANCHANAMALA. Noble Vasantaka, here are gifts for you in exchange for blessings from you.

*The* JESTER *approaches.* VASAVADATTA *offers him scents, flowers, and jewels.*

VASAVADATTA. For you, sir.

JESTER, *taking the gifts.* And my blessings upon you.

VOICE, *offstage.* The hour of dusk.
   O sun, going down behind the distant hill,
   Take the homage of the king as you do the homage of lotuses.
   Night is coming on.

SAGARIKA, *turning to look again at the* KING. Oh, is this the King Udayana to whom my father betrothed me? *Wistfully.* I never thought—

KING, *to* VASAVADATTA. The festival had stolen our minds away. Evening's here. See, dearest, how the beloved sun clings to his darling night.

SAGARIKA. They're leaving. I must be back before them. *She looks at the* KING *and sighs deeply.* Oh, that I wasn't aware earlier such beauty could exist!

KING. Dearest Vasavadatta, your lotus face shames the lotuses of the lake. Even the moon objects. . . . The songs are over; the bees, like embarrassed girls, are back in the bosomy buds. Let us go.

*All depart.*

C U R T A I N

## ACT II

### THE BANANA GARDEN

SUSAMGATA *enters, carrying a caged* sarika *bird.*

SUSAMGATA. Where has Sagarika disappeared? Poor little *sarika! She looks around.* Here's Nipunika, I'll ask her.

NIPUNIKA, *entering and speaking to herself.* I must give the message to the queen immediately. . .

SUSAMGATA. Nipunika, haven't you eyes? Can't you see me?

NIPUNIKA. Oh, Susamgata! My head's full of such exciting things! The holy man Srikhandadasa—you've heard of him?—he says he'll make trees blossom out of season, he says he'll bring flowers to the *navamalika* today. The queen sent me to inquire—but where are *you* going?

SUSAMGATA. Looking for Sagarika.

NIPUNIKA. Sagarika? I saw her entering the banana garden, with a box of colors, a painting board, and a paintbrush. She looked all flustered—I don't know why. But see, I'm in a hurry. You can find her.

*They both depart.* SAGARIKA, *wearing a lovesick expression and carrying her brush and board, enters and speaks with a sigh.*

SAGARIKA. Oh, my heart, stop! Why cry for the moon? When the moon won't come, there will be tears and sadness. . . . Yet my foolish heart hungers for a glimpse of the distant moon. Kamadeva, god of love, help me! *She folds her hands and prays tearfully.* O Kàmadeva, god of love, I am a helpless woman. . . . Leave me, leave me. *She looks at the painting board*. Will this help? I'll try. . . . *She concentrates, with a deep sigh.* My fingers tremble; but if this is the only way to have him, I will have him. *She sketches.*

SUSAMGATA, *entering and whispering to herself.* So lost she doesn't even notice me. . . . Let me see what she's painting. *She steals behind* SAGARIKA. Why, it's His Majesty! *Aloud.* It's beautiful, Sagarika! I didn't know you painted so well.

SAGARIKA, *sadly.* Only a painting—*She hides the board beneath a fold of her dress and smiles weakly.* Susamgata, my dear friend, Susamgata. . . sit here.

SUSAMGATA, *picking up the board.* All your own work? It's the king—but who are you portraying him as?

SAGARIKA, *blushing.* The god of love.

SUSAMGATA, *smiling.* You don't say! But you must put the goddess in too. *She picks up the brush and sketches quickly.*

SAGARIKA, *angrily.* But you're painting *me*.

SUSAMGATA, *laughing.* And why not? For every god a goddess. . .But come to the point. What are you doing, Sagarika? What's going on? The whole truth now!

SAGARIKA, *blushing and speaking to herself.* She knows. *Aloud.* Oh, Susamgata, I feel so ashamed. I can't help it—What shall I do now?

SUSAMGATA. Nothing. The whole thing's perfectly normal. You love handsomeness; you are beautiful. . . . Beauty loving handsomeness is good. But we'll have to go about it secretly. This *sarika's* going to give us trouble. She's picked up every word we've said, and if she blabs it out—

SAGARIKA, *sadly.* Nothing could be worse than the fire in my heart.

SUSAMGATA. Wait, I'll get you some cool leaves. *She goes offstage and returns quickly with a mat of woven lotus shoots, and with lotus leaves which she places on Sagarika's breasts.*

SAGARIKA. What good is a lotus mat? What good are lotus leaves? I love him but I can't have him. Oh, the dreadful inequality of love! He is great,

I am lowly. . .I am lost. Susamgata, I must die. *She hears a noise offstage.*
The monkey's loose!

VOICE, *offstage.* The stable monkey's loose, his gold chain jingling!
  He's in the palace now, frightening the ladies. . .
  The dwarf has scuttled inside the chamberlain's gown,
  The eunuchs and the harem guards have fled in fear.

SUSAMGATA, *taking* SAGARIKA *by the hand.* Quick, let's get out of here
before the monkey arrives.

SAGARIKA. Which way?

SUSAMGATA. This way—among these banana trees. *She looks back
fearfully.*

SAGARIKA. I've left the painting board behind.

SUSAMGATA. Let it be! That scamp of a monkey's opened the birdcage. . .
look, the *sarika*'s flown out! We'll have to follow her. She knows every
word we said, she'll start chirping it any moment.

SAGARIKA. What will happen, Susamgata?

JESTER, *offstage.* Brilliant! Brilliant!

SAGARIKA, *fearfully.* The monkey again!

SUSAMGATA. No, the jester.

JESTER, *entering.* Ha-ha! Srikhandadasa, fine fellow! Brilliant! Ha!-ha!

SAGARIKA *gazes curiously at him.*

SUSAMGATA. Let's go. We must look for the bird. Come. *They both
leave.*

JESTER. Good Srikhandadasa, you're a marvel! Your recipe is a marvel:
you've made the *navamalika* blossom—glistening, glorious flowers! This
news must go to the king—*He looks about.*—if the king does not go to
the news, for here he comes, beaming with joy. He must have seen the
creeper in bloom.

KING, *entering.* A lovely white creeper, as sweet as a woman's love.

JESTER, *approaching the* KING *and speaking excitedly.* The creeper's in bloom, sire. Srikhandadasa has performed a miracle!

KING. I never doubted the man's powers. Herbs and gems and charms are wonderful things. Where is the creeper?

JESTER, *importantly.* This way, sire. *They both proceed a short distance; then the* JESTER *stops suddenly, fearfully.* Sire, let's run. There's a—a—a—

KING. Speak up! What's wrong?

JESTER. A—a—a—s-s-s-spoook in this *vakula* tree.

KING. You're out of your head. Ghosts? Here? Bah!

JESTER. It—it's a spook, sire. I heard it. Listen, sire. Here. . . .

KING, *putting his ear near the* vakula *tree.* Yes. . .soft. . .and very sweet, like a girl's. . .oh, it's a bird, a *sarika.* . . . *He smiles.* It's a myna, you fool.

JESTER, *listening carefully.* A myna, sire?

KING, *laughing.* That's what I said.

JESTER. And you thought it was a spook? Ha-ha!

KING. *I* thought it was a spook? *You* thought it was a spook!

JESTER. I did? *I* did? No, don't stop me! *He raises his staff excitedly.* Why, you bloody *sarika,* you bitch of a myna, did you think I'd be frightened? A Brahmin be frightened! Wait till I knock you down, you rotten apple! *He prepares to strike.*

KING, *stopping him.* Don't be a fool! The bird's speaking. . .let's listen.

JESTER, *listening.* Did you hear that? "Who is he?" "The god of love." "But you're painting me!" "And why not? For every god a goddess. . . ." "Come to the point. . . . What are you doing? What's going on? The whole truth now!" Oho, oho, what's this?

KING. Some girl in love painting her handsome heart's desire—and her friend teasing her.

JESTER. Yes, that's it. Neat, very neat. *He snaps his fingers.*

KING. Ssssh. . .She speaks again.

JESTER. "You love handsomeness, and you are beautiful. . . . Beauty loving handsomeness is good. . . ." A pleasant morsel, sire, a juicy bit.

KING. Ssssh. . .Listen. This may lead to something.

JESTER, *with his ear to the tree*. Ha! Aha! Listen to this. . ."What good are lotus leaves, I love him but I can't have him. . . ."

KING. Warmer and warmer.

JESTER. Sire, listen. Riddles from the beak of a bitchy bird! "Oh, the dreadful inequality of love! He is great, I am lowly. . . . I am lost, I must die."

KING. Who but a Brahmin could speak like that? A Brahmin or a desperate lover.

JESTER. Ha-ha! That's a good one, sire. *He claps his hands and laughs loudly.*

KING, *looking up into the tree*. Stop, stop it! . . . Blast it, there goes the bird. . . . Where is she now? *He shades his eyes and squints.*

JESTER, *also squinting*. In the banana garden, sire. *He points.* Let us go there. *They move a few steps.* Here's the garden. *They enter.* Oh, what's the use? The bird has flown. Let's rest ourselves on this cool slab of stone under the shady banana trees. *They both sit down.*

KING. Children and parrots and mynas—dangerous things for lovers to have around them. Love will out, love will out.

JESTER. What's this? *He goes to pick something up.* A bird cage, sire! The myna's, I think. *He searches further.* And here! A painting board! Sire, look at this!

KING, *with curiosity*. What have you got?

JESTER. A spitting likeness of you, sire, painted as the god of love.

KING, *stretching out his hand*. Show it to me.

JESTER. No.

KING. Why?

JESTER. Not just your likeness, sire, but a lovely girl's. Are lovely girls shown free?

*The* KING *hands him a bracelet and takes the painting, which he studies intently.*

KING. Oh, but she's graceful and lovely, like a swan stirring in a lotus-filled lake.

SARGARIKA *and* SUSAMGATA *enter, but are screened from the* KING *and the* JESTER *by a vine.*

SUSAMGATA. We'll never find the bird, but let's get the painting board from the banana garden.

JESTER, *still looking at the painting.* Why does she appear so pale and lost?

SUSAMGATA, *listening.* The jester's voice. The king must be with him. Let's hide here, Sagarika, and listen. *The two girls hide themselves.*

KING. Oh, but she's graceful and lovely, like a swan stirring in a lotus-filled lake.

SUSAMGATA. Lucky you, Sagarika! Praise from His Majesty's lips!

SAGARIKA, *blushing.* You tease me, Susamgata.

JESTER. My question was not that, sire. I wanted to know why she looks so pale and lost.

KING. The bird answered that, didn't she? Why ask *me?*

SUSAMGATA. I knew the *sarika* would tell it all.

JESTER. And how do you find her, sire—pretty? Yes? . . . No? . . . . . . .

SAGARIKA, *to herself.* My heart hangs on his words.

KING. Pretty? The word is *lovely,* my friend. My slow eyes feast on her lovely thighs, pause on the delicate curves of her hips and waist, thirstily move up her heavy breasts, and rest tenderly in the peace of her tear-filled eyes.

SUSAMGATA. You heard, Sagarika?

SAGARIKA. He praises the skill of your painting.

JESTER, *looking again at the painting*. And you are so struck by her that you haven't a word for your own likeness?

KING. Why not? She did me honor by painting me. Look at that wet patch like a smudge of perspiration on my body—her tears that fell on the board while she painted, smudged where her palm touched them.

SUSAMGATA. I can't believe my ears. Lucky girl!

SARGARIKA *looks embarrassed*.

JESTER. Here's a lotus mat, sire, for a lovesick girl.

KING. You have quick eyes. And she lay on it: where it was touched by her breasts and hips it is faded, but the center is undisturbed where her soft body and arms enclosed it. And here lie two large lotus leaves, full of warmth still—the warmth they received when she placed them on her lovesick breasts.

JESTER. Here's a lotus shoot, sire.

KING, *placing it on his heart*. You must have slipped from between her breasts. How could there be a place for you there?

SUSAMGATA, *to herself*. This is the madness of love. He's talking nonsense. I'll have to think of something. . . . *Aloud*. Sagarika, the man you came for is here.

SAGARIKA, *with irritation*. Whom did I come for? Who's here?

SUSAMGATA, *laughing*. Oh, the painting. The man you painted. Take it.

SAGARIKA, *angrily*. Very clever. Let me go.

SUSAMGATA. Wait. I'll get the painting for you.

SAGARIKA. Nobody's stopping you.

SUSAMGATA *enters the banana garden*.

JESTER, *seeing* SUSAMGATA. Sire, the queen's maid Susamgata. Quick, hide it.

*The* KING *covers the painting with his cloak.*

SUSAMGATA. Sire, my homage.

KING. You are welcome, Susamgata. Sit here. SUSAMGATA *sits down.* How did you know I was here?

SUSAMGATA, *laughing.* But I heard all, sire—the painting, the whole story. . .the queen will be delighted to hear it from me.

JESTER, *in alarm; aside.* Stop her. She's a frightful gossip.

KING, *catching* SUSAMGATA'S *arm.* A joke, Susamgata, a gay little joke. The queen won't be interested, will she, Vasantaka? Take these. *He gives her his earrings.*

SUSAMGATA, *bowing and smiling.* Oh, I understand, sire. I was joking too. But I don't want earrings, sire. All I want is to join Sagarika, who is very angry, sulking behind that creeper there. You see, sire, Sagarika's very touchy, and you could help her—she's very angry because I painted her on that board—

KING, *rising hastily.* What! Where? Where is she?

SUSAMGATA *leads them to the creeper.*

JESTER. I'll keep the painting—it might come in handy someday.

SAGARIKA, *at first sight of the* KING, *speaks nervously and joyfully to herself.* I'm so nervous. I feel so silly. What shall I say?

JESTER, *catching sight of her.* A flawless gem! Paragon of beauties! A sight for the gods!

KING. You know, Vasantaka, I agree with you.

SAGARIKA, *speaking reproachfully to* SUSAMGATA. This is the painting you went to bring?

KING. Don't be angry: anger in your eye melts into gentleness. No, don't go yet.

SUSAMGATA. Take her hand, sire, she is very annoyed.

KING. Gladly, Susamgata. *He takes* SAGARIKA's *hand.*

SUSAMGATA. You shouldn't be angry now, Sagarika. The king has taken your hand.

SAGARIKA, *petulantly*. Stop it, Susamgata!

KING. Oh, but you shouldn't be angry with your friends.

JESTER. Sire, I see queen Vasavadatta.

*The* KING *quickly releases* SAGARIKA's *hand.*

SAGARIKA. What will I do now, Susamgata?

SUSAMGATA. Come, follow me—behind these banana trees.

*The two girls depart.*

KING. Where is Vasavadatta?

JESTER. Vasavadatta, sire?

KING. You said you saw her.

JESTER. Oh, sire, she looked so much like Vasavadatta I thought I saw Vasavadatta.

KING. Superidiot of idiots!—just when things were warming up. You would do something like that!

VASAVADATTA *enters with* KANCHANAMALA.

VASAVADATTA You said the *navamalika* is here?

KANCHANAMALA. Yes, my queen. *She sees the* KING *and is surprised.* Your Majesty! *She bows.*

VASAVADATTA. What a pleasant surprise, my husband!

KING, *aside*. Hide the damned picture!

*The* JESTER *covers it with his robe.*

VASAVADATTA. I heard that the *navamalika* is in full bloom.

KING. I was waiting for you. . . . Come, we'll go there together.

VASAVADATTA. But you look so happy, my husband, why do we need a *navamalika?* Let's stay here in the garden.

JESTER, *lifting his hand*. Good! Very good! *His robe slips, the painting is revealed, and the* KING *glowers at him. Aside.* Don't worry. I'll handle it.

KANCHANAMALA, *picking up the painting.* Look at this lovely painting, my queen.

VASAVADATTA, *to herself.* My husband. . .Sagarika. . .*Aloud.* What is this?

KING, *bashfully; aside.* What now?

JESTER. Oh, I was teasing him, Your Majesty—I said he couldn't paint if he tried. . .and he produced *that! He points to the painting.* Not bad, eh?

KING. He's right.

VASAVADATTA. And the girl there—her likeness must be your work, Vasantaka? No?

KING. Oh, no, no. . .pure imagination. . .a work of fancy. . .I did it out of my head. . .never saw her before. . . .

JESTER. By this holy thread, Your Majesty, I swear I never laid eyes on a girl with that face. I mean *we* never laid eyes—

VASAVADATTA, *aside.* Don't I know you, you double-crossing liar, Vasantaka, my sweet clown! *Aloud.* I feel so tired suddenly, my husband. I'll go lie down. *She rises and prepares to go.*

KING, *catching at her dress.* Did I do anything, Vasavadatta? Did I say something wrong? I'm sorry. Shall I say I won't do it again? . . . Won't do *what* again? I'm all confused. Did you mind? . . . Are you angry on account of me?

VASAVADATTA, *gently releasing her dress from her husband's grasp.* Oh, no, my husband. Just a little headache. One of those things. . .I think I should rest. *She leaves with* KANCHANAMALA.

KING. What a fool I've been! I've made her angry; it's true, even if she won't show it. A frown, a smile, a cool look, but no cruel words, not one insult or rebuff. There's good breeding for you. . . . Well, let us go to the queen.

*The* KING *and the* JESTER *depart.*

C U R T A I N

## ACT III

MADANIKA *enters in front of the curtain and turns to address someone offstage.*

MADANIKA. Is that Kausambika? Kausambika, where's Kanchanamala? You mean she came here and left? A long time ago? *She looks ahead.* Oh, never mind—she's here.

KANCHANAMALA, *entering; speaking to herself.* Vasantaka, your schemes would beat Yaugandharayana's!

MADANIKA, *smiling.* And why, dear Kanchanamala, is the jester accorded such golden praise from your lips?

KANCHANAMALA. Can you keep a secret, Madanika? You know you can't.

MADANIKA. Keep a secret? I swear by the queen I will. Tell me, tell me, Kanchanamala.

KANCHANAMALA. Well, come closer then. . . . *She lowers her voice.* This morning I saw the jester and Susamgata huddled together in conversation near the picture gallery. . .

MADANIKA, *impatiently.* Go on, go on.

KANCHANAMALA. You won't believe it, Madanika, but he told her there was no cure for the king's grief except Sagarika. . . .

MADANIKA. And she?

KANCHANAMALA. Well, you won't believe this either, but she said she would disguise Sagarika as the queen, and the king could meet her in secret near the *madhavi* creeper. "I'll dress up as Kanchanamala," she told him, "and you meet me near the picture gallery." I heard it all.

MADANIKA. The deceiving witch! Who ever thought Susamgata would play such a sly trick on the queen?

KANCHANAMALA. Be sure you keep it to yourself. Where were you going?

MADANIKA. To look for you. The queen sent me, because you took such a long time inquiring after His Majesty's health. How is he now?

KANCHANAMALA. Health! He's bursting with it! He's only a little love-sick, and a little worn out from trying to hide it under what he calls his indisposition. Let's tell the queen.

*They both depart. The curtain rises, revealing the* KING *in a lovesick attitude.*

KING, *sighing.* Burn in my heart, O fire!
  My heart, be scorched in the heat of love!
  The more fool I, having held her hand,
  To let it slip away without a protest.
  Yet the whole thing is a marvel—
  The mind's invisible, a state of flux,
  How could the god of love shoot at it?
  Five-arrowed Kamedeva, ruler of the world,
  Help me! . . .
  But no, not me, help innocent Sagarika,
  Open to the fury of the queen. . .
  Fear lives in her heart now, she does not notice people,
  Harmless talk becomes flaming gossip in her ears,
  Smiling friends confuse her,
  Poor Sagarika. . .
  Damn you, Vasantaka, what's keeping you?
  Haven't you news of her for me?

*The* JESTER *enters, beaming, speaking to himself.* Ha-ha! This news is worth twenty kingdoms! *He sees the* KING. Waiting for me, I see. *He approaches the* KING. And your wait, sire, has not been fruitless.

KING. You mean she is well?

JESTER, *teasingly.* I mean you'll see her soon.

KING. Again! When?

JESTER. Aren't you the king?

KING. *You*, sir, are the king. But tell me—when, where? *He listens as the* JESTER *whispers in his ear*. Oh, excellent! A good job! Take this. *He gives the* JESTER *a gold bracelet*.

JESTER, *placing the bracelet on his arm*. Gold! Thank you, sire. Now to my wife—who likes pure gold.

KING. Later to the wife who likes pure gold. It's not yet sunset.

JESTER. There—on that hill—the thousand-eyed sun, with love in his heart, is struggling toward the forest of the hilltop, where his beloved Evening calls. . . .

KING. Yes, you're right. . .it is sunset. Let us go to the *madhavi* creeper where she waits for me. Lead the way, Vasantaka.

*They go on their way.*

JESTER. We're in the dark of the honeyflower gardens, the trees thick around us. What now? I've lost my way.

KING. Use your nose. Champak scent; *sindhuvara* scent; the fragrant beds of *vakula;* the roses. . .This is the way.

JESTER. Sire, here is the *madhavi* creeper! Drunken bees and divine fragrance—oh, the scent, the scent! Wait here, sire, I'll bring Sagarika to you. She's dressed as the queen.

KING. Hurry!

JESTER. No more than a minute, sire. *He leaves.*

KING. Till she comes, loneliness. . .only these green stone slabs to sit on. *He sits down.* Stolen love is sweet—most delicious! . . . Damn the man, what's wrong with him? Has the queen got wind of it?

VASAVADATTA *and* KANCHANAMALA *enter, but are screened from the* KING'*s view by the creeper.*

VASAVADATTA. You mean she'll go to him dressed as *me?*

KANCHANAMALA. It's the truth, my queen. To prove it you have only to go and see Vasantaka waiting near the picture gallery.

VASAVADATTA. Take me there.

*They circle the stage. The* JESTER *enters, his head covered.*

JESTER. Footsteps! Sagarika! *He calls loudly.* Sagarika!

KANCHANAMALA. We are near the picture gallery, my queen. Watch. *She snaps her fingers.*

JESTER, *smiling.* Oh, is it you, Susamgata? I've been waiting for you. *He catches sight of* KANCHANAMALA. Perfect, Susamgata! Anyone would think you were Kanchanamala! Where's Sagarika?

KANCHANAMALA, *pointing to* VASAVADATTA. Here.

JESTER, *awe-stricken.* But that's the queen herself! No? What a perfect disguise! My lady Sagarika, follow me please. Let's hurry, my lady, the moon is up.

VASAVADATTA *looks significantly at* KANCHANAMALA, *and all three proceed around the garden.*

KING, *to himself.* I know she's coming. . .but the pain of waiting! Love oppresses most when near fulfillment, like a sweltering day before rainfall.

JESTER, *overhearing the* KING. My lady Sagarika—you hear how he loves you? Wait, I'll tell him you've come. *Scarcely waiting for* VASAVADATTA'*s nod, the* JESTER *approaches the* KING. Sire, she is here.

KING, *jumping up.* Where?

JESTER, *beckoning to* VASAVADATTA. Here.

VASAVADATTA *stands before the* KING.

KING. O dearest Sagarika, darling Sagarika,
Moon-faced Sagarika, lotus-eyed Sagarika,
Lotus-fingered Sagarika, lotus-armed Sagarika,
O Sagarika, lovely-thighed Sagarika,
Pleasure-giving Sagarika,
Come to me, Sagarika, and love me with your lips.

VASAVADATTA, *aside.* He's crazy—oh most strange! He's insane, Kanchanamala.

KANCHANAMALA, *aside*. He's in love.

JESTER. Good Sagarika, be kind to him. For his wife Vasavadatta speaks harshly to him, his ears are full of the queen's anger. Soothe him with the sweetness of your honeyed speech. . . .

VASAVADATTA, *ironically; aside*. *I* harsh, and Vasantaka most sweet—isn't that it, Kanchanamala?

KANCHANAMALA. He'll be sorry for those words some day.

JESTER. Your Majesty, look—the moon!

KING. Dearest Sagarika, see the moon!
  Oh, the wan moon robbed of her loveliness,
  Dearest Sagarika;
  Your beauty is richer.
  Oh, the envious moon, Sagarika!

VASAVADATTA. No more of this—this lunacy! *She snatches aside her veil.* "Sagarika! Dearest, darling Sagarika!"—Bah, where's Sagarika? I am the queen, Queen Vasavadatta!

KING, *confusedly*. Damnation! What's this?

JESTER, *sadly*. I'm ruined. . . .

*The* KING *kneels before* VASAVADATTA *and addresses her with folded palms.* O Vasavadatta, my darling, my dearest, forgive me—

VASAVADATTA. "My darling, my dearest—" To *me*! No, my husband—that's for Sagarika.

JESTER, *aside*. What now? *Aloud*. Oh, but you are noble, Your Majesty. You have a forgiving heart. Forgive him, Your Majesty, I beg you.

VASAVADATTA. I forgive *him*? He should forgive *me* for butting in on his mooning and spooning. I've spoiled the fun, haven't I?

KING. I am guilty. I know it, Vasavadatta. But I beg you, dearest, please forgive me. . .if there is a bit of pity and love in your heart. . . .*He falls at her feet.*

VASAVADATTA. No, my husband—don't. *She stops him.* How can I be angry when you are sorry? You are my husband. It is all right. . . . I must go now.

VASAVADATTA *and* KANCHANAMALA *depart.*

JESTER. Rise, Your Majesty. She's gone—no point in crying now.

KING, *looking up at him.* Gone? And she didn't forgive me after all.

JESTER. Of course she did—we're alive, aren't we?

KING. Shut up. No more of your damned jokes. *You* started the whole business. *You* made me do what I thought I'd never do in my life. The shame of it! . . . What must she think of me?

JESTER. It's not so much you, sire—consider Sagarika. What's going to happen to her?

KING. Dearest Sagarika!

SAGARIKA *enters, dressed as the queen, but is unnoticed by the* KING *and the* JESTER.

SAGARIKA, *speaking to herself anxiously.* No one saw me slip past the picture gallery. But where shall I go now? *She broods distractedly.*

JESTER. Oh, come off it! It's all over. What's the next step?

KING. There's only one—she must forgive us. Let us go to the queen. Maybe she will listen to me now.

*The* KING *and the* JESTER *take a few steps toward the exit from the garden.*

SAGARIKA, *still musing to herself.* Oh, I could kill myself: the queen knows all about me now. Hanging is all that's left. Death is better than disgrace. Oh, good asoka tree, I am coming. . . . *She walks toward the tree.*

JESTER, *in an attitude of listening.* Footsteps! I think the queen's coming back, sire. In a good mood—I hope!

KING. I *knew* she'd forgive me. She is noble by nature. Go see if she's coming.

*The* JESTER *peers through the stems of the creeper.*

SAGARIKA, *approaching the asoka tree.* A noose of the *madhavi* creeper —*She takes a tendril from the vine.*—and the hanging from the asoka. Oh, homeless, helpless, miserable. . .to die so young. . .*She places the noose around her neck.*

JESTER. Help! Help! The queen's hanging herself! Help, sire! Help!

*The* KING *runs to* SAGARIKA *and removes the noose from her neck.*

KING. Such foolishness! Are you insane? Oh, my darling, what made you do it?

SAGARIKA. Let me go, sire, let me go. Sagarika must die—she is a slave. Let me go! *She struggles to replace the noose around her neck.*

KING. Sagarika! *He is immediately overjoyed.* Don't be silly! Not a noose around your neck, lovely Sagarika, but a noose around my neck—a noose of your arms, lovely Sagarika! Not a noose of death, lovely Sagarika, but a noose of life! *He places her arms around his neck.* Ah! What joy! A shower with no clouds! Joy with no pain!

JESTER. That is to say, if Queen Vasavadatta doesn't appear. Then there'll be storm clouds!

VASAVADATTA *and* KANCHANAMALA *enter, but are screened from the others by the creeper.*

VASAVADATTA. It was cruel of me, Kanchanamala. Think of it—he fell at my feet and begged pardon, and I walked away.

KANCHANAMALA. If the king does wrong, should the queen do so too?

VASAVADATTA *and* KANCHANAMALA *circle the stage.*

KING. How long must you treat me like this, O heartless, O callous?

KANCHANAMALA, *overhearing.* It's the king—coming to entreat you again.

VASAVADATTA, *joyfully.* I'll surprise him from the back. . . .

JESTER. Good Sagarika, be kind to him.

VASAVADATTA, *angrily.* Sagarika! She here! *She peers through the creeper.*

SAGARIKA. But you love the queen, sire. Your words are mere courtesy.

KING. Love? . . . How little you know, dearest girl. She flamed in anger, I trembled. She was silent, I begged forgiveness. Her eyebrows shot up, I fell at her feet. You call that love?—old-world routine, royal affections. . . . I love *you*; my body thrills when you come near me, my dearest. . . .

VASAVADATTA, *surprising them and speaking irately*. Brilliant! Well done! A very pretty love scene!

KING, *taken aback*. Vasavadatta!—but you've misunderstood everything: I thought she was you. I didn't mean what I said. That is—*He falls at her feet*. I mean—

VASAVADATTA. You don't know what you mean! "Old-world routine, royal affections." Isn't that it? You may rise.

KING, *to himself*. She overheard that too! Well, the game's up. . . . *He stands shamefacedly, looking at the ground.*

JESTER. You've got it all wrong, my queen. I thought *she* was the queen —from the dress she's wearing—and I thought the queen was trying to hang herself, so of course I called the king to come and help me save her. If you don't believe it, look at this. *He shows her the noose.*

VASAVADATTA, *angrily*. Oh, I believe you all right. And we'll put the noose to good purpose too. Put it around the fool's neck, Kanchanamala, and take him to the palace. The foolish girl too. I'll see to them later.

KANCHANAMALA, *doing as she is told*. Lead on, Vasantaka. This way, Sagarika.

SAGARIKA, *to herself*. Oh, the shame, the shame!

JESTER, *looking sadly at the* KING. I *tried,* sire.

VASAVADATTA *leaves;* KANCHANAMALA, SAGARIKA, *and the* JESTER *follow.*

KING, *despondently*. The queen, her smile frozen into anger. And Sagarika, poor Sagarika, at the queen's mercy. And good Vasantaka, the noose around his neck. . .Whatever I think of is painful. What's the use of staying here? I must go to the queen. . .to soothe her displeasure. . . .

*He departs.*

C U R T A I N

# ACT IV

### THE MAGIC SHOW

SUSAMGATA *enters in front of the curtain, carrying a pearl necklace, sighing and speaking sorrowfully to herself. While she is speaking the* JESTER *enters, also speaking to himself, but joyfully and laughingly.*

SUSAMGATA. Poor Sagarika, so gentle, so noble, where are you now? *She sobs.* Oh, Fate, creating beauty, then shattering it. . .pitiless Fate. This pearl necklace—"Give it to some Brahmin," she said; it was her last wish. . . . But now where's a Brahmin? *She sees the* JESTER. The good Vasantaka!

JESTER. Oho! Ho-ho! The king has soothed the queen, the queen has soothed my stomach. . .cakes after prison, sweets after the noose, cooked all by herself! This silk robe too, ho-ho! And new gold earrings! . . . Where's the king?

SUSAMGATA, *approaching and speaking tearfully.* Noble Vasantaka!

JESTER. Susamgata—crying? Tsk-tsk. Why? . . . Is anything wrong— something to do with Sagarika?

SUSAMGATA. Sir, she's gone. . .poor girl. The queen packed her off to Ujjain at midnight.

JESTER, *looking concerned.* Cruel, most cruel.

SUSAMGATA. She wept and wept, and despaired of her life; and then she gave me this necklace and said, "Give it to noble Vasantaka." . . .Sir, I give it to you.

JESTER, *sadly.* No. . .how can I?

SUSAMGATA. Take it, sir. *She implores him with folded hands.*

JESTER. All right. . .perhaps it will console the king. *He looks at it.* But where did she get an expensive trinket like this?

SUSAMGATA. That's exactly what I asked her, sir.

JESTER. And what did she say?

SUSAMGATA. She looked up, sighed deeply, and began to weep, saying only, "You wouldn't understand."

JESTER. But this betrays royal rank, Susamgata, a necklace like this. Where is his Majesty?

SUSAMGATA. In the Crystal Room, sir. I saw him go there when he left the queen's rooms.

*They both depart. The curtain is raised, revealing the* KING *seated on the royal dais.*

KING. It wasn't my words and promises that did the trick, nor my confusion, my begging and pleading with the maids. It was her weeping that did it! Nothing like tears to dissolve anger: excellent washers of excess passion. *He sighs.* And now my heart begins to long again for Sagarika, lotus-soft Sagarika—gone as soon as she came to light my life. *He muses.* And Vasantaka snatched away too—no shoulder left for me to weep on.

*The* JESTER *enters, jubilantly.* Sire, it's me!

KING. Ah, Vasantaka! Come near.

JESTER, *embracing the* KING. The queen's let me off.

KING. I can see by your robe you've won her favor. Sit down. What news of our dearest Sagarika? *He notices that the* JESTER *looks worried.* Come, what's the news?

JESTER. Sire, I cannot—

KING. What is it? Is she ill? Angry? Is she—*He breaks off in horror.*

JESTER. No, no; not that.

KING. I'm prepared for the worst. Tell me.

JESTER. I'm told the queen's packed her off to Ujjain.

KING. Who told you? The queen is heartless.

JESTER. Susamgata, sire. And she gave me this—a pearl necklace, Sagarika's.

KING. Bring it here. *He looks at it and places it on his heart.* No more her loving hands. . .only a string of cold pearls. *He gives it back to the* JESTER. Take it. It hurts. Darling Sagarika!

JESTER. Sssh! Sire, the queen's spies are everywhere.

VASUNDHARA, *entering and bowing.* My homage, sire. Rumanvat's son Vijayavarman is at the gate with good news.

KING. Send him in.

VASUNDHARA *leaves and returns with* VIJAYAVARMAN.

VIJAYAVARMAN, *bowing.* My homage, sire. Rumanvat is victorious, sire.

KING, *joyfully.* Kosala is conquered?

VIJAYAVARMAN. Yes, sire.

KING. Well done, Rumanvat! A great victory! Tell me the details.

VIJAYAVARMAN. My father, on your orders, marched from here with a striking force of elephants, cavalry, and foot soldiers, and within a few days had brought siege against the fort of Vindhya. But the king of Kosala, incensed, brought forth a terrible army, consisting chiefly of elephants. With our arrows showering him, he charged us—fire flashed, blood flowed, helmets were dashed gorily on the ground! Then the king of Kosala attacked Rumanvat, my father; and my father slew him as he sat on his elephant, pierced by a hundred arrows.

KING. A brave king, Kosala. Even his enemies speak of his courage.

VIJAYAVARMAN. My father Rumanvat is now at the gates, leading the wounded elephants.

KING, *to* VASUNDHARA. Tell Yaugandharayana to look after him well, as befits a hero.

VASUNDHARA *leaves;* KANCHANAMALA *enters.*

KANCHANAMALA, *to* VASUNDHARA *in passing.* The queen wants a magician of hers to see His Majesty. *She sees the* KING. Sire, the queen says, "Here is an excellent magician named Sambarasiddhi, whom Your Majesty would like to meet."

KING. I always love magic. . .send him in.

KANCHANAMALA *leaves and re-enters with the magician, who is carrying a plume of peacock feathers.*

KANCHANAMALA. His Majesty.

SAMBARASIDDHI. May the king prosper! *He whirls his peacock feathers and continues in verse.*

> Bow to the feet of Indra, the Magician!
> Bow to Sambara!
> Sire, a word from you and the moon
> Flashes on earth,
> Hills float in the air,
> There is fire in water, darkness at noon.
> A word from you, sire,
> Brings your heart's desire.

JESTER. You talk big, my friend.

KING. Wait. Ask the queen to come here, Kanchanamala. We shall see the magic together. And clear the room of people.

KANCHANAMALA *leaves and re-enters with* VASAVADATTA.

VASAVADATTA. The magician is here? My husband––

KING. Good Vasavadatta, he's made himself hoarse promising the weirdest things. Do sit here, near me. *She sits down.* Proceed with the show, my friend.

SAMBARASIDDHI, *dancing and flourishing the feathers.* The gods, Hari and Hara and Brahman and Indra and the nymphs dancing—all behold!

KING, *stepping down from his seat.* Look! Look, Vasavadatta—

SAMBARASIDDHI. Brahma on his lotus,
> In the sky moon-touched Shankara,
> Indra on the holy elephant Airavata,
> The nymphs dancing—
> Jingle of anklets on tripping feet!

JESTER. Bah! Who wants gods and nymphs? Why, you damned son of a slave, can't you bring Sagarika here?

VASUNDHARA, *entering and bowing.* Sire, Yaughandharayana sends the minister of the king of Simhala and his chamberlain Babhravya to see you. It is urgent, he says, and the time is auspicious. He will follow soon.

VASAVADATTA. I think you should see them, my husband. They come from my uncle.

KING, *to* SAMBARASIDDHI. That's all for now. You may go.

SAMBARASIDDHI. But, sire, my best trick—

KING. All in good time, my friend, all in good time. I'll send for you later.

VASAVADATTA. Give him something, Kanchanamala.

KANCHANAMALA *and* SAMBARASIDDHI *depart.*

KING. Vasantaka, you'll have to go and welcome the minister Vasubhuti.

*The* JESTER *and* VASUNDHARA *leave, and the* JESTER *returns with* VA-SUBHUTI *and* BABHRAVYA.

JESTER. This way, sir. This way, sir.

VASUBHUTI, *aside, seeing the pearl necklace worn by the* JESTER. Isn't that the necklace His Majesty gave her.

BABHRAVYA, *aside.* It's the same. Shall I ask?

VASUBHUTI, *aside.* No, not now. There might be two here like that: this place has the look of luxury, hasn't it?

JESTER. His Majesty, King Udayana.

VASUBHUTI. My greetings, sire.

KING, *rising.* I welcome you, sir. A seat, Vasantaka.

*The* JESTER *brings a chair and* VASUBHUTI *sits down.*

BABHRAVYA. My homage, sire.

KING. You are most welcome, good Babhravya. Please sit down.

BABHRAVYA *does so.*

VASAVADATTA. I salute you, sir, and you, sir, and bid you welcome to my husband's palace.

KING. How is the king of Simhala, good Vasubhuti?

VASUBHUTI, *sadly*. Oh, sire, well, sire.

VASAVADATTA, *to herself*. I hope nothing's wrong.

KING. Speak up, Vasubhuti. What is it?

BABHRAVYA, *aside*. Tell him the truth. Now is the time.

VASUBHUTI, *sadly*. Sire, it's a long story. The princess Ratnavali knew that you wanted to marry her. So her father betrothed her to you when he heard that Queen Vasavadatta had perished in the fire, and—

KING, *aside to* VASAVADATTA. Is he mad? What's he saying?

VASAVADATTA, *aside; giggling*. Is he mad? . . . Oh, it's so funny.

JESTER. Well, go on.

VASUBHUTI. And Princess Ratnavali was drowned when our ship was wrecked. We were escorting her to you, Your Majesty. *He bows his head in shame.* It's all our fault.

VASAVADATTA, *in tears*. Sweet Ratnavali! Sweet cousin! Is she dead?

*Noise and shouting are heard offstage.*

VOICES. Fire! Fire in the palace! Flames in the golden turrets! Help! The garden is burning! The palace is burning! Help!

KING, *rising hastily from his seat*. The palace on fire? Vasavadatta!

VASAVADATTA. Sagarika's in there!—I kept her in chains. . . . Oh, save her!

KING. Sagarika? Where, which room?

JESTER, *catching hold of the* KING's *robe*. Sire, do not go.

KING, *pulling himself free*. Not go? With Sagarika in there? Let me go—
*He rushes out; the others follow cautiously.*

*Inner curtain is drawn, revealing* SAGARIKA *in chains and smothered in smoke.*

SAGARIKA. Oh, burn me, kill me, kind fire! Let me die in your arms!

KING. Sagarika! *He runs to her.* Here I am!

SAGARIKA. Help! Please. . .

KING. Wait, I'm here. . .it's all right. Your dress is burning! And this chain! Put your arms around my neck. *He tries to lift her.* That's strange. What's this? . . . No fire? Where's the fire? And the smoke? VASAVADATTA *enters.* Is that you, Vasavadatta? VASUBHUTI *enters.* Is that you, Vasubhuti? BABHRAVYA *enters.* It's you, Babhravya! *The* JESTER *enters.* My friend Vasantaka! Am I dreaming? What has happened? . . . There was a fire—

JESTER. No fire, Your Majesty. Just the last trick of the magician.

KING. And here, good Vasavadatta, is Sagarika.

VASAVADATTA. I know.

VASUBHUTI, *on first seeing* SAGARIKA, *speaking aside to* BABHRAVYA. The princess?

BABHRAVYA, *aside.* Princess Ratnavali!

VASUBHUTI. Sire, who is this lady?

*The* KING *looks at* VASAVADATTA.

VASAVADATTA. Yaugandharayana left her in my care. She is Sagarika, child of the sea.

KING, *to himself.* Yaugandharayana told me nothing.

VASUBHUTI, *aside.* The same necklace. . .Sagarika, child of the sea. . . *Aloud.* Princess Ratnavali!

SAGARIKA, *in tears.* Vasubhuti! Good Vasubhuti!

VASUBHUTI, *falling at her feet.* I am innocent, my princess. Forgive me.

SAGARIKA. Oh, Father, where are you? Mother—*She sobs uncontrollably.*

VASAVADATTA, *astonished.* Is she. . .is she my cousin—Ratnavali?

BABHRAVYA. Yes, Your Majesty.

VASAVADATTA, *embracing* SAGARIKA. Oh, Ratnavali—I didn't know.

KING. The daughter of the noble king of Simhala?

JESTER, *removing the necklace.* I knew this was worth something! *He places it around* SAGARIKA's *neck.*

VASAVADATTA. Don't cry, Ratnavali. Everything is over now.

RATNAVALI, *shamefully and confusedly.* But what I did to you—after what I did—

VASAVADATTA. Don't you worry now, Ratnavali. *She opens her arms and the two embrace again.* VASAVADATTA *then turns toward the* KING. Oh, my husband, I've behaved so horribly. . . . But Yaugandharayana never told me anything. . . . I didn't know. . . .

YAUGANDHARAYANA *enters in time to overhear the last of* VASAVADATTA's *excuses.*

YAUGANDHARAYANA. Let me explain, sire. When Queen Vasavadatta agreed to your taking a second wife, a new responsibility fell on me. Yet I was obliged to serve you, and I did what I thought was best in the circumstances. If I was wrong, sire, I implore you to pardon me.

KING. What do you think you did wrong, Yaugandharayana?

YAUGANDHARAYANA. Sire, please take your seat, and I'll explain. *Everyone sits down.* A great sage, whose words are truth itself, said of Princess Ratnavali when she was a child, "Whoever marries her will rule the world." But her father, the king of Simhala, would not agree that you should marry her, for he thought that Queen Vasavadatta—I beg your pardon, Your Majesty—would object. . . . But I kept trying; I spread the rumor that the good Queen Vasavadatta—I beg your pardon, Your Majesty—had perished in the fire at Lavanaka. Then Babhravya took the message to the king of Simhala, and—

KING. The rest we know. But why did you entrust Sagarika—I mean Ratnavali—to my wife's care?

JESTER. That's easy. So you'd see her and fall in love with her.

KING. Which I did. Yaugandharayana?

YAUGANDHARAYANA. Sire, I plead guilty.

KING. And the magician was your man too, eh? And the fire?

YAUGANDHARAYANA. Guilty again, sire. It was the only way. *He laughs.* Queen Vasavadatta, it's all in your hands now.

VASAVADATTA, *smiling.* What you mean, Yaugandharayana, is—why not give her to him? Isn't that it? Come, why don't you say so?

JESTER. He doesn't have to.

VASAVADATTA, *reaching out her hand.* Come, Ratnavali, come to me. You are my sister now, not cousin. *She decorates* RATNAVALI *with her jewels, and leads her by the hand before the* KING. My husband, here is Ratnavali. She is yours. And she is alone: console her in her loneliness. And you, Ratnavali, make a good queen!

YAUGANDHARAYANA. Sire, it is over. Sagarika, child of the sea, is with us, the queen is happy, the Kosalas are conquered, His Majesty is on the throne, and I—I am the proudest of ministers.

CURTAIN

# NOTES

———

# OTHER SANSKRIT PLAYS:
## A Short Reading List

———

# A PRONOUNCING GUIDE

# Notes

*Agastya,* the legendary sage (supposed to have been born in a jar, hence also called Kumbhayoni, "jar-born") who pioneered the Aryanization of southern India. To his pupil Rama he presented the invincible bow and inexhaustible quiver of Vishnu. (*The Later Story of Rama*)

*Airavata,* the holy elephant, vehicle of Indra, created by Brahma's seven chants. (*Ratnavali*)

*Arundhati,* wife of the great sage Vashishtha; in Hindu tradition she, along with Sita, represents the ideal wife. (*The Later Story of Rama*)

*"As Sita died, as Draupadi died,"* a confusion of legendary stories, indicating Sansthanaka's lack of cultivated taste. Sita is the heroine of the *Ramayana,* and does not, strictly speaking, "die." Draupadi, wife of the Pandava brothers in the *Mahabharata,* is the first to collapse on the way when, after successfully ruling their regained kingdom, they decide to trek to the Himalayas to offer their life's work to Brahma. (*The Toy Cart*)

*Avanti,* Ujjain, the capital of Malva, kingdom of Pradyota, Vasavadatta's father; also the surrounding territory. (*The Dream of Vasavadatta*)

*Bhagirath,* a descendant of Sagara, he brought the Ganga from heaven to the earth after a thousand-year penance, in order to purify the memory of his ancestors who were burned down by the wrath of the sage Kapila, founder of the Samkhya system of philosophy; hence the Ganges is also known as the Bhagirathi. (*The Later Story of Rama*)

*Bharata,* (1) a son of Dasharatha by Kaikeyi; (2) the author of the *Natyashastra;* (3) a son of Dushyanta and Shakuntala; (4) the eldest son of Rishabhadeva; hence India is called Bharatavarsha, "land of Bharata."

*Brahma,* the creative aspect of the Hindu trinity, born from a lotus out of the navel of Vishnu reclining on the waters; represented with four faces, standing for the four quarters, and the four parts of the mystic syllable *Om* (also, in flat representation, represented as the *Trimurti*).

*Ceremony of the would-be mother,* special clothes and jewelry and food are offered to the would-be mother, and a puja is performed before her by friends and relatives who are already mothers. This is different from the "puerperal longings" which the husband is supposed to satisfy. (*Shakuntala* and *The Later Story of Rama*)

*Chakravakas,* red geese or sheldrakes. These birds were supposed, in legend, to be ideally mated in the day but, as a result of a curse, during the night they bewailed each other's absence from the opposite banks of a river. (*Shakuntala* and *The Dream of Vasavadatta*)

*Chanakya,* the author of *Chanakya-niti* (*Laws of Chanakya*) and *Arthashastra* (*The Science of Success*). As minister of Chandragupta Maurya, his chief policy was to subdue the Nandas and annex their kingdom. Also known as Vishnugupta or Kautilya. (*The Signet Ring of Rakshasa*)

*Chandalas,* outcasts, specifically children of a Sudra father and a Brahmin mother. (*The Signet Ring of Rakshasa*)

*Dandaka,* a king of the solar dynasty who raped the daughter of his guru and was punished by having his kingdom turned into an impenetrable forest, Dandakaranya (*aranya* is Sanskrit for "forest"). (*The Later Story of Rama*)

*Dasharatha,* son of King Aja of the solar dynasty; father of Rama. His chief queens were Kaushalya, Sumitra, and Kaikeyi; after he had performed a special sacrifice under the direction of the sage Rishyasringa, Rama, Lakshmana and Shatrughna, and Bharata were born respectively to the three queens; his daughter was Shanta. He sent Rama to fourteen years' exile in order to honor a promise he had made to Kaikeyi, but died soon after of a broken heart. (*The Later Story of Rama*)

*Dharma,* an ethical code, way of life, social conscience, "the natural condition of things or beings, the law of their existence, truth, religious truth." From this is derived *sva-dharma,* taken to mean recognition of one's right to perform the duties dictated by one's nature and conscience.

*Draupadi,* daughter of King Drupada and wife of the five Pandava brothers; Krishna treated her as his sister and came to her help whenever she needed assistance. (*The Toy Cart*)

*Durvasas,* son of Atri, one of the seven great sages, and Anasuya. Proverbially hot-tempered, he cursed Shakuntala because she neglected to serve him. (*Shakuntala*)

*Dushyanta,* a king of the lunar dynasty. (*Shakuntala*)

*Five deadly sins,* killing a Brahmin, getting drunk, stealing, committing adultery with a guru's wife, and associating with any person guilty of any of these crimes. (*The Toy Cart*)

*"Five-Tufted Boy,"* refers to the sign of pupilhood, especially in one belonging to the Brahmin caste. (*The Later Story of Rama*)

*Gandharva,* literally, a celestial musician; but it also signifies marriage by exchange of garlands, a love union, recognized by Manu in his Shastras as one of the eight acceptable types of marriage. (*Shakuntala*)

*Ganga,* the name of India's most sacred river and its presiding deity (also called *Bhagirathi*); she was the first wife of Shantanu and came to the earth as the result of a curse, giving birth to eight sons, of whom Bhishma was the youngest.

*Goddess of the Sakya hills,* presumably Devi, Hinduism's mother goddess, whose other forms are Parvati, Uma, Durga, and Kali. She lives in the Himalayas and descends periodically to fertilize the plains. The Sakya hills are north of Magadha, in the foothills of the Himalayas in central India. (*The Toy Cart*)

*Hara,* Shiva, destroying aspect of the Hindu trinity.

*Hari,* Vishnu, preserving aspect of the Hindu trinity.

*Hastinapur,* the ancient site of Delhi, about thirty miles east of the modern Delhi in northern India, situated on the Ganges. (*The Later Story of Rama*)

*Horse sacrifice,* the Ashvamedha; a ritual performed by the absolute ruler of Bharata, to denote his unchallenged sovereignty over the land (see also the Preface to *The Later Story of Rama*)

*Ikshvaku,* the first king of the solar dynasty. (*The Later Story of Rama*)

*Indra,* the chief god of the Hindu pantheon of lower deities. He molested

Ahalya and was cursed by her husband, the sage Gautama; the thousands of sores that festered on his body as a result later became so many eyes. He is also, as the god of rain, the dispenser of blessings.

*Janaka,* king of Mithila, foster father of Sita, called "best among Brahmins" because of his extraordinary performances of charity and penance. (*The Later Story of Rama*)

*Jatayu,* eagle-son of Aruna, the charioteer of the sun god. In Hindu myth he is the king of birds and dies trying to save Sita from the clutches of Ravana. (*The Later Story of Rama*)

*Kaikeyi,* daughter of Kekaya and one of the three chief queens of Dasharatha. (*The Later Story of Rama*)

*Kama,* the god of love; his wife is Rati and his friend the season *vasanta* (spring). He was shriveled into cinders by the eye of Shiva, who was practicing penance and disliked Kama's stirring passion in him for his wife Uma, and reborn as Pradyumna.

*Kamboja,* the territory to the east of Kashmir and beyond the Himalayas.

*Kanva,* a sage, foster father of Shakuntala. (*Shakuntala*)

*Kashyapa,* a sage who, by marrying the thirteen daughters of Daksha, became the progenitor of the inferior deities (*devas*), demons, human beings, beasts, and reptiles.

*Kayastha,* member of the Kshatriya, the second, warrior and administrator caste. (*The Signet Ring of Rakshasa*)

*Khara,* a demon, half brother of Ravana, who was killed by Rama. (*The Later Story of Rama*)

*Koel,* or *kokila,* a cuckoo. In Sanskrit, it is called *parabhrita,* "brought up by another," because the female koel leaves her eggs in the nest of a crow to be hatched. The koel's song expresses the sad sweetness of frustrated or alienated love. (*The Toy Cart*)

*Kosala,* the territory along the banks of the river Sarayu which had two capitals, Kushavati (for south Kosala) and Sravasti (for north Kosala).

*Krishna,* the eighth incarnation of Vishnu. Born to Vasudeva and Devaki, he was brought up by Nanda and Yashoda, and killed his maternal uncle, the wicked Kamsa. He was a friend of the Pandavas during their exile, charioteer of Arjuna, and hero of the *Gita*.

*Kshatriya*, see *Kayastha*. (*Shakuntala*)

*Kuru*, a legendary monarch, ancestor of the Kauravas and Pandavas.

*Kusha grass*, a tapering soft grass (*eragrostis cynosuroides*) considered sacred and used in all Hindu religious rituals. (*Shakuntala* and *The Dream of Vasavadatta*)

*Lotus*, a symbolic flower in Indian religion and literature. Brahma is born out of the lotus in the navel of Vishnu; the Buddha is always depicted as sitting on a lotus; the Tibetan prayer chant is *Om mani padme hum*, "I salute the jewel in the lotus." Growing in stagnant village ponds, it symbolizes emergence into selfhood from the temptations of sensual life; the leaves, unaffected by water, symbolize the atman uncontaminated by the interplay of the gunas; and its daytime opening and nighttime closing within itself suggest the eternal day and night of Brahma in the framework of Hindu metaphysical belief.

*Madana*, Kama, or Kamadeva, god of love. (*Ratnavali*)

*Magadha*, the territory around southern Bihar, in central India. In Dasharatha's time, it was ruled by Shurasena (c. 4000 B.C.); during the time of the Pandavas, by Jarasandha; during Chandragupta's reign (fourth century B.C.), its annexation became part of the minister Chanakya's grand political design. (*The Signet Ring of Rakshasa*)

*Mahendra*, from Sanskrit, *maha*, great, and *Indra*, it is another name for Indra.

*Malaya*, the southern portion of the Western Ghats, a mountain range forming the eastern boundary of Travancore in southern India.

*Marichi*, son of Sunda and Tadaka, he was ordered by Ravana to assume the form of a golden deer to lure away Rama and enable Ravana to abduct Sita.

*Matali*, the charioteer of Indra.

*Maya,* in Vedantic philosophy, "the cosmic illusion on account of which the One appears as many, the Absolute as the relative." It may also be defined as the ignorance that prevents man's realization of his identity with Brahman, leading to increasing involvement in the bewildering multiplicity of mirrors created by the senses. On the esthetic plane, maya governs the realm of rasa, the principle of all forms of artistic relish. Zimmer associates maya with shakti, the creating and binding force in the phenomenal world.

*Menaka,* the heavenly nymph who seduced the sage Vishvamitra; her daughter is Shakuntala. She was sent by the gods to distract Vishvamitra from his yoga, because excessive practice of moral discipline gave him power over the deities. Since he was a Kshatriya, Dushyanta (also a Kshatriya) finds it perfectly proper to marry Shakuntala. (*Shakuntala*)

*Mithila,* the capital of Videha, the kingdom of Dasharatha.

*Nanda,* king of Magadha. Its capital was Pataliputra, the modern Patna. (*The Signet Ring of Rakshasa*)

*Nirvana,* literally, "a snuffing out"; in Buddhism, the extinction of all forms of desire, achieved through the practice of the eightfold path which cures the cause of *dukkha,* "sorrow." (*The Toy Cart*)

*"Offering water to ancestors,"* the eldest son offers water and balls of rice to his ancestors at prescribed intervals to preserve their state of blessedness in the next birth. (*Shakuntala*)

*Prakrit,* from *prakriti,* "primordial nature"; hence, "not cultivated, vulgar", hence, all vernaculars or dialects which derive from the Sanskrit (meaning "cultivated to perfection"). (*The Signet Ring of Rakshasa*)

*Puru,* founder of the lunar dynasty. (*Shakuntala*)

*Poison girls,* girls employed as spies by Chanakya, with specific instructions to poison suspected enemies of the king. (*The Signet Ring of Rakshasa*)

*"Radha's son, Pandu's son,"* a muddle of legends again, to indicate Sansthanaka's lack of good breeding. Pandu, father of the Pandavas, is in the *Mahabharata,* while Radha is the gopi (cowherdess) whose love for

Krishna symbolizes, *Song of Solomon* style, the atman's search for union with Brahman. (*The Toy Cart*)

*Raghu,* founder of the solar race, the dynasty of Rama, who is therefore called a Raghava.

*"Rama kissed Draupadi,"* another muddling of mythology, reflecting Sansthanaka's neglected education. Rama, the hero of the *Ramayana,* has nothing to do with Draupadi, the common wife of the five Pandava brothers in the earlier epic, the *Mahabharata.* (*The Toy Cart*)

*Rasa,* a mythical river in the sky; also a theory of dramatic purpose and effect as propounded by Bharata; more broadly, the central principle in Hindu esthetics. In the Aitareya Upanishad occurs the sentence: *Raso vai sah,* "The well-carved is the well-loved," in the sense that "Perfection alone is delectable." The ineffable nature of rasa is suggested in its intimate association with the dance of the divinely inspired gopis who, in honor of Krishna with whom they desire union, perform the *rasa-lila* to the accompaniment of his fluting in the moonlight.

*Ravana,* the demon king of Lanka; he had ten heads and twenty arms, and the power to assume any form he wished. (*The Later Story of Rama*)

*"Released from further lives,"* the attainment of moksha, or release from the cycle of rebirth, through the performance of the pure act (as distinct from the good, evil, or absurd act) conceived in terms of a harmony between social duty and private conscience, is a basic tenet of Hindu belief. (*Shakuntala*)

*Ritual birth-knot,* one of the thirteen samskaras (religious observances) which a Hindu is expected to perform in the course of his life. (*The Later Story of Rama*)

*"Round this fire,"* fire is the basic Aryan religious symbol, water the Dravidian; Hinduism harmonizes both within its world-view. Birth, marriage, departure, death—all require a form of fire ritual. (*Shakuntala*)

*Sacred thread of a Brahmin,* the *upavita,* worn by upper-caste Hindus, which is a cotton thread of three strands, given to the boy by his guru during the initiation ceremony, which takes place when he is between eight and twelve years old. The sacred thread makes a boy *dvija* (the twice-born), the first birth being a purely physical one, the second symbolic of his entry into the complex Hindu process of moksha, or salvation in the sense of release from rebirth. (*The Toy Cart*)

*Shakuntala,* daughter of Vishvamitra and Menaka. Abandoned on the banks of the Malini when Menaka returned to heaven, she was looked after by *shakuntas* (birds)—hence the name—until the sage Kanva found and adopted her.

*Shankara,* another name for Shiva. (*Ratnavali*)

*Shanta,* daughter of Dasharatha; wife of Rishyasringa, the sage who successfully performed the ritual of penance for the sonless Dasharatha. (*The Later Story of Rama*)

*Simhala,* Lanka, or Ceylon, the island kingdom of Ravana. (*Ratnavali*)

*Soma,* the milkweed plant; also the sacred wine used in Vedic times during the performance of rituals; sometimes personified as the god of the moon. (*Shakuntala*)

*"Son of Kunti,"* presumably Arjuna is meant (Bhima and Yudhishthira are her other two sons). Kunti was the wife of Pandu, the regent king because his elder brother Dhritarashtra was blind; Pandu's second wife Madri had two sons, Nakula and Sahadeva. (*The Toy Cart*)

*Tadaka,* a female demon killed by Rama.

*"Thief scatters special seeds,"* since expert thieving is one of the arts of civilization, there are shastras (science, prescribed rules, scriptures) available in Hinduism explicitly designed to promote efficiency in the practice of stealing. (*The Toy Cart*)

*Three worlds,* in Vedic conception *triloka,* or the universe consisting of the earth, the middle space or atmosphere, and the ether or sky. It also signifies the world of men, the world of semidivine creatures, and the world of the gods; also heaven, earth, and Patala (the world of the demons). The "three-forked river flowing into heaven" mentioned in *Shakuntala* refers to the descent of the Ganga from heaven into the matted locks of the supreme yogi, Shiva, who received it on the earth.

*Trishanku,* a king of Ayodhya (the modern Oudh) of the solar dynasty who asked Vashishtha to perform a sacrifice that would enable him to ascend to heaven with his mortal body. Vashishtha refused and condemned him as a chandala. The sage Vishvamitra, however, agreed, in spite of the repeated objections of the gods and Brahmins. Indra hurled Trishanku down through space, but Vishvamitra, with his extreme penance, stopped the fall; as a result Trishanku hangs in midspace, one of the stars in the sky. (*Shakuntala*)

*Urmila,* wife of Lakshmana.

*Urvashi,* the celestial nymph who came to the earth as the result of a curse, married Pururavas, and had a son, Ayus.

*Vali,* brother of Sugriva and monkey ruler of Kishkindha. So powerful he even defeated Ravana, he was killed by Rama at Sugriva's request.

*Valmiki,* legendary author of the *Ramayana.* Born a Brahmin, he lived by stealing until Narada, the sage of the gods, set him right. It is said that he burst into song when he saw a hunter's arrow shoot down a mating bird; from *soka,* "grief", came *sloka,* "poetry."

*Vashishtha,* the family priest of the Ikshvakus, the solar dynasty. The holy cow Kamadhenu was his property and because Vishvamitra tried to take the cow away from him by force, the two never got on well together.

*Vedanta,* literally, "consummation (*anta*) of the Vedas"; the nondualistic philosophy of Shankaracharya, the eighth-century Aquinas of Hinduism. See *Maya.*

*Vedas,* the earliest Hindu scriptures, psalmlike in structure and spirit. There are four collections of these songs: Rig-Veda, Yajur-Veda, Sama-Veda, and Atharva-Veda; sometimes the Brahmanas and Upanishads are also included.

*Vibhishana,* Ravana's brother. When Ravana refused to restore Sita to Rama at his request, he joined forces with Rama who appointed him king of Lanka after Ravana's death.

*Videha,* territory identified as that around the south of Nepal, in central India.

*Vishnu,* preserving aspect of the Hindu trinity; he has ten chief incarnations, but whenever the balance of the natural moral order is upset, he "bodies himself forth" in order to restore stability by destroying the excess of evil. He is said to have been born out of the forehead of Brahma, as Brahma is born out of the lotus in his navel.

*Vishvamitra,* a great sage; son of Gadhi of the lunar dynasty. His name means literally, "friend of the world." Vishvamitra's title is "Brahmarshi" or "Sage of Brahma," because his thousand-year yoga is said to have given him Brahma-like powers. He is also called Kaushika.

OTHER SANSKRIT PLAYS:
A Short Reading List

**KALIDASA**

1. "Malavika and Agnimitra"
   [Translated by Arthur Ryder, University Press, Berkeley, 1915]

2. "Vikrama and Urvashi"
   [Translated by H. H. Wilson in "Select Specimens of the Theatre of the Hindus", Vol. I, 1871]
   [Translated into verse as "The Hero and the Nymph", by Aurobindo Ghosh, Calcutta, 1911]

**BHASA**

3. "Yaugandharayana's Vows"
   [Translated by A. S. P. Ayyar, Madras, 1941]

4. "Pratima Nataka"
   [Edited and translated by R. P. Kangle and F. C. Trivedi, Vasanta Printing Press, Ahmedabad, 1927]

**BHAVABHUTI**

5. "Malati and Madhava"
   [Translated by H. H. Wilson in "Select Specimens of the Theatre of the Hindus", Vol. II, 1871]

   [Translated by M. R. Kale, Gopal Narayan and Co., Bombay, 1928]

**HARSHA**

6. "Nagananda"
   [Translated by R. D. Karmarkar, Vishvanatha & Co., Bombay, 1923]

MAHENDRAVARMAN

7. "Matta Vilasa Prahasana"
   [Translated by L. D. Barnett, "Bulletin of the School of Oriental
   Studies", Vol V, Part IV, pp. 697–717, 1930]

ANTHOLOGIES

8. *Six Sanskrit Plays in English Translation,* edited and with an intro-
   duction by Henry W. Wells (Asia Publishing House, New York,
   1964)
   [Contains the following—"Shakuntala", tr. by A. Hjalmar Edgren.
   "Vikrama and Urvashi", tr. by Sri Aurobindo. "The Toy Cart",
   tr. by Revilo P. Oliver. "Nagananda", tr. by Palmer Boyd. "The
   Dream of Vasavadatta", tr. by A. C. Woolner and Laksman
   Sarup. "The Later Story of Rama", tr. by N. C. Joshi]

9. *Three Sanskrit Lighter Delights,* translated by C. C. Mehta (Baroda
   M. S. University, 1969)
   [Contains the following one-act plays—"Bhagavad-ajjukiyam" or
   "The Monk and the Courtesan", "Matta-vilasa-prahasana" or
   "The Farce of the Drunk Monk", "Ubhayabhisarika" or "The
   Infatuated Damsel"]

10. A full Bibliography of Sanskrit plays translated into English has
    been prepared by V. Raghavan. See "Indian Literature", Vol. 3
    No. 1, Oct. 1959–Mar. 1960, pp. 141–153 (Sahitya Akademi, Gov-
    ernment of India, New Delhi).

# A PRONOUNCING GUIDE

*The system of pronunciation employed here is based on that of*
Webster's New International Dictionary, *Second Edition*

| | |
|---|---|
| Abhayadatta | ă·bhă·yă·~~th~~ă'·thă |
| Achala | ä'·chă·lă |
| Aditi | ä'·~~thē~~·thē |
| Agastya | ă·găs'·thyă |
| Ahinta | ă·hĭn'·thă |
| Anasuya | änă·sü'·yä |
| Angaravati | ăn·gă·ră·vă·thē |
| Aparajita | ă·pă·rä'·jē·thă |
| Arundhati | ă·rün'·dhă·thē |
| Aruni | ä'·rü·nē |
| Aryaka | ăr'·yă·kă |
| Asana | ä'·să·nă |
| Ashtavakra | ăsh'·tä·văk·ră |
| Atreyi | ä'·thrā·ē |
| Avantika | ăv·ăn'·thĭ·kä |
| Avidhava-Karana | ă·vĭ'·~~th~~hă·vä'-kă'·ră·nă |
| Ayodhya | ă·yō'·~~th~~yä |
| | |
| Babhravya | băbh·räv'·yă |
| Balagupta | bä'·lă·güp·thă |
| Balhikas | bäl·hē·käs |
| Bhadrabhata | bhă~~th~~·ră·bhă·tă |
| Bhagirathi | bhä'·gē·ră·thē |
| Bhagurayana | bhä'·gü·ră·yă·nă |
| Bhandayana | bhän'·dä·yă·nă |
| Bharata | bhä'·ră·thă |
| Bhargava | bhär'·gă·vă |
| Bhasa | bhä'·să |
| Bhasuraka | bhä'·sü·ră·kă |
| Bhavabhuti | vă·bhü'·thē |
| Bhima | bhē'·mă |
| Bibhatsaka | bĭ·bhäth'·să·kă |
| Bilvapatra | bĭl·vă·păth·ră |
| Brahmadatta | brăh'·mă·~~th~~ă·thă |
| Buddha | bü'·~~th~~hă |
| | |
| Chanakya | chä'·nă·kyă |
| Chandanadasa | chăn·dă·nă·dä'·să |
| Chandrabhanu | chăn·~~th~~ră·bhä'·nü |
| Chandragupta | chăn'·~~th~~ră·güp·thă |
| Chandraketu | chăn·dră·kā'·thü |
| Chandralekha | chăn·~~th~~ră·lā'·khä |
| Charudatta | chä'·rü·~~th~~ă·thă |

| | |
|---|---|
| Chitrakuta | chĭth · ră · kü′ · tă |
| Chitravarman | chĭth · ră · văr′ · măn |
| Chutalatika | chü · thă · lă · thĭ · kä′ |
| | |
| Dandaka | dăn′ · dă · kă |
| Dandapasika | dăn · dă · pä′ · sē · kă |
| Danu | dä′ · nü |
| Darduraka | thăr′ · thu · ră · kă |
| Darsaka | thăr′ · shä · kă |
| Daruvarman | thä′ · rü · văr · măn |
| Dhanasena | thhä′ · nă · sä · nă |
| Dingarata | dĭn′ · gă · ră · thă |
| Dirgaraksha | thēr′ · gă · răk · shă |
| Draupadi | throu′ · pă · thē |
| Durjaya | thür′ · jă · yă |
| Durmukha | dür′ · mü · khă |
| Durvasas | thür · vä′ · shăs |
| Dushana | thü · shä′ · nă |
| Dushyanta | thü · shyăn′ · thă |
| | |
| Gandharva | găn · thhăr′ · vă |
| Ganga | găn′ · gä |
| Gautami | gou′ · thă · mē |
| Ghoshavati | ghōsh′ · ä · vă · thē |
| Godavari | gō · thä′ · vă · rē |
| Goha | gō′ · hă |
| | |
| Hanuman | hă · nü · män′ |
| Harsha | hăr′ · shă |
| Hastinapur | hăs · thē · nä′ · pür |
| | |
| Ikshvaku | ĭksh · vä′ · kü |
| Indra | ĭn′ · thrä |
| Indusarman | in′ · thü · săr · măn |
| Ingudi | ĭn · gü′ · thē |
| | |
| Jajali | jä′ · jä′ · lē |
| Janaka | jă′ · nă · kă |
| Januka | jä′ · nü · kă |
| Jatayu | jă · tä′ · yü |
| Jirnavisa | jēr′ · nă · vē · shă |
| Jivasiddhi | jē′ · vă · sĭth · thē |
| Jrimbhika | jrĭm · bhē′ · kä |
| | |
| Kadamba | kă′ · thăm · bă |
| Kalidasa | kä · lĭ · thä′ · să |
| Kalindi | kä · lĭn′ · dē |
| Kalpasika | kăl · pä′ · sē · kă |
| Kama | kä′ · mă |

| | |
|---|---|
| Kamboja | kăm·bō'·jă |
| Kambojas | kăm·bō'·jäs |
| Kampilya | kăm·pĭl'·ă |
| Kanchanamala | kăn·chă·nă·mä'·lä |
| Kaushalya | kou·shăl'·yă |
| Kanva | kăn'·vă |
| Karabhaka | kă·ră·bhă·kă |
| Karnapuraka | kär·nă·pü'·ră·kă |
| Kashyapa | kă'·shyă·pă |
| Kayastha | kä'·yăs·thă |
| Khara | khă·rä' |
| Kirata | kĭ·rä'·tă |
| Kiratas | kĭ·rät'·ăs |
| Kraunchavata | krounch'·ä·vă·thă |
| Krishasva | krĭ·shăs'·vă |
| Kumbhilaka | küm·bhē'·lă·kă |
| Kunti | kün'·thē |
| Kusha | kü'·shă |
| | |
| Lakindi | lă·kĭn·dē' |
| Lakshmana | lăksh'·mă·nă |
| Lava | lă'·vă |
| Lavana | lă'·vă·nă |
| Lavanaka | lă'·vă·nă·kă |
| Lopamudra | lō'·pă·müth·ră |
| | |
| Madanika | mă·thă·nē·kä' |
| Madhavi | mä'·thhă·vē |
| Madhavika | mä'·thhă·vē'·kä |
| Madhukarika | mă·thhü·kä'·rĭ·kä |
| Magadha | mă·gă·thhă |
| Mahasena | mä'·hä'·sä·nä' |
| Maitreya | mă'·thrä·ă |
| Malayaketu | mä·lă·yă·kä'·thü |
| Malyavat | mä'·lyă·văth |
| Mandakini | män'·dă·kē·nē |
| Mandavi | män'·dă·vē |
| Manthara | măn·thă·rä' |
| Marichi | mä'·rē·chē |
| Markandeya | mär·kăn·dä'·yă |
| Matali | mä'·thă·lē |
| Matanga | mă·tăn'·gä |
| Mathura | mä'·thü·ră |
| Maurya | mour'·yă |
| Megha | mā'·ghă |
| Meghanada | mā·ghă·nä'·thă |
| Menaka | mā'·nă·kă |
| Mithila | mĭ·thĭ·lä' |
| Mleccha | mlā'·chchă |

| | |
|---|---|
| Murala | mü · rǎ · lä′ |
| | |
| Nanda | năn′ · t̶h̶ǎ |
| Narada | nä′ · rǎ · t̶h̶ǎ |
| Narmada | nǎr · mǎ · t̶h̶ä′ |
| Navamalika | nǎ · vǎ · mä′ · lē · kä |
| Nipunaka | nĭ′ · pü · nǎ · kǎ |
| Nipunika | nĭ · pü · nĭ · kä′ |
| Nishada | nĭ′ · shǎ · t̶h̶ǎ |
| Nishadas | nĭ · shä′ · t̶h̶ǎs |
| | |
| Padmavati | pǎth · mä′ · vǎ · thē |
| Padminika | pǎt̶h̶ · mē · nē · kä′ |
| Palaka | pä′ · lǎ · kǎ |
| Pallavaka | pǎl′ · lǎ · vǎ · kǎ |
| Pampa | pǎm · pä′ |
| Panchavati | pǎn · chä′ · vǎ · thē |
| Pandu | pän′ · dü |
| Parabhritika | pǎ · rǎ · bhrē · thē · kä′ |
| Parasikas | pä′ · rǎ · shē · käs |
| Parvataka | pǎr′ · vǎ · thǎ · kǎ |
| Parvateshvara | pǎr · vä · thäsh′ · vǎ · rǎ |
| Pataliputra | pät′ · lē · püth · rǎ |
| Prakrit | präk′ · rĭth |
| Pramodaka | prǎ · mō′ · t̶h̶ǎ · kǎ |
| Prasravana | prǎs · rä′ · vǎ · nǎ |
| Praviraka | prä · vē′ · rǎ · kǎ |
| Prithvi | prĭth′ · vē |
| Priyamvada | prē · yǎm · vǎ · t̶h̶ä′ |
| Priyamvadaka | prē′ · yǎm · vǎ · t̶h̶ǎ · kǎ |
| Puru | pü′ · rü |
| Purushadatta | pü · rü · shǎ · t̶h̶ǎ′ · thǎ |
| Pushkaraksha | püsh′ · kǎ · rǎk · shǎ |
| Pushpaka | püsh′ · pǎ · kǎ |
| Pushpakaranda | püsh · pǎ · kǎ · rǎn′ · dǎ |
| | |
| Radanika | rǎ · t̶h̶ǎ · nē · kä′ |
| Radha | rä · t̶h̶hä′ |
| Rajasena | rä · jǎ · sä′ · nǎ |
| Rajasina | rä′ · jǎ · sē · nǎ |
| Rajgriha | räj′ · grē · hǎ |
| Rakshasa | räk′ · shǎ · sǎ |
| Rama | rä′ · mǎ |
| Ravana | rä′ · vǎ · nǎ |
| Rebhila | rä′ · bhē · lǎ |
| Rishyasringa | rĭsh · yǎ · shrĭn′ · gǎ |
| Rohasena | rō · hǎ · sä′ · nǎ |
| Rohitaksha | rō′ · hē · thǎk · shǎ |

| | |
|---|---|
| Sagaradatta | sä' · gä · rä · thä · thä |
| Sagarika | sä' · gä · rĭ · kä |
| Sakatadasa | shä · kä · thä · thä' · sä |
| Sambara | shäm' · bä · rä |
| Sambarasiddhi | säm · bä · rä · sĭth' · thhē |
| Sambuka | shäm' · bü · kä |
| Sami | sä' · mē |
| Samiddhartaka | sä · mĭth · thhär' · thä · kä |
| Saudhataki | shou · dhä' · thä · kē |
| Sansthanaka | säns · thä' · nä · kä |
| Saradvata | sä · räth' · vä · thä |
| Sarika | shä' · rē · kä |
| Sarngarava | särn' · gä · rä · vä |
| Sarvarthasiddhi | sär · vär · thä · sĭth' · thĭ |
| Sataketu | shä · thä · kä' · thü |
| Satananda | sä · thä' · nan · thä |
| Sena | sä' · nä |
| Sephalika | sä' · fä · lĭ · kä |
| Shakas | shä' · käs |
| Shakuntala | shä · kün' · thä · lä' |
| Shankara | shän' · kä · rä |
| Shanta | shän' · thä |
| Sharvilaka | shär' · vē · lä · kä |
| Shatrughna | shäth · rügh' · nä |
| Shikharasena | shĭ · khär · ä · sä' · nä |
| Shudraka | shü' · thrä · kä |
| Shyama | shyä' · mä |
| Siddharthaka | sĭth · thhär' · thä · kä |
| Simhabala | sĭm · hä · bä' · lä |
| Simhala | sĭm · hä' · lä |
| Simhanada | sĭm · hä · nä' · thä |
| Sindhusena | sĭn' · thhü · sä' · nä |
| Sindhuvara | sĭn' · thhü · vä · rä |
| Sinhananda | sĭn · hä · nän · thä |
| Sita | sē' · thä |
| Sonottara | sō · nō' · thä · rä |
| Sramana | shrä' · mä · nä |
| Srikhandadasa | shrĭ · khänd' · ä · dä' · sä |
| Sringavera | shrĭn · gä · vä' · rä |
| Srutakirti | shrü · thä · kēr' · thē |
| Stavakalasha | sthä' · vä · kä · lä · shä |
| Sthavaraka | sthä' · vä · rä · kä |
| Suchaka | sü · chä' · kä |
| Suganga | sü · gän' · gä |
| Sumantra | sü · män' · thrä |
| Surpanakha | sür' · pä · nä · khä |
| Susamgata | sü · säm' · gä · thä |
| Tadaka | thä' · dä · kä |

| Tamasa | thă·mă·sä′ |
| Trishanku | thrē·shän′·kü |
| Trisura | thrĭ·shü′·ră |

| Udayana | ü′·thă·yă·nă |
| Udumbara | ü·thüm′·bă·rä |
| Ujjain | üj·jän′ |
| Urmila | ür·mĭl·ä′ |

| Vairochaka | vä·rō′·chă·kă |
| Vajraloman | văj·ră·lō′·măn |
| Vakranasa | văk·ră·nä′·să |
| Vakula | vă′·kü·lă |
| Valmiki | väl′·mē·kē |
| Vanjula | văn·jü′·lă |
| Varaha | vă·rä′·hă |
| Vardhamanaka | văr·thhă·mä′·nă·kă |
| Varvaraka | văr′·vă·ră·kă |
| Vasantaka | vă·săn′·thă·kă |
| Vasantasena | vă·săn·thă·sä′·nä |
| Vasanti | vä′·săn·thē |
| Vasavadatta | vä′·să·vă·thă·thă |
| Vasubhuti | vä′·sŭ·bhü·thē |
| Vasundhara | vä·sün·thhă·rä′ |
| Vedanta | vä·thän′·thă |
| Vibhishana | vĭ·bhē′·shă·nă |
| Vijaya | vĭ·jă·yä′ |
| Vijayapala | vĭ·jă·yă·pä′·lă |
| Vijayarama | vĭ·jă·yă·rä′·mă |
| Vijayavarman | vĭ·jă·yă·văr′·măn |
| Vinayadatta | vĭ′·nă·yă·thă·thă |
| Vindhya | vĭn·thyă |
| Viradha | vĭr·ä′·thhă |
| Viradhagupta | vĭ·rä′·thhä·güp·thă |
| Viraka | vē′·ră·kă |
| Vishakadatta | vĭ·shä′·kă·thă·thă |
| Vishnudasa | vĭsh·nü·thä′·să |
| Vishvavasu | vĭsh′·vă·vă·sü |
| Visvavasu | vĭsh′·vă·vä·sü |

| Yaugandharayana | you·găn·thhă·rä′·yă·nă |
| Yavanas | yă′·vă·năs |